THE LESBIAN REVOLUTION

The Lesbian Revolution argues that lesbian feminists were a vital force in the Women's Liberation Movement (WLM). They did not just play a fundamental role in the important changes wrought by second wave feminism, but created a powerful revolution in lesbian theory, culture and practice. Yet this lesbian revolution is undocumented.

The book shows that lesbian feminists were founders of feminist institutions, such as resources for women survivors of men's violence, including refuges and rape crisis centres, and that they were central to campaigns against this violence. They created a feminist squatting movement, theatre groups, bands, art and poetry and conducted campaigns for lesbian rights. They also created a profound and challenging analysis of sexuality which has disappeared from the historical record. They analysed heterosexuality as a political institution, arguing that lesbianism was a political choice for feminists and, indeed, a form of resistance in itself. Using interviews with prominent lesbian feminists from the time of the WLM, and informed by the author's personal experience, this book aims to challenge the way the work and ideas of lesbian feminists have been eclipsed and to document the lesbian revolution.

The book will be of key interest to scholars and students of women's history, the history of feminism, the politics of sexuality, women's studies, gender studies, lesbian and gay studies, queer studies and cultural studies, as well as to the lay reader interested in the WLM and feminism more generally.

Sheila Jeffreys is a Professorial Fellow in the School of Social and Political Sciences at the University of Melbourne, Australia. In 1973, in the UK, she became involved in the Women's Liberation Movement and became a lesbian in 1977. She moved to Australia in 1991, where she became a Professor of Feminist Politics at the University of Melbourne, and has authored numerous books on the history and politics of sexuality, the global sex industry, lesbian feminism, harmful beauty practices, religion and women's rights and the politics of transgenderism. She moved back to the UK in 2015.

ROUTLEDGE STUDIES IN RADICAL HISTORY AND POLITICS

Series editors: Thomas Linehan, Brunel University, and
John Roberts, Brunel University

The series *Routledge Studies in Radical History and Politics* has two areas of interest. Firstly, this series aims to publish books which focus on the history of movements of the radical left. 'Movement of the radical left' is here interpreted in its broadest sense as encompassing those past movements for radical change which operated in the mainstream political arena as with political parties, and past movements for change which operated more outside the mainstream as with millenarian movements, anarchist groups, utopian socialist communities, and trade unions. Secondly, this series aims to publish books which focus on more contemporary expressions of radical left-wing politics. Recent years have been witness to the emergence of a multitude of new radical movements adept at getting their voices in the public sphere. From those participating in the Arab Spring, the Occupy movement, community unionism, social media forums, independent media outlets, local voluntary organisations campaigning for progressive change, and so on, it seems to be the case that innovative networks of radicalism are being constructed in civil society that operate in different public forms.

The series very much welcomes titles with a British focus, but is not limited to any particular national context or region. The series will encourage scholars who contribute to this series to draw on perspectives and insights from other disciplines.

Titles include:

Migrant Britain
Histories and Historiographies: Essays in Honour of Colin Holmes
Edited by Jennifer Craig-Norton, Christhard Hoffmann and Tony Kushner

The Lesbian Revolution
Lesbian Feminism in the UK 1970–1990
Sheila Jeffreys

For more about this series, please visit: www.routledge.com/Routledge-Studies-in-Radical-History-and-Politics/book-series/RSRHP.

THE LESBIAN REVOLUTION

Lesbian Feminism in the UK
1970–1990

Sheila Jeffreys

LONDON AND NEW YORK

First published 2018
by Routledge
2 Park Square, Milton Park, Abingdon, Oxon OX14 4RN

and by Routledge
711 Third Avenue, New York, NY 10017

Routledge is an imprint of the Taylor & Francis Group, an informa business

© 2018 Sheila Jeffreys

The right of Sheila Jeffreys to be identified as author of this work has been asserted by
her in accordance with sections 77 and 78 of the Copyright, Designs and Patents Act 1988.

All rights reserved. No part of this book may be reprinted or reproduced or utilised
in any form or by any electronic, mechanical or other means, now known or
hereafter invented, including photocopying and recording, or in any information
storage or retrieval system, without permission in writing from the publishers.

Trademark notice: Product or corporate names may be trademarks or registered trademarks,
and are used only for identification and explanation without intent to infringe.

British Library Cataloguing in Publication Data
A catalogue record for this book is available from the British Library

Library of Congress Cataloging in Publication Data
Names: Jeffreys, Sheila, author.
Title: The lesbian revolution : lesbian feminism in the UK, 1970–1990 / Sheila Jeffreys.
Description: Abingdon, Oxon ; New York, NY : Routledge, 2018. |
Series: Routledge studies in radical history and politics |
Includes bibliographical references and index.
Identifiers: LCCN 2018012144 | ISBN 9781138096561 (hardback) |
ISBN 9781138096578 (pbk.) | ISBN 9781315105253 (ebook)
Subjects: LCSH: Lesbians–Political activity–Great Britain–History–20th century. |
Feminism–Great Britain–History–20th century.
Classification: LCC HQ75.6.G7 J44 2019 | DDC 306.76/63–dc23
LC record available at https://lccn.loc.gov/2018012144

ISBN: 978-1-138-09656-1 (hbk)
ISBN: 978-1-138-09657-8 (pbk)
ISBN: 978-1-315-10525-3 (ebk)

Typeset in Bembo
by Out of House Publishing

This book is dedicated to Ann Rowett. We met in 1987, when some elements of a lesbian feminist movement still existed, and have been together ever since. We saw the movement disappear and now we are seeing the beginnings of a rebirth. I am very grateful to Ann for her wise counsel on this volume, as well as all the love and strength she has given me in my writing and in my life.

CONTENTS

Biographies of interviewees	*ix*
Acknowledgements	*xiii*

	Introduction	
	Lesbian feminism: hidden from history	1
1	The origins of lesbian feminism	13
2	Lesbian culture	34
3	Separatism	55
4	The lesbian perspective	76
5	Political lesbianism and heterosexuality	96
6	Sadomasochism: The challenge to the politics of sexual equality	115
7	The gender backlash: Butch/femme role-playing	135
8	Identity politics and the destruction of lesbian feminism: 'The CIA couldn't have done it better' (Rahila of Southall Black Sisters, 1986)	152

viii Contents

9   Grief: The demise of lesbian feminism   170

   Postscript: The erasure of lesbians   186

Bibliography   *195*
Index   *212*

BIOGRAPHIES OF INTERVIEWEES

Lynn Alderson

Lynn Alderson discovered the hidden world of lesbian clubs in the late 1960s before finding her true home in the Women's Liberation Movement a little later. She was a founder member of Sisterwrite Bookshop and very involved in the rich world of feminist publishing and newsletters, a member of Onlywomen Press, involved in Catcall and a founding member of the radical feminist magazine *Trouble and Strife*. A career in equalities work in local government followed. In 1997 she adopted her daughter after a two-year battle through the courts, which set the case law for lesbian and gay adoption in England and Wales. In 2010 she was part of an initiative to create a new network of 1970s WLM activists and is now part of two older women's groups, one of them lesbian. She is particularly keen to pass on consciousness-raising as a radical tool for both younger women and those who want to experience the last segment of their lives as part of a vibrant and permanently awkward sisterhood. She lives in Devon and, having been a cat woman for many years, is now besotted with her dogs.

Rosemary Auchmuty

Rosemary Auchmuty came to London from Australia, where she grew up, in 1978. In the 1980s she worked in adult education, teaching history and women's studies, co-founded the Lesbian History Group with Sheila Jeffreys and studied law at the Polytechnic of Central London, now the University of Westminster, where she went on to teach from 1989 to 2007. Since then she has been Professor of Law at the University of Reading. She researches and writes about feminist approaches to property law, feminist legal history, sexuality and law and girls' fiction.

Linda Bellos

Linda Bellos discovered she was a lesbian in 1979, and then questioned the politics of sexuality and immediately became a feminist. She is honoured to have been

x Biographies of interviewees

involved in the Women's Liberation Movement and learnt a great deal about process and inclusion, which she took into her activism in the Labour Party. During those years she was proud to be an out Lesbian and a feminist, and she still is. Years ago she suggested that there should be a lesbian grandmothers' group; now is the time.

Julie Bindel

Julie Bindel became a lesbian in 1977, aged 15, and a feminist soon afterwards, when, aged 17, she moved to Leeds in search of like-minded women and found the Leeds Revolutionary Feminist Group and Women Against Violence Against Women (WAVAW). She is an investigative journalist, writer and broadcaster. She has been active in the global campaign to end violence towards women and children since 1979 and has written extensively on surrogacy, rape, domestic violence, sexually motivated murder, prostitution and trafficking, child sexual exploitation, stalking and the rise of religious fundamentalism and its harm to women and girls. Her 2014 book *Straight Expectations* looks at the state of the lesbian and gay movement in the UK. Her latest book is *The Pimping of Prostitution: Abolishing the Sex Work Myth* (2017).

Al Garthwaite

Al Garthwaite is a lesbian feminist activist and campaigner. She helped draw up the four (eventually seven) demands of the Women's Liberation Movement, performed street theatre at the first International Women's Day march and co-founded the UK's 'Reclaim the Night'. Focusing especially on combating sexual and physical violence against women, she has also campaigned on women's health and reproductive rights, media representation on screen and behind the camera, equal pay and education/workplace opportunities, and nurseries and childcare. She initiated and, with others, set up a holiday centre for women and children in the Yorkshire Dales. As a founder of the feminist-run production company Vera Media she has made over 100 films, including *Video 28*: a celebration and a record of lesbians' fight against section 28 of the Conservative government's 1988 Local Government Act (later repealed by Labour), which forbade local authorities to "promote homosexuality as a pretended family relationship".

Sibyl Grundberg

Sibyl Grundberg came to the UK in 1971 from Boston and New Mexico. Drawn into a vibrant Women's Liberation Movement in London, she fell in love with women through admiration for their strength and purpose. She was initially active in the co-counselling network, lived with groups of women in London, Wales and Sussex and was involved with The Women's Press in its early years. She was a member of the Lesbian Line collective from 1981 to 1985, at the same time training as an osteopath and naturopath. She practises in London.

Lynne Harne

Lynne Harne joined the Women's Liberation Movement in 1971. By 1972 she had become a lesbian, lived in the lesbian feminist squatting community in Hackney and attended early lesbian conferences. By the early 1980s she had become a revolutionary feminist and was involved in activism against male sexual violence and pornography. She became the first lesbian custody worker at Rights of Women and worked in mainstreaming lesbian feminism and challenging heterosexism at the Greater London Council. She has been in Lesbians in Education and joined the Lesbian History Group in the early 1990s. Since then she has worked as a lecturer and researcher, including on violence against women and children. She co-edited a book on the demise of radical lesbian feminism, *All the Rage*, in 1996. She has written other books on male violence and on lesbian mothers and child custody. More recently she has helped revive the Lesbian History Group and challenged lesbian erasure, including setting up the Lesbian Rights Alliance.

Elaine Hutton

Elaine Hutton has been a lesbian feminist activist since the mid-1970s. She has been involved in many campaigns and groups over the years, including Rape Crisis (Newcastle upon Tyne and Bristol), Women Against Violence Against Women, Lesbians in Education and the Lesbian History Group. She has run Workers' Educational Association classes in women's writing (1978, 1990s), was a member of Onlywomen Press in the early 1980s and has both edited a book about lesbian writing, *Beyond Sex and Romance* (1998) and contributed to another, *All the Rage* (1996), both published by The Women's Press. In her working life she often worked in women-only situations – women's centres, young women's projects – and created women-only groups within other working environments. More recently she has been one of the women who have reactivated the Lesbian History Group, recognising the importance of reaching out to younger lesbians and recording lesbian history, and, in the same context, she is part of the growing number of lesbians challenging lesbian erasure by recreating a strong lesbian presence and lesbian visibility, through statements, meetings and action.

'Kate'

'Kate' became involved in the WLM in 1978. She came from a solid, working-class socialist background, the values of which she's never lost. She was aware of the obdurate sexism of many 'lefty' men within socialist politics, however, and she found it difficult to challenge. At the beginning of an academic career, with a marriage on the rocks and two small girls, life was frantic. But, just as it seemed that things could not get worse, she fell in love with another woman and promptly got landed with a lesbian custody case. Feminist friends and colleagues were incredibly supportive, giving financial as well as emotional support. She attended a women's liberation conference in which there was a strand on patriarchy. At last her life and her struggles made sense, and, theoretically, she was able to 'see' and challenge. She joined the Patriarchy Study Group and was serious. She broke the law and found it hilarious to surreptitiously squirt superglue into the locks of sex shops and to ruin pornographic calendars with her mum in Leicester Square. The ensuing years have seen the development of Kate's career and the arrival of four grandchildren. And so the challenges continue.

xii Biographies of interviewees

Jan McLeod

Jan McLeod became involved in lesbian and feminist activism and work against male violence when she joined the Rape Crisis movement in 1977. She has been involved in a range of work based in Scotland, including: support for women who have experienced violence and abuse, or whose children have been sexually abused; campaigning against pornography and commercial sexual exploitation; the design and delivery of training on violence against women to improve service responses; and strategic and policy work at local and national level. Jan works with the Women's Support Project, and is a member of the board of directors of Rape Crisis Scotland.

Sandra McNeill

Sandra McNeill joined the WLM in 1975. A former anarchist and trade unionist, she became a revolutionary feminist in 1977. She was involved in setting up East Leeds women's workshops, Women Against Violence Against Women, Justice for Women and, most recently, Support After Rape and Sexual Violence Leeds (the Leeds Rape Crisis Centre). She is a trustee of Feminist Archive North – remember us with your memorabilia. In 2009 she was awarded the Emma Humphreys Memorial Prize. She remains a feminist activist.

Femi Otitoju

Femi Otitoju came out as a lesbian in the late 1970s and helped set up the first Black Lesbian Group in the early 1980s. After a short, ill-advised association with the Wages for Housework and Wages due Lesbians campaigns, and an even shorter stint at London Lesbian Line, she volunteered for London Lesbian and Gay Switchboard for about 13 years, led its Training Group for two years and was chair for two years. She continued to serve the lesbian and gay communities through membership of the management committees of the London Lesbian and Gay Centre, the Black Lesbian and Gay Centre and Stonewall Housing Association. A keen writer, she contributed to magazines, including *Spare Rib*, *Outrage Magazine* and *Outwrite*, and books such as *Being Active Citizens* and *Radical Records: Thirty Years of Lesbian and Gay History, 1957–1987*; she was also a member of the Women's Liberation Newsletter Collective and a *Capital Gay* columnist. Femi worked for the Greater London Council in the Women's Committee Support Unit from 1984 to 1986 and became a 'professional lesbian' as a founding member of staff at the Haringey Lesbian and Gay Unit from 1986 to 1988. She launched her own equality and diversity consultancy Challenge in 1988, which she still runs, as well as being co-chair of National Women's Aid.

ACKNOWLEDGEMENTS

The interviews with my lesbian feminist sisters lie at the heart of this book. It could not have been written without them, their memories and their wisdom. They are: Lynn Alderson, Rosemary Auchmuty, Linda Bellos, Julie Bindel, Al Garthwaite, Sibyl Grundberg, Lynne Harne, Elaine Hutton, 'Kate', Jan McLeod, Sandra McNeill and Femi Otitoju. Sandra McNeill and Lynne Harne helped me immeasurably by reading chapters and giving their advice. It is a heavy responsibility to record this lesbian revolution, and I have needed all the help I can get to make this book as accurate as possible. I am grateful to all those who created lesbian feminism in the UK, some of whom have died already. I hope that through this book their inspiration will live on and enliven the next generation. My thanks go to all my friends and sisters back in Australia and here in the UK of all ages, who have helped to keep my lesbian feminist hopes and dreams alive and to keep lesbian ethics in action. May there be many times ahead in which we can sing, dance, roar with laughter together and make revolution once more.

INTRODUCTION

Lesbian feminism: hidden from history

This book is about the lesbian revolution that took place in the 1970s and 1980s in the UK. The history of lesbian feminism in the UK has never been written, despite its importance to the Women's Liberation Movement (WLM) and feminism in general. This book seeks to make up for this omission. I was involved in lesbian feminism in this period. I made the choice to become a lesbian because of my politics, and took part in the writing of some of the significant texts of lesbian feminism at that time, from the 'Political Lesbianism' paper, in *Love Your Enemy?* (Onlywomen Press, 1981), to the Lesbian History Group book *Not a Passing Phase* (Lesbian History Group, 1989). I was a member of the London Lesbian Offensive Group, the Lesbian History Group, the Lesbian Archive collective, Lesbians Against Pornography and Lesbians Against Sadomasochism. Lesbian feminism transformed my life. When it went into gradual decline from the mid-1980s onwards, I grieved – along with many others.

It is reasonable to speak of a 'lesbian revolution' because of the extraordinary changes that were brought about by the mobilising of lesbian feminists during this time. Lesbian feminists came out of the Gay Liberation Front (GLF) and the Women's Liberation Movement to create a rich culture and a rich social and political community, in which all feminists could immerse themselves so thoroughly that they had little need to have recourse to the resources of the 'malestream' world. Lesbians created culture through setting up feminist and lesbian presses and bookstores, feminist art projects, theatre groups, bands, discos, dances and concerts. They wrote and published copious books of theory, fiction, poetry, self-help and history. Lesbians took the lead roles in creating innumerable resources to resist male violence, refuges for women battered by men in their homes, incest survivors' groups and rape crisis centres. Involvement in creating and running these resources led to many more women deciding to become lesbians. Lesbians were much involved in organising political groups, events and conferences for hundreds and thousands of

2 Introduction

women at a time. Lesbians also organised groups and activities for lesbians only. The result was that a lesbian feminist living in London, for instance, could go to several meetings a week and several conferences a month and conduct a social life entirely in feminist and mostly women-only spaces, bookstores, arts centres, women's centres and discos. Importantly, the facilities and community created by lesbian feminists formed the base from which the Women's Liberation Movement for social change was able to draw its energy and nurturance.

Although this book is about lesbian feminism in the UK it will include material about the US when necessary. Authors such as Mary Daly and Adrienne Rich were very influential in creating lesbian feminist theory, which was embraced in many countries. Black lesbian feminism was inspired in the UK by Black lesbian theorists such as Audre Lorde ('Black' was capitalised in WLM writings, to emphasise the importance of Black feminist politics, and I continue that tradition here). The ideas, practices and achievements of lesbian feminism shared many similarities in the US and the UK. The American lesbian feminist Adrienne Rich expressed the centrality of lesbian feminism to the Women's Liberation Movement in the US in a speech in 1977:

> In this country, as in the world today, there is a movement of women going on like no other in history. Let us have no doubt; it is being fueled and empowered by the work of lesbians. Lesbians are running presses; starting magazines and distribution systems; setting up crisis centers and halfway houses; creating political dialogues; changing our use of language; making a truly lesbian and female history available to us for the first time; doing grassroots organizing and making visionary art.
>
> *(Rich, 1977: 6)*

Lilian Mohin, an American lesbian feminist who lived in London in the 1970s and 1980s and contributed greatly to the creation of lesbian culture through Onlywomen Press, expressed the importance of lesbian feminism in the UK thus: 'It's crucial that we assert the necessity for lesbianism as a means of freeing all women from the oppression of all men. Lesbians have provided most of the vitality that fuels the WLM and it's time we acknowledge that rather than politely refrain from mentioning it' (Mohin, 1984: 8). In fact, the written history of the WLM does politely refrain from mentioning this.

Texts written about the WLM in the 1990s and even into the 2000s could not envisage that the spectacular edifice that was lesbian feminism in general would ever disappear. In 1993, for example, American lesbian historians Verta Taylor and Leila Rupp identified lesbian feminist communities and culture as forming a reservoir which will serve as a base to harbour lesbian feminist politics in times of retreat: 'The culture of lesbian feminist communities both serves as a base of mobilization... and provides continuity from earlier stages of the women's movement to the future flowering of feminism' (Taylor and Rupp, 1993: 34). In 2005 Taylor was still optimistic, writing: 'During periods without visible movement campaigns, many activists gravitate to cultural activities and alternative institutions such as battered women's shelters, rape crisis lines, feminist bookstores, women's music festivals, spirituality groups, theater performances, writers' groups, and presses… Such cultural and service activities maintain feminist collective identity' (Staggenborg and Taylor, 2005: 44).

In fact, bookstores and presses describing themselves as feminist or lesbian scarcely survived in the US or the UK by 2005, and those that remained mostly disappeared in the succeeding decade, which may have been the lowest point for feminism in the last 50 years. Lesbian feminist organisations disappeared completely in the UK, so that today, although there are signs of a revival of feminism, lesbian feminism is in a parlous state. The London Lesbian History Group (LHG), which I was involved in setting up again after decades of hiatus in 2015, is the only resource of its kind that young lesbians in London say they are able to find which uses the word 'lesbian' in its title and provides a space for lesbians to meet face to face. Lesbian spaces, or the women-only spaces that nurture lesbians, are virtually non-existent. The cultural reservoir did not survive, and lesbian feminism is having to be created anew from scratch. The wiping out of lesbian feminism that has taken place could not have been envisaged while vestiges of the movement and culture still existed. In the last decade, however, the very word 'lesbian' either became invisible or came to be seen as offensive and old-fashioned in comparison with terms which obscured the womanhood of those claiming them, such as 'queer' and 'non-binary'. Lesbians were, as the US feminist journal *Trivia* stated in 2010, 'becoming extinct' (Weil, 2010).

Today the bookstores and presses are almost entirely gone from both the UK and the US. Few books of feminist theory, let alone lesbian theory, appear. Women-only spaces are conspicuous by their absence. The demise of the WLM and lesbian feminism took place in tandem, and, as this book will show, the date of the demise is variously calculated from as early as the late 1970s to as late as the 1990s. This book concentrates on the period 1970 to 1990 because it was between these dates that a recognisable WLM and lesbian feminism existed. The lesbians I interviewed for this book place the demise at various points between the mid-1980s and the mid-1990s. Certainly, many of the institutions and practices I cover here still existed in some form in the 1990s – some bookstores and presses, for instance. But the forces I discuss, which led to the demise of lesbian feminism, such as identity politics, the 'sex wars' – i.e. the eroticising of power differences between lesbians, the revival of butch/femme role-playing, the direct targeting of lesbian and gay organisations and politics by a right-wing government – had all wreaked such damage by 1990 that I have chosen that date as the point at which the hopes and dreams of lesbian feminists of being able to create a great social transformation had mostly crashed to earth.

Lesbian feminism came from radical and revolutionary feminism

A variety of feminist perspectives will be mentioned in this book, and I will explain the ways in which I use the terms 'liberal feminism', 'socialist feminism', 'radical feminism' and 'revolutionary feminism' here. In the 1970s, when lesbian

4 Introduction

feminism was born in the UK, there were two major theoretical streams within the WLM: socialist feminism and radical feminism. These were not always clearly differentiated in the early 1970s. Women like myself who joined WLM campaigning and consciousness-raising groups in these years may not have adopted either label or understood there to be a difference, but we were all likely to be socialists. There was not a strong tradition of 'liberal feminism' in the country, a term that applies to feminists such as Betty Friedan, who wrote the important founding text of US feminism *The Feminine Mystique* in 1963 and founded the National Organization of Women (NOW). Liberal feminists seek equal opportunities with men in the public world rather than a profound social, and socialist, transformation (Friedan, 1963). Radical feminism in the US and the UK developed out of socialist feminism (see Morgan, 1977). Although they retained their socialist perspective, radical feminists grew exasperated by the sexism of men on the Left. They outgrew the idea that the oppression of women was something that served the interests of capital and would wither away after the revolution, and focussed on the role of men individually and as a group in enforcing women's subordination. Mohin explains radical feminism as recognising that men oppress women: 'Radical feminists became an identifiable political grouping…on the grounds that we understood that it is *men* who oppress women and that we were/are prepared to say so, and go on saying so, and act on that analysis' (Mohin, 1984: 6, emphasis in original).

Radical feminists theorised the ways in which the 'personal' is political, through examining the way women are objectified by beauty practices and oppressed by the men they lived with in the bedroom and the kitchen, and argued that women constitute a 'sex class', oppressed by men in a way similar to that in which the bourgeoisie oppresses the proletariat in Marxist economic theory. The radical feminist theorist Catharine MacKinnon developed her very influential theoretical approach directly from a criticism of Marxism (MacKinnon, 1989). She states that women's oppression is organised through sexuality in the same way that class oppression is organised through work. She explains that 'the molding, direction, and expression of sexuality organizes society into two sexes: women and men' so that 'as work is to Marxism, sexuality is to feminism' (ibid.: 3).

I too outgrew socialism, but, in my case, I did not become a 'radical feminist'; rather, I developed my own tendency of 'revolutionary feminism'. The first group I joined in the WLM was a socialist feminist one in Manchester in 1973, and I joined another socialist feminist group in London when I moved there in 1976. By 1977, though, I had become critical of the ideas and practices of socialist feminism and was asking why it was not possible to analyse men as the oppressors instead of concentrating on 'women and' issues that fitted women into the concerns of the male Left – e.g. women and Ireland, women and imperialism. I wrote a paper for the National Women's Liberation Conference which took place in 1977 in London, entitled 'The Need for Revolutionary Feminism: Against the Liberal Takeover of the Women's Liberation Movement' (Jeffreys, 1977). After the conference workshop that discussed the paper, women started to describe themselves as 'revolutionary feminists', and a new tendency was born. Revolutionary feminism shared the analysis of radical feminism that women constituted the subordinate sex class under male supremacy. But it was a tendency more committed to theorising sexuality and heterosexuality, as well as to direct action, and it was most instrumental in campaigns against male violence and pornography (Rees, 2010; Mackay, 2014). Whilst most radical feminists were and remained heterosexual, revolutionary feminists all were or became lesbians. Lesbian feminism had its roots in radical and revolutionary feminism. Many socialist feminists were lesbians and saw themselves as lesbians and feminists, but the term 'lesbian feminist', in which those two words crucially affect each other, was adopted primarily by those who saw women as a sex class and sexuality as the organising principle of women's oppression.

Writing the history of lesbian feminism

Interest in recording the history of the WLM in the UK is in its infancy, and the history of lesbian feminism is undocumented. The situation is different in the US, where the WLM has been much more thoroughly documented and the history of lesbian feminism is a little more prominent. There have been a number of autobiographies and general histories giving good insights into the origins and practices of the movement, and some of these include coverage of lesbian feminist ideas (Brownmiller, 2000; Rosen, 2000; Echols, 1989). Alice Echols' *Daring to be Bad* (1989) provides an account of the theorising of heterosexuality by lesbian feminists in the US in the early 1970s and the controversy that this occasioned. Kristan Poirot has addressed this issue in the US in a more recent account (Poirot, 2009). Such an account does not exist for the UK, however. Until recently the little history of the WLM in the UK that was recorded has tended to represent the activities and personalities of socialist feminism (Rowbotham, 1997; Coote and Campbell, 1982; Segal, 1987). Radical feminism and revolutionary feminism, in which lesbian feminism had its origins, are not generally recorded, or the absence of these perspectives and the personalities associated with them remarked upon. The domination of the historiography by socialist feminist historians and commentators has meant that those issues and activities pursued by radical/revolutionary feminists, critiques of sexuality and heterosexuality, campaigns against male violence, sexual violence and pornography and the critique of heterosexuality have received much less coverage. The vast majority of the written and oral history, therefore, has concentrated on ideas and campaigns most relevant to heterosexual women, such as the abortion campaign, or on the workplace struggles of working-class women. One example is *A Century of Women* (1997), by the socialist feminist historian Sheila Rowbotham, which does not even contain the word 'lesbian' in the index.

An ambitious attempt to record the history of the WLM in the UK is similarly deficient. This is the Sisterhood Project, with the aim of documenting and recording oral histories from those involved in the WLM, which was embarked upon in 2012 by a team of feminist historians in concert with the British Library

6 Introduction

(British Library, n.d.). The British Library project, which is the first attempt to try to cover the WLM in its entirety, has an extensive website providing a fairly detailed timeline of the WLM in the UK. But the timeline does not, at the time of writing, include any reference to events concerning lesbians, though it does record the setting up of publishing collectives; the election of the first Black woman to the House of Commons; and, in 1988, 'Women in Black formed in Israel', an event which does not even relate directly to the UK. The words 'lesbian' or 'lesbianism' appear in the text three times in lists of topics covered by a magazine or in relation to the sixth demand of the WLM adopted at the 1974 conference – 'An end to discrimination against lesbians'. In the list and description of WLM campaigns, no lesbian campaigns, for child custody, for instance, appear. On page 39 of 42 pages, when I first consulted it in 2015, there was a heading 'Gay and lesbian liberation politics and choice about sexuality', under which two short paragraphs appeared. By 2016 this section had been expunged, so no trace of what lesbian politics might entail remained. Lesbians and lesbianism are not otherwise mentioned.

In the last decade there has been a change in academic feminist history. A new generation of feminist researchers is producing research that has bucked the trend of concentration on campaigns and personalities seen as significant by socialist feminists. These include Eve Setch's work on the London Women's Liberation Workshop (Setch, 2002), Jeska Rees's work on revolutionary feminism (Rees, 2010), Sarah Browne's work on the WLM in Scotland (Browne, 2012; 2014), Finn Mackay's work on the history of radical feminism in general (Mackay, 2014; 2015) and Bridget Lockyer's work on the WLM in Bradford, Yorkshire (Lockyer, 2013). Lesbian feminists were very prominent and may well have comprised the majority of those involved in the WLM activities and groups covered in this research. Sarah Browne's work, for instance, shows that the St Andrews group she writes about was perceived as full of lesbian feminists and had a concentration on producing theory on sexuality and lesbianism, in comparison with other local WLM groups in Scotland (Browne, 2012). Browne points out that the historiography of the WLM has concentrated on the works of prominent public socialist feminists but not the grassroots activities of feminists in local groups, though information about these is available in newsletters and conference papers and, potentially, through oral history. This more recent research, very useful though it is in documenting aspects of the UK WLM that have received little attention, notably radical and revolutionary feminism, offers little information about lesbian feminism specifically, even though the protagonists who the research focuses on included or mainly comprised lesbian feminists. The index of the lesbian feminist Finn Mackay's book *Radical Feminism: Feminist Activism in Movement* (Mackay, 2015) lists the phrase 'lesbian feminism' as appearing on just two pages in the book, and the word 'lesbian' on its own does not appear.

Eve Setch points out that, although the accounts of the WLM 'divide the movement into two polarized sides, socialist and radical, seeing radical feminists as instigating the movement's fall' (Setch, 2002: 171), there were never two clearly opposing sides. Nonetheless, the dominance of socialist feminists in the historiography does mean that lesbian feminism has received little attention. Radical feminism in general is described by socialist feminist commentators as 'extremist' (Setch, 2002: 172), and revolutionary feminism as "'divisive', 'elitist', 'reactionary' and 'a politics of despair and retreat'" (Rees, 2010: 145). There is little space in accounts of this kind to pay attention to lesbian feminism.

Documenting lesbian history

Lesbian historians have pointed out why it is important to document lesbian history. The first book on lesbian history in the UK was published in 1988 by the London LHG, which was founded by one of my interviewees, Rosemary Auchmuty, and me in 1984. The introduction says,

> For lesbians themselves, the need for lesbian history is self-evident. Every social group needs access to its own history. Knowledge of our past gives us cultural roots and a heritage with models and experiences to learn from and emulate, or to choose not to follow. Lesbians have been deprived of virtually all knowledge of our past.
>
> *(Lesbian History Group, 1989: 2)*

It goes on to point out that our history 'gives us a context in which to place ourselves in the world and a basis for our efforts to change things', as well as giving women and girls who are not yet lesbians the chance to imagine becoming such, because they can 'reassess their own lives and the choices available to them'. The LHG used a quotation from the US lesbian feminist poet and theorist Adrienne Rich to emphasise the importance of our history to lesbians: 'The denial of reality and visibility to women's passion for women, women's choice of women as allies, life companions, and community…meant an incalculable loss to the power of all women *to change the social relations of the sexes, to liberate ourselves and each other*' (quoted in Lesbian History Group, 1989: 3, emphasis in original).

The LHG explained that documenting lesbian history is difficult because lesbians did not usually leave a record that they were lesbians and, if they did, their families were likely to erase it after their deaths. In some cases, historians made up boyfriends for lesbians to normalise them – ones that died in the war, perhaps. At the time we wrote the book it did not occur to us that the history of those of us involved in lesbian feminism could suffer a similar fate to that of lesbians in earlier periods. But this is what has happened. The lesbian feminists who the present book is about are not in the same position as lesbians before the WLM, who preferred to remain closeted. They have been happy to embrace the word 'lesbian' and have their lives and loves made public, but there were still difficulties for me in recording this history. Some women I know to be lesbians did not want to be so identified, and some groups which were composed only of lesbians did not use the word. One lesbian who was asked if I might include her as a lesbian in the book said that it was fine, but that it was the first time she had been 'out'. New forms of 'disappearance'

8 Introduction

are taking place. Lesbians in the WLM have been obscured by different means from those used to deny or conceal the lesbianism of those who loved women before us, but obstacles still exist.

A new obstacle is what I have called elsewhere the practice of 'transnapping' lesbians from history and re-identifying them as 'trans' rather than as lesbians, though there is no evidence that they thought they were actually any sex other than female. These reclassified lesbians include the British novelist Radclyffe Hall, the American jazz trumpeter Billy Tipton, and Brandon Teena, a young American lesbian who dressed occasionally in masculine attire and was murdered in Nebraska in 1993 (Jeffreys, 2014; Brownian, 2016; Gage, 2010). The transing of history enables lesbians to disappear, as if they were really men all along.

Methodology

The methodology of this research is twofold: interviews and archival research. I interviewed women who were active lesbian feminists in the 1970s and 1980s and conducted research in feminist archives in London, Glasgow and Leeds to examine materials that were not published in mainstream fora, such as newsletters, minutes of meetings and conference papers. The 12 oral history interviews were conducted with lesbians who I know from that time who were politically active in various branches of feminist and lesbian feminist work, campaigns against violence against women, Black lesbian activism, the lesbian child custody campaign, feminist bookshops and feminist publishing, girls' work, running women's centres, the Lesbian History Group, the Lesbian Archive and lesbian studies. These lesbians do not necessarily represent a full range of political views held by lesbians who were feminists at the time. They are mainly those who called themselves radical or revolutionary feminists, and, most importantly, lesbian feminists – i.e. they saw their lesbianism as fundamental to their feminism, rather than incidental, and were involved in challenging heterosexuality as an oppressive institution. Most were 'political lesbians', in the sense that they became lesbians as a result of their involvement in the WLM and exposure to lesbian feminists and lesbian feminist ideas. This practice of feminists choosing lesbianism as a form of resistance to male supremacy may seem foreign to common notions about lesbianism today, even within feminist circles, which are that lesbianism is something essential, not something that can be chosen, and with no particular relevance to feminism (Gottschalk, 2003).

My own involvement in lesbian feminism has enabled me to create questions and suggest topics to my interviewees from my knowledge of what was happening at the time. As Sue Bruley comments in relation to her research using oral history interviews with members of a Clapham consciousness-raising group in 1970s London that she was herself involved in, she was 'aware that being both a historical actor and a narrator is problematic' (Bruley, 2013: 718). My research is not in any sense an autoethnography, in that I do not make my own experience a focus. I do include certain useful details that are not recorded in published histories, such as my own knowledge of the role of conference papers in the formation of ideas, for instance, but my own experience is not otherwise used except as a prompt to questions to be asked of the sources and as a touchstone for the accuracy of written accounts. The very little research now being done on revolutionary feminism, or on groups that were formed by or fundamental to lesbian feminism, is by researchers who have no personal knowledge of lesbian feminism to alert them to issues and questions to ask (Rees, 2010; Setch, 2002; Lockyer, 2013). This small amount of research is most welcome, but I consider that my work, as someone involved, will add an important element to the documentation of the lesbian feminist movement. It also means that my interviewees showed me a good deal of trust and goodwill.

I conducted archival research in the Women's Library in London, which has now been incorporated into the Library of the London School of Economics; in the Women's Library in Glasgow; and in the Feminist Archive North, which is based in the Special Collections of Leeds University Library (the Brotherton). I also made great use of my extensive personal collection of papers, which includes journals, press cuttings, conference papers and minutes of meetings from groups that I was involved in, such as the London Lesbian Offensive Group and the Lesbian Archive collective.

Structure of the book

The first half of the book looks at the situation of lesbians before the development of lesbian feminism, how lesbian feminism came to exist and the changes that it wrought. It examines the central role of lesbian feminists within the WLM, particularly in creating women-only spaces, such as women's centres, and resources to counter violence against women. It also looks at the culture that lesbian feminists created for feminists in general, not just lesbians, through women's music and musical venues, theatre and art that were in fact largely created by lesbians. The culture was informed by the theory and politics of lesbian feminism, by ideas, novels and poetry that were not just the product of lesbian feminists but also arose from a distinctive lesbian perspective, a view of the world that started from a critique of heterosexuality as a political institution and envisaged and created a new world for women. The crucial critique of heterosexuality and the establishment of a politics in which many women could and did choose to be lesbians as an act of resistance, transforming their lives, has a chapter of its own.

The second half of the book is directed towards understanding why lesbian feminism declined. Many of the reasons for the demise of lesbian feminism were the same as those which caused the WLM in general to decline. I shall concentrate in this book on those which relate to specifically lesbian feminist concerns or which involved mainly lesbian feminist actors. One was the intense backlash against the radical/revolutionary feminist analysis of sexuality and sexual violence, which was largely created by lesbian feminists and encapsulated the lesbian perspective. The enemies of lesbian feminism used the promotion of sexualised hierarchies of power through sadomasochism and butch femme role-playing to attack the new and revolutionary ethics and ideas that lesbian feminists had created about the importance of equality in sex

10 Introduction

and relationships. I shall look also at the internecine warfare around identity politics that created divisions around class, race and disability, which led to the destruction of the revolutionary impulse in the mid- to late 1980s. It led to the stultification and eventual collapse of many important institutions of lesbian and feminist politics and culture, such as the *London Women's Liberation Newsletter* and the Lesbian Archive. The actors involved where this struggle was at its most heated were mostly lesbians. None of these conflicts would have been so effective in trashing lesbian feminism and the WLM without the changed political context that was brought about by the Conservative government led by Margaret Thatcher and its neoliberal, individualist policies, which led to the abolition of the Greater London Council and the passing of legislation that prohibited local councils from engaging in the 'promotion of homosexuality'. These political changes are described in the final chapter.

Scope

This book is the first to be written about lesbian feminism in the UK. It cannot possibly do justice to the richness of what took place. I am sure that many lesbian feminists from those days will feel that important organisations, campaigns and cultural institutions have been neglected or omitted. I hope that the book will not just enrage with what it has left out, but stimulate much more in the way of memoir and research both from those who were involved and from the new generation of lesbian feminists now emerging. I hope that others will cover many more aspects and provide detail that was not possible here and that research will be done on lesbian feminism outside London. This book concentrates on what was happening in London mainly because that was where I, and most of my interviewees, lived and took part in feminist politics, and because lesbian feminism in London is better documented than that which took place elsewhere. My research focussed on the *London Women's Liberation Newsletter*, for instance, and the national newsletter *WIRES* (*Women's Information and Referral Enquiry Service*), but did not extend to regional resources.

The ambition of the book

I did not simply write this book because I consider lesbian feminism to be in need of rescue from its annihilation in the histories of the UK WLM, though I do think this is very important. I have written it with the hope that knowledge of what went before will inspire a new generation of feminists who are becoming lesbians today to imagine what can be done, to be proud of their history and to strive to create a new lesbian feminist movement.

Bibliography

British Library (n.d.). Sisterhood and After. British Library. www.bl.uk/sisterhood# (accessed 30 January, 2018).

Browne, Sarah (2012). 'A Veritable Hotbed of Feminism': Women's Liberation in St Andrews, Scotland, *c*.1968–*c*.1979. *Twentieth Century British History*, 23 (1): 100–123.

Browne, Sarah (2014). *The Women's Liberation Movement in Scotland*. Manchester: Manchester University Press.

Brownian, Carrie-Ann (2016, 31 October). Transing the Dead: The Erasure of Gender-Defiant Role Models from History. 4th Wave Now. https://4thwavenow.com/tag/radclyffe-hall.

Brownmiller, Susan (2000). *In Our Time: Memoir of a Revolution*. New York: Dial Press.

Bruley, Sue (2013). Consciousness-Raising in Clapham: Women's Liberation as 'Lived Experience' in South London in the 1970s. *Women's History Review*, 22 (5): 717–738.

Coote, Anna, and Campbell, Beatrix (1982). *Sweet Freedom. The Struggle for Women's Liberation*. Oxford: Basil Blackwell.

Echols, Alice (1989). *Daring to Be Bad: Radical Feminism in America 1967–1975*. Minneapolis: University of Minnesota Press.

Friedan, Betty (1963). *The Feminine Mystique*. New York: W. W. Norton.

Gage, Carolyn (2010). The Inconvenient Truth about Teena Brandon. Trivia: Voices of Feminism. www.triviavoices.com/the-inconvenient-truth-about-teena-brandon.html (accessed 28 October 2017).

Gottschalk, Lorene (2003). From Gender Inversion to Choice and Back: Changing Perceptions of the Aetiology of Lesbianism over Three Historical Periods. *Women's Studies International Forum*, 26 (3): 221–233.

Jeffreys, Sheila (1977, 5 April). The Need for Revolutionary Feminism: Against the Liberal Takeover of the Women's Liberation Movement. Paper presented at 9th National Women's Liberation Conference, London. Available at Feministes Radicales: www.feministes-radicales.org/2012/05/20/the-need-for-revolutionary-feminism (accessed 19 December 2017).

Jeffreys, Sheila (2014). *Gender Hurts: A Feminist Analysis of the Politics of Transgenderism*. Abingdon, UK: Routledge.

Lesbian History Group (ed.) (1989). *Not a Passing Phase: Reclaiming Lesbians in History 1840–1985*. London: Women's Press.

Lockyer, Bridget (2013). An Irregular Period? Participation in the Bradford Women Liberation Movement. *Women's History Review*, 22 (4): 643–657.

Mackay, Finn (2014). Reclaiming Revolutionary Feminism. *Feminist Review*, 106: 95–103.

Mackay, Finn (2015). *Radical Feminism: Feminist Activism in Movement*. Basingstoke, UK: Palgrave Macmillan.

MacKinnon, Catharine A. (1989). *Toward a Feminist Theory of the State*. Cambridge, MA: Harvard University Press.

Mohin, Lilian (1984). Lesbian Radical Feminism: The Only Radical Feminism? (Letters). *Trouble and Strife*, 3: 6–8.

Onlywomen Press (1981). *Love Your Enemy? The Debate between Heterosexual Feminism and Political Lesbianism*. London: Onlywomen Press.

Poirot, Kristan (2009). Domesticating the Liberated Woman: Containment Rhetorics of Second Wave Radical/Lesbian Feminism. *Women's Studies in Communication*, 32 (3): 263–292.

Rees, Jeska (2010). A Look Back at Anger: The Women's Liberation Movement in 1978. *Women's History Review*, 19 (3): 337–356.

Rich, Adrienne (1977). *The Meaning of Our Love for Women Is What We Have Constantly to Expand: Speech at New York Lesbian Pride Rally June 26, 1977*. New York: Out & Out Books.

Rosen, Ruth (2000) *The World Split Open: How the Modern Women's Movement Changed America*. New York: Viking.

Rowbotham, Sheila (1997). *A Century of Women: The History of Women in Britain and the US.* London: Viking.

Segal, Lynne (1987). *Is the Future Female? Troubled Thoughts on Contemporary Feminism.* London: Virago.

Setch, Eve (2002). The Face of Metropolitan Feminism: The London Women's Liberation Workshop, 1969–1979. *Twentieth Century British History*, 13 (2): 171–190.

Staggenborg, Suzanne, and Taylor, Verta (2005). Whatever Happened to the Women's Movement? *Mobilization*, 10 (1): 37–52.

Taylor, Verta, and Rupp, Leila J. (1993). Women's Culture and Lesbian Feminist Activism: A Reconsideration of Cultural Feminism. *Signs*, 19 (1): 32–61.

Weil, Lise (2010). Are Lesbians Going Extinct? (Editorial). *Trivia: Voices of Feminism*, 10. www.triviavoices.com/issue-10-are-lesbians-going-extinct-1.html.

1

THE ORIGINS OF LESBIAN FEMINISM

The revolution that was lesbian feminism transformed the meaning and practice of lesbianism. Lesbianism went from being a largely underground and stigmatised form of sexual deviance to a form of resistance by proud and out lesbians who were intent upon changing the world. Lesbian feminists put the spotlight upon hetero-sexuality, the institution that founds and organises the subordination of women, as a problem. They were the solution. In this chapter, I will examine the way that lesbianism was understood and lived before the Women's Liberation Movement and the changes that lesbian feminism wrought. I will explain the ways in which lesbian feminism developed in relation to the WLM. Differences of class, education and race affected the way that lesbian feminism developed, as did political differences around the way that lesbianism and feminism related to each other, between socialist feminists and radical feminists in particular. I will explain why lesbians separated off from mixed struggles that included gay men, and why they found it necessary, in many situations, to organise separately from heterosexual feminists.

Lesbianism before the flood

Lesbian feminism developed as part of the Women's Liberation Movement. Before the WLM, feminist historians point out, it is likely that the majority of women knew little of women's ability to express sexual love for each other (Faderman, 1985; Jeffreys, 1997 [1985]). There was no concept of the lesbian – i.e. a woman who chooses to love women – in popular culture. If women did come to love each other, and indeed to express this sexually, there was no lesbian 'identity' to which they could attach themselves. They are likely to have considered their love to be an eccentric and individual phenomenon. Lesbian historians argue that we should be careful about the way in which we name women who loved other women in the nineteenth century (Faderman, 1981: Jeffreys, 1989). Some women did behave

14 The origins of lesbian feminism

towards each other in ways that we would be likely to call 'lesbian' today and lived with women partners all their lives. Some even left a record (and this is extremely rare) of their sexual encounters with other women (Whitbread, 1988). Most women were unable to choose to live with and love other women because they did not have independent means. They were forced to marry, or to live under the protection of a male relative who would support them.

But women did find ways to love each other. Lillian Faderman and other feminist historians have traced a history of what they call 'women's romantic friendships', in which middle-class women would engage in long-term relationships with best friends which could last a lifetime, and could include sleeping in the same bed and forms of passionate physical affection, though there is usually no record to suggest how far this went (Rosenberg, 1975; Faderman, 1981). Such friendships seem to have been common and unremarkable. The women were not stigmatised, and they were not seen as sexual deviants or social outcasts. These women would likely not have called themselves lesbians or any other word which would indicate same-sex sexual relationships. They may not have known that women could relate to each other except in terms of friendships, which were often conducted alongside their marriages to men.

Those women who were able to choose for women because they were financially independent of men did have some models of women-loving women to whom they could compare themselves, and therefore create something which could now be seen as related to a lesbian identity. The wealthy, independent landowner Ann Lister, for instance, who conducted a number of sexual relationships with women in Yorkshire, where she lived, uses the example of Sappho when talking of her relations with women in her diaries from the 1820s (Whitbread, 1988). There is nothing in her diaries to suggest that she knew other women who identified with Sappho, however, or that she was part of a community rather than an isolated individual. Other women in the early nineteenth century, such as the teachers at a Scottish girls' school who were the protagonists in Faderman's book *Scotch Verdict*, may not have had a model to relate to, but seem to have managed to carry on relationships nonetheless (Faderman, 1985).

In this period there were likely to have been differences between the ways in which middle- and upper-class women who loved women thought about themselves and practised their love and the ways in which working-class women did. The difficulty for historians is that, although there is some record kept by educated middle-class women in diaries and letters of their love for women, working-class women did not keep such records, and the shape of such relations as they had with other women is not clear. Middle- and upper-class women were more likely to be literate and to live independent lives and practise their lesbianism more freely. They were able to write down information that enables us to have some insight into their lives.

Lesbian historians suggest that a golden age of romantic friendships for middle-class women was brought to an end by the work of the sexologists or scientists of sex in the late nineteenth century and early twentieth (Faderman, 1981). The

The origins of lesbian feminism **15**

sexologists created hostile stereotypes of what Henry Havelock Ellis called 'female inverts', which led to the stigmatisation of lesbian relationships as deviant (see Jeffreys, 1997 [1985]). Ellis based his insights on his own wife, Edith Lees Ellis, who was a lesbian. Lesbian feminist historians have argued that the sexologists were engaged in an ideological backlash against the powerful feminist movement of that period, which made women's friendships that had once seemed harmless into a threat to male dominance. Women started to enter occupations, such as teaching and typing, which enabled some independence. Women with an income were in a position to reject men and choose each other as life companions. Ellis's work circulated amongst a certain class of women, and by the 1920s lesbians such as Vita Sackville-West, who was married to a homosexual, and the novelist Radclyffe Hall possessed extensive libraries of his work and other sexology texts. The sexological version of the lesbian was of a woman who was masculine because she possessed the soul of a man in the body of a woman. Homosexuality was explained by sexual inversion – i.e. the 'germs' of one sex finding their way mysteriously into the body of the other. This appealed to some lesbians in the period before the First World War and the period between the wars, because it provided an explanation for their inclinations and a way to defend themselves. If lesbianism was the work of god-given biology, then lesbians should be tolerated rather than condemned. Radclyffe Hall, whose 1928 novel *The Well of Loneliness* is a plea for tolerance, has her heroine Stephen say: 'God's cruel, he let us get flawed in the making' (Hall, 1982 [1928]: 207).

In the 1920s manly dress was adopted by certain fashionable women of the middle classes in the UK, with the effect that those lesbians who wore breeches were less likely to stand out and attract opprobrium (Doan, 2001). In the case of working-class women in the UK, the adoption of masculine attire was less a fashionable affectation and more a matter of survival and necessity (Oram, 2007). These lesbians had to be taken for men if they wanted to get remunerative employment, and in such a guise they were able to live with other women without remark. The lesbian historian Alison Oram found examples of such practice until the 1950s (Oram, 2007). She explains that, when those taken to be men were revealed to be women, there was no public outcry against them as lesbians; rather, they were seen as curiosities. There was no category of 'the lesbian' in popular culture into which observers might place them. Rebecca Jennings explains that a lesbian subculture in which lesbians could socialise and create community did not exist before the 1920s. Men had had a gay subculture and particular clubs and bars long before this time, but there were cultural norms against women drinking, women had less money and there were restrictions on women's freedom of movement in public spaces (Jennings, 2007). In the 1920s a lesbian culture was developing around particular pubs and clubs that were usually mixed. This began to change, and the Gateways Club in London, which had started out as a Bohemian venue in the 1930s, catered almost entirely to lesbians by the 1950s (Gardiner, 2003). It was less class-specific than the venues of the 1920s, in which upper-class lesbians had been able to socialise. Nonetheless, until the late 1960s most lesbians would have had recourse

16 The origins of lesbian feminism

only to mixed gay clubs, and the lesbian culture available therein would likely have been one of butch/femme role-playing.

A working-class lesbian from Newcastle describes the clubs in which lesbians socialised and found partners in the 1960s, just before the advent of gay liberation and the WLM, as the 'dives' (Farnham, 1990: 50). It was not a positive environment, because '[t]here was no women-only things. It wasn't that you weren't out as a lesbian it was just that the pubs were all you had, and they were grotty, overcharged and mixed.' The pub she used, she says, 'was a dive, where all sorts of people went, you had gays and petty criminals and prostitutes, so you mixed shoulders with everybody. This was the middle sixties.' The predominant way in which lesbians interacted was through butch and femme roles: 'I was into the three-piece suits and the butch thing. [...] And no way could I ever see myself as a femme. God, no. It was the high heels... You felt you were either one or the other' (ibid.). Even well into the 1970s, in places where there were no 'discos' (alternative venues run by lesbians where women danced to music selected by lesbian disc jockeys and often run as benefits for women's organisations), the alternatives for a social life were dire. My interviewee Al Garthwaite describes the situation thus: 'You had to go into these, the Gateways, holes in the ground with lesbians in them, or places that were frankly low life' (Al Garthwaite, interview 2013).

The 1960s: a change of climate

In the 1960s there was a change in the climate which affected the way that lesbianism was thought about by lesbians themselves and in popular culture. A move towards a more collective identity replaced the idea of individual deviance. The more liberal sexual climate encouraged wider public discussion of the issue of homosexuality and enabled the setting up of homosexual rights groups. A campaign to repeal the legislation that criminalised male homosexual activity began after the Wolfenden report was published in 1957 (Home Office, 1957). The report was commissioned as a result of a wave of police persecution, arrests and imprisonment of gay men in the early 1950s. It recommended that a private/public distinction should be applied to male homosexuality, such that homosexuality in private should not be within the concerns of the law. In response, the Homosexual Law Reform Society (HLRS) was set up to campaign for law reform, which led to repeal in the 1967 Sexual Offences Act. Greater public awareness and toleration made homosexuality a respectable topic for media discussion, as in the two television documentaries by Bryan Magee in 1964 and 1965, the second of which was on lesbians (Jennings, 2007: 100).

Lesbian sex was not criminalised in the same way, but lesbians were involved in the HLRS to support gay men. The first stage in what Rebecca Jennings calls 'the negotiation of collective lesbian identities' was the publication of a specifically lesbian magazine, *Arena Three*, whose editor, Esme Langley, remained in post until its demise in 1971 (Jennings, 2007: 130). Out of this an organisation, the Minorities Research Group (MRG), was set up by Langley, Cynthia Read, Julie Switsur and

The origins of lesbian feminism **17**

Diana Chapman, to publish the magazine and to 'conduct and to collaborate in research into the homosexual condition, especially as it concerns women; and to disseminate information and items of interest' to a variety of actors (ibid.: 138). There was an example to emulate, in the shape of the first specifically lesbian organisation set up in the US a decade earlier, the Daughters of Bilitis (ibid.). The MRG agenda was egalitarian rather than feminist, meaning that it focussed on promoting the idea that male and female homosexuals were really just like anyone else and should be supported in integrating seamlessly into malestream society and culture.

In an interview, Diana Chapman explains how men reacted when *Arena Three* was set up. She says that the organising group had not realised that, for men, lesbianism was a source of sexual excitement: 'We hadn't realised that there was this interest in lesbianism as pornography and that we found quite shocking. We'd have men knocking at the door or ringing up' (Hall Carpenter Archives, 1989). Men's desire to sexually access lesbians probably results from the fact that lesbians are women who specifically reject men's advances and provide the exciting challenge of violating boundaries. This problem bedevilled lesbian organising from this time onwards. Its counterpart today is the pretence by male heterosexual cross-dressers that they are 'lesbians' and the demand that lesbians submit to penetration by these men to avoid accusations of 'transphobia' (see Jeffreys, 2014). Chapman explains that the lesbians who produced *Arena Three* wanted it to be 'a proper, decent magazine and that there should be no overt sex, nothing that could be remotely described as titillating'. The times were so conservative that 'we wouldn't send it out to any married woman who didn't have her husband's approval because I think we had one or two letters from raving husbands more or less threatening to sue us for alienation of affection' (Hall Carpenter Archives, 1989: 53).

The MRG was determined to present a respectable image, and some members were dismayed that there were women attending meetings in masculine attire. An issue of the MRG magazine *Arena Three* from its first year contains what the writer called a 'complaint' in a section entitled 'MRG News', about the way that some lesbians who attended meetings chose to dress:

> We must regretfully voice a complaint. A good many members who have attended the first two M.R.G. meetings have been somewhat piqued by the exhibitionist tendency of one or two others, and want to know if it is really absolutely necessary to turn up to these meetings dressed in what is popularly known as 'full drag'. As the majority of women homosexuals are not 'transvestites'…we shall be glad if at future meetings there will be no further cause for wounded sensibilities.
>
> *(Arena Three, 1964, 1 (6): 14)*

A contributor called K.H. comments: 'Would anyone take the H.L.R.S. seriously if all the male homosexual members turned out in full female finery?' Chapman comments that, when the social group Kenric was set up out of the MRG, 'we

18 The origins of lesbian feminism

had a very bitter debate on whether women should come dressed as men', but says that this role-playing was not de rigueur because 'there were always people like me and Esme who just dressed in slacks and shirt' (Hall Carpenter Archives, 1989: 55). The MRG and *Arena Three* were important in providing the first public voice for lesbians, and providing a support network. The magazine became steadily more feminist in orientation until its demise in 1971 under the influence of the burgeoning WLM.

Lesbian feminism and the WLM

Lesbian feminism was a development from the Women's Liberation Movement, which began in the UK in 1969/70. Lesbian feminism transformed the idea and practice of lesbianism from being simply a sexual practice to a revolutionary way of living, as the US lesbian feminist philosopher Janice Raymond explains: 'Lesbian feminists have…expanded the range and reality of what has been perceived as a sexual category – lesbian sexuality – far beyond the physical body to a social and political reality' (Raymond, 1986: 14). Women's liberation got under way sooner in the US. Susan Brownmiller recounts, in her autobiographical account of its early years, that women's groups were being formed in the late 1960s, mainly by women activists who had been involved in the civil rights movement and on the Left (Brownmiller, 2000). By the early 1970s many feminist publications had already been started up, including the foundational feminist magazine *MS* in 1971. The American example helped to spark the beginning of women's liberation in the UK, which got under way a couple of years later than in the US.

As in the US, the women who began the WLM in the UK came from the Left. Sheila Rowbotham says that it was an awareness of a women's movement beginning in the US and Germany reaching the UK in 1968 and an uprising of working-class women that sparked the WLM in Britain (Rowbotham, 1972). The first women's rights group was formed in Hull in the spring of 1968, around a campaign by fisherman's wives to demand improved safety after the loss of two trawlers on which their husbands worked. This stimulated what Rowbotham calls 'left middle class women' to form an equal rights group. Gradually women on the Left started to talk about their 'specific oppression', Rowbotham explains, and tried to link this to Marxism. They created an edition of the revolutionary paper *Black Dwarf* which included an article by Rowbotham on how to 'relate how you encountered sexual humiliation to marxism' (ibid.: 93). Another women's group formed in Tufnell Park in London, and it was involved in setting up the London Women's Liberation Workshop to create a network of activist groups. The workshop at first had only four groups across London under its aegis. By the end of the 1970s there were more than 300 groups and it was acting as an umbrella organization, as well as being an office for information and contacts, a bookshop and meeting place and the base for the *London Women's Liberation Newsletter* (Setch, 2002).

During the rest of 1969 various women's groups were set up, particularly at universities such as Essex and Coventry. As Eve Setch explains in her history of the London workshop, 'By the end of 1969 groups had come together across the country and a coordinated Women's Liberation Movement was growing' (ibid.: 172). Rowbotham and others held a meeting at Ruskin College, Oxford, to discuss holding a conference on women's history, and out of it came what is seen as the first Women's Liberation Conference. Rowbotham comments, 'It was really from the Oxford conference in February 1970 that a movement could be said to exist' (Rowbotham, 1972: 97). Thereafter, a national WLM conference was held every year in different cities until 1978.

In these early years feminists were likely to call themselves socialist feminists and endlessly debate the question of how forms of women's oppression could be fitted into Left understandings. The most problematic issues for socialist analysis were those which related to women's oppression by individual men. Socialists were more open to discussion of the ways in which the state or capitalism oppressed women – e.g. equal pay and factory gate politics, and issues relating to benefit payments, women and housing. Such issues as male violence against women, sexual violence and lesbianism did not fit in, but increasingly feminists were taking up these issues and began to call themselves radical rather than socialist feminists. It was from this latter group, the radical feminists, that lesbian feminism emerged.

Lesbian separation from gay men

Lesbian feminism was created by lesbians issuing from two directions: from mixed gays organising in groups such as the Campaign for Homosexual Equality and the Gay Liberation Front; and from the WLM. Lesbians joined gay organisations in the 1960s and 1970s out of the assumption that they would have common cause with gay men as a result of shared oppression. Even those who had nothing to do with straight men fondly believed that gay men would be different and less sexist. It did not turn out that way, and lesbians involved in working with gay men began to get exasperated on many fronts. The assimilationist politics of lesbian and gay organisations in the US and the UK were beginning to change in the late 1960s, towards a more self-confident and challenging approach. The advent of Gay Liberation is usually dated to the time of the Stonewall rebellion in Greenwich Village, New York, in 1969, but gay historians acknowledge that the ideas that were to form gay liberation politics were already gestating in groups and communities within the US before that time (Jeffreys, 2003). The WLM developed in the US ahead of gay liberation, with the effect that Gay Liberation Front ideas on the politics of the personal were strongly influenced by feminism. The GLF also developed alongside and reflected the anti-capitalist and anti-racist ideas emanating from Black politics, student politics and the new Left. These gay activists were radical, and committed to creating the revolution now by transforming interpersonal relations (Jay and Young, 1992 [1972]). They rejected role-playing and the exploitative nature of the gay social scene, which revolved, in the US, around making money from selling drink into a captive market to profit Mafia interests.

20 The origins of lesbian feminism

When the GLF got going in the UK in 1971, it incorporated the same ideas. The GLF rejected the culture in which lesbians and gay men had been forced to live up till then – i.e. socialising in poky, hidden and sometimes literally underground bars with exorbitant prices and conditions. They were determined to come out of the closet into the public realm. Role-playing had been part of both the gay and lesbian scene, and UK gay liberationists rejected this entirely, saying that it was simply a form of acting straight, imitating the harmful practices of male dominance in which relationships were organised around male power and women's submission (Walter, 1980). Alternative venues were set up which were non-exploitative and in which the mores of the patriarchy could be rejected. These included discos and socials in community centres and student unions where there was full light instead of semi-darkness and women and men could socialise without deafening music and alcohol.

Men hugely outnumbered women, and there was no recognition that lesbians might have separate concerns. Activists tended to focus on issues of male gay concern, such as cottaging, which was still illegal. In this practice men lurked about in public lavatories to find sexual partners, leaving them vulnerable to arrest by policemen engaged in a form of entrapment through pretending to be interested in sex with them (Jeffreys, 2003). Cottaging, and sex in public places generally, were not activities or a cultural form that was part of lesbian culture or history. Lesbian feminists were angered by the way in which gay men dominated and imposed their priorities with no consideration about how lesbian issues might be different or even in conflict. The fact that some of these gay men considered that wearing items of women's clothing was revolutionary, because it challenged the notion that men should be masculine, was infuriating (ibid.). Lesbians were challenging femininity, the idea that women had to wear dresses, only to discover that some of their brothers considered the wearing of dresses to be the revolution in action. Moreover, the whole tradition of drag, in which gay men wore what they saw as women's clothing to imitate and make fun of women, made lesbians and feminists angry.

The practice of drag is based upon the idea that women are so hilarious that a man with balloons up his jumper is engaged in a jolly jape. Feminists did not see women as essentially hilarious and were not delighted that some gay men were prepared to adopt the clothing of the subordinate class in order to be alluring and outrageous to their fellows. UK lesbian feminist Sheila Shulman describes the only time that she encountered gay liberation: 'There was a gay "be-in" of some species at Essex University…including discussions and a dance. The lesbians told the gay blokes that it was obvious that men and women couldn't work together even if we were all gay.' She had 'a long argument with one of the blokes there who was in drag. He was dressed in black fishnet stockings and red satin skirt and God knows what and telling me it was a tribute to his mother! Which was balderdash, total misogyny!' She calls it misogyny because 'it was a parody of a woman' (Shulman, 1983: 55).

Another problem for lesbians in working with gay men was the construction of gay male sexuality, which was different from the construction of malestream male sexuality only in choice of partner. The aspects of male sexuality that endangered girls and women through sexual assault and rape – i.e. objectification and aggression – persisted in a gay male sexuality that was focussed on the eroticising of power difference. UK lesbian feminist Liz Stanley was the women's organiser for the Campaign for Homosexual Equality, which was a more traditional organisation than Gay Liberation, from 1972 to 1976. She writes incisively of the reasons she abandoned mixed organising, one of which was gay men's sexual behavior:

> Gay men treated each other in what seemed an almost invariably sexist way. By this I mean treating each other as sexual objects, objectifying the young and stereotypically attractive, and making use of involvements with new members in order to exploit them sexually.
>
> *(Stanley, 1982: 197)*

These new members were often young and in need of considerable support as they came out as homosexual for the first time so they were ripe for exploitation. It was not just that gay men saw women as irrelevant to their concerns that annoyed lesbians, but their clear and rancid misogyny. Stanley explains,

> Persistently I and other women in the WCC [Women's Coordinating Committee] received complaints that the women in local groups smelled. This was a feature of all women, who, literally, stank. Women's cunts were suppurating wounds, full of crawling worms. They should not be permitted in the same rooms with men.
>
> *(ibid.: 199)*

Over her years of working in CHE she was 'as the "name" associated with the women's campaign, constantly attacked, vilified, insulted and, quite literally, hated by hundreds, possibly even thousands, of gay men in this country – and not just those in CHE either' (ibid.).

The US lesbian feminist philosopher Marilyn Frye explained with admirable clarity in a talk in 1981 why lesbians and gay men could not form a united political community, despite the fact that both are subject to discrimination and hatred on the grounds of who they choose to love (Frye, 1983). The main reason was that gay men, as men, have as their first loyalty, men and masculinity and this places them in direct opposition to feminism and lesbian feminism. The principles of male supremacy to which male gay rights movements and male gay culture are entirely congruent, she points out, are: the presumption of male citizenship, worship of the penis, male homoeroticism or man-loving, compulsory male heterosexuality and the presumption of general phallic access. She concludes that male homosexuality is 'congruent with and a logical extension of straight male-supremacist culture' (Frye, 1983: 144). The 'feminist lesbian', Frye argues, has values that are entirely 'noncongruent' with all this because she does not love men; she does not preserve all passion and significant exchange for men. She does not hate women. She presupposes the equality of female and male bodies, or even the superiority or normativeness of the female body. She has no interest in penises beyond some reasonable concern about how men use them against women.... She is not accessible to the penis.

(ibid.)

Another fundamental difference, she stresses, is that gay men do not believe sexuality can be subject to conscious choice whereas that is precisely the 'political policy' of lesbian feminists who 'present ourselves publicly as persons who have chosen lesbian patterns of desire and sensuality' (Frye, 1983: 149). For all these reasons, lesbians who were becoming involved in feminism and the WLM left mixed organising in the early 1970s and did not return until the 1980s, when some started to work with gay men again out of compassion over the ravages of AIDS on the gay male community.

Development of lesbian feminism

At the birth of lesbian feminism, in the early 1970s, women from gay liberation were becoming involved in the WLM and women who were already in WLM groups were beginning to come out as lesbians or deciding to become lesbians. All of this caused ructions in the early WLM as heterosexual feminists reacted with discomfort or hostility. This happened in the US women's liberation movement too (see Abbott and Love, 1972). As lesbians started to come out in the National Organisation for Women (NOW), the founder, Betty Friedan, called lesbianism a 'lavender herring' that would distract from women's rights and bring NOW into disrepute. Reactions were similar in the UK. Although lesbians were present in early WLM groups and conferences, their reception if they tried to raise lesbianism as an issue for feminism was not always positive. Al Garthwaite describes going to a women's liberation meeting in Oxford at the beginning of 1971 and finding that lesbianism was still an unmentionable subject. She says that a woman got up at the meeting

and said that she was going to a Gay Liberation Front social and event in London, and would anyone like to go with her? And there must have been 40, 45 women in the room, and you could have heard a pin drop. Complete shocked; amazed silence. And Ros looked round and said, 'Oh, I can see not,' and sat down again. I thought that was very brave, and I really admired her.

(Al Garthwaite, interview 2013)

As early as 1972 lesbians writing and organising meetings in the *London Women's Liberation Newsletter* (*LWLN*) or attending meetings of the London Women's Liberation Workshop were referring to themselves as 'gay' and talking about the Gay Liberation Front, which had been formed in the UK the previous year. In a

The origins of lesbian feminism **23**

January 1972 issue of the *London Women's Liberation Newsletter*, the nomenclature of gayness was used by a woman seeking to organise a meeting to talk about the discrimination suffered by women who were 'gay' in the London workshop. The announcement asked, 'Is it good to be "gay" in the Workshop. Feel isolated, ignored, suppressed in your Workshop group? Many of us are scared to tell our sisters that we are gay. Want to talk about "gaiety" vis-à-vis Workshop with other women? Let's get together and stop feeling guilty' (LWLN 65, 1972, 9 January). A couple of weeks later the meeting had been arranged, and it was called a 'think-in' to discuss 'the relationship of the Gay Women's Group of GLF to the London Women's Liberation Workshops and also to GLF itself where many sisters feel oppressed by the sexism and male chauvinism within the movement' (LWLN 68, 1972, 30 January).

These lesbians were on the way out of the GLF and into women's liberation.

> Several sisters are feeling the necessity to establish a separate Gay-Women's-Group (along the lines of Radicalesbians, New York) that will be relatively autonomous of the heavily-male-dominated G.L.F. And would like to discuss this along with the possibility of establishing a separate office/center for Gay-sisters and the production of a non-censored or edited radical feminist/lesbian newspaper.
>
> *(ibid.)*

The separate Gay Women's Group which was set up in February was called 'Red Lesbians' (LWLN 70, 1972, 13 February). By January 1973 the word 'lesbian' had generally replaced the word 'gay', and a 'Lesbian Liberation' meeting was held at Radnor Terrace, a women's squat (LWLN 115, 1973, 7 January). Houses that were reclaimed for use by the women's squatting movement were often used as centres for activities such as meetings or music rehearsals.

Lesbianism and radical feminism were controversial issues at the time when the London Women's Liberation Workshop, which had previously had no premises, made plans to set up its first geographical location in a building in Earlham Street. The minutes of a meeting of the workshop at Covent Garden Community Centre in November 1973 show this. There was discussion of two connected issues. One was whether lesbians were making women (presumably heterosexual) feel uncomfortable and should tone down their presence, and the other was the question of whether the bookshop, which was to be part of the workshop at the newly secured premises, should be women-only. It had already been decided that the workshop itself was to be women-only. The lesbians were seen to be the ones arguing most forcefully for the women-only principle. A paper was read from the Balham WLM group, which said that 'Women's Liberation is not lesbianism. This idea makes many women feel threatened' (minutes, London Women's Liberation Workshop meeting, 1973, 3 November: 10, Lynne Keys' collection). One woman said, 'The real argument is whether the movement identifies with Radical Feminism or Gay Liberation or whether it remains as Women's Liberation' (ibid.). In response, a lesbian answered that it had taken her 21 years to find herself and she couldn't

24 The origins of lesbian feminism

bear to go back, but she was answered by another woman who was worried about lesbians and said that many women 'feel alienated from the Workshop because of emotional blackmail that has been taking place by the Lesbian group' (ibid.). When one woman argued that 'there are many women who won't come into the bookshop if men are excluded', another replied, 'This is moral blackmail,' and added: 'This is a power struggle, you would not ask a TU guy to ask a factory owner to solve his problems' (ibid.: 11). When the vote finally took place on whether the bookroom should be women-only, 117 voted for, 30 against and 20 abstained (ibid.: 13).

There seems to have been a strong lesbian/heterosexual split at this meeting. The lesbians were referred to indistinguishably as either 'lesbians' or 'radical feminists'. One woman proclaimed that she felt 'dominated by certain extreme women here. This is turning into a witch hunt.' Another said that 'there is a situation in which some women feel threatened within the Movement. And feel that women who are not radical feminists are witch hunting them for that.' The political split continued, as the minutes from an April 1974 bi-annual meeting of the now Earlham Street Workshop indicate. There was discussion of how 'dress and life-style differences are seen as divisive' (minutes of the bi-annual meeting of the Earlham St. Workshop, 1974, 21 April: 16, Lynne Keys' collection). There was a suggestion at the meeting that 'radical feminists' should not be workers 'because of the distance they have to travel to see how new people respond to something'; in other words, they would alienate other women (ibid.: 17). At the same meeting, a discussion took place about whether there was a 'gay/straight' problem, and a woman responded that it was not a 'gay/straight' split but 'Marxist feminists v. radical feminists' (ibid.: 19).

The lesbians, though, were getting organised. Specialised lesbian groups were being set up, such as the Jewish Lesbian Feminist Group in 1974 (LWLN 46, 1974, 12 June). The first lesbian conference, still called a Gay Women's Conference in the publicity (LWLN 30, 1974, 13 February), took place in April 1974 and was an important milestone. Sheila Shulman was interviewed about it in 1983 in a piece called 'When Lesbians Came Out in the Movement' (Shulman, 1983: 51). Shulman was born in the US but spent all her WLM years in the UK. She described herself as 'lesbian, radical feminist, and Jewish'. Although the conference was not explicitly called 'lesbian feminist', Shulman explains, she and all her friends were definitely attending as lesbian feminists. The conference was notable for being the first time that lesbians cast off some or all of their clothes to dance and socialise. Shulman says, 'I was so exuberant – I who am normally totally inhibited was without my shirt and dancing!' (ibid.: 52). There were, she says, 'a whole lot of naked ladies around, it was quite wonderful. The whole tone of the conference was "My God, look at us" – "we're all here, look how many of us" (ibid.). Relationships were a big focus of the conference because, Shulman explains, lesbians usually had to be inhibited when discussing them in front of heterosexual women. This was because lesbians were conscious that their relationships were very different and because the relationships of heterosexual women, and their difficulties with men, were the focus of consciousness-raising in the WLM. Lesbians had to fend for themselves and invent new ways of thinking and relating.

The issue of lesbian visibility in the WLM was much discussed, with the result that the conference put in a demand to the organisers of the next National Women's Liberation Conference, in Edinburgh in the same year, that there should be block workshops on lesbianism. The result was that everyone had to spend a full afternoon at the Edinburgh conference talking about lesbianism. The demand arose from the fact that 'we felt that we had been invisible in the movement, even to ourselves in some way' (ibid.: 52). Lesbians felt, Shulman says, 'a quite beleaguered minority' at the event (ibid.: 53). They wanted a 'lesbian' demand to become one of the official demands of the WLM, and were successful. The sixth demand of the WLM was adopted in the form of 'the right to a self-defined sexuality' and 'an end to discrimination against lesbians', though the first half was split off at the 1978 national conference and placed as a preface in front of all the other demands. Shulman explains that the new 'lesbian' demand was 'meant to be a recognition of our presence and the necessity for women to confront their own sexuality – for heterosexual women to confront their own sexuality' (ibid.). Al Garthwaite explains there was still clear hostility about public discussion of lesbianism at the conference, which was shown in relation to the adoption of the sixth demand. There was, Al said,

> some opposition from some women who said that it would discredit the movement, it would put off 'ordinary women' (in inverted commas) from joining the movement, if that demand was there, because they would be put off by the idea of lesbians. I mean, that argument didn't sway the conference. But that was still being had, that sort of discussion, then. And it wasn't just screamed down, as maybe a few years later it would have been. Or thought of as disgraceful that that sort of prejudice would be airing itself.
>
> (Al Garthwaite, interview 2013)

Although lesbian feminists were not saying at the time that radical feminists should become lesbians, the assumption was there, Shulman says, that 'perhaps if women did confront all the issues of their own sexuality they would naturally become lesbians. I think it was a hope.' She says that in 1974 there were not yet specifically lesbian groups, though the 'constituency' of radical feminist groups was lesbian. She says, 'Most of the lesbians I knew were calling themselves radical feminist, and the consciousness raising groups I was in were all lesbian' (Shulman, 1983: 53).

The hostility lesbians faced is exemplified in the behaviour of Erin Pizzey, the woman who set up the first refuge for women escaping battering by male partners. Pizzey was not a radical feminist, and she was worried when her thunder was stolen by a developing radical feminist refuge movement which became Women's Aid. Women's Aid was set up by lesbians, as so many of the campaigns against male violence and facilities such as rape crisis centres were. In 1975 Pizzey sent letters

26 The origins of lesbian feminism

to a number of local authorities accusing Jo Sutton, a lesbian feminist and the first national organiser of Women's Aid, who had been working at the Chiswick refuge that Pizzey set up, of having dangerous links with women's liberation and Gay Women's Liberation, a group that did not exist (Sutton and Hanmer, 1984). This was an attempted anti-lesbian smear campaign.

A newsletter in August 1974 shows that the divisions developing in the WLM were between those variously called 'radical feminists' and 'lesbians' and those called 'Marxist feminists' (*LWLN* 56, 1974, 15 August). It contains sections of the preface to a piece called 'In Defence of Feminism', which turns out to be a critique of radical feminists by some Marxist feminists. They complain that, instead of writing their ideas down, radical feminists write bad poetry instead. Radical feminists, they say, control and destroy women's centres, and though they cannot destroy 'the movement' they may give it a 'bad name among women'. 'Their ideology,' the Marxist feminists argue, 'reduces itself to two articles of faith, two shibboleths: (1) hate all men (2) love all women.' Moreover, they say the radical feminists were contemptuous of heterosexual women:

> Despite an ideology of love, on the level of practice there are many and growing signs of an anti-woman attitude among Rad Fems. Because they look down on women who are in heterosexual relationships and who are 'taking shit' from men, they look down on most women in or out of the movement.
>
> *(ibid.)*

The setting up of a phone helpline, Lesbian Line, by lesbian feminists in 1977 was a pivotal moment in the development of lesbian feminism (Bishop, 1992). At that time lesbians were trying to survive as volunteers on mixed gay phone lines, of which there were several. There were four women on a collective of 25 at Icebreakers and five women and 75 men at Gay Switchboard. Women from both these organisations joined with other lesbian feminists to create what was originally called the Gay Women's Switchboard, before the name was changed to Lesbian Line. Lesbian Line offered the same help to lesbians that other mixed helplines offered mostly to men, such as support in coming out and information about where to meet other lesbians. Collective members held 'Sunday afternoon socials' for 'callers who wanted to meet other lesbians or to have the chance for a longer discussion face-to-face [sic]' (Bishop, 1992). The organisation formed a hub for the promotion of lesbian visibility and lesbian feminist ideas and practice. By this point a lesbian feminist movement was well under way.

The historical context

Social movements need to be understood in their historical contexts. The history of class and race, for instance, affect the way in which movements develop and who is in a position to join them. These became very important issues in the WLM.

Class and education

The UK of the 1960s and 1970s was riven by a rigid class structure that had a considerable effect on which women were in a position to discover feminism and get involved. This affected the way in which class identity politics was deployed, with destructive results within the WLM in the late 1970s and 1980s. The education system created major fault lines, whose harmful effects were felt amongst and between feminists. Secondary schools were divided into grammar schools and secondary moderns, and children were selected for them on the basis of a test, the 11-plus. The great majority of girls, 75 per cent, did not get to grammar schools because of the impact of social class, which affected the educational level of their parents, the area they came from and the school they attended (Sisterhood and After Research Team, 2013). They were unlikely to receive an education beyond the school-leaving age, which was raised to 15 from 1947 and to 16 in 1972. They were not able to acquire qualifications that could take them to university. Most grammar school students were middle class because their educated middle-class parents provided them with educational aspirations and resources that ensured this. Some working-class children did get to grammar schools and received an elite education which was structured to educate a class of persons who would fill the administrative posts in the state. This deliberate creation of social inequality created barriers between women.

There was a major expansion in university student numbers in the 1960s, with a doubling in seven years, partly attributable to the introduction of a maintenance grant system in the 1962 Education Act. In the early 1960s only one in 20 women went to university, but by the 1980s it was one in ten. This is still a very different percentage from the 51 per cent of women in 2010, however (Coughlan, 2010). The women who formed the Women's Liberation Movement were most likely to have been those who had been to grammar schools and to university, because they had easier access to the books and ideas that made women into feminists. Some working-class women were able to find their way to feminism through workplace activism and trade unionism, as Helen Lilly did in Newcastle (Farnham, 1990).

The great majority of my interviewees had attended grammar schools and universities but were the first in their families to do so. They were part of the opening up of university to women which happened in the 1960s. It took place at the same time as very important social movements were being formed around them, and discussed and organised with great energy in the student unions they frequented. These movements included the student movement itself, the Situationists in France and protests against the Vietnam War. The women who came to create early WLM groups and later came out as lesbians and lesbian feminists were not as steeped in anti-racist struggle as those in the US who took part in civil rights politics, but they were involved in radical questioning and dissent. The great wave of women entering universities in a context of protest movements launched women's liberation. But this new generation of university women was not necessarily secure in their middle-classness. They came from working-class backgrounds or from

28 The origins of lesbian feminism

working-class parents who were embourgeoising themselves. Stuck between the great majority of women, who did not get to grammar schools and could not imagine going to universities, and more securely middle-class women, who took these things for granted as their parents had, they collected – as we shall see in a later chapter – a good deal of the ire of their working-class sisters at class inequality.

Black lesbian feminism

There is no information on how many Black feminists and/or lesbian feminists took part in the WLM in the UK, but there is likely to have been a considerable disparity between the UK and the US in the numbers available to do so in the early years. In the US the Black and ethnic minority population was much larger as a percentage of the total population in the 1970s and 1980s, when the WLM was at its height. This was because of the history of slavery and a more open system of immigration. The UK had a great involvement in slavery, but the slavery took place overseas. Thus, the percentage of Black British people when slavery was abolished who became a regular part of the British population was not on the same scale as in the US. There were always Black people in Britain, as historians make plain, but the number was small (Fryer, 1984). In the post-war period there was a consider-able movement of Black people to the UK from the Caribbean and from Asia in response to the opening up of immigration and the direct recruitment of (mainly) men to fill jobs in low-paid areas of the economy, a practice which enabled the post-war boom. Immediately before this new immigration, in 1950, the number was estimated to be between 20,000 and 30,000. This rose sharply in the next two decades, but women were slower to arrive, and the numbers of children born in the early years would have been quite limited. This meant that the number of second-generation girls and young women who were in a position to join the WLM was small compared with a similar cohort in the US. Perhaps for this reason, Black feminists did not begin to write their own theory and history until considerably later, in the early 1980s, compared with the mid- to late 1970s in the US.

In the UK, the first Black women's group to be founded was the Brixton Black Women's Group, in 1973. Amina Mama gives a brief history of Black women's organising in the 1970s and 1980s in her book *Beyond the Masks* (Mama, 1995). She explains that the Brixton group, which she joined in 1979, was formed by women who had been involved in Black Power politics and were 'angered by the suppression of gender issues' (ibid.: 3). A new cohort of women joined later who were infuriated by the 'reluctance of women in the Women's Liberation Movement (WLM) to address the realities of racism both within and beyond their ranks' (ibid.). Black women's groups were subsequently set up all over Britain. A national umbrella group was set up in 1978, originally called the Organisation of Women of Africa and African Descent, and later the same year changed to Organisation of Women of African and Asian Descent in recognition of the fact that half the 'non-white' popu-lation in the UK were Asian. OWAAD held annual conferences from 1979 to 1982. The announcement of the 1982 OWAAD conference stated that there was a shift in direction from focusing on the wider Black liberation movement and socialism, and the role of Black women in fighting imperialism and racism, to a focus on developing a Black feminism, 'welcomed by some of us as being long overdue, and resisted by others who thought it could be diversionary from other aspects of our struggle. Discussions were to include sexuality, violence against Black women, development of Black women's culture, and "the definition of Black feminism"' (*Outwrite*, 4, July 1982). After OWAAD broke up, a Black Feminist Conference was held in 1984.

In March 1982 *Outwrite*, a newspaper, was founded. The first issue explains that four Black women and two white women had got together to write a newspaper for women. From the beginning *Outwrite* showed a determination to cover news relevant to Black women. It covered aspects of racism in the UK as well as women's rights in a range of other countries in Asia, Africa and South America. It contained a wide coverage of lesbian content too, usually in the form of news such as lesbian rights issues in the UK and the persecution of lesbians in other countries. In particular, it featured continuous coverage of the Lesbian Custody campaign, detailing legal cases about whether lesbians leaving marriages were to be allowed to take their children with them and related issues. It covered cases in which women were sacked for being lesbians in the UK, such as from nursery work, and the court cases that resulted. This compared very favourably with other feminist outlets at the time, which contained little news relevant to lesbians.

In 1985 a series of conferences and groups were set up to represent lesbian feminists who did not fit into the usual white and gentile profile of the WLM. In January a Jewish Lesbian conference took place in Birmingham and in October 1985 the first national Black Lesbian Conference took place in London. This latter was an important landmark for Black lesbian feminism in the UK. It was not a source of unalloyed celebration for all attendees, however. A letter in *Outwrite* the next month from an Asian lesbian explained that she did not feel welcome. She said she had 'feelings of pain' from the conference. She had expected unity between Afro-Caribbean and Asian lesbians because she had grown up in a situation of harmony between these groups in the community, but what she found was that 'Black' was interpreted to mean Afro-Caribbean, and as an Asian lesbian she did not fit in: 'The term Black was used to denote racial origin rather than "political strands and directions"' (*Outwrite*, 41, November 1985). Moreover, there was actual prejudice shown against Asian women: 'Myths about Asian people were "voiced". There was a "free for all" airing of offensive prejudice. ...I know that at least some of the Asian women there, already a minority, felt pushed out.'

The definition of 'Black lesbian' had to be extended in the late 1980s to cover women from a greater range of cultural and ethnic backgrounds. Whereas the lesbians who set up the original Black lesbian groups and conferences were mainly Afro-Caribbean and Asian, a much greater diversity of lesbians existed in the UK who did not fit comfortably into a white ethnicity and cultural background. As soon as the first Black lesbian groups were set up in the mid-1980s, many other groups of lesbians who did not feel that they fitted within a 'Black' umbrella started

30 The origins of lesbian feminism

to set up their own groups too. In March 1986 a Turkish Lesbian Group began meeting in London, and in May a group for Black Lesbians of Asian descent. A piece in the radical feminist journal *Trouble and Strife* in 1987 by Zehra, a Turkish lesbian, makes this clear (Zehra, 1987). Zehra interviewed 39 lesbians from a 'variety of different backgrounds', including Afro-Caribbean, Jewish, half-Jewish/half-Irish, Asian, Turkish Cypriot, Greek, Arab, Spanish, Irish, Iranian, Chinese, Gibraltarian, Russian, American, Latin American, mixed-race and Italian. The fact that there were lesbians in the UK from such a variety of backgrounds, the interviewees said, was not obvious from '[a]ny kind of lesbian thing you read', which 'just does not mention you anywhere, it is like you don't exist' (ibid.: 12).

The lesbians all spoke about having felt different because they did not fit in to white communities. Sonya explained that she did not fit into 'Black culture' because she was raised in a white community and had the wrong accent. It was also because she was Guyanese and a 'lot of the community was Jamaican so we weren't seeing eye to eye'. Linda explained that Black women have 'differences and diversities' because

> we may be from Pakistan, Nigeria, Jamaica or St. Lucia, and as the Black lesbian movement grows, those differences will have a greater chance to develop which, to my mind, is a source of strength to us. By defining as Black we arm ourselves to fight the racism we collectively and individually experience, but we must also give each other space to explore the cultural differences between us
>
> *(ibid.: 13)*

Lee said she found it harder to handle the homophobia she experienced when it came from within the Black community than from the white community, because she needed the Black community more (ibid.).

But, as well as recognising differences between themselves and white lesbians, they saw themselves as having common concerns with white lesbians on issues of lesbian oppression, such as 'hospital visiting rights to bereavement, inheritance, housing', and wanted more positive images of lesbians in the media and for lesbian works to be in the school curriculum. They were also 'very concerned' about custody issues around their children, rights to have artificial insemination to become pregnant and rights to adopt and foster children. There were considerable complexities to the issue of race within WLM theory and practice.

Naming lesbians

In the 1970s, my interviewees pointed out, they were more likely to call themselves radical or revolutionary feminists than lesbian feminists. In the early 1970s dozens of lesbian magazines, journals and newsletters that were developing lesbian feminist theory were set up in the US, and these began to circulate in the UK. Not all were explicitly lesbian feminist but most were, including such iconic titles as *The*

Furies, Amazon, Killer Dykes and *Lavender Woman* in 1971; *Amazon Quarterly* in 1972; *Dykes and Gorgons, Lesbian Feminist, Lesbian Tide* and *One to One: A Lesbian/Feminist Journal of Communication* in 1973; *Quest: A Feminist Quarterly* and *Lesbian Connection* in 1974; *Dyke: A Quarterly* in 1975; *Sinister Wisdom* in 1976; *Trivia* in 1982; and *Common Lives/Lesbian Lives* in 1981.

Lesbian feminist publications were not so prolific in the UK and did not start as early, but feminists were familiar with the lesbian theory coming out of the US because it was reproduced in newsletters and magazines or as pamphlets. As in the US, publications with general feminist titles might be produced entirely by lesbians and have clearly lesbian content. By the mid-1970s, though, around the time of the first National Lesbian Conference in 1974, specifically lesbian groups and lesbian publications were beginning to spring up around the country. Some examples are the *Leeds Lesbian Newsletter,* which was set up in 1975 out of the Leeds Lesbian Campaigning Group (formed in 1974); the *National Lesbian Newsletter,* which was established in 1975; and the *Lesbian Teachers' Newsletter,* also set up in 1975. The *Revolutionary and Radical Feminist Newsletter,* which was produced by lesbians and recognisably a lesbian newsletter from its content, was produced for the first time in Leeds in 1978 and continued until 1990.

Several of my interviewees said that they did not use the term 'lesbian feminist' to describe themselves before the 1980s. Lynne Harne explained when women began to call themselves lesbian feminists: 'Yes, I think we began calling ourselves lesbian feminists around about 1974, 1975. Before that, I think we were lesbians and feminists' (Lynne Harne, interview 2013). Julie Bindel said that she 'always used the term lesbian feminist. I've never really used one without the other. I used to say I was a revolutionary feminist, and then that got completely co-opted' (Julie Bindel, interview 2013). But 'Kate', on the other hand, said she had never put the two terms together ('Kate', interview 2013). Political difference was more important than race or ethnicity in determining what lesbians called themselves, and what they thought about issues such as separatism and political lesbianism. The lesbians who called themselves lesbian feminists came from a radical feminist background, whereas those who aligned themselves with socialist feminist politics were unlikely to adopt this name.

This distinction is clear in a discussion between four Black lesbians that was published in the journal *Feminist Review* in 1984 (Carmen, Gail, Shaila and Pratibha, 1984). Of the four lesbians, two identified as radical feminists and lesbian feminists, and the two who did not were of a socialist feminist persuasion. Carmen says she called herself a 'Black lesbian feminist' because 'my lesbianism is not just about who I sleep with or just about anti-heterosexuality as an institution, it's also about an understanding of all the oppressions that we face' (ibid.: 65). She did not agree, she says, that the relations of production are 'dominant'. She does say that working in mixed Black organisations would be possible for socialist feminists, whereas it was not for her, 'although I am not saying that all men are responsible for all the shit, I think they have got a definite responsibility', and men cannot accept that (ibid.). Shaila also calls herself a lesbian feminist, saying: 'I would define myself as a Black

32 The origins of lesbian feminism

lesbian feminist who is also a socialist and an anti-imperialist.' What that means is that

> yes, men as men, have power over women, as women… I won't accept that capitalism is the root cause of oppression of all types the world over. I won't accept that a man who rapes his wife or daughter has necessarily got anything to do with the capitalist system existing in this country… To me that is male power over a woman.
>
> *(ibid.: 67)*

Gail, however, who was a socialist feminist, says she couldn't 'call myself a "lesbian feminist" because to me it is a whole concept that says you subsume everything to patriarchy' (ibid.: 69).

Lesbian feminist culture and community

By the early 1980s many more groups, publications and organisations were identifying themselves as specifically lesbian in the UK, and some of these, such as lesbian studies courses, the Lesbian Archive and the Lesbian History Group, will be discussed later in this volume. As lesbian resources, groups, organisations and institutions were established, a lesbian community and culture was created in which lesbians could gain succour, gird their loins for the political struggle, find lovers and lesbian 'family', nurture themselves with poetry and novels, hone their political understanding with books, newsletters and journals of lesbian feminist theory and access entertainment that celebrated lesbians at discos, plays and art exhibitions. This rich and diverse 'women's culture' of the time, which lesbians created and which reinforced their pride and confidence, will be examined in the next chapter.

Bibliography

Abbot, Sidney, and Love, Barbara (1972). *Sappho Was a Right-On Woman: A Liberated View of Lesbianism*. New York: Stein & Day.

Bishop, Helen (1992). Writing Our Own History: Dial-a-Dyke. *Trouble and Strife*, 25: 45–52.

Brownmiller, Susan (2000). *In Our Time: Memoir of a Revolution*. New York: Dial Press.

Carmen, Gail, Shaila and Pratibha (1984). Becoming Visible: Black Lesbian Discussions. *Feminist Review*, 17: 53–72.

Coughlan, Sean (2010, 10 April). University Applications up 16.5 Percent. BBC News. http://news.bbc.co.uk/1/hi/education/8619922.stm.

Doan, Laura (2001). *Fashioning Sapphism: The Origins of a Modern English Lesbian Culture*. New York: Columbia University Press.

Faderman, Lillian (1981). *Surpassing the Love of Men: Romantic Friendship and Love between Women from the Renaissance to the Present*. New York: William Morrow.

Faderman, Lillian (1985). *Scotch Verdict*. London: Quartet.

Farnham, Margot (1990). Tyne and Tide: A Lesbian Life Story. Margot Farnham interviews Helen Lilly. *Trouble and Strife*, 18: 47–52.

Frye, Marilyn (1983). *The Politics of Reality: Essays in Feminist Theory*. Freedom, CA: Crossing Press.

Fryer, Peter (1984). *Staying Power: The History of Black People in Britain*. London: Pluto Press.

Gardiner, Jill (2003). *From the Closet to the Screen: Women at the Gateways Club, 1945–1985*. London: Pandora.

Hall, Radclyffe (1982 [1928]). *The Well of Loneliness*. London: Virago.

Hall Carpenter Archives Lesbian Oral History Group (1989). *Inventing Ourselves: Lesbian Life Stories*. London: Routledge.

Home Office (1957). *Report of the Committee on Homosexual Offences and Prostitution* [known as the Wolfenden Report]. London: Her Majesty's Stationery Office.

Jay, Karla, and Young, Allen (eds.) (1992 [1972]). *Out of the Closets: Voices of Gay Liberation*. New York: New York University Press.

Jeffreys, Sheila (1989). Does It Matter If They Did It? In Lesbian History Group (ed.), *Not a Passing Phase: Reclaiming Lesbians in History 1840–1985*. London: Women's Press, 19–28.

Jeffreys, Sheila (1997 [1985]). *The Spinster and Her Enemies: Feminism and Sexuality 1880–1930*. Melbourne: Spinifex Press.

Jeffreys, Sheila (2003). *Unpacking Queer Politics*. Cambridge: Polity Press.

Jeffreys, Sheila (2014). *Gender Hurts: A Feminist Analysis of the Politics of Transgenderism*. Abingdon, UK: Routledge.

Jennings, Rebecca (2007). *Tomboys and Bachelor Girls: Narrating the Lesbian in Post-War Britain 1945–71*. Manchester: Manchester University Press.

Mama, Amina (1995). *Beyond the Masks: Race, Gender and Subjectivity*. London: Routledge.

Oram, Alison (2007). *Her Husband Was a Woman! Women's Gender-Crossing in Modern British Popular Culture*. Abingdon, UK: Routledge.

Raymond, Janice G. (1986). *A Passion for Friends: Towards a Philosophy of Female Affection*. London: Women's Press.

Rosenberg, Carroll Smith (1975). The Female World of Love and Ritual: Relations between Women in Nineteenth Century America. *Signs*, 1 (1): 1–20.

Rowbotham, Sheila (1972). The Beginning of the Women's Liberation Movement in Britain. In Wandor, Michelene (ed.), *The Body Politic: Women's Liberation in Britain 1969–1972*. London: Stage 1, 91–102.

Setch, Eve (2002). The Face of Metropolitan Feminism: The London Women's Liberation Workshop, 1969–1979. *Twentieth Century British History*, 13 (2): 171–190.

Shulman, Sheila (1983). When Lesbians Came Out in the Movement: Interview by Lynn Alderson. *Trouble and Strife*, 1: 51–56.

Sisterhood and After Research Team (2013). Girls in Formal Education. British Library. www.bl.uk/sisterhood/articles/girls-in-formal-education.

Stanley, Liz (1982). Male Needs: The Problems and Problems of Working with Gay Men. In Friedman, Scarlet, and Sarah, Elizabeth (eds.), *On the Problem of Men: Two Feminist Conferences*. London: Women's Press, 190–212.

Sutton, Jo, and Hanmer, Jalna (1984). Writing Our Own History: A Conversation about the First Years of Women's Aid between Jo Sutton and Jalna Hanmer. *Trouble and Strife*, 4: 55–60.

Walter, Aubrey (ed.) (1980). *Come Together: The Years of Gay Liberation 1970–73*. London: Gay Men's Press.

Whitbread, Helena (ed.) (1988). *The Secret Diaries of Miss Anne Lister*. London: Virago.

Zehra (1987). Different Roots, Different Routes. *Trouble and Strife*, 10: 11–15.

2
LESBIAN CULTURE

The birth of the Women's Liberation Movement was accompanied from the outset by the development of a women's culture. This was a revolutionary creation in its own right, and it formed the necessary foundation for activism. This women's culture was not specifically lesbian, though lesbians were the instigators and provided much of the work and leadership that formed it. The women's culture was not necessarily inspired by radical feminism either, though radical feminists were heavily involved in its creation. But the women's culture provided the amniotic fluid in which lesbians and lesbian feminism could thrive and grow. This culture was supported by feminist and lesbian bookshops and publishers, discos, arts centres, poetry readings, theatre events, women's nights at bars, women's music events, squats, the Lesbian History Group, the Lesbian Archive and lesbian studies, and these were overwhelmingly women-only events. The poems, songs and plays promoted political ideas, which were often specifically the product of lesbian feminism, such as songs about loving women and hating men. They carried common understandings to thousands of women. The women's culture created spaces in which lesbians could safely meet, be inspired and love. Lesbians dominated the 'women's culture', though this was rarely mentioned at the time, and created the ambience as well as the common cultural understandings. Although heterosexual feminists took part in women's culture, they had an alternative, malestream/mainstream culture in which to live their lives and seek succour, and they would likely be restricted in how many events they could attend. Boyfriends and husbands constituted an impediment to total immersion which lesbians did not face.

This chapter will introduce some of the richness of the cultural and social life of lesbian feminists in London in the 1970s and 1980s. The importance of women's culture to lesbianism is well expressed by the US lesbian feminist literature scholar Bonnie Zimmerman: 'I would go so far as to say that without a culture and a politics, we wouldn't have lesbians, only women who have sex with women' (Zimmerman,

2007: 46–47). The patriarchal culture in which women and lesbians live creates serious obstacles to the possibility of developing lesbian and feminist ideas and practice. As Adrienne Rich explains in her iconic essay from 1980, 'Compulsory Heterosexuality and Lesbian Existence', 'lesbian existence' was unthinkable in a culture in which lesbians were invisible in literature (Rich, 1984 [1980]). For a few decades this was redressed by the creation of a women's and lesbian culture.

Before the creation of a lesbian culture there was virtually no mention of lesbians in films or television and very little mention of lesbians in literature. When lesbians did appear, they were painted in negative terms and usually suffered a sad fate. This was so even when the novelists who wrote about them were lesbians, as in Radclyffe Hall's *The Well of Loneliness* (Hall, 1982 [1928]). But in the late 1960s the beginnings of a positive lesbian literature were evident. As Zimmerman explains, when the first novel of this kind appeared in 1969, Isabel Miller's *A Place for Us*, later published as *Patience and Sarah* (Miller, 1971): '[I]t was as yet unthinkable that two women could love each other and be rewarded with a home and happiness rather than condemned to marriage or death' (Zimmerman, 1990: xii). Lesbian feminists set up feminist presses to publish lesbian literature. For there to be a lesbian literature, Zimmerman points out, lesbians had to develop a collective identity as lesbians (ibid.). The word 'lesbian', for the writers of the 1970s, 'represented a point of view', she says, 'rather than a sexual behaviour or innate identity', and it was out of this feminist point of view that 'a 'distinctive lesbian, or lesbian feminist culture' was created (ibid.: 12). She uses the term 'culture' to refer to 'more than literature, music, theatre and art… Culture also encompasses the ideals and ethos of a group, all the intangibles that distinguish it from other groups' (ibid.). She explains that lesbians need to create their own culture because, unlike ethnic groups, they are not born into a culture that they can identify with (ibid.: 14). Writing in the late 1980s, she was able to say with confidence that, 'when a woman comes out as a lesbian, she has an identity and belief system waiting for her should she choose to embrace it' (ibid.: 14).

The lesbian feminist community was so rich in institutions, events, conferences, theatre groups and music groups that it would not be possible to do justice to all this in a single chapter. I will attempt only to give an indication of what was available and of its significance to lesbian feminism and feminism in general. This chapter will document the variety of cultural institutions created largely or entirely by lesbian feminists, the feminist presses and bookstores, arts centres, lesbian centres and women's centres. It will show the extent of the social and entertainment options available to lesbian feminists at this time, the bars, clubs and discos, all run by lesbians and mostly created by lesbian feminists, with a lesbian feminist philosophy, women-only and supportive of women's music.

The chapter will also go some way to document the different ways of living that lesbian feminists were experimenting with at the time, such as the lesbian squatting movement in London. The richness of this culture was such that lesbians were able to live almost entirely within it. If they had jobs, these were likely to be in the malestream world, but the rest of the time could be spent entirely with

36 Lesbian culture

women and lesbians, in their squats or other women-only living spaces, in meetings, at conferences, at the discos which took place in London on every night of the week, at the women's holiday centres, at plays, poetry nights and music events. The breadth of merchandise available at women's bookstores, conferences and events meant that lesbians could have posters and artwork on their walls, jewellery, T-shirts and music that would make lesbian feminist spaces out of their homes. Common cultural referents were turned into artwork, with which lesbians proudly decorated their persons as well as their walls.

The creation of the different aspects of women's and lesbian culture took place simultaneously, and it is not possible to place the development of poetry before music, for instance. I shall begin with the written word, but that does not mean that it should logically be seen to pre-date the other cultural forms.

Literature

A new women's and lesbian literature, which included fiction, poetry and theory, was a fundamental part of the new culture. This tide of literature began with self-publishing or took the form of pamphlets, newsletters and Gestetnered sheets. Many speeches and conference papers were later published through women's print shops. Then feminist and lesbian presses or women's imprints of malestream publishing houses were set up, and the books were sold through women's bookstores. The UK socialist feminist lesbian Beatrix Campbell describes the salience of the written word thus:

> We ate the literature that was pouring out of the Women's Liberation Movement, we ate it… [I]t was an extraordinary relationship to the written word… [A]ll of these tracts and texts and books, we consumed as soon as they came out. And, whether you were an intellectual or not, you just read every-thing and it impacted massively on your life.
>
> *(interview with Campbell, quoted in Delap, 2016: 171)*

The lesbian fiction inspired by the WLM included many forms, from coming-out stories to historical novels, romances, science fiction and crime novels. Bonnie Zimmerman provided, in her 1990 book *The Safe Sea of Women*, an account of lesbian literature from its origins in 1969 to 1989. She says that lesbian novels were read by lesbians to 'affirm lesbian existence', whilst, '[c]onversely, the books a woman reads are what make her a lesbian feminist, or a member of a "lesbian community"' (Zimmerman, 1990: 15). She defines the purpose of lesbian fiction as being to 'map out the boundaries of female worlds – of Lesbian Nation – and in this way assist women in coming out, provide models for behavior, and encourage us to feel good about ourselves' (ibid.: 21). She points out that fantasy or science fiction novels were particularly important in achieving these ends. More than any other genre, science fiction enabled lesbian writers to imagine a world without men in which women could be strong and self-sufficient and create new values and ways

Lesbian culture **37**

of living. These novels offered women visions and fantasies to enable lesbian feminist dreams. It is hard to envisage very radical transformation without any idea as to what it might encompass. Elaine Miller, the British lesbian feminist and member of the London Lesbian History Group, in a study of lesbian wonderlands and utopias, argues, 'The literature of "imagined worlds" has obvious attractions for both lesbian writers and readers wanting to protest about the way things are and to explore and promote different ways of being.... They contain our experience, express our anger, validate our ideals and consistently place us at the centre' (Miller, 1998: 152). Such utopias include *The Female Man* (1975), by Joanna Russ; *The Wanderground* (1978), by Sally Miller Gearhart; *Daughters of a Coral Dawn* (1984), by Katherine Forrest; and *Bulldozer Rising* (1987), by Anna Livia.

Romance novels and historical novels affirmed lesbian existence and provided positive role models, but crime novels and science fiction did more. Where science fiction in the form of women-only utopias gave us ways to imagine different worlds in which women could escape male domination and lesbians could create communities of lovers, crime novels gave women lesbian heroes and allowed women to imagine forms of justice against male violence and oppression. When lesbian detective fiction emerged as a genre in the 1980s, with lesbians such as Val McDermid in the UK and Sarah Dreher, Barbara Wilson, Valerie Miner and Katherine Forrest in the US, lesbian feminists were offered comforting scenarios of good lesbians catching bad men, embedded in positive visions of lesbian community. Both genres fulfilled crucial functions for the nascent lesbian feminist community and movement and were deeply satisfying.

The Black American lesbian feminist Audre Lorde invented a new style of writing that reads like a novel but is in fact a form of memoir mixed with mythology, which she called 'biomythology', to write about her experience growing up as a Black child and young woman and becoming a lesbian in the years before the WLM: *Zami: A New Spelling of My Name* (1982). Her influence was very considerable in contributing to the nascent Black lesbian movement in the UK, through explaining how racism worked for women and lesbians and how it manifested in the WLM itself. She contributed to lesbian feminist literature in many ways, including through poetry and essays. In the UK there was a dearth of Black lesbian literature before the 1980s. An early book by a Black lesbian feminist in the UK was similarly unusual in its format: *Feminist Fables: A Retelling of Myths*, by Suniti Namjoshi (1981). It was published by the feminist publisher Sheba, which explains that it was set up with a commitment to 'diversity, to difference'. Sheba was proud of publishing the book, and stated, '[W]hen lesbian-feminists were universally assumed to be white, and Indian women universally assumed to be heterosexual, *Feminist Fables* called into question this cosy compartmentalization' (Sheba Feminist Publishers, accessed 18 December 2017). The 1980s saw a blossoming of Black women's writing in the UK, inspired by feminism and lesbian feminism as well as Black liberation politics. The Black lesbian Barbara Burford wrote plays, poetry, short stories and a novella. She published short stories with Sheba, under the title *The Threshing Floor* (1986), and published poetry with other Black women,

38 Lesbian culture

such as the UK lesbian feminist Jackie Kay, under the title *A Dangerous Knowing: Four Black Women Poets* (1984).

By the 1990s the retreat from feminism was having harsh effects upon lesbian literature. Lesbian utopias went extinct, perhaps because the times were no longer hopeful enough to imagine a world of women. Lesbian detective novelists tended to abandon lesbian heroes altogether, as Val McDermid did (Radford, 1998). Her first heroine, Lindsay Gordon in the late 1980s, was a lesbian, a feminist and a socialist, who examined crimes in those political contexts. McDermid moved on to a heterosexual heroine, Kate Brannigan, and the political context was lost. By 1995 she had introduced a hero, Tony Hill, who works with a female counterpart, and her work became malestream. The feminist presses declined and disappeared, and lesbian authors were less and less likely to produce work with lesbian contexts as they sought to make a living in the malestream publishing world.

Poetry

Poetry written by lesbians was a potent source of inspiration and strength for those involved in the women's community. The lesbian-run UK publisher Onlywomen Press published anthologies of lesbian and feminist poetry which included both UK- and US-based poets through the 1970s and 1980s, such as *One Foot on the Mountain* (Mohin, 1979) and a book of specifically lesbian poetry in 1986, *Beautiful Barbarians* (Mohin (ed), 1986). The press was founded by women from a women writers' group who specifically wanted to publish their poetry. The more prolific outpourings of lesbian feminists from North America were published and consumed in the UK too, and helped to create the cultural norms of the community. Poets whose works were admired and followed included Nicole Brossard from Canada and Judy Grahn, Pat Parker and Adrienne Rich from the US.

It is not possible to cover all the lesbian poets who provided an inspiration to a generation of feminists and lesbians here, so I shall focus on Judy Grahn as a US lesbian poet whose work has been recognised as of outstanding import-ance throughout English-speaking lesbian and women's culture. She wrote a prose piece about the punishment of a lesbian in the mental health system in 1964, 'The Psychoanalysis of Edward the Dyke', which is famous as being an extraordinarily out and proud poem about lesbianism from the period before the WLM, and many other poems that delighted lesbians and feminists. Grahn says she was 'absolutely thrilled' by the outpouring of lesbian and feminist poetry that took place during the WLM. Here she speaks of the early days of this fountain of feminist and lesbian poetry in 1972:

> [T]he feminist movement was a movement of poets initially – women could easily write their expressions in some kind of poetic form and so they did. It's the most time-conservative method. And it doesn't cost anything. And there were those of us who were making the anthologies – we just wanted to know

what women thought. We were burning to know their thoughts. And they had them, buried in their dresser drawers: poems about their very own lives.

(Moore, 2013)

One of Grahn's most famous poetry series was entitled *The Common Woman* (published in 1969), inspired by her participation in a consciousness-raising group. One of these, 'Carol, in the Park, Chewing on Straws', begins 'She has taken a woman lover, whatever shall we do…' and ends 'She walks around all day quietly, but underneath it she's electric; angry energy inside a passive form. The common woman is as common as a thunderstorm.' Grahn laments the destruction of the lesbian feminist poetry movement by what she sees as anti-feminism: 'It was so powerful – all the way through the '80s – and then it appeared to vanish. I mean, I can only speak for myself, but I'm sure there were other people who felt the backlash surge of "Let's just dump the feminist"' (ibid.).

Feminist bookstores

Hundreds of feminist bookstores and many feminist presses were created out of the wave of creative energy that was the WLM in the US and the UK (Delap, 2016). The bookstores did not just enable women to find theory, novels and poetry with women-centred and feminist themes and politics; they also functioned as community hubs and meeting places. They provided venues where women could go for readings, have coffees and meet and discuss ideas and literature. Hundreds of political pamphlets and feminist journals and newsletters were for sale, and women could buy their posters and labrys earrings (labryses were double-headed axes associated with goddess worship in ancient Minoan culture, and much worn and flourished by lesbian feminists). They were sources of information on women-centred resources in local areas and internationally. They served as recruitment centres for feminism and lesbianism, places where women could come anonymously to find information and inspiration. As the historian Lucy Delap explains, 'Bookshops played a crucial role in publicizing and spatially locating the women's movement, making available its texts, and facilitating its social networks and intellectual exchanges' (ibid.: 173).

No specialist feminist bookstores exist in the UK today. The two significant London feminist bookstores, set up by mainly lesbian energy, were Sisterwrite in Islington (1978–1993) and Silver Moon in the West End (1984–2001). Sisterwrite was set up by three women, two of whom were lesbians, including my interviewee Lynn Alderson (personal communication, Lynn Alderson, 11 May 2017). Silver Moon was set up by two lesbians, Sue Butterworth and Jane Cholmeley (see Cholmeley, n.d.). When they both closed there were no comparable community resources in the city. All the feminist cultural forms that were created in the 1970s originated in the counterculture on the Left at that time. The bookshops came out of the alternative or radical bookstore movement, and some of the women who set up feminist bookstores started their careers in the alternative ones. They carried with them values that went on to inform the 'distinctive feminist culture of

40 Lesbian culture

co-operative decision-making, collective position-taking and taking responsibility', which was 'innovative, time-consuming and sometimes fraught' (Delap, 2016: 173). Like many other elements of the women's culture, feminist bookstores and presses would have found it very difficult to function without support from public funds, such as the Arts Council and regional arts associations, development agencies and local government.

The withdrawal of this support in the late 1980s was a significant factor in their demise. In addition, the bookshop workers depended on paying very low rents for their living spaces, because their wages were so low. Like women band members, they were supported by the benefits system. For the women who set up Sisterwrite, '[s]quatting and social welfare benefits allowed them to sustain the venture until it had become economically viable' (ibid.: 178; see also Alderson, 2016). As Delap points out, feminist bookstores experienced complications from trying to run businesses on feminist principles. One such principle was that feminist newsletters which stipulated that they were to be read only by women could not ethically be available for perusal by or sale to men. Moreover, Silver Moon and Sisterwrite both had cafés that were women-only. Silver Moon used the 1975 Sex Discrimination Act's provision for private, non-profit clubs to enable women-only provision. Jane and Sue hoped that the café would be 'a means that regular folk who worked in offices would come in for lunch. That never happened because they thought it was a den of lesbian iniquity – which it was! Oh my God, I could have run a dating agency out of that café, I tell you!' (Cholmeley, n.d.).

Lynn Alderson, one of the founders of Sisterwrite, describes their activities as 'trying to operate as a centre for knowledge and activity for the WLM' (Alderson, 2016). Women's groups were able to meet there, and the shop provided 'newsletters that would tell you what was happening' and notices 'for groups or somewhere to live'. Women could find 'the latest book or article, the one everyone was discussing at the time; or find something totally obscure – books on medieval women or women in Victorian literature; lesbian books and newsletters'. Some of the material was under the counter, such as

> Down There, the guide to self-exam by Sophie Laws of Onlywomen, sold with a speculum to do it yourself, and here is one of those speculums! – And if I remember rightly there are some lovely photos of my cervix in there, not an easy photo-shoot; or Betty Dodson's Liberating Masturbation – very popular that was, we sold many copies.
>
> *(ibid.)*

The shop also 'sold badges and lovely silver women's symbol earrings and pendants… and labrys/axe pendants, and badges, of course' (ibid.).

The women's bookstores had to deal with violence and harassment from men, and even from some women who disagreed with the centring of women. Jane Cholmeley said there was 'general hostility', including having books thrown at her, and 'men would come in and shout at us'; also 'some guy wanked off on the carpet downstairs' and 'one of our customers was subject to a knife attack'. There was also an 'arson threat' from an 'Islamic group saying that we should be burnt down and sent back to the kitchen' (Cholmeley, n.d.). Some women complained that the café was women-only. In the end the café had to be closed, Cholmeley explains, because the planning authorities would not accept that the café was and would continue to be women-only and demanded that there should be a men's toilet, for which there was no room. Feminist bookstores did not survive in the UK or the US. In the US and Canada in the mid-1990s there were 120, but by 2014 there were only 13 (Enjeti, 2014). The forces that extinguished them came largely from outside, including political and economic changes, which will be considered in the final chapter.

Feminist presses

Feminist presses were essential to the creation of women's and lesbian culture. Some of these were entirely independent of the malestream publishing industry, such as Onlywomen and Virago. Some were attached to malestream publishers, such as Pandora and The Women's Press. All performed a vital function in publishing feminist novels, poetry, history and theory. Onlywomen Press was the only one which was started by out lesbians, however, and it evolved into a publisher which was focussed on lesbian writing. It was founded in 1974 and conceived in a women writers' group which wanted to publish poetry. The founders wanted to control the whole printing process, so three women, Lilian Mohin, Sheila Shulman and Deborah Hart, went to college to learn how to print. The original name was The Women's Press, until that was taken over by a new press linked to malestream publishing and they had to rename themselves Onlywomen. The founding statement made their feminist mission clear: 'In order to create a Women's Liberation Movement reality, we need discussion and the development of political analysis unhindered by patriarchal values. We need a means of establishing our own culture' (Delap, 2016: 173).

Onlywomen published original poetry, theory and novels from the UK and reprinted material from the US. The publisher did not publish books with spines until 1979, when it outsourced its printing. The first book was an anthology of poetry called *One Foot on the Mountain* (Mohin, 1979). Before that, though, they published political theory in an important series of pamphlets which circulated both UK and US ideas around the WLM. The usual method of circulating and discussing ideas before the age of social media and the Internet was the distribution of Gestetnered conference papers, usually no more than 1,000 words in length. Alternatively, significant papers were printed on Gestetner machines, stapled together and distributed through feminist and alternative bookstores. Pamphlets from Onlywomen allowed more extensive coverage of issues between glossy covers. The first pamphlets were theoretical works by lesbians, such as *Women and Honour: Notes on Lying* by the US lesbian feminist Adrienne Rich (1979). In the 1980s the pamphlet series continued with the very controversial *Love Your Enemy?* (Onlywomen Press, 1981), which contained the 'Political Lesbianism' paper from

42 Lesbian culture

Leeds Revolutionary Feminists, which argued that lesbianism was a necessary political choice for feminists, and responses to it from the *WIRES* newsletter. Onlywomen also reproduced Adrienne Rich's iconic lesbian feminist treatise 'Compulsory Heterosexuality and Lesbian Existence' (Rich, 1984 [1980]). There was no way that such important debates could have been accessible so widely across a whole movement without Onlywomen's publication of these works.

In the 1980s Onlywomen published a number of important volumes that gave extensive coverage to what were seen as the most urgent practical and theoretical issues of the day, such as men's violence against women and lesbian feminist separatism. *Women against Violence against Women* (Rhodes and McNeill, 1985) was a collection of papers from three feminist conferences, which had taken place in 1980 and 1981, on men's violence against women. Another significant compendium from Onlywomen is *For Lesbians Only* (Hoagland and Penelope, 1988), a collection of writings from the US on lesbian feminist separatism. It is a thick and heavy volume, and it is not likely to have been attractive to publishers. Certainly, no publisher could be found in the US, but Onlywomen was brave enough to publish a book on such a controversial volume. There were many other important volumes too, such as *Changing Our Minds* (Kitzinger and Perkins, 1993), which was a lesbian feminist critique of psychology. Two publishers focussed upon books by women exist in the UK today: Virago, which started in 1973 and describes itself as an 'international publisher of books by women', is still going, and Persephone, which was set up to reprint 'neglected fiction and non-fiction by mid-twentieth century (mostly) women writers'. But no lesbian feminist publisher exists.

Squatting

Underpinning the work of many of the lesbians who created the women's culture was the practice of squatting. Squatting provided premises for cultural enterprises, free housing for lesbians on benefits or low wages in the women's sector and a community in which ideas, music and theatre could be nurtured. Like other aspects of the alternative political culture of the period from which the women's culture developed, lesbian squatting grew out of and reflected the political values of the counterculture of the late 1960s and 1970s. But, whilst the malestream squatting movement has been documented, lesbian squatting has not. Chris Wall, who was involved in lesbian squatting herself in the 1970s, has sought to right this bias through her own research, interviewing lesbians who squatted and documenting the practice (Wall, 2017). Wall explains that women's squatting was essentially lesbian feminist squatting: 'The collective energy of young lesbian feminists underpinned the many women-only households and squatting communities which appeared in Inner London at the time' (ibid.: 1).

Squatting was motivated and aided by several historically specific factors. The population of London was shrinking rapidly, leaving many properties which were often left empty whilst inner city councils worked on redevelopment plans for houses they considered inadequate because they lacked basic amenities. The number of persons squatting in mid-1970s London was reckoned to be between 30,000 and 40,000. The political climate created out of the radical social movements of the time, Wall writes, 'opened the way to communal and other non-traditional and anti-establishment ways of living' (ibid.). The main lesbian squatting areas were in Hackney, around London Fields and Broadway Market, Ladbroke Grove, Caledonian Road in Kings Cross, and Vauxhall. Lynne Harne describes the alternative values that informed the lesbian squatting community she was involved with: '[T]he childcare was shared and everything, which was wonderful, and…even our clothes were shared, so if you didn't get there early enough, you got the worst clothes' (quoted in ibid.: 2). Harne also points out that, even if women who moved into these squats were not lesbians at the time, they swiftly became so.

An important aspect of lesbian squatting was the way in which women had, perforce, to learn and practise DIY skills. This necessity led to campaigning for women's entry to the hitherto entirely male industry of the building trades. By the mid-1970s there were women electricians and plumbers who had developed their skills through having to make squats habitable. The organisation Women and Manual Trades was set up to support women in the trades and to promote their skills and businesses. By the 1980s directories were available of women in the trades covering plumbing, electrical work, carpentry, building work and car maintenance. The trades were fiercely defended by men as male-only enclaves because they offered decent incomes that women could not achieve in any other jobs outside the professions. The pioneering work of lesbians in the WLM did not make a permanent inroad, however, as the proportion of women in the trades today stands at barely 2 per cent (Peachey, 2015). In 2016 Women and Manual Trades was re-established under a new name, Women on the Tools (Womensgrid, 2016).

Squatting provided an impetus to and premises for the nurturance of women's music. Frankie Green, a significant figure in the development of women's music, explains its importance. She says that it was the lesbians involved in the Gay Liberation Front who set up women-only households in squats. They saw the opening of the houses as a political act, 'seeing housing as a way to gain control over the material basis of their lives and providing the means to live collectively and share resources' (Green, 2012). There were six squats near Kings Cross on the Caledonian Road in the late 1960s, and Frankie lived in one which was 'turned into a women's centre by putting up a sign outside saying it was a centre and offering free pregnancy tests'. The squats provided crucial spaces in which women could share instruments, rehearse and engage in songwriting sessions at no cost, and thus formed an 'essential part of the newly emerging women's music scene' (ibid.). The squats were also spaces for the creation of other women's services, such as the first refuges from male violence. The cheap housing that they offered enabled lesbians to endure the low wages available in feminist enterprises such as women's bookshops and presses. They formed part of what Wall calls an 'alternative economy'. The lesbians involved in squatting used facilities created through alternative politics. A community-run print shop in Hackney, which opened in 1975, enabled women to learn photography and printing and to produce posters and pamphlets. The lesbian squatting

Music

There was a proliferation of women's bands, singers and music in the 1970s in the UK, though there might not have been such a profusion of women's music as there was in the US because women's music festivals were less common. Bonnie Morris argues in her book *The Disappearing L* (Morris, 2016) that women's music in the US, nurtured through a plethora of such festivals, spread the political ideas of lesbian feminism and formed the basis for the creation of lesbian feminist culture. The longest-lasting and largest of these festivals, in Michigan, came to an end only in 2015, and a wealth of material exists from before and after its demise attesting to its importance as a centre of lesbian culture and community (ibid.). In the US many of the festivals were yearly events in different parts of the country and attracted many thousands of women. They supported the bands and musicians, as well as the exchange and promotion of common ideas through the sale of merchandise, T-shirts and badges, jewellery such as labryses and other artefacts. The space to make and sell products into lesbian culture helped to create a supportive lesbian economy. The US supported more women's music festivals than the UK did because the size of the lesbian population allowed for economies of scale and there was land which could be bought or rented cheaply for women's activities, which was not the case in the small, tightly held spaces of rural UK. Nonetheless, women's music was very important in the UK. Morris explains that the vast majority of those involved in women's music in the US, as musicians, singers, engineers and enablers of all kinds, were lesbians. This seems to have been the case in the UK too, where women may have been heterosexual when they first became involved but were likely to become lesbians quite quickly as a result of being surrounded by lesbian energy not just in the bands but at the events, which were overwhelmingly women-only and spaces where lesbianism and lesbian feminism spread rapidly and furiously.

Dozens of women's bands were formed in the late 1970s and 1980s in the UK as an emanation from the passion and fury of the Women's Liberation Movement. The musicians were mostly self-taught and challenged the sexism and exclusion of the contemporary music scene. Their lyrics were political and feminist, and most of those who set up or got involved in the bands were lesbians. Frankie Green, who helped to set up the Women's Liberation Music Archive online in 2013, where the stories of these bands and samples of their music are stored, was one such. She has told the story of how women's bands developed. The first one was formed, she says, by women who had 'met through Women's Liberation and the Gay Liberation Front' in London in 1972 and formed the London Women's Liberation Rock Band, which was 'shortly followed by the Northern Women's Liberation Rock Band'

(Green, 2012). Band titles did become catchier as the decade progressed, and she was later in Jam Today. She describes a time in the 1970s when 'whole terraced houses' were squats in Vauxhall, and housed a 'dyke community' with 'one of London's first feminist discos in a local pub and the first South London Women's Art Centre in one of the houses in Radnor Terrace'. Music was at the centre of this cultural scene.

Green explains that music-making was not just a form of entertainment but a form of 'progressive cultural activism' that was a key component of movements for profound social change (ibid.). The manifesto of the Northern Women's Liberation Rock Band in 1974 explained the politics of women's music at that time very well:

> [M]usic…contains a certain view of life, supports a certain order of things. Unless we use music to express women's fight against oppression, to encourage other women to stand with us, it will support the established order… [W]e are trying to create music that expresses the new values and relationships the movement is creating, of women standing up against male domination…about women's relationships in the home, at work…, fighting back, having a good time together without men, about how we want to be… [T]he women's movement, not the commercial circuit, has made our music.
>
> *(Green, 2014)*

The feminist politics that inspired the bands was evident in their names, which included 'the Harpies, Devil's Dykes, Frigging Little Bits, Brazen Hussies, PMT, Ova, Proper Little Madams, the Mistakes, Mother Superior and the Bad Habits, Jam Today, Sisters Unlimited' (Green, 2015).

Ova was the longest-lived of the women's bands. It was formed by Jana Runnalls and Rosemary Schonfeld, who worked together for 13 years, from 1976 to 1989. At the beginning their partnership went under different names. They first called themselves the Dykier, than Sky High Forever Band, making it clear that they were out and proud lesbians from the beginning. Then they called themselves the Lupin Sisters and played briefly with other women musicians before becoming a duo. Ova were remarkable, Schonfeld explains, in being 'two young radical lesbian musicians, surviving for thirteen years, touring internationally, writing and producing four albums, and setting up a women's recording studio and music resource in London' (Schonfeld, 2017). 'No other group or individual in the lesbian music scene' in the UK, she says, 'lasted as long or achieved as much'. As with other lesbian and feminist ventures at the time, they were aided by squatting and the benefits system. Schonfeld says 'the squatting and short life housing culture in the 1970s made this possible', because 'we could rehearse in our own homes', as well as pay low rent. They 'signed on' at first, meaning that they lived on state benefits, or did 'office temping' so that they 'could devote nearly all our time to making music'. In addition, like other such ventures, they gained a grant from the Greater London Council (GLC) in 1983, which enabled them to set up a women's recording studio and music resource that employed four women. They could not have kept up their 'momentum', she says, without GLC support.

46 Lesbian culture

Ova's experience was similar to that of other women's bands and enterprises. They formed in reaction to the exclusion of women from any significant roles in the music industry at the time, a situation not markedly different today, and were subjected to violence from men. On one occasion, Schonfeld says, she and Runnalls were beaten up by a man who lived on the floor below in the same squat, who was aided by three of his friends. They did not get much sympathy from friends on the Left, because the man was Irish and 'they said we got what we deserved because we were English'. They swiftly became politicised and met other lesbian feminists. They took the name Lupin Sisters, after a tendency in the gay community to take the surname 'Lupin', on the basis of a Monty Python sketch. They realised there was a 'real hunger for political songs written and performed by lesbians'. This was a time when women were still not 'allowed the freedom of forming and leading bands'. They were supposed to be 'eye-candy', fronting a band of men, or to 'play the flute'. Taking over roles arrogated to men could lead to violence, and Schonfeld recalls that 'Terry Quaye, the percussionist, told the story of a drummer threatening to break her wrists'. The problem for women seeking to break into the music industry, like women seeking to enter the manual trades and other fields that men saw as their preserves and specifically masculine, was not just discrimination but the real threat of physical violence. 'Open lesbianism,' Schonfeld says, 'was absolutely forbidden' (ibid.).

Most of their gigs were for women only, and their audiences could be very large. Schonfeld describes playing to as many as 2,000 women in Germany when they were on tour. She explains the crucial importance of women-only gigs: 'This was a time in history when women only space was essential for all of us to discover who we were, what we wanted, our strengths, our weaknesses, without the pressures of heterosexual normality and male judgement.' The nurturing of women's skills in traditionally male areas was an important part of their mission. They sought to be autonomous of the male industry, trained themselves in sound technology and provided their own PA equipment. They wanted to record lesbian music because this was very rare at the time: 'We were aware of how much music was being made by lesbian feminists, and that there were very few recordings. No British lesbian band/musician apart from us had made an album.' So they saved up to make their first full-length recording, which they produced with the help of other women musicians and a woman sound engineer. Their photography and typography were by women too.

Their politics was unashamedly feminist, and, like many feminist creative artists at the time, they were campaigners against men's pornography and sexual and physical violence against women. Rosemary Schonfeld's song *Self-Defence* is an angry anthem to women's right to kill men who assault them, which was extremely popular with her women audiences: 'One day I'm gonna kill a man in self-defence, One day I'm gonna kill a man... But I've been beaten and dragged by my hair, because I dared to answer back, And every time you beat a woman, You beat me, you hurt me' (Schonfeld, 1982 [1979]).

Singing was an important part of activism at that time, and women sang on marches and at events to express their anger and bond with other women. The

Lesbian culture **47**

revolutionary feminist group in London that I was in, like many other groups, made up new lyrics to already existing tunes so that they were easy to sing with gusto. One of these, which gives a flavour of the politics, was 'Women Are a Girl's Best Friend', to the tune of 'Diamonds Are a Girl's Best Friend'. The lyrics, which refer to what might take place in the back row of the stalls in the cinema, are as follows:

> He may seem nice when he buys you a choc ice, but women are a girl's best friend. He won't seem so fantastic when he fiddles with your elastic, women are a girl's best friend. Men grow bald when they grow old. They all lose their charms in the end. All men are wankers, said Christabel Pankhurst. Women are a girl's best friend.

Such songs, including a stirring, transmogrified version of 'There Is Nothing Like a Dame', which gave suggestions as to what 'dames' might do to show their anger at men, were sung through megaphones on marches.

Discos

When the women's culture was strong, lesbians could experience total immersion, living all the parts of their lives that did not require paid work in malestream enterprises, amongst women. Social life could be lived through the very numerous clubs and discos, some regular weekly events and many others arranged as fundraisers for campaigns or women's services. All around the country lesbians organised women-only discos, where women could dance, socialise and find lovers. In London in March 1978, for instance, the discos advertised in the *London Women's Liberation Newsletter*, and often in malestream magazines such as *Time Out* and *City Limits*, included the Cauldron at the Sols Arms pub on Tuesdays, the Women's Disco at the Prince Albert pub on Wednesdays, the Lesbian Line Women's Disco on Sundays, Eaves Disco at the New Lewisham Women's Center on Thursdays, the Other Women's Disco at the Prince Albert on Saturdays, Sappho Discos at the Sols Arms (LWLN 58, 1978, 29 March). Where possible the discos played music by women or with woman-positive themes. The 1975 Equal Opportunities Act created challenges for women who sought to conduct public events separately from men, but the discos suffered too from all the hostile forces that coalesced against women-only spaces over succeeding decades.

Feminist politics shaped the many forms in which women's music culture could be experienced. In 1976 an initiative called the Women's Monthly Event was started. These 'events' provided an alternative to traditional concerts and discos, which were dogged by a heavy drinking culture and music so loud that conversation could not take place. The advertisement was as follows:

> A regular event for women; a real alternative to the disco scene where there is space for women to play, sing and listen to live women's music; read poems; share paintings, photos etc.; dance talk, sell things they've made, posters,

48 Lesbian culture

> literature etc.; we hope there will be facilities for a bar, coffee, and food, and
> that money made will go into women's causes.
>
> *(LWLN 44, 1976, 20 October)*

These periodic events continued to take place in venues such as community centres, where different rooms could be dedicated to a variety of activities.

By the 1980s these events had changed to become more like the rest of the commercial music scene and the bands had loud PA systems. I wrote in the *London Women's Liberation Newsletter* about what I saw as a worrying change in feminist entertainment, towards emulating masculine aggression from the women's band Tour de Force at a Women's Monthly Event, which had diverged considerably from the countercultural style in which it was first set up. I said that I had been 'engaged in the fight against male violence now for several years' and could not 'ignore the connection between the music of violence and aggression and the culture of men's violence in which as women we struggle to survive' (LWLN 258, 1982, 9 March). I wanted music which encouraged connectedness and community between women instead of preventing it, music which allowed women to think and even to speak to each other: 'How many women felt peaceful, relaxed and able to massage themselves in the balm of their friends' company on Saturday night? Why are we allowing ourselves to suffer in atomised, alienated silence, the onslaught of aggressive, male music?'

Other women wrote similar complaints. Women's music survived into the 1980s, but it was not necessarily infused with precisely the same countercultural principles.

Women's and lesbian theatre

Women's theatre was another aspect of the women's culture that was dominated by lesbian feminists. Some theatre groups also incorporated music, and some, such as Siren, performed both as a theatre group and a band. The names of the women's theatre groups of the 1970s suggest their rebelliousness, humour and feminist politics. They included Beryl and the Perils (1978), the Devil's Dykes (1978), Hormone Imbalance (1979) and many others. Like the bookshops and presses, they were formed out of an alternative political culture of the time which featured socialist theatre groups and gay theatre groups. The politics of these mixed groups was alternative. They were organised as collectives, they were non-profit and they performed at benefits for socialist and alternative causes and organisations, but they were not woman-friendly or feminist. Beryl and the Perils state that they formed because they were '[v]ery, very unhappy... [F]rustrated with the number of women on stage and the role for women and...the initial impetus was to redress the balance' (Unfinished Histories, 2013a). The Perils performed at women's refuges, as well as Rock Against Racism and Rock Against Sexism events. As they say in an interview,

> [W]e were radical and we were very scared, we didn't know we were
> radical and didn't know we had anything to say. And that was what was so

extraordinary, there was a kind of a crest of a wave and we were on it... [I]t became something that spoke to a lot of women, it was a political tool.

(ibid.)

The Perils were seen as so scary, indeed, that they gained the attention of the police: 'We were underground, you know we were dangerous, we were subversives and... just after we put our second show together were investigated by the Special Patrol Group... [T]hey were a branch of the police that looked at political subversives' (ibid.).

Siren, which comprised four lesbian feminists, Natasha Fairbanks, Debs Trethewey, Jane Boston and Jude Winter, was both a theatre company and a band (Unfinished Histories, n.d. – a). They started out as a band in Brighton called Devils Dykes in 1978 (the Devil's Dyke is a valley in the South Downs north of the city), and then became Bright Girls before becoming Siren. Like the lesbians involved in many of the other feminist and lesbian enterprises covered in this chapter, the Siren lesbians survived through being on benefits and doing part-time low-paid work. As Jude Winter expresses it in an interview: 'We felt very justified about signing on and performing... [W]e worked our butts off! We worked! And we all worked as washers-up. We...had a rota in a fish restaurant and we used to just do washing up to try and survive' (ibid.).

Hormone Imbalance was formed in 1979 and was a specifically lesbian theatre group. The members gave as their motivation '[a] desire to create a style of lesbian theatre that was more edgy and provocative than the predominantly earnest style of lesbian feminist theatre that was – of necessity – being created in the mid-1970s. It was, in effect, an alternative to the alternative.' They produced, they said, work that was 'Lesbian feminist with a twist'. The core group was composed of six lesbians brought together by the lesbian playwright Sara Hardy. The explosion of women's music and theatre in the 1970s was enabled by the system in which unemployed people could get unemployment or other benefits without being punished. Hardy, who was a leading light of feminist and lesbian theatre in the 1970s before moving to Australia in 1981, explains: 'I "signed on" for unemployment benefits during much of this era, as did most of my colleagues – it was the arts funding you got when you weren't getting any arts funding!' (Unfinished Histories, 2013b).

Lesbians were central to women's theatre in other ways too, not just by doing the writing and acting. Kate Crutchley was a director and impresario as well as an actor. She directed productions for the gay theatre company Gay Sweatshop and was the co-organiser of the Women's Festival at the alternative theatre venue, the Drill Hall, in 1977, which took place over three weeks and comprised '[t]heatre, music, dance, craft, arts, photography, workshops by and for women' (Unfinished Histories, n.d. – a). The Drill Hall also held a women's bar and a vegetarian café for women only on one night per week. From 1980 Crutchley was the theatre programmer for the Oval House, another alterative theatre venue which staged a great deal of women's and lesbian theatre in the 1980s (Unfinished Histories, n.d. – b). Lesbian feminism featured in the work of the Theatre of Black Women (founded 1982), which was an

50 Lesbian culture

aspect of the blossoming of Black women's literature and arts in the 1980s. Jackie Kay's play *Chiaroscuro*, which was performed by the company in 1986, featured Black lesbian experience.

Conferences

In the 1970s and 1980s much of lesbian social life took place at political events, particularly conferences. At conferences women made friends, created networks, found lovers, created supportive bonds. Conferences were very frequent and could take place for the whole of one day or over a weekend. They included national and local WLM conferences. There were many more conferences on specialised issues, such as rape and sexual violence, revolutionary feminism and lesbian motherhood. These conferences created opportunities for the development of theory and campaigns but also, importantly, for the creation of community. Conferences regularly included discos on the Saturday night for women to relax and socialise. Whilst these discos were for all women, they provided different functions for heterosexual and lesbian feminists. Lesbian feminists could find partners and friends based upon their lesbianism, while heterosexual women could discover lesbianism, and many did.

The activities advertised in the 75th issue of the LWLN give an indication of the range of events that feminists could choose to attend in the month of July 1978. There were meetings of the Women's Arts Alliance collective; the Women are an Endangered Species group, which collected details of incidences of violence against women and girls from newspapers in order to argue that there should be as much concern about what was being done to women as there was for the preservation of whales; the Women and Mental Health group; housing co-op meetings; a demonstration against the misogynist work of the sculptor Allen Jones; plays; exhibitions; a National Abortion Campaign day school; Brent Women's Centre Festival; a Women Against Nukes meeting; a Women in Manual Trades meeting; a Women Against Rape meeting; a Latin American Women's Group meeting; a book bus meeting to talk about setting up a bus to take feminist literature around Britain; a Women and Caring Jobs meeting; Laurieston Hall Women's Arts Festival in Scotland; a Workers' Educational Association summer school on women's rights; and a planning meeting for a women's conference in Sheffield (LWLN 75, 1978, 28 July). Outside London there are likely to have been many other meetings that the London newsletter does not cover.

Cultural institutions

Lesbian culture and politics were promoted and supported by important cultural institutions which were set up in the late 1970s and early 1980s, and all of which disappeared in the 1990s. Lesbian Line, the phone support service which was founded in 1977, was one of these (Bishop, 1992). Apart from providing emotional support and help in meeting other lesbians, Lesbian Line was an institution at the heart of lesbian community and served other social and political functions. The existence of the line provided an important symbolic role in establishing lesbian existence. The practice of Lesbian Line was embedded in feminist politics, and the rejection of the eroticising of power through sadomasochism – important to lesbian feminists – was fundamental. Helen Bishop explains that, early on, Lesbian Line adopted a policy against S/M and would not recruit volunteers or workers who identified as S/M dykes (ibid.). Lesbian Line excluded from its services cross-dressing men who wanted to find lesbians to have sex with. It addressed issues of male violence which were specific to women, girls and lesbians and applied theory and practice developed with lesbians and radical feminists. It developed thinking about the experience of lesbian survivors of incest and violence as children, and survivors of this male violence were in the collective.

Another aspect of Lesbian Line that was common to the feminist and lesbian organisations that were set up at this time was a determined resistance to professionalisation and the idea that volunteers, or workers (after the line got funding from the GLC to employ one worker in 1983), should be women with specialist counselling skills. The Lesbian Line collective was based on the principle of equality and the belief that any woman with experience of an issue is in a position to listen to and support another in a similar situation: 'There was a suspicion of women who had professional counselling skills', which, Sibyl Grundberg explains, was a result of the way 'psychiatry and psychology were associated with trying to socialise us out of sexuality and out of sexual and life choices' (Sibyl Grundberg, interview 2013). This principle extended to not allowing a woman with professional counselling skills to join the collective. Lesbian Line, like other lesbian and feminist organisations also tried to adhere to identity politics – i.e. exercising a preference for volunteers from one of the correct categories: 'working class', 'Black', 'women with disabilities'. The policy had to be abandoned because it led to a difficulty recruiting volunteers such that the rota could not be filled. Lesbian Line contributed to creating positive images of lesbians by doing outreach and appearing in the media. It also contributed to lesbian cultural and community life by staging regular fundraising events with 'women's bands, poetry reading, comic duos' (Bishop, 1992).

Two significant cultural institutions which were set up by lesbian feminists in the early 1980s show the sophistication of lesbian culture at that time: the Lesbian History Group and the Lesbian Archive. They show the extent to which we were valuing our history, wanting to research, write about and discuss it and record it for posterity. The Lesbian History Group developed out of the frustration that lesbian historians, including me, were experiencing at the lack of attention to lesbianism and lesbian feminist analysis in the Feminist History Group. It was set up in the summer of 1984, after the Lesbian Studies Conference of that year, by my interviewee Rosemary Auchmuty and me, and was composed of lesbians with an interest in history rather than professional historians. It organised lesbian history walks and visits to places of lesbian interest, such as Sissinghurst in Kent, home of Vita Sackville-West. It held discussions and talks by lesbian authors and historians, and conducted quizzes. The group also edited the book *Not a Passing Phase: Reclaiming*

52 Lesbian culture

Lesbians in History 1840–1985 (Lesbian History Group, 1989), the first collection on lesbian history to be published in the UK. The Lesbian Archive in London, also founded in 1984, came out of the determination to preserve the lesbian history that was being created at that time. Before the dispute developed which led to the end of the archive (covered in Chapter 8), the archive was a women-only space, open daily, which put out a newsletter and sponsored speakers in concert with the Lesbian History Group. It was an important community resource for lesbians.

The women's culture was a glorious and unprecedented outpouring of women's creativity. It was not an add-on to WLM activism but the vital background against which it took place. It was dominated by lesbian creative talents in music, poetry, theatre, political ideas. The politics of lesbian feminism was spread by all the means described here, and the songs, plays and poetry echoed the theory and helped to create it. The women-only venues of women's centres, bars, discos and theatre and music nights were crucibles in which lesbians could form political and love relationships and develop the strength and self-belief that being in the company of remarkable women can engender. It stands out in disturbing contrast to the present, when women's bookstores and publishing houses, discos, bands and theatre scarcely exist, and women and lesbians are forced to survive in the interstices of a viciously masculinist culture, whose dominating forms, from Internet pornography to an abusive social media, could not have been imagined when women broke out to create their own world to live in 50 years ago. Most of the community resources that this chapter describes were based on women-only principles. Separatism is the necessary foundation of lesbian culture, and lesbian feminist understandings and practices of separatism will be examined next.

Bibliography

Alderson, Lynn (2016, 8 December). Sisterwrite Bookshop. Lesbian History Group. https://lesbianhistorygroup.wordpress.com/2016/12/08/sisterwrite-bookshop-lynn-alderson.

Bishop, Helen (1992). Writing Our Own History: Dial-A-Dyke. *Trouble and Strife*, 25.

Burford, Barbara (1986). *The Threshing Floor*. London: Sheba Feminist Publishers.

Burford, Barbara, Pearse, Gabriela, Nichols, Grace, and Kay, Jackie (1984). *A Dangerous Knowing: Four Black Women Poets*. London: Sheba Feminist Publishers.

Cholmeley, Jane (n.d.). Oral Histories/Jane Cholmeley. London Metropolitan Archives. www.speakoutlondon.org.uk/oral-histories/jane-cholmeley (accessed 5 January 2018).

Delap, Lucy (2016). Feminist Bookshops, Reading Cultures and the Women's Liberation Movement in Great Britain, c. 1974–2000. *History Workshop Journal*, 81: 171–196.

Enjeti, Anjali (2014, 9 May). The Last 13 Feminist Bookstores in the US and Canada. Paste Magazine. www.pastemagazine.com/blogs/lists/2014/05/the-last-13-feminist-bookstores-in-the-us-and-canada.html.

Gearhart, Sally Miller (1978). *The Wanderground: Stories of the Hill Women*. Watertown, MA: Persephone Press.

Green, Frankie (2012). Talk given at the 'Music and Liberation' exhibition at Space Station 65 Gallery, London, 1 December. https://womensliberationmusicarchive.co.uk/talks-presentations-interviews.

Green, Frankie (2014). Talk given at the 'Feminist Archives and Activism: Knowing Our Past – Creating Our Future' workshop at the 'Feminism in London' conference, London, 25 October. https://womensliberationmusicarchive.co.uk/talks-presentations-interviews.

Green, Frankie (2015). Talk given at the 'History of Feminist Activism' event, London, 11 March. https://womensliberationmusicarchive.co.uk/talks-presentations-interviews.

Hall, Radclyffe (1982 [1928]). *The Well of Loneliness*. London: Virago.

Hoagland, Sarah Lucia, and Penelope, Julia (eds.) (1988). *For Lesbians Only: A Separatist Anthology*. London: Onlywomen Press

Kitzinger, Celia, and Perkins, Rachel (1993). *Changing Our Minds: Lesbian Feminism and Psychology*. London: Onlywomen Press.

Lesbian History Group (ed.) (1989). *Not a Passing Phase: Reclaiming Lesbians in History 1840–1985.* London: Women's Press.

Livia, Anna (1987). *Bulldozer Rising*. London: Onlywomen Press.

Lorde, Audre (1982). *Zami: A New Spelling of My Name*. Freedom, CA: Crossing Press.

Miller, Elaine (1998). Zero Tolerance in Wonderland: Some Political Uses of Imagination. In Hutton, Elaine (ed.), *Beyond Sex and Romance? The Politics of Contemporary Lesbian Fiction*. London: Women's Press, 152–174.

Miller, Isabel (1971). *Patience and Sarah*. New York: McGraw-Hill.

Mohin, Lilian (ed.) (1979). *One Foot on the Mountain: An Anthology of British Feminist Poetry 1969–1979*. London: Onlywomen Press.

Mohin, Lilian (ed.) (1986). *Beautiful Barbarians: Lesbian Feminist Poetry*. London: Onlywomen Press.

Moore, Lisa L. (2013, 23 August). It Is an Apple. An Interview with Judy Grahn. Los Angeles Review of Books. https://lareviewofbooks.org/article/it-is-an-apple-an-interview-with-judy-grahn/#!.

Morris, Bonnie (2016). *The Disappearing L: Erasure of Lesbian Spaces and Culture*. New York: New York University Press.

Namjoshi, Suniti (1981). *Feminist Fables: A Retelling of Myths*. London: Sheba Feminist Publishers.

Onlywomen Press (1981). *Love Your Enemy? The Debate between Heterosexual Feminism and Political Lesbianism*. London: Onlywomen Press.

Peachey, Paul (2015, 22 August). Women in Manual Trades: Pioneering Tradeswoman's Charity Faces Closure despite Shortage of Skilled Construction Workers. *The Independent*. www.independent.co.uk/news/uk/home-news/women-in-manual-trades-pioneering-tradeswomans-charity-faces-closure-despite-shortage-of-skilled-10467368.html.

Radford, Jill (1998). Lindsay Gordon Meets Kate Brannigan – Mainstreaming or Malestreaming: Representations of Women Crime Fighters. In Hutton, Elaine (ed.), *Beyond Sex and Romance? The Politics of Contemporary Lesbian Fiction*. London: Women's Press, 81–105.

Rich, Adrienne (1979). *Women and Honour: Notes on Lying*. London: Onlywomen Press.

Rich, Adrienne (1984 [1980]). Compulsory Heterosexuality and Lesbian Existence. In Snitow, Ann Barr, Stansell, Christine, and Thompson, Sharon (eds.), *Desire: The Politics of Sexuality*. London: Virago, 212–241.

Rhodes, Dusty, and McNeill, Sandra (eds.) (1985). *Women against Violence against Women*. London: Onlywomen Press.

Russ, Joanna (1975). *The Female Man*. New York: Bantam Books.

Schonfeld, Rosemary (1982 [1979]). Self-Defence. In *Out of Bounds* [album]. London: Ova Music.

54 Lesbian culture

Schonfeld, Rosemary (2017, 15 September). Ova: The Radical Feminist Band. Lesbian History Group. https://lesbianhistorygroup.wordpress.com/2017/09/15/ova-the-radical-feminist-band-rosemary-schonfeld.

Unfinished Histories (2013a). Beryl and the Perils. www.unfinishedhistories.com/history/companies/beryl-and-the-perils.

Unfinished Histories (2013b). Hormone Imbalance. www.unfinishedhistories.com/history/companies/hormone-imbalance.

Unfinished Histories (n.d. – a). Kate Crutchley. www.unfinishedhistories.com/interviews/interviewees-a-e/kate-crutchley.

Unfinished Histories (n.d. – b). Siren. www.unfinishedhistories.com/interviews/interviewees-a-e/siren.

Wall, Chris (2017, 18 May). Sisterhood, Sawdust and Squatting: Radical Lesbian Lives in 1970s Hackney. Lesbian History Group. https://lesbianhistorygroup.wordpress.com/2017/05/18/sisterhood-sawdust-and-squatting-radical-lesbian-lives-in-1970s-hackney-christine-wall.

Womensgrid –Women's Groups News (2016, 9 May). Women and Manual Trades Relaunches as Women on the Tools! www.womensgrid.org.uk/groups/?p=4201.

Zimmerman, Bonnie (1990). *The Safe Sea of Women: Lesbian Fiction 1969–1989.* Boston: Beacon Press.

Zimmerman, Bonnie (2007). A Lesbian-Feminist Journey through Queer Nation. *Journal of Lesbian Studies*, 11 (1/2): 37–52.

3

SEPARATISM

The Women's Liberation Movement and lesbian feminism could not have developed on the scale and in the ways in which they did if they had not been based upon separatist principles. In this chapter I will examine the theory and practice of separatism that was adopted across the Women's Liberation Movement in the UK from the early 1970s onwards. Today the idea that women would want to meet separately from men to discuss feminist ideas, to plan and carry out feminist activism, to hear feminist speakers or women's music, to dance, to march and to protest is likely to be controversial. During the Women's Liberation Movement, however, this most fundamental form of 'separatism', the creation of women-only space, was fundamental and unproblematic amongst both heterosexual and lesbian feminists. Many lesbian feminists took separatism much further, to the extent of living in women-only houses and creating women-only culture. They chose to have very little interaction with men except as the necessity to earn a living or attend to family responsibilities might dictate. Some went so far as to live on women-only land and seek to be self-sufficient, so that they were able to live, as far as possible, without male contact. Separatism meant different things to different women, but there was little controversy about the principle that spaces and events should be women-only. Today any attempt to create women-only space is challenged and sometimes threatened by men's rights activists and men who transgender (Jeffreys, 2014). The historical struggle to create such space and the reasons why it was, and remains, crucially important to feminism have been forgotten.

When I asked my interviewees about whether they had been separatists, their answers depended on what they took separatism to mean. They all agreed that they attended women-only events and meetings and lived, for the most part, women-only social lives. But those who understood separatism to mean going to live on women's land, and seeking to live lives as separate as possible from men, sought to make it clear that they had never agreed with this as a political tactic. Not many

56 Separatism

women were able to choose to live on 'women's land' in the UK, because it is a small, crowded country and offers no cheap land. The US situation was different, because it offered more possibility of geographical separation, and women's lands in the US have been very important reservoirs of lesbian culture and politics and as places of respite and safety for women. For the most part, this chapter will focus on separatism in the UK, where 'women's land' was less common.

Theory of separatism

Separatism as a political practice, a philosophy or a way of life is different from acts of separation. Acts of separation are fundamental to feminism, particularly intellectual separation, since women would be unable to imagine an end to women's subordination without it. The whole edifice of Western male thought, encompassing religion, academic disciplines, such as the social sciences, and medicine, was, when the WLM came into existence, constructed by men in their own interests. The literary canon, with a few exceptions, consisted of novels by men; the movies were written by men and had male directors; and mind sciences such as psychoanalysis and psychology were almost entirely male in their personnel, and contained the insights of men's prejudices about what women were and what they were for. Politics was understood as men in movements and in parliaments. Much of this remains unchanged. In order to create the Women's Liberation Movement, feminists had to separate intellectually from the ideas that derived from male power and authority, often called by feminists the 'man' or the 'male in the head' (see Holland et al., 1998), challenge them and start to construct their own systems of meaning.

All colonised peoples have to separate intellectually in order to struggle for their liberation, a process which was called by Paulo Freire, the Brazilian Marxist education theorist, 'conscientization' (Freire, 1970). Those involved in liberation movements have to go through a process of identification of the thought processes instilled into them through oppression, in order to reject them and create revolutionary ideas and practices. The 1960s and 1970s were daring times in which many peoples, including women, were able to separate from the oppressor in the head and engage in intellectual insurrection. Lesbian feminists had to do this twice over, however. They were likely to have been in women's liberation groups that did consciousness-raising, a technique used in liberation movements at the time to enable activists to throw off the yoke of oppressive ideas by describing their experience and articulating their thoughts in small groups in order to identify the mechanisms of oppression. They separated from male supremacist thought, to become feminists, but then had to engage in a second separation from what Monique Wittig, the French lesbian philosopher, called the 'straight mind', or heteropatriarchal thought, in order to take pride in their lesbianism and plot their resistance (Wittig, 1980). The straight male mind did not just promote hostile ideas about women, but created sciences and humanities that were founded on the idea that heterosexuality, marriage and the family were natural and inevitable, and that any attempt by women to leave these confines to love women was a sign of a mental disorder. Lesbians had to commit thought crime against the masculine, established, intellectual order so that they could be proud lesbians and feminists.

Intellectual separation is the first step in separatist practice. The American separatist Sydney Spinster identifies a handful of lesbian feminist theorists as providing the founding ideas of separatism, all of whom emphasised the need to separate from male modes of thought and from male language. She explains, 'Most of the Lesbians I know who have named ourselves Separatist after '76 or so were greatly influenced by the writings of Separatist teachers like Mary Daly, Marilyn Frye, Julia Penelope, and Sarah Hoagland' (Spinster, 1988: 107). She quotes Mary Daly on the importance of separation from male culture and ideas, or 'internal' separatism, as a core necessity for the practice of separatism:

> It is Crone-ological to conclude that internal separation or separatism, that is, paring away, burning away the false selves encasing the Self, is the core of all authentic separations and thus is normative for all personal/political decisions about acts/forms of separatism.
>
> *(Daly, quoted in Spinster, 1988: 110)*

Separation from male language is important too. Lesbian separatist Julia Penelope explains that thought is constructed through language and it is men who have constructed what she calls PUD, the patriarchal universe of discourse (Penelope, 1990). She explains that feminists and lesbian feminists need to reject male language and invent their own because 'patriarchal thought controls and limits the ways we live in the world' and the structure of the English language perpetuates 'men's descriptions of what our lives are like and what the world is like' (ibid.: xxxvii). Lesbian feminists Monique Wittig and Sandre Zeig seek to create a new lesbian language and dictionary in *Lesbian Peoples: Material for a Dictionary* (Witt and Zeig, 1979). Many feminists take this journey of internal separation from men's culture, ideologies and language without recognising it as having any relationship to 'separatism'.

Women-only space and organising

Similarly, the principle of women-only organising and women-only space was axiomatic in the WLM and not necessarily seen as connected to 'separatism'. The pamphlet *Free Space*, from the very beginning of WLM organising in the US (Allen, 1970), takes it for granted that the group it describes, and all other feminist groups, were composed only of women. It usefully explains why the women-only principle was universal: 'We do not allow men in our movement because in a male supremacist society, men can and do act as the agents of our oppression' (ibid.: 40). There is no mention of lesbianism in the pamphlet, and it is directed at a heterosexual audience, but it demonstrates very well that that which would be seen as controversial today was the very basis, the sine qua non, of the earlier wave of feminism. In its explanation of how the feminist small group should work, examining women's

58 Separatism

personal experience and using that as the material from which to develop theory and plan action, it provides some indication as to why so many women from these small groups became lesbians. The analysis of experience led to criticism of heterosexuality, and the exciting atmosphere created by an intimate circle of women provided the possibility of choosing women.

All my interviewees spoke of living lives that were, to a large extent, women-only, in terms of meetings, conferences, discos, parties and demonstrations. They all said that the principle of women-only organising and socialising in these ways was crucial and uncontroversial at the time of the WLM. The women-only principle was not necessarily seen as separatist, though; it was simply how the Women's Liberation Movement worked. The fact that women's refuges from men's violence, rape crisis centres, health services, women's centres should be women-only, for instance, was unquestioned. The battle for women-only organising was decisively won, and the principle well accepted in the WLM by the mid-1970s, as Sandra McNeil comments: 'The battles had been won. By the time I started going to women-only things in '75 or '76 it was just accepted that there were women-only socials, women-only parties, unlike today' (Sandra McNeill, interview 2013).

The adoption of this principle did not happen straightaway, and in many instances it was adopted pragmatically, as a reaction to the way men behaved. There is evidence in newsletters that there was sometimes a serious struggle on the issue. An issue of *WIRES*, which was the national WLM newsletter, from February 1976 reports on a planning meeting for that year's International Women's Day march. The question of whether men should be allowed on the march was not settled at this point, and a decision reached at one meeting could be reversed at the next one. At the meeting on 21 January, 22 women voted to have no men, 11 voted for men to be present and four women abstained. A statement by one woman in the newsletter explains why the decision to exclude men was taken (*WIRES* 8, 1976: 10). She says that on the previous year's march men made sexist remarks to women when asked to march at the back. One lesbian was told by a man that she should not be on the march because she was not a 'real' woman. Other women, she said, were angry that groups of men from the Left were shouting loudly, and taking up a lot of space at what was supposed to be a Women's Day march. The decision to exclude men, on the basis of their behaviour, was taken overwhelmingly at the first meeting of the planning group; then it was overturned by women from 'mixed' groups who deliberately came 'en masse'; and then, in a third meeting, men were again voted out. The struggle was between socialist feminists who were involved in the male Left, and wanted access to women's space for their male comrades, and radical and lesbian feminists who prioritised women.

The women-only principle was outlawed in spaces open to the public in the 1975 Equal Opportunities Act, however. Equal opportunities legislation is supposed to enhance women's rights but in fact it creates insurmountable obstacles because it does not recognise, except in some very particular situations, that members of a subordinate group that suffers consistent violence from members of the dominant group should have the right to exclude them. Such power dynamics are not acknowledged in this form of liberal individualism. The problem became clear in 1984 in a dispute around the Fallen Angel pub in London. The proprietors of this gay venue put on a women-only night on Tuesdays, and a group of angry gay men took them to court under the equal opportunities legislation in response. They were successful, and the women's night came to an end (Clews, 2017). Thereafter, lesbian clubs and discos often had to engage in subterfuge, such as making the venues private by offering membership cards to women at the doors, so that they would not fall under the Act, but women-only spaces of this kind did operate well into the 1990s in various ways. Now none such exist, mainly as a result of the demands for entry by male cross-dressers, who call themselves transwomen.

Despite the legislation, meetings in public venues were regularly advertised as women-only in subsequent years. The launch of Andrea Dworkin's book *Pornography: Men Possessing Women*, which took place at Conway Hall in London in 1981, was advertised by the publisher, The Women's Press, as being women-only (LWLN 238, 1981, 13 October). Women-only space and organising were seen as important for several reasons. One is the obvious fact that women would not be able to voice ideas that were critical of men if men were present. They would be constrained in their imagination, the ability to envisage not just how the world should be changed but what sort of world could be built for women outside male dominance. As is the case in other liberation struggles, challenging and profound oppositional ideas and strategies could not be constructed with the oppressor present, to interrupt, get upset, demand women's loyalties or even threaten violence or exposure. The need for a place of greater safety is another prime reason for separate women-only spaces. There is plentiful evidence that women, girls and lesbians are at risk of violence from men in mixed spaces (Romito, 2008). Men's violence against women is so egregious and so extensive that women need refuges from it for their safety. These include places where women can live with others beyond the control of violent husbands and partners, fathers and other male relatives. But they also include places where women can dance, perform and be joyful without the eyes of men who leer, comment, harass and rape. As an example of the urgent need for separate places of entertainment that persists today, Sweden's largest music festival, Bråvalla, was cancelled for 2018 because of the prevalence of sexual violence, including four rapes and 23 sexual assaults that took place at the 2017 event (AFP, 2017). Valentine Louise, writing in the American lesbian separatist anthology *For Lesbians Only*, expresses the importance of this motivation thus: 'Radical lesbianism is the reclamation of our most intimate power, the right to walk the planet free from the scourge of patriarchal terror' (Louise, 1988: 182).

Another highly important reason from the point of view of lesbian feminism is that women-only spaces enable women to become lesbians. They provide examples of women being strong, capable and entertaining, for other women to admire and love. The rush of female energy that is present in women-only spaces is also lesbian energy, for it creates a woman-loving high. Lesbianism is marginalised and difficult to access when women are kept apart by the interpellation of men, even

60 Separatism

ones who are not troublesome. Mary Daly explains eloquently why women-only organising creates lesbianism: 'The Presence of Enspiriting Female Selves to each other is a creative gynergetic flow that may assume different shapes and colors. The sparking of ideas and the flaming of physical passion emerge from the same source' (Daly, 1979 [1978]: 373). My interviewee Sandra McNeill agrees, saying that it was the women-only spaces that 'allowed thousands of us who were heterosexual to become lesbians' (Sandra McNeill, interview 2013). Some women resisted the flame, but many saw no reason to.

Going too far?

Going Too Far is the title of a collection of essays by *Ms* magazine founder Robin Morgan about her journey away from the Left and mixed-sex, political organising towards radical lesbian feminism (Morgan, 1977). The forms of separatism that were seen by some critics as going too far were those that went much further than a change of consciousness and women-only spaces, towards more profound changes in the way that lesbians lived their lives. Lesbian feminist theorists hoped that lesbian separatism would hollow out the support structures of male domination and thus contribute to ending it. Julia Penelope, the American lesbian feminist linguist and philosopher, describes this more profound form of separatism thus:

> Separatists, for example, maintain that the only way to free ourselves from male domination is for all females to withdraw from men, to withhold from them our energy, our nurturing, our care-taking of them; only in this way, we believe, we can erode the foundation of male power and control over us.
>
> *(Penelope, 1988: 526)*

British lesbian feminists commonly became separatists in this more thoroughgoing way. Their separatism took different forms but usually involved a series of incremental acts. UK lesbian feminist Janet Dixon describes the practice of separatism like this: 'It is the centre, the beating heart, the essence' of feminism. She left separatism, but it did not leave her: 'My involvement with separatism lasted five years, but in a very real sense it will never leave me' (Dixon, 1988: 69). She explains her accession to separatism thus:

> One by one the men in our mixed household left or were thrown out. We stopped going to GLF (Gay Liberation Front), and to mixed gay discos and on mixed demos. We sold all our male records, stopped reading the newspaper and watching the telly. When I wrote letters home I addressed them to my mother only. I sat alone in the canteen at college, I stopped drinking in pubs and chatty male bus conductors and shop assistants were met with blank stares.
>
> *(ibid.: 78)*

Dixon saw this as strategic: 'To ignore men was to cut the umbilical cord once and for all, to deny them their very lifeforce.' Julie Bindel speaks in her interview of making similar decisions as she became a separatist: 'I would go to the extent that I wouldn't even get on a bus with a male conductor – which I thought was hilarious' (Julie Bindel, interview 2013). She says she 'walked a lot' and 'would tell off men who called me 'love', all of those kinds of things which take your energy'. Sheila Shulman, an American lesbian feminist resident in London, describes her move towards separatism: 'A lot of my separatism involved an enormous effort at unlearning everything that I had learned, which was unfortunately a great deal and all of it male culture. I think I'd been peculiarly steeped, and I had to scrub my head out' (Shulman, 1983: 54). She describes 'the struggle involved' in her effort to separate: 'I had enormous anguishes about could I listen to Beethoven or not… What could possibly be my relationship to all this, a lot of which I really loved. Also, I didn't want to be in men's presence if I could possibly avoid it' (ibid.).

These forms of separatism, in which lesbians sought to live their lives with little contact with men but continued to live in cities and usually to work alongside men, were common amongst my interviewees. But some said they had rejected what they thought of as separatism at the time of the WLM, and these lesbians had a rather different and special understanding of what it meant. They saw it as a removal to the countryside and an exodus from political involvement, and they judged it to be counter-revolutionary and a diversion from the tough task of ending male supremacy. Lynn Alderson, for instance, says she never defined herself as a separatist, but nonetheless believed in women-only spaces and organising:

> I thought it was a political cul-de-sac. I really did. I felt that women's space was important, our right to choose our own space, to do things as women, our autonomy – all of that was important. But I did not feel that the answer to everything was a separatist life for everybody.
>
> *(Lynn Alderson, interview 2013)*

Julie Bindel was similarly passionate in her repudiation of 'lifestyle' separatism. She says: 'Oh gosh, I hated that. I hated lifestyle separatism. I couldn't bear the idea of removing yourself from a political struggle. And then presenting it like some did as though it was part of the revolution. And I could never understand why they did that' (Julie Bindel, interview 2013). Julie's understanding of the way that lesbians who chose geographical separatism lived their politics may not be entirely accurate. This form of what was disparagingly referred to at the time and in my interviews as 'lifestyle' separatism was rare in the UK, such that I cannot remember ever coming across it.

Sandra McNeil was similarly dismissive of lifestyle separatism: 'So I associated it with this trying to live… Well, you heard about it in the States: women's land, women went and lived on women's land and had nothing to do with men' (Sandra McNeill, interview 2013). The more ordinary kinds of separatism that she practised,

62 Separatism

which did not involve moving to women's land, she did not include in the definition. She explains:

> We meant putting all our positive energy into women, but we weren't calling that 'separatist', or I wasn't calling it 'separatist'; I was calling that "lesbian feminism'. Putting most of your energy into women, not having male friends. And not having male lovers. And putting all your energy into women's things and doing things for individual women.
>
> *(ibid.)*

Separatism does not mean isolation

The form of separatism that was most commonly practised in the UK was not geographical, and separatists were much involved in feminist organising with other women, and often with members of such malestream organisations as trade unions or even local branches of the Labour Party. The Leeds Revolutionary Feminist Group, of which I was a member, wrote a paper explaining what we called 'tactical separatism', for a revolutionary feminist conference in Leeds in 1979 (Leeds Revolutionary Feminist Group, 1979, author's collection). We distinguished between 'tactical' separatism and 'cultural' separatism, and explained that we saw tactical separatism as a separation from men which would enable us to fight male dominance better. We defined it thus: '[N]ot living with men, not fucking them, not talking to them about Feminist politics, not treating them as individuals to give (priority) time and emotional support to, not feeling obliged to make their day brighter.' We would, however, use men in situations when we needed information – 'e.g. on genetic engineering' or for 'resources or skills'. Tactical separatism, we said, 'is the way we live our personal lives, as a means to an end' that was 'vital to our political struggle, not an optional extra'. It included 'supporting women' and 'having fun'. We would conserve and increase our revolutionary energies by focusing on women only, and be better equipped for the fray.

Many American separatists had a similar approach. The American separatist and feminist philosopher Joyce Trebilcot explains that, for her, lesbian separatism

> excludes participating in relationships with men for their own sake, but it does not preclude political action that confronts men and their institutions. Sometimes directly facing men is necessary or worthwhile in order for us to establish our rights, to obtain the resources we need, or to defend and support other women. Many separatists are regular organizers of and participants in political actions that involve dealing with men both in confrontation and in coalition.
>
> *(Trebilcot, quoted in Hoagland, 1988: 6)*

It was a 'misunderstanding of separatism', she stresses, 'to suppose that it is always or usually similar to the withdrawal of some Germans into an "interior life" during the Third Reich' (ibid.). American Black separatist Bette Tallen makes the same point: 'Separatism is based on both a resistance to and a rejection of the dominant oppressive culture and the imperative for self-definition… [N]ot about the establishment of an independent state, it is about the development of an autonomous self-identity and the creation of a strong, solid lesbian community' (Tallen, 1988: 141). Janice Raymond provides an elegant way of understanding the way in which many separatists chose to live; as 'insider outsiders', they continued to work in the malestream world but were consciously outsiders to it: 'The insider outsider lives in the world with worldly integrity, weaving the strands of feminist wisdom into the texture of the world' (Raymond, 1986: 232).

Separatism and lesbianism

Forms of separatism that went beyond internal separation and women-only space were not available, of course, to heterosexual feminists. Men were central to their existence, as the objects of their love and attention or the partners in their beds and lives. Lesbian separatists were able to move men out of their lives to a greater or lesser extent, but always in ways not open to their heterosexual sisters. They withdrew their love and attention at the same time as closing access to their bodies, homes and intimate lives. In the hostility that developed towards separatism from critics at the time, and today, it is likely that straightforward anti-lesbianism often lies at the root. Indeed, lesbianism and separatism were not always clearly differentiated by their critics. Janet Dixon points out that they were attacked together at WLM conferences in the UK in the 1970s: '[T]he lesbians in general, and the separatists in particular, were accused of being elitist, divisive, of tearing the women's movement apart and taking energy away from 'the real struggle'' (Dixon, 1988: 73). This association of lesbianism with separatism is not surprising, since lesbianism constitutes an act of separation in its own right. Women who choose for women, instead of allowing men access to their bodies and their love, are engaging in a fundamental separation in a society in which men rely on such access to women to control women and children and exploit their labour to provide the necessities of their existence. American lesbian feminist philosopher Marilyn Frye explains that 'heterosexuality, marriage and motherhood' are 'the institutions that most obviously and individually maintain female accessibility', and they 'form the core triad of antifeminist ideology' (Frye, 1983: 108). Lesbians inevitably do separate, even though they may not see themselves as feminists. Societal hatred and disparagement of lesbians shows just how threatening they are to the power structure of male domination whether they politicise their practice or not.

Frye explains why separatism was so controversial in her influential essay 'Some Reflections on Separatism and Power', first published in 1977 (Frye, 1983 [1977]). She explains that she needed to write about this issue because it was plain to her that the idea and practice of 'separation' was fundamental to feminism, in 'everything from divorce to exclusive lesbian separatist communities, from shelters for battered women to witch covens, from women's studies programs to women's bars,

64   Separatism

from expansion of daycare to abortion on demand' (ibid.: 96). But it was much contested and controversial, so, she asks, what makes separation 'so basic and so sinister, so exciting and so repellent?' (ibid.). Feminist separation, she says, consists of 'separation of various sorts or modes from men and from institutions, relationships, roles and activities which are male-defined, male-dominated and operating for the benefit of males and the maintenance of male privilege – this separation being initiated or maintained, at will, by *women*' (ibid., emphasis in original).

Frye explains that feminist separation is completely different from 'masculine separation', which is 'the partial segregation of women from men and male domains at the will of men' (ibid.). Men separate from women in order to consolidate their power and network to preserve their privileges in parliaments, gentlemen's clubs, the Freemasons. This form of separation to create and preserve power by men is under threat as women demand entry or representation. Men's religions and customs have traditionally separated women from men because women were seen as inferior, polluting, unsuitable for power or influence, or as rivals. The Catholic and Greek Orthodox Churches, orthodox Judaism and mainstream Islam still enforce the segregation of women (Jeffreys, 2012). Women have been segregated from men in convents and in other institutions or organisations which were invented by men to serve their own purposes. Separatism, on the other hand, is the choice by women to separate from men in order to resist male domination.

Men have had the resources to live independently, so separating from women, except so far as they might need servants to cook and clean, was something they could choose at will in ways that occasioned no negative criticism. Gay men are one group that can do this. UK lesbian feminist Liz Stanley describes how she became aware of this through her involvement in mixed gay organising in the early 1970s. She explains:

> I would say that perhaps the majority of gay men in this country who are in contact with other gay men, through gay groups and the commercial 'gay scene', live separatist lives. Women are not only absent from their lives in terms of friendship, but absent in other ways because few postmen, electricity men, television repair men, and so on are women. They have no need to have women in their lives *at all* unless they want to, and most decidedly do not.
>
> *(Stanley, 1982: 199, emphasis in original)*

This choice of separatism on the part of such gay men could be associated with their extreme opposition to feminism. Stanley illustrates this with the behaviour of a man in CHE (Campaign for Homosexual Equality), the mixed organisation she was involved with, who opposed the 'women's campaign' and accused her of 'separatism', but admitted that 'I was the first woman to enter his house in the two years he had lived there' (ibid.). On the other hand, Stanley says, the number of men who had entered her house, for one reason or another, was too great to count.

The controversial nature of separatism and the fact that, to many women, it seems so scary that they must publicly repudiate it is, Frye argues, a result of the fact that it is a threat to male power and 'blatant insubordination' (Frye, 1983 [1977]: 103). Women, she says, fear 'punishment and reprisal' for such behaviour. The 'women-only meeting' is, she says, 'a fundamental challenge to the structure of power' (ibid.: 104). It is an example of the slave rising up against the slave owner: 'It is always the privilege of the master to enter the slave's hut. The slave who decides to exclude the master from her hut is declaring herself not a slave' (ibid.). Frye explains that women and girls are maintained in a situation of accessibility to men so that, if women deny men access to their persons, emotions and support, this is seen by the powerful class as a dangerously and revolutionary assumption of control: 'When we start from a position of total accessibility there must be an aspect of no-saying (which is the beginning of control) *in every effective* act and strategy, the effective ones being precisely those which *shift power*, i.e., one which involved manipulation and control of access' (ibid.: 106, emphasis in original). It is when women do this that there is likely to be a vicious reaction and attempted reassertion of male control: 'It is our experience in the movement generally that the defensiveness, nastiness, violence, hostility and irrationality of the reaction to feminism tends to correlate with the blatancy of the element of separation in the strategy or project which triggers the reaction' (ibid.: 107).

Was separatism a luxury for white women?

The question of whether Black lesbian feminists should separate was passionately discussed, and both in the US and the UK some Black lesbian feminists did identify with separatism. This is not necessarily clear from the way in which the history of the WLM is written, which often suggests that Black feminists rejected separatism out of hand. In the US, passionate advocacy against separatism has tended to obscure the complexity of the discussion in which Black feminists and Black lesbian feminists were involved. Lesbian separatism has been accused by its Black lesbian and feminist critics of being a white and middle-class idea (Combahee River Collective, 1983 [1978]; Johnson Reagon, 1983). The practice is racist according to some, because Black women and Black lesbians do not have the privilege of being able to separate from men in the way that white women do. Their oppression as Black, such critics say, is shared by Black men, and to confront it they need to work with their political brothers.

In the vehement critique by Bernice Johnson Reagon, for instance, separatism, in the form of the creation of women's spaces, is an anathema: 'We've pretty much come to the end of a time when you can have a space that is "yours only" – just for the people you want to be there. Even when we have our "women only" festivals there is no such thing' (Johnson Reagon, 1983: 357). She goes on, 'There is nowhere you can go and only be with people who are like you. It's over. Give it up' (ibid.). She takes a hectoring tone towards lesbians who might like to create lesbian-friendly spaces in which women can feel comfortable expressing affection in public. That would exclude women who are anti-lesbian, Johnson Reagon says, and is therefore not acceptable: 'There is an in-house definition so that when you say,

66 Separatism

"women only", most of the time that means you had better be able – if you come to this place to handle lesbianism and a lot of folks running around with no clothes on' (ibid.: 360). She says that, to include Black women in women-only space, it is necessary to admit women who are homophobic and then 'challenge them about it. Can you handle it? This ain't no nurturing place no more' (ibid.: 367). Another famous statement of Black lesbian politics from the US contains determinedly anti-separatist sentiments. The Combahee River Collective Statement from 1978 says, '[W]e feel solidarity with progressive Black men and do not advocate the fractionalization that white women who are separatists demand' (Combahee River Collective, 1983 [1978]: 275). They explain that they need to have solidarity with men around the issue of race and therefore do not have the privilege of being separatists.

Black separatists, on the other hand, have countered these ideas by arguing that they are themselves both Black and separatist, and that there is no necessary contradiction involved. The range of ideas and practices around separatism in the UK is well covered in a discussion between four Black lesbians in the socialist feminist journal *Feminist Review* in 1984. The authors use only their first names, which was very unusual and may reflect the particular challenges faced by Black women who came out as lesbian at that time. There was general acceptance by Black feminists in the UK of the need for women-only groups. As Black feminists they were often involved in extricating themselves from layer after layer of mixed organising. They may have been in mixed-sex Black organising which was separate from the mainly white Left, have left that for women-only groups and conferences, and have left them to set up lesbian-only groups. They set up Black women's groups often as a result of their dissatisfaction with trying to work with Black men in mixed anti-racist work (Carmen, Gail, Shaila and Pratibha, 1984). Carmen explains, 'There is so much violence among the men that it really puts me off thinking that I can begin to start talking about where I am… Just to get yourself heard you have to become like them which I am not prepared to do' (ibid.: 64).

Black lesbian feminists also set up their own separate Black lesbian groups as a result of finding that their lesbianism was rejected in some Black women's groups and conferences. This is explained in the *Feminist Review* discussion. Pratibha explains that she 'came out publicly' at a Black women's conference in 1981 organised by OWAAD. She reports that she was asked by a woman in the lunch queue which workshop she was going to, and that when she said the Black lesbian one '[s]he looked at me blankly and then turned away' (ibid.: 55). Shaila, who was at the same conference, said she found the anti-lesbianism 'really painful':

> It was a process that all of us had to go through… I felt that we were exposed in a terrible way. I felt so disappointed that we were under attack, in a sense, at this conference where we should have experienced a feeling of togetherness… We were up at the top on this gallery…where everyone could look up at us and there was such a feeling of hostility coming towards us.
>
> *(ibid.)*

Pratibha notes that the Black lesbian workshop was the 'beginning of something important', which was the Black Lesbian Group. Shaila comments that there were very few 'visible Asian lesbians' at the conference, and that she knew only 12. There were many more Afro-Caribbean lesbians that she knew, and she wished that 'more Asian women' were 'able to come out' (ibid.: 56).

The four lesbians disagreed about separatism because they had different politics. Two, who defined as lesbian feminists or radical feminists, were positive, whereas the two who defined as socialist feminists, and put the class struggle before women's liberation, were not. Thus Gail, a socialist feminist, was critical: 'Separatist political strategies are always simplistic and I believe essentially reactionary. […] I could never define myself as a radical/revolutionary feminist. I do, though, respect the fact that Black women who define themselves so are in the business of challenging racism amongst radical feminists' (ibid.: 60). In a later version of the same discussion Gail is much more forthright in her rejection of separatism, calling 'separatist political strategies' 'simplistic', 'reactionary' and 'facile' (Carmen, Gail, Neena and Tamara, 1987: 226). But Gail is upfront about the problems Black lesbians faced when working with heterosexual Black women. She says of the Brixton Black women's group, 'It has been incredibly hard because the group has been so rabidly homophobic' (ibid.: 62). This anti-lesbianism existed in Black politics in the US too, as Black lesbian feminist Cheryl Clarke describes. She says the 'black male so-called left' was 'vehement in its propagation' of homophobic beliefs, and that there was a 'homophobic cult of black men' in Black politics (Clarke, 1983: 201). The particular challenge that Black lesbian feminists faced in working with some heterosexual Black women may be related to the profound hatred of homosexuality in the Rastafarian movement and in Jamaican culture. This problem persists today, according to the psychology lecturer Keon West, who has conducted research into attitudes in Jamaica (West, 2014).

Carmen, who was in a local Black women's group, took a different position on separatism, however. She says, 'It seemed such a contradiction, you would be in a Black feminist group and then outside of that you live your life with men. What we were putting up with from men seems incredible now' (Carmen, Gail, Shaila and Pratibha, 1984: 60). Carmen explains that her circle of Black lesbian feminists liked the ideas of the Leeds Revolutionary Feminist Group, particularly the political lesbian paper (discussed at length in Chapter 5), which argued that feminists should separate from men and become political lesbians, a separatist strategy. The paper sparked intense debate and much agreement: 'We read this pamphlet 'Love Your Enemy'…which we'd never seen the likes of before… [T]alked through every argument and personal experience for four days. By the end of it we couldn't bring any reasons forward for continuing relationships with men and that was it' (ibid.: 61). But they felt 'very isolated because in that part of London, we didn't know any other Black lesbians at all. We did hear about the Black Lesbian Group, but just as we were deciding to get involved it packed up' (ibid.: 61). For some Black lesbian feminists, their separatism encompassed avoiding relationships with white women too. Shaila disagreed with this tactic, and expresses it thus: 'I know some women

68 Separatism

who are so insistent that Black lesbians must not have relationships with white lesbians and if you do, that it was sleeping with the enemy. I do find that over the top because I could see *lots of other enemies around...*' (ibid.: 62, emphasis in original).

The *Feminist Review* discussion covered the problem of Black lesbians finding their energies stretched too thin if they sought to work in mixed Black groups, Black women's groups, as Black lesbians and in the WLM generally. Carmen explains,

> But it's really a question of priorities, isn't it? Because we have only got so much energy. I am very interested to hear what is happening with the mixed Black organisations and how they are developing, but I am not prepared to put my energies there at the moment... I think there is definitely enough work to do with Black women.
>
> *(ibid.: 64)*

Shaila agrees: 'I have not had a political history of organising with men, and it would be in "crisis" situations that I would consider temporary alliances. I want us to be working with women, for women, because if we don't who will?' (ibid.: 65).

One of my interviewees, the Black lesbian feminist Femi Otitoju, explains what separatism meant to her. She embraced separatism, she says, in the 1980s, but she still 'worked in the mainstream', so she didn't live a 'women-only life' (Femi Otitoju, interview 2013). Her 'house was female', however, and '[w]e had a brief summer of absolute separatism – postmen asked to leave things at the end of the corridor and...milkmen asked to leave things at the end of the corridor'. The reason for her separatism was that 'we just didn't want men in our lives', and she felt this particularly strongly because she was 'at the very sharp end of the effects of sexism, the very literal effects', because she was 'very young. I was slim and attractive, and I was... pretty, so men would walk into my consciousness every minute of every day, and so it was the obvious thing for me to do, to walk away from that.' When asked whether she continued to call herself a separatist, Femi says, 'You know, technically I don't, but in reality, when I look through my life, I probably am.'

Carmen, one of the Black lesbians in conversation in *Feminist Review* in 1984, points out that it is the political difference between radical or lesbian feminism and socialist feminism that creates the different attitudes towards separatism. She says, 'Some Black women...are able to work with mixed Black organisations because of having a socialist feminist line' (Carmen, Gail, Shaila and Pratibha, 1984: 65). She couldn't be comfortable in the way that a socialist feminist could, because of her different understanding towards men's culpability for the oppression of women: 'Although I am not saying that all men are responsible for all the shit, I think they have got a definite responsibility' (ibid.).

Lesbian separatism and other separatisms

One way in which lesbian separatists have answered accusations that their separation from men is classist and racist is to point out that lesbian separatism forms part of a tradition in which oppressed peoples have chosen separation from the cultures and communities that have denigrated and persecuted them (Hess, Langford and Ross, 1988 [1980]). Women came into feminism and lesbian feminism from backgrounds in Left politics and other social movements, particularly, in the US, the civil rights movement. Some of the US separatists have pointed out that there is a proud history of separation amongst beleaguered communities in the US that have suffered racism and exclusion. Bette Tallen compares lesbian separatism with Black separatism, and says that 'American history, from its inception, consists of the stories of many separatisms' (Tallen, 1988 [1983]: 140). Jewish separatists explain that in some cases their mothers had been part of Jewish separatism, when the community functioned quite separately from the mainstream world, with its own shops and services and social life, and self-help against a hostile world. The American separatist Billie Potts, for instance, in a piece called 'Owning Jewish Separatism and Lesbian Separatism', explains that she was born into a Jewish Orthodox separatism (Potts, 1988 [1982]: 150). This Jewish separatism, she explains, was for the purpose of preservation and self-definition, as well as resulting from experience of abuse, exploitation and ghettoization. These other forms of separatism have not been criticised in the same way as lesbian separatism, probably because separatism that includes men is not a threat to male dominance.

Women's separation is fundamentally different from other incarnations, however, because women's oppression is carried out in families and love relationships, and women give birth to their oppressors. Whereas other social groups can retreat to their families or communities to gain support, women are not in a position to do so. Most of men's exploitation of women and violence against women and girls takes place in the home (MacKinnon, 1989). Women's oppression is based upon the exploitation of women's bodies in childbearing, and women are required to produce children for men under men's control. When seeking to separate, women face the problem of their love for their boy children and family members, and the task of leaving them is hard. This makes the phenomenon of lesbian separatism even more extraordinary, as women are the only oppressed group that faces such a challenge. It also makes it more unacceptable, because women's bodies and work underlie the success of men and male networks across all social groups. Lesbian separatism is very different from other forms.

Boy children

Another way in which separatism was criticised was for the exclusion of boy children. Al Garthwaite says that the issue of whether boy children should be allowed into women's spaces was 'very contentious' (Al Garthwaite, interview 2013). Al describes her experience with a Yorkshire women's holiday centre that she was involved with:

> And there was a big debate about boys, about male children. And how far and whether they should be involved in women's discos, for example, or up to

70 Separatism

> what age. I was among a group who started the Women's Holiday Centre in Horton-in-Ribblesdale, and we had a lot of debate about to what age women would be able to bring their sons to that centre. We finally fixed on the age of ten, on the grounds that above that age…it wouldn't be suitable, and the boys themselves probably wouldn't want to come anyway.
>
> *(ibid.)*

She adds that mothers could, however, feel 'got at', as she put it, and might find themselves shut out of women's events if they could not find or afford childcare. Lynn Alderson explains that the issue of boy children was likely to create difficulties for women who wanted to be part of the WLM but happened to have boy children as a result of their heterosexual past: 'You know, you couldn't just tell them to hate their children and…that they should not have had boy children, you know; it was a completely unhelpful thing to do… It was partly about how you work with people' (Lynn Alderson, interview 2013).

There were strong arguments in support of the exclusion of boys, however. One reason for having a low age limit for boy children, or forbidding them altogether, was the idea that girl children deserved to be made a priority in terms of their safety from boys' harassment and demands, and so that mother and daughter time could be maximised. As Al explains,

> And yet, girls really, really benefited…from girl-only space; there was absolutely no doubt about that. I took my daughter and another, and an older girl from the communal living situation, to a women and girls' weekend out in Silverdale, and the girls when they arrived said: "Are there really no boys here? Really no boys?" And it was wonderful. 'Cos they were putting up with boys…in the school playground every single day… [T]hey really liked it.
>
> *(Al Garthwaite, interview 2013)*

American Black separatist Anna Lee puts it this way: 'When we invite male children into our spaces we devalue our daughters' (Lee, 1988 [1981]: 314). She responded to the argument sometimes made by the mothers of boy children that they could raise them differently so that they were not sexist by saying that there was no point trying to change male children because, in the last analysis, boys would find having power more attractive than whatever their mothers were offering: 'What we as wimmin can offer little boys is not power. If you were a little boy which would you choose – power or sensitivity? Be honest' (ibid.: 313).

Some feminists left their children with their fathers when they decided to become lesbians, particularly if they were boy children. That might appear controversial, but the abandonment of children to the care of their mothers by men who for any reason decided not to continue in a relationship was not, and probably would not now, be worthy of remark. One woman who did this, Al Garthwaite explains, was the influential feminist peace campaigner Helen John, who left her five sons with their father permanently and, according to Al, had the view that 'men have always left their families for war; I left my family for peace' (Al Garthwaite, interview 2013; Docuaddict, 2012).

Transsexualism

Another controversial issue for lesbian separatists was the inclusion of male cross-dressers who transgender, who were called transsexuals at the time of the WLM. Today there is a powerful 'transgender' activist movement, made up primarily of men who oppose the right of women and lesbians to meet separately from them (Jeffreys, 2014). The Women's Liberation Movement was not much troubled by these men, however, mainly because there were very few of them at that time. The transgender movement of the 1990s, spawned by the Internet and the specialist pornography that appealed to cross-dressing men, had not yet begun (ibid.). Cross-dressers mostly still kept their proclivities secret, and they were not claiming to be women or lesbians. Furthermore, the feminist politics of the time was strong. The very basis of the WLM was a belief in the importance and strength of womanhood, which was based on women's biology and honed through growing up to face oppression as a girl and as a woman. There was an overwhelming sense, at least as revealed in the *London Women's Liberation Newsletter* in the late 1970s, that the handful of male interlopers who sought to gain entry to women's discos could never be women and should be determinedly excluded.

The lesbian feminist Maria Katyachild, for instance, wrote in the LWLN in 1979 that a male cross-dresser claiming to be a woman had attended a women's disco:

> On Saturday night a formerly accepted 'womin' confessed…to being a transsexual (male-to-constructed female) – i.e. a man who has had his prick cut off! […] I personally am *not* a humanitarian, I am a feminist, there's a difference! […] It is a totally political issue…which must…be worked out once and for all.
>
> *(LWLN 104, 1979, 24 January)*

In the next newsletter, Pauline Long, later known as Asphodel, writes in support of Maria: 'And all of us say NO. Putting on skirts and make-up, even having "the" operation doesn't turn a man into a woman. What makes us women is the put-down since birth' (LWLN 105, 1979, 31 January). She expresses herself with much feeling, saying: 'I am born a woman, and I reflect the pain that millions of women as well as myself have borne. I will not be put down by this new kind of person… He does not and cannot feel it. He invades the Women's mysteries. He degrades us' (ibid.). Like other feminists at the time who sought to protect their women-only spaces, she exhorts these men to form their own groups to further their own interests. They should not 'muscle in on us'. She says, 'Do not divide us… Transsexual infiltration

72 Separatism

of our groups is just one more male ploy to get us down' (ibid.). My interviewee Sandra McNeill wrote a piece in the newsletter at this time entitled 'Transsexuals and the Women's Liberation Movement', in which she rejects the idea that such men should be admitted to women's spaces in no uncertain terms. She writes,

> The issue is men.... Whether there is a place for men in the Women's Liberation Movement.... [I]t is an insult, an insult greater than a white choosing to wear blackface, an insult greater than a member of the middle class choosing to drop out and not use their money or education to call themselves working class, an insult to the suffering and oppression of all women for these ex oppressors to claim to be women. To accept male-to-constructed female transsexuals as women is to allow men to reassert their control over women.
>
> *(LWLN 106, 1979, 8 February)*

Lesbian feminist theory on transsexualism was honed by the first feminist book on the subject, which was published later in the same year: *The Transsexual Empire*, by the American lesbian feminist philosopher Janice Raymond (Raymond, 1994 [1979]). The issue of the right of men who cross-dress to enter women's spaces continued to be the subject of passionate commentary in the newsletter. On 25 July 1979 there was a one-day workshop entitled 'Transsexuals – Men or Women' at the London women's centre, organised by A Woman's Place (AWP). The policy of AWP was not to allow transsexuals to have access. The report back said that there were 25 women present and transsexuals were excluded (LWLN 131, 1979, 8 August). The majority of those at the meeting were firmly against the idea that men could become women. Furious discussion continued in the newsletter.

In August Mary Stott, feminist journalist, first and longest-serving editor of the *Guardian* 'Women's Page' (set up in 1956) and later a chair of the Fawcett Society and one of its original trustees, wrote a piece arguing that transsexuals should be in the WLM (LWLN 134, 1979, 29 August). Stott's views were those of an older generation of feminists whose politics were very different from the radical and lesbian feminists of the WLM. The historian June Purvis describes her as a 'liberal feminist' (Purvis, 2004). I joined in the discussion in October, stating that, whether these men thought they were 'women, ducks or Boeing 707s', they were actually simply men and had no place in the WLM (LWLN 141, 1979, 17 October). The vast majority of the opinions in the newsletter rejected the idea that these men should be admitted. The issue continued to be important, such that adverts for events in succeeding years specifically stated that they excluded transsexuals. The National Lesbian Conference, for instance, in January 1981 stated that they would not admit them (LWLN 199, 1981, 18 January). This degree of unanimity is hard to imagine today, when a powerful movement of transgender activists has, in the absence of a strong feminist movement, made strides towards the inclusion of male cross-dressers not just in women's meetings but in women's toilets, prisons, refuges and sport (Jeffreys, 2014).

The end of separatism?

It is hard to imagine how most of the important aspects of the WLM could have existed without the women-only principle. Although some of my interviewees still considered themselves to be separatist at the time of interview, most were no longer so, or not in the same way that they used to be. Julie Bindel explains why she was a separatist when the WLM was still going on but has abandoned it now: 'When I was younger and when it was more possible – in other words, when I didn't have a formal job and I was more fiery' (Julie Bindel, interview 2013). This was no longer the case so: 'Uh, but now I'm not. I s'pose, for practical reasons, it seemed to become less necessary.' But there are other reasons now why feminists and lesbian feminists may not be separatists. Separatism was likely to lead to isolation when there was no longer a WLM to support the practice and provide a lesbian feminist community and culture. The comfort of women's friendship may be harder to find, and women's spaces such as discos, women's centres, meetings and conferences have become almost non-existent. If lesbians want to dance or sing in choirs today they are likely to have to do this with men. Even what would once have been women-only dyke marches are now mixed, with male cross-dressers front and centre. Separatism was the basis for the creation of a women's community and became anachronistic in its absence. The creation of a new women's liberation movement, though, would require a rebirth of separatism. The panoply of lesbian feminist political thought and philosophy could not have developed without separatism, and this is the subject of the next two chapters.

Bibliography

AFP (2017, 3 July). Sweden's Bråvalla Music Festival Cancelled Next Year after Sex Attacks. *The Guardian*. www.theguardian.com/world/2017/jul/03/swedens-bravalla-music-festival-cancelled-next-year-after-sex-attacks.

Allen, Paula (1970). *Free Space: A Perspective on the Small Group in Women's Liberation*. New York: Times Change Press.

Carmen, Gail, Shaila and Pratibha (1984). Becoming Visible: Black Lesbian Discussions. *Feminist Review*, 17: 53–72.

Carmen, Gail, Neena and Tamara (1987). Becoming Visible: Black Lesbian Discussions. In Feminist Review (ed.), *Sexuality: A Reader*. London: Virago, 216–244.

Clarke, Cheryl (1983). The Failure to Transform: Homophobia in the Black Community. In Smith, Barbara (ed.), *Home Girls: A Black Feminist Anthology*. New York: Kitchen Table Press, 190–201.

Clews, Colin (2017). *Gay in the 80s: From Fighting for Our Rights to Fighting for Our Lives*. Leicester: Troubador Press.

Combahee River Collective (1983 [1978]). The Combahee River Collective Statement. In Smith, Barbara (ed.), *Home Girls: A Black Feminist Anthology*. New York: Kitchen Table Press, 272–282.

Daly, Mary (1979 [1978]). *Gyn/Ecology: The Metaethics of Radical Feminism*. London: Women's Press.

Dixon, Janet (1988). Separatism: A Look Back at Anger. In Cant, Bob, and Hemmings, Susan (eds.), *Radical Records: Thirty Years of Lesbian and Gay History*. London: Routledge, 69–85.

74 Separatism

Docuaddict (2012, 31 May). The Road to Greenham 'Changed the Course of My Life'. Disarming Grandmothers. https://disarminggrandmothers.wordpress.com/2012/05/31/the-road-to-greenham-changed-the-course-of-my-life.

Freire, Paulo (1970). *Pedagogy of the Oppressed*. New York: Herder and Herder.

Frye, Marilyn (1983 [1977]). Some Reflections on Separatism and Power. In *The Politics of Reality: Essays in Feminist Theory*. Freedom, CA: Crossing Press, 95–109.

Frye, Marilyn (1983). *The Politics of Reality: Essays in Feminist Theory*. Freedom, CA: Crossing Press.

Hess, Katharine, Langford, Jean, and Ross, Kathy (1988 [1980]). Comparative Separatism. In Hoagland, Sarah Lucia, and Penelope, Julia (eds.), *For Lesbians Only: A Separatist Anthology*. London: Onlywomen Press, 125–131.

Hoagland, Sarah Lucia (1988). Introduction. In Hoagland, Sarah Lucia, and Penelope, Julia (eds.), *For Lesbians Only: A Separatist Anthology*. London: Onlywomen Press, 1–14.

Holland, Janet, Ramazanoglu, Caroline, Sharp, Sue, and Thomson, Rachel (1998). *The Male in the Head: Young People, Heterosexuality and Power*. London: Tufnell Press.

Jeffreys, Sheila (2012). *Man's Dominion: The Rise of Religion and the Eclipse of Women's Rights*. Abingdon, UK: Routledge.

Jeffreys, Sheila (2014). *Gender Hurts: A Feminist Analysis of the Politics of Transgenderism*. Abingdon, UK: Routledge.

Johnson Reagon, Bernice (1983). Coalition Politics: Turning the Century. In Smith, Barbara (ed.), *Home Girls: A Black Feminist Anthology*. New York: Kitchen Table Press, 356–368.

Louise, Valentine (1988). Fear. In Hoagland, Sarah Lucia, and Penelope, Julia (eds.), *For Lesbians Only: A Separatist Anthology*. London: Onlywomen Press, 181–186.

MacKinnon, Catharine A. (1989). *Toward a Feminist Theory of the State*. Cambridge, MA: Harvard University Press.

Morgan, Robin (1977). *Going Too Far: The Personal Chronicle of a Feminist*. New York: Random House.

Penelope, Julia (1988). The Mystery of Lesbians. In Hoagland, Sarah Lucia, and Penelope, Julia (eds.), *For Lesbians Only: A Separatist Anthology*. London: Onlywomen Press, 506–546.

Penelope, Julia (1990). *Speaking Freely: Unlearning the Lies of the Fathers' Tongues*. New York: Pergamon Press.

Potts, Billie (1988 [1982]). Owning Jewish Separatism and Lesbian Separatism. In Hoagland, Sarah Lucia, and Penelope, Julia (eds.), *For Lesbians Only: A Separatist Anthology*. London: Onlywomen Press, 149–158.

Purvis, June (2004). Inspiring Women: Remembering Mary Stott (1907–2002). *Women's History Review*, 13 (4): 517–520. www.tandfonline.com/doi/pdf/10.1080/09612020400200408.

Raymond, Janice G. (1986). *A Passion for Friends: Towards a Philosophy of Female Affection*. London: Women's Press.

Raymond, Janice G. (1994 [1979]). *The Transsexual Empire: The Making of the She-Male*. New York: Teachers' College Press.

Romito, Patrizia (2008). *A Deafening Silence: Hidden Violence against Women and Children*. Bristol: Policy Press.

Shulman, Sheila (1983). When Lesbians Came Out in the Movement: Interview by Lynn Alderson. *Trouble and Strife*, 1: 51–56.

Spinster, Sydney (1988 [1982]). The Liberation of Lesbian Separatist Consciousness. In Hoagland, Sarah Lucia and Penelope, Julia (eds.), *For Lesbians Only: A Separatist Anthology*. London: Onlywomen Press, 97–121.

Stanley, Liz (1982). Male Needs: The Problems and Problems of Working with Gay Men. In Friedman, Scarlet, and Sarah, Elizabeth (eds.), *On the Problem of Men: Two Feminist Conferences*. London: Women's Press, 190–212.

Tallen, Bette S. (1988 [1983]). Lesbian Separatism: A Historical and Comparative Perspective. In Hoagland, Sarah Lucia, and Penelope, Julia (eds.), *For Lesbians Only: A Separatist Anthology*. London: Onlywomen Press, 132–143.

West, Keon (2014, 6 June). Why Do So Many Jamaicans Hate Gay People? *The Guardian*. www.theguardian.com/commentisfree/2014/jun/06/jamaica-music-anti-gay-dancehall-homophobia.

Wittig, Monique (1980). The Straight Mind. *Feminist Issues*, 1 (1): 103–111.

Wittig, Monique, and Zeig, Sandre (1979). *Lesbian Peoples: Material for a Dictionary*. New York: Avon.

4

THE LESBIAN PERSPECTIVE

Lesbian feminists were involved in all the different areas of feminist activism in the 1970s and 1980s, but their way of seeing things was likely to be different from that of their heterosexual sisters. This was because of their outsider status, as they existed outside the institution of heterosexuality in all its forms and were able to observe it critically. In addition, though, their separation from men – sexually and often in their living situations, political groups and cultural events – enabled the development of a specifically lesbian perspective, uninflected by keeping menfolk happy and by men's interventions in their theory and practice. Lesbian feminists were very important from the beginning of the WLM in creating the theory of feminism and radical feminism. So many of the theorists who created the principles of radical feminist thought were lesbians that an argument could be made that these foundational works did, in themselves, represent the lesbian perspective. Such radical feminist theorists included Kate Millett (1972 [1970]), Mary Daly (1979 [1978]), Susan Griffin (1981), Andrea Dworkin (1981), Adrienne Rich (1977), Janice Raymond (1986), Audre Lorde (1984) and many more. The works of theory they created, such as Kate Millett's *Sexual Politics* (first published in 1970) and Mary Daly's *Gyn/Ecology* (first published in 1978), have not generally been recognised as works of lesbian feminist theory, but, whether the works specifically addressed lesbians – as Daly's did – or not, they were refracted through a lesbian point of view.

In this chapter, I will focus on an area of feminist theory and practice which is not usually seen as susceptible to the lesbian perspective: men's sexual violence. Lesbian feminists were greatly over-represented in theorising sexual violence, in campaigns against it and in the creation of resources, such as refuges and rape crisis centres to help women to escape and survive it. This is likely to be because, as my interviewees argue, lesbian separation from men enabled them to be profoundly critical of men's behaviour in a way that was much harder for women who had men in their lives who they loved and wanted to exempt from analysis. Today there

The lesbian perspective **77**

is a useful acronym used in social media discussions to sum up the argument often used by heterosexual women to protect their male intimates from any aspersions of being implicated in male violence: NAMALT, or 'Not all men are like this'.

In the rest of this chapter I concentrate on thinking that was consciously created from a lesbian perspective. I shall consider the first objects of lesbian feminist scrutiny, which were lesbianism itself and women's relationships with other women in general, including women's friendships and women's love for women. The lesbian perspective was particularly prominent, too, in relation to the construction of sexuality. One good example of the unique lesbian perspective, for instance, is the theorising of heterosexuality as a political institution, a way of organising women's oppression. Heterosexual feminists who were involved in this institution often did not think of themselves as 'heterosexual', as the 1993 research by lesbian feminist scholars Sue Wilkinson and Celia Kitzinger discovered (Wilkinson and Kitzinger, 1993). For them, heterosexuality just seemed natural, rather than political. The lesbian perspective, the view from outside, was necessary to analyse the way that heterosexuality worked. The theorising of heterosexuality is examined in the next chapter. In the 1980s there was the blossoming of a field of thought that was called in the US 'lesbian ethics'. This directed a conscious lesbian perspective to the ways in which lesbians did and should relate to each other, and I shall look at this important development here. It is not possible to give any more than a brief introduction here to the rich universe of lesbian feminist theory, and I have had to make for this chapter a small selection of the writers and themes that it encompasses.

Inventing lesbian feminist thought

Lesbian feminist philosophers knew that lesbians had to think in very different and unprecedented ways if they were to understand and transform the world of male dominance. Mary Daly, the American lesbian feminist theorist, calls this new thinking 'pyrotechnics' and says that it is possible when relating to other 'wild' women (Daly, 1979 [1978]). This created the space for a world view that was not what Monique Wittig, a French lesbian feminist who lived in the US, calls the 'straight mind' (Wittig, 1992). This new point of view is called by the American lesbian feminist philosopher Julia Penelope the 'lesbian perspective' (Penelope, 1992 [1990]). Penelope points out that there is not just one kind of lesbian or one kind of lesbian thought, but the situation of all lesbians gives them a viewpoint which is distinguishable from the heterosexual world view. She explains,

> Given the depth of the differences in the ways we understand ourselves, can there be such a being as 'The Lesbian'? I think yes. Our perspective inheres in all our works… I want to emphasize the unique potential inherent in the Lesbian experience, a potential so dangerous to the heterosexual body politic that it's exhilarating.
>
> *(ibid.: 39)*

78 The lesbian perspective

In her introduction to Julia Penelope's collection of writings, *Call Me Lesbian* (Hoagland, 1992), lesbian feminist philosopher Sarah Lucia Hoagland describes the contribution Penelope has made to defining the lesbian perspective. Lesbian thought sees women differently: 'Women, or lesbians, become our focus in a way not conceived in heteropatriarchy' (ibid.: xi). It originates in a sense of difference because lesbians occupy outcast status, and 'is born of, encourages, and even demands deviant and unpopular thinking' (ibid.). Penelope, she says, explained the way in which lesbians

> internalise heteropatriarchal values and so keep bringing them into lesbian space – 'the pig in the head,' we used to call it – and we need an analysis that helps us sort them out. That a particular thing feels good, that it feels familiar and so secure, that it has meaning for us, that we do it, is not enough.
>
> *(ibid.: xv)*

As Hoagland explains, 'We need the lesbian perspective to initiate the creation of new value but we need the feminist analysis to guide the rejection of patriarchal structures' (ibid.: xvi).

Lesbian feminist thought was a development of radical feminist thought. Unlike other kinds of feminists, radical feminists did not see women's oppression as coming from capitalism, or some unfortunate accident of history. Radical feminists named men as the oppressors and understood women to be subordinated as a 'sex class' by the ruling class of men. We rejected the systems of thought developed by the great thinkers of male domination, such as Karl Marx and Sigmund Freud, and later Michel Foucault and Jacques Lacan. We saw men's ideas as created out of their position of dominance and their specific interests as the ruling class in relation to the subordinate class of women. They could not be useful to creating our theory, except inasmuch as criticising them helped advance our own thinking, because they did not consider women as fully human like themselves (MacKinnon, 2006). This book will not examine the ideas of these male thinkers in detail to show that their views are inappropriate for the creation of feminist theory. This has been done elsewhere (Millett, 1972; MacKinnon, 1989), and there is no space in a book dedicated to the ideas of lesbian feminists. Other varieties of feminists did not do this wholesale rejection; rather, they considered that they could adapt the ideas of the masters by adding women into the analysis – a position that has sometimes been called 'Add women and stir'. Socialist feminist theorists sought to adapt Marxism or Freudianism (Mitchell, 1974; Hartman, 1979). We sought to overthrow these ideas and create, from our own experience, a whole new way of thinking. We unearthed this experience in consciousness-raising, the practice of examining women's experience in small groups, to understand how women's oppression worked to construct our everyday lives (see MacKinnon, 1989a: chap. 5).

Lesbian feminist theory applies the revelations of radical feminist thought to lesbians. Lesbian feminist philosophers such as Mary Daly (1979 [1978]), Monique Wittig (1992), Julia Penelope (1988), Sarah Lucia Hoagland (1988a) and Audre

Lorde (1984) have explained that the ways in which the known world was constructed through the master thinkers of male domination and their assistants and disciples – i.e. priests, sexologists and therapists – made lesbianism unthinkable. These men described and constructed the world out of masculinity and femininity, the behaviours of male dominance and female subordination which they considered to be natural and inevitable, and created language to match their view of reality. Through their efforts the animal 'kingdom', heterosexuality, the family, clothing and beauty rules were constructed to follow what purported to be natural male domination and female subordination, and when the facts did not fit the fairy tale they were forced to do so. The behaviours of male and female non-human creatures do not fit well into the romance of male domination, though the male sexologists, such as Henry Havelock Ellis, wrote as if they did, to support their ideas about dominant male and subordinate female sexual behaviour (Ellis, 1936). The heterosexual imperative was axiomatic. Lesbians could not exist in this picture; they burst the mould.

British lesbian feminist thought was greatly influenced by the work of the significant American lesbian feminist philosophers mentioned above. Their books were eagerly awaited and discussed, and their ideas informed the ways in which our thinking developed. The work of the American lesbian philosopher Mary Daly was very influential in the UK. Her early work consisted of a feminist critique of religion (1985a [1968]; 1985b [1973]), since she came from a Catholic background and needed to offload that baggage before she went on to write her lesbian feminist classics (Daly, 1979 [1978]; 1984). In her most influential book, *Gyn/Ecology*, she was consciously creating lesbian feminist theory, writing in the preface: 'The Journey of this book, therefore, is (to borrow an expression from the journal *Sinister Wisdom*) "for the Lesbian Imagination in All Women"' (Daly, 1979 [1978]: xiii). The book makes it clear how profound a revolution in thought was required for lesbians to make new sense of the world and sets out to establish some parameters for this new way of thinking. Much of the book is devoted to unravelling the lies of what she calls the male 'mythmasters and enforcers' who conceal or justify the subordination of women (ibid.: 53).

Daly stands out from other feminist theorists in her use of language, in her fury and in the depth and extent of her critique of the ideologies and practices of the masters that keep women down. It is hard to select just a few bons mots from the gathering storm that is her way of writing, but the following might be illustrative. She describes males as 'necromancers', 'dancing with death', out to destroy the natural world and women, and lesbian feminism as 'biophilic', loving the natural world of which women are a part. She roars against 'phallocratic technology', saying,

> The insane desire for power, the madness of boundary violation, is the mark of necrophiliacs who sense the lack of soul/spirit, life-loving principle with themselves and therefore try to invade and kill off all spirit, substituting conglomerates of corpses. This necrophilic invasion/elimination takes a variety of forms. Transsexualism is an example of male surgical siring which

80 The lesbian perspective

invades the female world with substitutes. Male-mothered genetic engineering is an attempt to create without women.

(ibid.: 70)

She creates proud and powerful language for feminists and lesbians to use through reclaiming words that had become pejoratives but often had much more positive origins. The feminists and lesbian feminists involved in the rejection of the masters she calls 'Revolting Hags/Crones' and 'pyrotechnists' (ibid.: 57). She refers throughout to feminists as 'spinsters' who require, in a play on the title of Virginia Woolf's feminist essay *A Room of One's Own*, a 'loom of our own' – a place to spin our theory and creativity. This powerful use of language is illustrated here:

> Crones expect and en-courage [sic] each other to become sister pyrotechnists, building the fire that is fueled by Fury, the fire that warms and lights the place where we can each have a loom of our own, where we can spin and weave the tapestries of Crone-centred creation.
>
> *(ibid.: 384)*

Daly's work creates not just an alternative language but also strong imagery, which sparks (to use her term) lesbian imaginations and helps to create lesbian art and culture.

This sort of lesbian feminist theory was very influential in the UK, but British lesbian feminist thought did concentrate on some new areas and develop ideas that originated in the US in new ways. One new direction was the rigorous analysis of male sexuality that was undertaken by British lesbian feminists active in campaigning against violence against women, in books, articles and the *Revolutionary/Radical Feminist Newsletter* (*RRFN*), as we shall see below. In addition, British lesbian feminists contributed new perspectives in the theorising of heterosexuality in the political lesbian paper, for instance, which will be considered in the next chapter (Onlywomen Press, 1981). British lesbian feminist theory paid more attention to analysing the behaviour of men than our counterparts in the US did.

What is a lesbian?

The first object of lesbian feminist thought was, necessarily, the question: what is a lesbian? Before lesbian feminists began to define lesbianism for themselves, the male sexologists were in charge of the script (Jeffreys, 1997 [1985]). Many of the men who wrote about homosexuality before the WLM did not mention lesbians at all in their books, presumably because lesbianism did not occur to them, and in other texts they were an add-on at the end of a chapter. When lesbians were made the object of study by these men, the results were the creation of extraordinarily hostile stereotypes. The American sexologist Frank Caprio's book *Female Homosexuality* is a good example of this (Caprio, 1954). Caprio says that lesbians were likely to commit serious crimes or be psychopaths, to 'manifest pronounced sadistic and psychopathic trends' and to be kleptomaniacs (ibid.: 304). In the period before the First World War, the origin of what was seen as an unfortunate abnormality or deviation was described as a biological mix-up in which men's brains ended up in women's bodies (Ellis, 1927). Later, as Freudian ideas took hold, lesbianism was attributed to bad relationships with parents. Caprio suggests a variety of what he calls 'environmental influences' – 'broken homes, maladjusted parents, a sadistic feeling attitude toward the opposite sex, death of a parent, predisposition to masculinity and precocious sexuality' (Caprio, 1954: 304). The most urgent task for lesbian feminists was to create a new meaning for lesbianism that would create lesbian pride and make lesbianism a really desirable way of life. So, lesbian feminists took back the definition of lesbianism into lesbian hands.

Lesbian feminists defined lesbianism as constituting a great deal more than just a sexual practice. Heterosexuals do not define themselves simply by what they do with their genitals, but have a heterosexual lifestyle and heterosexual culture and remain heterosexual even if not currently in a sexual relationship and doing sex. For lesbian feminists, too, lesbianism is understood as going far beyond genital connection. Lesbian feminists gave lesbianism a political, and potentially revolutionary, dimension. The clearest early expression of this new definition comes from the womanifesto of Radicalesbians in the US:

> What is a lesbian? A lesbian is the rage of all women condensed to the point of explosion. She is the woman who, often beginning at an extremely early age, acts in accordance with her inner compulsion to be a more complete and freer human being than her society...cares to allow her.
>
> *(Radicalesbians, 1972 [1970]: 172)*

She is a rebel against 'the limitations and oppression laid on her by the most basic role of her society – the female role' (ibid.). The lesbian, then, is a feminist revolutionary par excellence because she refuses to be hobbled by the barbarities of femininity, such as harmful beauty practices and the requirements of deference to men.

The Black American lesbian feminist Cheryl Clarke makes a similar argument, but adds into the social structures that the lesbian rebels against those of slavery and colonialism:

> For a woman to be a lesbian in a male-supremacist, capitalist, misogynist, racist, homophobic, imperialist culture, such as that of North America, is an act of resistance... No matter how a woman lives out her lesbianism – in the closet, in the state legislature, in the bedroom – she has rebelled against becoming the slave master's concubine, viz. the male-dependent female, the female heterosexual... The lesbian has decolonised her body. She has rejected a life of servitude implicit in Western, heterosexual relationships and has accepted the potential of mutuality in a lesbian relationship – roles notwithstanding.
>
> *(Clarke, 1981: 128)*

82 The lesbian perspective

Adrienne Rich reminds us that just being a lesbian in itself is not enough. She says that when a woman chooses a woman lover there is a 'nascent feminist political content', but 'for lesbian existence to realise this political content in an ultimately liberating form, the erotic choice must deepen and expand into conscious woman-identification – into lesbian/feminism' (Rich, 1984 [1980]: 236). This woman-loving is, Rich observes, the foundation for the feminist revolution: 'Woman-identification is a source of energy, a potential springhead of female power, violently curtailed and wasted under the institution of heterosexuality' (ibid.: 234). Seeing lesbians as the vanguard of the revolution is a positive and proud redefinition which turns on its head the sexological model of sinfulness, stigma and masculinity. But lesbian feminists went further than this, to valorise all the loving and affectionate ways in which women relate to each other, in opposition to men's attempts to divide and isolate them, and to show how lesbians are the model for womanloving or 'gyn/affection'.

Lesbian friendship

The way in which women relate to each other was a fundamental concern to lesbian philosophers. Lesbian theorists argued that one major organisational method of male domination was the prevention of love and friendship between women, and, indeed, the fomentation of distrust and rivalry, so that women could not create collective resistance. Women's love was to be only for men, and relationships between women could be tolerated only so long as they did not endanger women's focus upon men as the central interest and source of authority in their lives. The lesbian philosopher Marilyn Frye, for instance, points out that manloving is the cement that undergirds the edifice of male domination, and womanloving threatens this. Men, straight and gay, and women are expected to adhere to this principle alike:

> If manloving is the rule of phallocratic culture, as I think it is, and if, therefore, male homoeroticism is compulsory, then gay men should be numbered among the faithful, or the loyal and law-abiding citizens, and lesbian feminists are sinner and criminals, or, if perceived politically, insurgents and traitors.
>
> *(Frye, 1983: 135–136)*

Lesbians are the only ones who refuse this imperative. From the beginning of the WLM in the US, the importance of affection and solidarity between women was emphasised as vital to women's liberation. As Janice Raymond points out, 'The slogan "Sisterhood is powerful" signalled a coming together of women formerly separated from each other... Different schools of feminism all stressed the necessity to build a strong solidarity of sisterhood' (Raymond, 1986: 28). This was called woman-identification in the important 1970 paper 'The Woman-Identified Woman' (Radicalesbians, 1972 [1970]).

Janice Raymond has written a stirring paean of praise to women's friendship in her influential book *A Passion for Friends: Toward a Philosophy of Female Affection*

(Raymond, 1986). The book examines the history of women's friendship and the obstacles to it that are created by 'heteroreality', which she describes as the 'world view that woman exists always in relation to man' (ibid.: 3). She creates the useful term 'gyn/affection' to describe love between women, and explains why this is vital to feminist politics: 'In addition to being a personal space, Gyn/affection is a political space, a female enclave created by conscious female effort in the world that men have fabricated' (ibid.: 232). In this space, 'friendship can be built where women appear to our Selves and each other, where there is finally an audience for female creation, and where Gyn/affection no longer needs to hide itself or be labelled abnormal, it is a profoundly political act' (ibid.). *A Passion for Friends* is an uplifting and optimistic book about the potential power of women's friendships, stating: 'Female friendship gives women the context in which to be "life-glad". It creates a private and public sphere where happiness can become a reality. It provides encouragement and environment for the full use of one's powers' (ibid.: 238). The philosophers of lesbian feminism wrote about the way in which lesbians might relate to each other differently, outside the parameters of what Mary Daly calls the 'sadosociety' that men have created. Bonding between women, as Daly points out, is frightening to patriarchs because women could bond against them or see through their ruses: '[T]he bonding of our Selves is perceived by the warriors as the Ultimate Threat to be shot down with every big gun available' (Daly, 1979 [1978]: 370).

Theorising sexual violence: the influence of lesbian feminists

The lesbian perspective went beyond the ways in which lesbians understood themselves and their relationships with other women. It was of fundamental importance in relation to men's violence against women, an issue at the heart of radical and revolutionary feminist politics. Lesbian feminists created theory and practice against men's violence against women in numbers disproportionate to their presence in the WLM. This is likely to be because lesbians are not constrained by the compromises made by heterosexual feminists in order to have relationships with men. Lesbian feminists were free to think beyond the bounds of the heterosexual system, and this is important in recognising the extent and form of men's violence against women. Whilst heterosexual feminists might feel under pressure to say that 'not all men' do that, in order to protect the men that they love from any suspicion of collusion in male violence, lesbians are not so constrained. They can, and do, engage in profound analysis of the entire edifice of male sexuality. They explain that sexuality lies at the very foundation of women's oppression, being the grounds on which members of the ruling class of men and the subordinate class of women most intimately interact, and the basis on which their relations are organised in marriage and relationships (Jeffreys, 1997 [1985]; 2011 [1990]). They analysed the ways in which male sexuality constructs the world in which women work, walk in the street, dress and relate to others. My book *Beauty and Misogyny*, for example, is an analysis of the way in which beauty practices from make-up to high-heeled shoes enforce

84 The lesbian perspective

women's subordination and construct them into sex objects to pleasure male observers (Jeffreys, 2014 [2005])). I consider that book to be the expression of a lesbian perspective.

The book written by five UK lesbian feminists, including me, from the Patriarchy Study Group, *The Sexuality Papers*, is an example of lesbian feminist analysis of male sexuality (Coveney et al., 1984). We set out to understand why male sexuality takes the form it does, such as why men practise sexual 'perversions', whilst women do not. We explain that the form taken by male sexuality is constructed out of men's position of dominance. This status creates difficulties for them when they try to act out sexually with women, who they have learnt are not only their inferiors but also dirty and polluting. Our analysis helped us to understand men's sex industry pursuits such as mud wrestling, in which men become excited by watching women covered in dirt, a practice related to what sexologists call 'saliromania'. The contortions that plague men's sexual expression can be understood if seen as constructed in such a political crucible. The forensic examination of how male sexuality and men's sexual violence are constructed was a responsibility that lesbian feminists took very seriously in the 1980s.

My interviewees considered that lesbian feminists were in a better position than their heterosexual sisters to analyse violence against women. Kate says, 'I think if you were still in a strong relationship with a bloke and you've got sons, it would be very difficult' (Kate, interview 2013). Femi Otitoju was of a similar mind; she says that 'many [sic] violence against women groups would not have existed' but for 'the lesbian presence'. She says this was partly because at that time lesbians were not generally choosing to have children, and so 'we were the ones who were free', but also we were not troubled by the 'dichotomy' of feeling as though

> we were betraying the people we were raising and the people we were living with, the people we were supporting. It was much easier to be critical…of man, plural, from a lesbian perspective than it would be from a heterosexual perspective. Everybody wants to say that their particular man is different, that their child won't grow up in that way.
>
> *(Femi Otitoju, interview 2013)*

Jan McLeod also says that lesbians 'have more freedom to speak out' (Jan McLeod, interview 2013). She says that lesbians were extremely influential in creating and running anti-male-violence groups, and wonders whether this would now be known. She argues that it should be documented: '[I]t was hugely unacknowledged, and I do wonder if younger women now who are joining these organisations appreciate the extent to which they were shaped by lesbians… I think it's really important that it's captured.' She says that 'lesbians definitely strengthen…feminism' and that 'lesbians were leaders…in their analysis and the sheer amount of time that they put in' (ibid.).

Elaine Hutton agrees that lesbians were greatly over-represented in organisations fighting men's violence, saying that all those working in Women Against Violence

The lesbian perspective **85**

Against Women in the early 1980s and all those working at Brent Women's Aid were lesbians (Elaine Hutton, interview 2013). Sandra McNeill says that the fact that women organised separately from men in women-only groups was crucial to fighting pornography and violence against women, because 'women weren't worried about offending Fred, pissing off Paul and so on and could just argue with each other and debate with each other, socialise with each other without narking Nigel' (Sandra McNeill, interview 2013). Some feminists who chose to work in groups and services against men's violence to women were already lesbians and many more became lesbians as a result of working in such positive lesbian company. They chose to work in anti-violence groups because of their commitment to all women, as Sandra explains: 'We love women, we care about women... [T]hat's what our whole life is about: caring about women' (ibid.).

Lesbian feminists in the US were major participants in the theorising of men's violence against women and men's sexual violence in the 1970s and 1980s. They included Andrea Dworkin (1981; 1988 [1977]), Diana Russell (1975), Kathleen Barry (1979), Pauline Bart (in Bart and Moran, 1993) and Susan Griffin (1981). Although Andrea Dworkin chose to live with a gay man, John Stoltenberg, she identified as a lesbian (Dworkin, 1988 [1977]: 111). Janice Raymond, whose book *A Passion for Friends* was inspirational for lesbian feminists in the 1980s, by the 1990s was a leading figure in the Coalition Against Trafficking in women. The same pattern of lesbians being well, if not over-, represented in theory and activism against male violence is clear in the UK. Jalna Hanmer, for instance, was a leading figure in the refuge movement and the theorising of men's violence against women in the home (see Hanmer and Saunders, 1984). Liz Kelly (1988) and Jill Radford (see Radford and Russell, 1992) have produced important theory and research. Very many others were involved in writing conference papers that advanced feminist thinking on different aspects of violence against women. Many founded, worked in or directed refuges, rape crisis centres and other anti-violence services from the 1970s to, in some cases, the present day, my interviewee Jan McLeod being one. Lesbian feminists were key to WLM activism in many other areas, but it is their contribution to theorising and working against violence against women that was most influential in the long run.

Lesbian feminists extended the analysis of sexual violence to new areas, with a range and profundity of understanding that has not been matched in recent times. This breadth of analysis is clear in the 1985 volume *Women against Violence against Women* from the UK, which was edited by lesbians and full of papers that were mainly by lesbians, from three conferences on men's violence (Rhodes and McNeill, 1985). Papers from the first conference covered in the book relate to pornography, sexual initiation as rape, the problem of sex therapy, everyday heterosexual sex, prostitution, indecent exposure, mixed wards in hospitals, psychiatry, the age of consent and much more, all analysed as forms of, or contributing to, male sexual violence. Another set of papers was from a conference on sexual violence against girls, and the third from a 1981 conference on general violence against women which covered sexual fantasies, sexual pleasure, pressure to be heterosexual,

86 The lesbian perspective

marriage, rape in marriage, sexual harassment at work, fashion as violence against women, language as violence and action against male violence. These papers, too, were overwhelmingly written by lesbian feminists.

Lesbian feminist theory on sexuality and sexual violence was developed out of activism around these issues. Lesbian feminists in the UK, for instance, were heavily involved in the first group working against pornography, the London Revolutionary Feminist Anti-Pornography group, of which I was a member (see London Revolutionary Feminist Anti-Pornography Group, 1985 [1978], the latter year being when it was written as a conference paper). The group formed in 1977, and, of the women involved in the group, most were heterosexual when it was set up but only one remained so when it disbanded. Studying men's pornography was a good disincentive to being sexually involved with men. In fighting violence against women, lesbian feminists have mainly been working for and with heterosexual women on forms of battery and rape from men which lesbians are unlikely to suffer. We have understood that harm done to one woman affects us all and have been committed to liberating all women from the most immediate and brutal threats. As Janice Raymond puts it, 'If we are lesbian feminists, we feel and act on behalf of women as women... We feel and act for all women because we are women, and even if we were the last ones to profess this, we would still be there for women' (Raymond, 1989: 155). Lesbian feminist activism and theory, which challenged men's eroticising of dominance and submission and violence, accompanied a determination to create a sexuality of equality between lesbians themselves.

Lesbian ethics

Lesbian ethics emerged from the fundamental principle of the WLM that the personal and the political should reflect each other. Feminist ideas in this respect were derived from ways of thinking on the Left, where most of those who entered the WLM had cut their political teeth. In the new Left of the 1960s and 1970s, many socialist thinkers talked about what they called 'living the revolution now', meaning the way in which activists and revolutionaries should conduct their 'private lives' in consonance with their political beliefs and aims (Zaretsky, 1976). They talked about prefigurative forms – i.e. creating forms of practice that would prefigure what would happen after the revolution. For those on the Left, this related to issues such as the rejection of private property, the squatting movement (which enabled access to housing without owning it), non-monogamy (which was seen as opposing ideas of ownership of other people) and sharing resources (which was a way to counter poverty).

Radical feminists in the WLM accepted the principle that the personal was political and used this idea to argue that a feminist revolution must start from creating equality in relations between women and men in daily life, love and relationships. Lesbian feminists went further, and set out to create a quite new ethics for the new lesbian culture they were creating. We were engaged in a radical social experiment. Whereas the culture of male supremacy was based on domination, subordination and brotherhood, lesbian ethics was designed to create a new world view based upon equality, cooperation and sisterhood. During the 1970s these new ideas were debated at conferences and in conference papers, magazines and newsletters. In the 1980s lesbian feminist writers in the US, in particular, named these ideas 'lesbian ethics', and they became a hot topic in specially created journals and books. In the US the journal *Lesbian Ethics* was published from 1984 into the 1990s. In the UK the journal *Gossip: A Journal of Lesbian Feminist Ethics* was published from 1986 onwards by Onlywomen Press in response to the US version. Lesbian ethics was understood to cover the analysis and theoretical exploration of issues concerning lesbian personal lives, sexuality and relationships.

An examination of the US journal *Lesbian Ethics*, published by Jeanette Silveira in California, shows the scope of the discussion. It published articles by many of those involved in developing what we in the UK were probably still calling the politics of the personal, such as Julia Penelope, Bev Jo, Sidney Spinster and the UK novelist Anna Livia. One article was from the Bloodroot Collective, which ran (and continues in 2018 to run) the feminist vegetarian café and bookstore in Connecticut and first delivered its papers in the lecture series the 'Women's Intellectual Terrorist Conspiracy from Hell' (W.I.T.C.H.) in Boston (Bloodroot Collective, 1988). *Lesbian Ethics* featured a regular 'Readers' Forum', offering short pieces by many contributors on special topics set in advance. Memorable topics were 'Non? Monogamy?' (1: 2, Spring 1985); 'Lesbian Therapy' (3: 3, Fall 1985); 'Femme and Butch' (2: 2, Fall 1986); 'Sex' (2: 3, Summer 1987); and 'Separatism' (3: 2, Fall 1988). Articles covered topics such as lesbian nuns, sadomasochism, 'Dyke Economics', fat oppression, lesbian violence and the possibility of lesbian community. Although the term 'lesbian ethics' did not become common currency in the lesbian feminist community in the UK, the journal *Gossip* was created by Onlywomen Press to mirror the discussion that was taking place in the US. It republished some of the articles from *Lesbian Ethics*, notably Julia Penelope's series 'The Mystery of Lesbians' and pieces on lesbian role-playing, on separatism, AIDS and fat oppression.

By the late 1980s, in the US, lesbian ethics had become a field of enquiry in philosophy departments in universities where lesbian feminists were teaching. Philosophy in the academy seems to have taken a rather different form in the UK, where universities have not nurtured feminist philosophers. In the US, however, many academic lesbian feminists were able to incorporate issues such as sadomasochism into the remit of philosophy in a way that I think would have been unthinkable in the UK. These remarkable and exciting US academic lesbian feminist philosophers include Marilyn Frye, Sarah Lucia Hoagland, Claudia Card, Joyce Trebilcot and Jeffner Allen. Hoagland, for example, published her book *Lesbian Ethics* in 1988, Claudia Card published *Lesbian Choices* in 1995 and Jeffner Allen's collection *Lesbian Philosophies and Cultures* was published in 1990. Under the banner of lesbian ethics, lesbian feminists engaged in a rigorous analysis of sexuality and relationships, discussing what was, and what was not, consonant with lesbian feminist revolution.

88 The lesbian perspective

Lesbian feminist sex

Lesbian ethics was concerned particularly with how lesbians should love, conduct their relationships and do sex. The object was to identify and reject heteropatriarchal forms and engage with one another in ways that would prefigure the lesbian feminist revolution. The experience of lesbian feminists in working against pornography and men's sexual violence made us acutely aware of the problems that resulted from constructing sexuality around dominance and submission. Sexuality had to be entirely refashioned, we considered, to eroticise equality. Mary Daly argued that there was a fundamental difference between the way men defined erotic love and friendship and what was possible for women. Men understood erotic love to be based on a sadomasochist model: 'Male defined erotic love involves loss of identity and is inherently transitory. It involves hierarchies, ranking roles – like the military – on the model of S and M' (Daly, 1979 [1978]: 373). Women, on the other hand, understood erotic love to be an extension of friendship rather than a battleground:

> For female identified erotic love is not dichotomized from radical female friendship, but rather is one important expression/manifestation of friendship. Women loving women do not seek to lose our identity, but to express it, discover it, create it… [T]he Presence of Enspiriting Female Selves to each other is a creative gynergetic flow that may assume different shapes and colours. The sparking of ideas and the flaming of physical passion emerge from the same source… It is biophilic bonding.
>
> *(ibid.)*

I approached this in a slightly different way in my book *Anticlimax* (1990), and argued that there was no possibility of women's freedom whilst it was precisely women's subordination that was eroticised as 'sex' for both women and men. I called the eroticising of difference of power 'heterosexual sex', and the eroticising of equality of power 'homosexual sex', whether practised in relationships between women, between men and women or between men and men. Lesbian feminists were committed to creating relationships of equality amongst ourselves, and the rejection of eroticised power difference fuelled lesbian feminist analysis of our sexual practice. We rejected butch and femme role-playing and sadomasochism and wrote about how different our ways of loving could be from those that aped the hierarchical patterns of the heteropatriarchy.

Other lesbian feminist theorists developed swingeing critiques of the way sex was constructed under male domination and pointed out that lesbians could not fit into the frame. In an incisive essay entitled 'Lesbian Sex', the US lesbian feminist philosopher Marilyn Frye shows how the entire understanding of what constituted sex under the rule of the Church, sexologists, popular culture and sex advice literature is irrelevant to what lesbians do (Frye, 1993). She points out that the malestream notion of sex is of an activity that revolves around the penis, in which the sexual act is seen as beginning with the rising of the penis, taking place through

The lesbian perspective **89**

the insertion of the penis in a vagina or other orifice, and ending with ejaculation. For this reason, she says, the question posed in sex surveys, 'How many times a week do you "have sex"?', has meaning for heterosexuals as the number of times this sequence takes place. This view of sex does not take into account whether the woman received pleasure, or whether this was what she wanted to do. The sex is done to her, not by her. Lesbians cannot fit into this paradigm. The pleasure lesbians have with each other does not depend upon penetration, cannot easily be done to another person who is dissociating to survive, is not marked or ended by the satisfaction of one partner, as in male ejaculation, can take place over hours and can involve all sensitive areas of the body. The question 'How many times' in this case does not make sense. Three hours of ecstatic sensual communication may not even constitute 'one time' by patriarchal accounting.

The US Black lesbian feminist poet and author Audre Lorde writes that the understanding of 'the erotic' needs to be greatly extended in order to encompass that which lesbians experienced with one another (Lorde, 1984 [1978]). The masculine logic of sexology and pornography is that the erotic is the same as sex and constitutes male use of women's bodies for sexual pleasure. This is indicated in the fact that a variety of pornography, usually that which purports to be less violent, is called 'erotica' but does not differ from other forms in the activity it portrays. Audre Lorde, on the other hand, argues that the erotic should be seen as a form of life force which infuses women's relationships with themselves and each other: 'The erotic is a resource within each of us that lies in a deeply female and spiritual plane, firmly rooted in the power of our unexpressed or unrecognized feeling' (ibid.: 53). The erotic is also 'an assertion of the lifeforce of women; of that creative energy empowered, the knowledge and use of which we are now reclaiming in our language, our history, our dancing, our loving, our work, our lives' (ibid.: 55). The erotic, she considers, is an 'electrical charge' which 'can give us the energy to pursue change within our world', which will be away from 'the pornographic' to that which is 'female and self-affirming in the face of a racist, patriarchal, and anti-erotic society' (ibid.: 59). When Lorde gave this speech in 1978 there was still a strong optimism within the WLM and lesbian feminism that sexuality could be transformed.

Two issues relating to how lesbians should conduct their emotional and sexual lives with one another were central to lesbian ethics: non-monogamy and lookism. The idea that non-monogamy was a revolutionary practice had its origins with sexist men on the Left who wanted widespread sexual access to women. They were able to pretend to be progressive and overcome women's inhibitions by lecturing non-compliant women that they were too hung up on seeking ownership and property in another person and deeply bourgeois 'romantic love', rather than 'free love'. Within heterosexuality these ideas benefited men, but not women so much. But the idea that non-monogamy was progressive was absorbed in the WLM and lesbian feminism, and was much written about in newsletters and discussed at conferences at the time (Lesbian Ethics, 1985).

Most of my interviewees considered that non-monogamy caused great hurt and trouble between women and was not ultimately a progressive course for lesbians.

90 The lesbian perspective

Julie Bindel says that it was 'very common' but it caused 'loads of trouble' (Julie Bindel, interview 2013). Lynn Alderson says that 'because we were challenging everything' lesbian feminists challenged monogamy too, but 'in most cases it was fairly disastrous. Most women stopped doing it.' It caused, she says, 'a lot of distress', but also 'a lot of fun as well'. Lesbian feminists did, she emphasises, have 'a good laugh around these things as well', which gives the lie to the common idea that feminists are 'humourless', and she remembers 'laughing a hell of a lot' (Lynn Alderson, interview 2013). Sandra McNeill explains that she was inoculated against the attractions of non-monogamy because she had come across it when she was in anarchist politics, 'where there were some men who thought that women should just sleep with any man and that there shouldn't be monogamy, and it was all about men getting sexual access to lots of women, …pressurising women'. Men would extract sexual access by saying things such as: 'You're actually holding up the revolution by not having sex with me.' So, she was 'a bit suspicious' when she came across similar ideas in lesbian feminism (Sandra McNeill, interview 2013).

Sibyl Grundberg describes having been involved in non-monogamy in the early 1970s: 'I was involved in non-monogamy from my very first lover, who was already in a relationship, so I embraced the whole thing and, you know, struggled to live it for as long as I did, but it doesn't seem to me to come naturally to the human condition, and particularly the female mind.' The practice for feminists was, she says, based on 'good ideas', which were 'that we didn't own anybody else, and that we could express ourselves freely', but it was 'very much a continuation of the sexual revolution, I'm afraid'. She was non-monogamous for only a few years because it was 'emotionally very difficult', probably for everyone involved, but 'we were all very busy not admitting it' and 'being brave' (Sibyl Grundberg, interview 2013). Kate chose not to engage in it, saying that 'activities' that 'really hurt other women' were not 'justifiable' because, 'if morality isn't about trying not to hurt other people, I don't know what it is about'. She says that it was 'all '60s sexual revolution stuff, wasn't it? It wasn't women's invention, as far as I know. I can't see what is liberating about adopting the practices of men.' Such practices 'came in as part of the uncritical copying of what was going on in all sorts of so-called freedom movements. That particular one, I really believe, operated in the interests of men. They got access to more women than they could possibly hope for, without any caring responsibility' ('Kate', interview 2013).

Another idea that was taken up by lesbian feminists was the unacceptability of 'fancying', because it was seen to be based on lookism or the objectification of women. It existed within gay liberation too, and a piece in the GLF magazine *Come Together* in March 1972 by a gay man, 'Nick', is entitled 'The Myth of Sexual Attraction' (Nick, 1980 [1972] : 176). Nick considered it 'sexist', saying that, 'if people are going to clear all the sexist shit out of their heads once and for all, they have to go to the root of the problem and destroy the idea of sexual attraction', since it is this idea that underpins the 'whole sexist structure'. Lesbian feminists were opposed to what they were likely to call 'objectification', the process whereby women are reduced by men to objects for their sexual excitement, particularly in practices such as pornography and street harassment, and this caused them to be critical of the ways in which they were attracted to other women. We discussed whether it was possible to 'fancy' another woman without objectifying her. Sandra McNeill says that you were not supposed to talk about 'fancying people' at the time, because that was 'certainly politically unsound' and 'too much like heterosexuality', but 'there was clearly 'a lot of sexual attraction going on' (Sandra McNeill, interview 2013). Femi Otitoju says that lesbians were 'always talking' about who one could reasonably have a 'sexual relationship' with; the politics of potential lovers was important, for instance. In addition, though, there was 'an unwritten rule about not colluding with, you know, this objectification of women that men had been doing' (Femi Otitoju, interview 2013). Lynn Alderson says that concern about fancying did exist but was, 'of course', 'ridiculous'. There was a good deal of concern with appearance at the time, she continues, particularly on occasions when women took their shirts off. She comments that it was in this area of the politics of appearance amongst lesbians that 'we most profoundly failed' (Lynn Alderson, interview 2013). The politics of how lesbians should relate to each other was very important to lesbian feminists, however, and occupied many discussions, conference workshops and papers.

The rejection of therapy

An important aspect of the system of patriarchal ethics that lesbian feminists sought to overthrow was therapy. Freud and the other fathers of psychoanalysis were seen by feminist writers as the authors of profoundly misogynist attitudes and practices that were aimed at the control of women and the enforcement of conformity to the dictates of male domination. The earliest feminist texts after the Second World War identified Freud and his followers as having been greatly influential in the creation of hostile ideologies about women (Klein, 1946; de Beauvoir, 1972 [1949]; Figes, 1970). There was an attempt by some socialist feminists to rehabilitate psychoanalytic theory, both that of Freud and his later disciples such as Lacan, in the 1970s (Mitchell, 1974; Coward, 1982; Barrett, 1980). Radical feminists were extremely critical of this move. The UK radical feminist sociologist Stevi Jackson argued that socialist feminists recuperated psychoanalysis because it solved a theoretical difficulty for them. It created 'a space for theorizing gender relations and sexuality in their own right without challenging pre-existing Marxist concepts and categories' (Jackson, 1983: 41). They could account for the oppression of women without recognising that men oppressed women in everyday life; rather, women's troubles were all in their own heads, stemmed from childhood and were very difficult to repair.

The greatest threat to feminist theory and practice in the late 1970s and 1980s, however, was not psychoanalysis itself but therapy, which was influenced by Freud and his followers and developed in the 1960s into the 'growth movement'. As Sarah Scott and Tracey Payne explain in the UK radical feminist journal *Trouble and Strife*, the founding idea of therapy is the belief in an 'essential self' (Scott and Payne, 1984). This belief was counter-revolutionary, they contend, because it meant that 'people have a core self, a human essence which exists before and outside of the

92 The lesbian perspective

human society in which we live' (ibid.: 32). The task of therapy was to rediscover this self. This idea does not recognise, as feminists do, that women and girls are created within male domination and are profoundly influenced by its precepts, or that the most effective 'therapy' for women was likely to be involvement in the WLM and consciousness-raising.

An industry of therapy developed in the 1970s, first in the US, where the culture of individualism was most developed, and subsequently in the UK. It was taken up by many lesbians and took the place of consciousness-raising groups, casting women back onto contemplation of their navels instead of how to create political change. A new generation of 'feminist' therapists argued that their techniques were consonant with feminism and carried none of the baggage of their male progenitors. Their principles of liberal individualism meant that they promoted tolerance and diversity in sexual practice rather than lesbian ethics. Amongst feminists and lesbian feminists concerned with lesbian ethics, the idea that therapy could be positive for feminism was rejected. The challenge to therapy as a feminist practice was taking place in the in the 1970s (Sarachild, 1978), and by the late 1980s and early 1990s the harms of therapy for feminist politics were clear. The US journal *Lesbian Ethics* held a 'Readers' Forum' on therapy in 1985 (*Lesbian Ethics*, 1985) which raised questions not just about whether therapy was generally useful for feminists but about the problems its practice created for lesbian relationships and lesbian friendship. A major matter of concern was the fact that a power relationship inevitably inhered in therapy, whereby one person paid another for their expertise, whether they were both women and lesbians or not. The American lesbian feminist philosopher Janice Raymond was scathingly critical of what she called 'therapism' in her book *A Passion for Friends* (1986). She argues that therapy was very damaging to women's friendships: '[W]omen in continuous therapy purchase friendship by the hour from those in the therapeutic role' (ibid.: 158).

The aim of UK lesbian feminists Celia Kitzinger and Rachel Perkins in their book *Changing Our Minds* was to 'draw attention to the political problems inherent in the very idea of "feminist therapy" or "feminist psychology" (Kitzinger and Perkins, 1993: 3). They explain that it was 'common' for feminists and lesbians to 'strenuously oppose psychology as a discipline' in the early years of the WLM. Feminists argued that psychology was a masculine set of ideas; as Naomi Weisstein put it, '[A] pseudo-scientific buttress for patriarchal ideology and patriarchal social organisation' (Weisstein, quoted in ibid.: 5). By the time that Kitzinger and Perkins wrote their book, in 1993, three out of four lesbians in the US had been in therapy and 'lesbian' therapy was burgeoning as a practice and an industry. Lesbians had, they say, 'changed their minds', but the problem was that the mind of the WLM and lesbian feminism was changed too. They reject therapy because it is about internal and individual change. It causes women with problems often caused by seeking to live under oppression to adjust mentally, rather than seeking political change. Therapy thus creates quietism, and women blame themselves for their unhappiness. Therapy also, they point out, transforms the ways that feminists are able to think. The language of therapy invaded feminism with depoliticising terms such as 'lesbophobia', which implies that the hatred of lesbians is a mental illness rather than a tool of male domination, and 'empowerment', a term which implies that power is something an individual woman can acquire all on her own, even though she is the victim of male power under an oppressive political system. My interviewee Lynne Harne identified the growth of therapy as a significant force in what she calls the 'dispersion' of lesbian feminism.

The lesbian perspective is a revolutionary way of looking at the world from the point of view of lesbian experience. It creates meaning and value outside the laws and ideologies of the fathers about who lesbians are, about women's friendships, about sexuality and violence against women. In the form of lesbian ethics it prospered in universities in the US in the 1980s and 1990s and was developed in many discussions, conference papers and journals in the UK. This glorious flowering created new ways of thought for a generation of lesbian feminists that have affected the ways that they have lived their lives. It gradually lost currency, however, and was not taken up by new generations. Outside forces such as the therapeutic profession and ideology undermined the new ways of life and thinking that lesbians were creating. Lesbian feminist insights about sexuality did not survive the creation of a lesbian sex industry and a sadomasochist movement, which overwhelmed the new ways of thinking with the imperatives of male sexual violence and sexual exploitation, as we shall see in later chapters.

Bibliography

Allen, Jeffner (ed.) (1990). *Lesbian Philosophies and Cultures*. Albany, NY: State University of New York Press.

Barrett, Michèle (1980). *Women's Oppression Today: Problems in Marxist Feminist Analysis*. London: Verso Books.

Barry, Kathleen (1979). *Female Sexual Slavery*. New York: New York University Press.

Bart, Pauline, and Moran, Eileen Geil (eds.) (1993). *Violence against Women: The Bloody Footprints*. Newbury Park, UK: Sage.

Bloodroot Collective (1988). Bloodroot: Brewing Visions. *Lesbian Ethics*, 3 (1): 3–22.

Caprio, Frank (1954). *Female Homosexuality*. London: Peter Owen.

Card, Claudia (1995). *Lesbian Choices*. New York: Columbia University Press.

Clarke, Cheryl (1981). Lesbianism: An Act of Resistance. In Moraga, Cherríe, and Anzaldúa, Gloria (eds.), *This Bridge Called My Back: Writings by Political Women of Color*. New York: Kitchen Table Press, 128–137.

Coveney, Lal, Jackson, Margaret, Jeffreys, Sheila, Kay, Lesley, and Mahony, Pat (eds.) (1984). *The Sexuality Papers: Male Sexuality and the Social Control of Women*. London: Hutchinson.

Coward, Rosalind (1982). Sexual Violence and Sexuality. *Feminist Review*, 13: 9–22.

Daly, Mary (1979 [1978]). *Gyn/Ecology: The Metaethics of Radical Feminism*. London: Women's Press.

Daly, Mary (1984). *Pure Lust: Elemental Feminist Philosophy*. London: Women's Press.

Daly, Mary (1985a [1968]). *The Church and the Second Sex*. Boston: Beacon Press.

Daly, Mary (1985b [1973]). *Beyond God the Father: Toward a Philosophy of Women's Liberation*. Boston: Beacon Press.

De Beauvoir, Simone (1972 [1949]). *The Second Sex*. London: Penguin Books.

Dworkin, Andrea (1981). *Pornography: Men Possessing Women*. London: Women's Press.

94 The lesbian perspective

Dworkin, Andrea (1988 [1977]). Biological Superiority: The World's Most Dangerous and Deadly Idea. In Dworkin, Andrea, *Letters from a War Zone: Writings 1976–1987*. London: Secker & Warburg, 110–116.

Ellis, Henry Havelock (1927). *Sexual Inversion*. Philadelphia: F. A. Davis.

Ellis, Henry Havelock (1936). *Studies in the Psychology of Sex*, vol. I. London: William Heinemann Medical.

Figes, Eva (1970). *Patriarchal Attitudes: Women in Revolt*. New York: Stein & Day.

Frye, Marilyn (1983). *The Politics of Reality: Essays in Feminist Theory*. New York: Crossing Press.

Frye, Marilyn (1993). Lesbian Sex. In Frye, Marilyn, *Willful Virgin: Essays in Feminism*. New York: Crossing Press, 76–92.

Griffin, Susan (1981). *Pornography and Silence*. London: Women's Press.

Hanmer, Jalna, and Saunders, Sheila (1984). *Well-Founded Fear: A Community Study of Violence to Women*. London: Hutchinson.

Hartman, Heidi (1979). The Unhappy Marriage of Marxism and Feminism: Towards a More Progressive Union. *Capital and Class*, 3 (2): 1–33.

Hite, Shere (1977). *The Hite Report: A Nationwide Study of Female Sexuality*. Sydney: Summit Books.

Hoagland, Sarah Lucia (1988). *Lesbian Ethics: Toward New Value*. Palo Alto, CA: Institute for Lesbian Studies.

Hoagland, Sarah Lucia (1992). Introduction. In Penelope, Julia, *Call Me Lesbian: Lesbian Lives, Lesbian Theory*. Freedom, CA: Crossing Press, xi–xvii.

Jackson, Stevi (1983). The Desire for Freud: Psychoanalysis and Feminism. *Trouble and Strife*, 1: 32–41.

Jeffreys, Sheila (1997 [1985]). *The Spinster and Her Enemies: Feminism and Sexuality 1880–1930*. Melbourne: Spinifex Press.

Jeffreys, Sheila (2011 [1990]). *Anticlimax: A Feminist Perspective on the Sexual Revolution*. Melbourne: Spinifex Press.

Jeffreys, Sheila (2014 [2005]). *Beauty and Misogyny: Harmful Cultural Practices in the West*. Abingdon, UK: Routledge.

Kelly, Liz (1988). *Surviving Sexual Violence*. Cambridge: Polity Press.

Kitzinger, Celia, and Perkins, Rachel (1993). *Changing Our Minds: Lesbian Feminism and Psychology*. London: Onlywomen Press.

Klein, Viola (1946). *The Feminine Character: History of an Ideology*. London: Kegan Paul.

Koedt, Anne (1974 [1970]). The Myth of the Vaginal Orgasm. In The Radical Therapist Collective (ed.), *The Radical Therapist*. London: Penguin Books, 133–142.

Lesbian Ethics (1985). Non? Monogamy? A Readers' Forum. *Lesbian Ethics*, 1 (2): 79–105.

London Revolutionary Feminist Anti-Pornography Group (1985 [1978]). Pornography. In Rhodes, Dusty, and McNeill, Sandra (eds.), *Women against Violence against Women*. London: Onlywomen Press, 13–18.

Lorde, Audre (1984). *Sister Outsider: Essays and Speeches by Audre Lorde*. Freedom, CA: Crossing Press.

Lorde, Audre (1984 [1978]). Uses of the Erotic: The Erotic as Power. In Lorde, Audre, *Sister Outsider: Essays and Speeches by Audre Lorde*. Freedom, CA: Crossing Press, 53–59.

MacKinnon, Catharine A. (1989). *Toward a Feminist Theory of the State*. Cambridge, MA: Harvard University Press.

MacKinnon, Catharine A. (2006). *Are Women Human? And Other International Dialogues*. Cambridge, MA: Harvard University Press.

Millett, Kate (1972 [1970]). *Sexual Politics*. London: Abacus.

Mitchell, Juliet (1974). *Psychoanalysis and Feminism: A Radical Reassessment of Freudian Psychoanalysis*. London: Allen Lane.

Nick (1980 [1972]). The Myth of Sexual Attraction. In Walter, Aubrey (ed.), *Come Together: The Years of Gay Liberation 1970–73*. London: Gay Men's Press, 176–177.

Onlywomen Press (1981). *Love Your Enemy? The Debate between Heterosexual Feminism and Political Lesbianism*. London: Onlywomen Press.

Penelope, Julia (1988). The Mystery of Lesbians. In Hoagland, Sarah Lucia, and Penelope, Julia (eds.), *For Lesbians Only: A Separatist Anthology*. London: Onlywomen Press, 506–546.

Penelope, Julia (1992 [1990]). The Lesbian Perspective. In Penelope, Julia, *Call Me Lesbian: Lesbian Lives, Lesbian Theory*. Freedom, CA: Crossing Press, 39–51.

Radford, Jill, and Russell, Diana (1992). *Femicide: The Politics of Woman Killing*. Farmington Hills, MI: Twayne Publishers.

Radicalesbians (1972 [1970]). The Woman-Identified Woman. In Jay, Karla, and Young, Allen (eds.), *Out of the Closets: Voices of Gay Liberation*. New York: New York University Press, 172–177.

Raymond, Janice G. (1986). *A Passion for Friends: Towards a Philosophy of Female Affection*. London: Women's Press.

Raymond, Janice G. (1989). Putting the Politics Back into Lesbianism. *Women's Studies International Forum*, 12 (2): 149–156.

Rhodes, Dusty, and McNeill, Sandra (eds.) (1985). *Women against Violence against Women*. London: Onlywomen Press.

Rich, Adrienne (1977). *The Meaning of Our Love for Women Is What We Have Constantly to Expand: Speech at New York Lesbian Pride Rally June 26, 1977*. New York: Out & Out Books.

Rich, Adrienne (1984 [1980]). Compulsory Heterosexuality and Lesbian Existence. In Snitow, Ann Barr, Stansell, Christine, and Thompson, Sharon (eds.), *Desire: The Politics of Sexuality*. London: Virago, 212–241.

Russell, Diana (1975). *The Politics of Rape: The Victim's Perspective*. New York: Stein & Day.

Sarachild, Kathie (1978). Psychological Terrorism. In Redstockings (ed.), *Feminist Revolution*. New York: Random House.

Scott, Sarah, and Payne, Tracey (1984). Underneath We're All Lovable. *Trouble and Strife*, 3: 20–24.

Wilkinson, Sue, and Kitzinger, Celia (eds.) (1993). *Heterosexuality: A Feminism and Psychology Reader*. London: Sage.

Wittig, Monique (1992). *The Straight Mind and Other Essays*. Boston: Beacon Press.

Zaretsky, Eli (1976). *Capitalism, the Family and Personal Life*. New York: Harper & Row.

5
POLITICAL LESBIANISM AND HETEROSEXUALITY

Lesbian feminist theorising of heterosexuality was the greatest challenge to malestream ideology. The idea that heterosexuality requires its own explanation and analysis, rather than being just a natural and biological sexual preference, was a fundamental insight of lesbian feminism. We pointed out that heterosexuality as an institution is created and enforced under male dominance to enable the extraction of women's labour and to effect the control of women and children. Many lesbian feminists went further than criticising heterosexuality, and argued that lesbianism is also socially constructed and can be chosen as a political tactic and form of resistance in the struggle to end women's oppression: feminists can become 'political lesbians'.

This idea was controversial at the time, and is even more so today when there is little or no feminist theorising of heterosexuality, and lesbianism is frequently seen – even by a new generation of feminists – as biologically ordained and unchangeable. This chapter will examine these radical analyses and include a case study of an important paper from 1979 which made the argument that feminists should become political lesbians: 'Political Lesbianism: The Case against Heterosexuality' (see Onlywomen Press, 1981). The paper was written by the Leeds Revolutionary Feminist Group, and I was one of the authors. An examination of the paper and the controversy that surrounded its publication will show just how radical and challenging these ideas were at their inception.

Heterosexuality as a political institution

Lesbian feminists argued that heterosexuality is not the result of biology or just a sexual orientation but, rather, a political institution that forms the very foundation of male domination. Instead of accepting the boundaries for lesbianism that male supremacists created – i.e. that we were simply a deviant minority – we turned the critical gaze back upon heterosexuality and threw all its justifications and practices into question. In malestream sociological theory, social institutions are understood as the systems of behaviour that underpin and organise societies and perform important functions (Giddens, 2009 [1986]). Sociologists identify the family as the most important example of an 'institution'. The family is seen as a social formation which exists for particular purposes rather than being the result of biology. Feminist theorists pointed out that the family is the institution through which women's oppression is organised and women's labour is extracted (Delphy and Leonard, 1992). Most violence against women takes place in the 'family', and it is in the 'family' that women's human rights – to freedom of movement and expression, for instance – are most likely to be constrained (Okin, 1989). The family is the crucible in which women's subordination is inculturated. The feminist political theorist Susan Moller Okin explains that the family is a 'school of justice' in which children are placed into the power relations of male dominance (ibid.: 17). The idea that the family is a social institution is widely accepted by sociologists, though not necessarily seen as political or as an arena of male power, but the idea that heterosexuality itself is an institution is not.

Heterosexuality is not seen as an institution in the same way, but perceived as natural, the expression of an innate desire, and as a quintessentially private and non-political area of life. Lesbian feminists challenged the naturalness of heterosexuality, pointing out that the family is just the main way in which heterosexuality is organised: there are other forms, after all, such as the brothel, the harem and other forms of female sexual slavery. Heterosexuality, as the organising principle of male domination, underlies all these forms in which women are subjected for men's use, whether that be reproductive, productive, emotional, sexual. From early on in the Women's Liberation Movement the idea that heterosexuality was a political institution was crucial to the way in which lesbian feminists understood themselves, their politics and the object of their struggle.

This analysis was already clear in 1972 in the writings of the US group the Furies, which included Rita Mae Brown, Charlotte Bunch and Roxanne Dunbar. The title of Brown's piece in *The Furies* magazine, 'Roxanne Dunbar: How a Female Heterosexual Serves the Interests of Male Supremacy', politicises and problematises heterosexuality (Brown, 1972). Bunch explains that heterosexuality is a necessary foundation of male supremacy and that women can make the political choice to leave it and become a lesbian: 'Whether consciously or not, by her actions, the lesbian has recognized that giving support and love to men over women perpetuates the system that oppresses her... Women-identified lesbianism is, then, more than a sexual preference, it is a political choice' (Bunch, 1972: 8). When women make such a choice, she says, they withdraw their support from the institution of heterosexuality: 'Being a lesbian means ending your identification with, allegiance to, dependence on, and support of heterosexuality' (ibid.: 9). She expresses the revolutionary potential of this choice: 'Lesbianism is a threat to the ideological, political, personal, and economic base of male supremacy' (ibid.).

The understanding that lesbianism was a political choice and a form of resistance (Clarke, 1981), and that heterosexuality was a support system for male supremacy,

98 Political lesbianism and heterosexuality

continued to be a formative idea of the lesbian feminist movement. Important papers were written on the subject in the 1980s, including Adrienne Rich's iconic 'Compulsory Heterosexuality and Lesbian Existence' (1984 [1980]) and 'Separatism and Radicalism' by the French-Canadian lesbian feminists Ariane Brunet and Louise Turcotte (1988 [1982]). Brunet and Turcotte express the political function of heterosexuality particularly clearly:

> Feminism has never confronted heterosexuality as a political institution that enables the male class to oppress and exploit the female class. This institution defines woman as sexually accessible to male power, as a reproducer of men and the nourisher of their power. Heterosexuality is the institution that creates, maintains, and supports men's power.
>
> *(ibid.: 454)*

How is heterosexuality constructed?

Adrienne Rich, in her well-known article 'Compulsory Heterosexuality and Lesbian Existence' (first published in 1980), starts from the understanding that 'heterosexuality...needs to be recognized and studied as a political institution' (Rich, 1984 [1980]: 226). She says that heterosexuality is enforced 'as a means of assuring male right of physical, economical, and emotional access' (ibid.). She writes from her anger that lesbianism is excluded as a possibility from the significant feminist texts on motherhood, psychoanalysis and health. If it is ignored within feminism and within the feminist academy, she says, what chance do lesbians have of seeing their existence recognised in culture? This 'erasure' of lesbians from art, literature and film is one of the 'cluster of forces' that she describes as making heterosexuality 'compulsory'. She describes this practice of erasure as 'the rendering invisible of the lesbian possibility, an engulfed continent that rises fragmentedly to view from time to time only to become submerged again' (ibid.: 226). She says that erasure is combined with 'idealization of heterosexual romance and marriage' to constitute 'control of consciousness', which prevents women from deviating from a heterosexual trajectory (ibid.: 220). Another mechanism of erasure, she argues, is the disappearance of lesbians into male homosexuality so that lesbians cannot be recognised as women, or as having a specific and different oppression: 'Lesbians have historically been deprived of a political existence through "inclusion" as female versions of homosexuality' (ibid.: 228). Other ways that she pinpoints as culturally enforcing heterosexuality are as various as child marriage and pornography.

She suggests why it might be hard for heterosexual feminists to recognise that their heterosexuality is not innate but constructed and enforced, '[T]o acknowledge that for women heterosexuality may not be a "preference" at all but something that has to be imposed, managed, organized, propagandized, and maintained by force is an immense step to take if you consider yourself freely and "innately" heterosexual' (ibid.: 226). But, she says, failing to recognise this is similar to the failure to recognise that other oppressive systems exist which heterosexual feminists would have no trouble identifying: 'The failure to examine heterosexuality as an institution is like failing to admit that the economic system called capitalism, or the caste system of racism, is maintained by a variety of forces, including both physical violence and false consciousness' (ibid.).

Lesbian feminist researchers have identified other forces in the enforcement of heterosexuality too, such as the system of 'gender' in which girls are required to embody femininity, the status of subordination, through appearance and behaviour, and boys the status of domination, thus providing the framework for constructing heterosexuality. The idea of 'gender difference' ordains that men and women should occupy different but complementary roles and have different but complementary personalities. Janice Raymond has explained how this creation of difference, such that a member of one sex is disabled and unable to deal with life's exigencies unless hitched up to the other, means that a 'masculine' person has to come together with a 'feminine' person (Raymond, 1986). The learnt helplessness, whereby women are trained not to be strong and physically capable, and boys are not trained to be able to cook and to feed themselves, enforces heterosexual union. It also makes heterosexuality seem natural: simply the coming together of opposites to make one functioning whole.

In her book *Loving to Survive*, the US lesbian feminist psychologist Dee Graham offers a particularly cogent account of the way in which gender creates heterosexuality (Graham, 1994). She argues that women enter heterosexuality out of the need to survive men's violence. She says, 'I do not see women's femininity, love of men, and heterosexuality as biologically determined and thus inevitable. Rather, I see them as the consequences of social conditions characterized by male violence against women, and particularly against women's (physical and psychic) sexual beings' (ibid.: 184). Her explanation as to how 'gender' is acquired is that women under male dominance have to adopt the behaviour of hostages in siege situations to survive male violence and threat. Like other hostages, they have to work out how to please the captor and make themselves attractive and submissive in order to avoid punishment. The hostage behaviour is what is then understood to constitute 'natural' femininity, which includes deference, keeping men happy and not being challenging or independent – the necessary bulwarks of heterosexuality as an institution.

Graham explains that masculinity is the behaviour of the dominant group of men and femininity of the subordinate group of women, and that the behaviours expected of these two categories precisely mirror this power structure (ibid.). Men express their masculinity through their body language. They take up space because they are the powerful class (Henley, 1977). They may 'manspread' on public transport, on sofas in the home. Women must sit with their knees together, enforced further by the fact they are required to wear clothing that reveals their underwear to men's gaze if they do not do so, and take up as little space as possible. Men may touch women at will, but women may not touch back lest they be seen as sexually available and open to assault. Men may stare at women but staring back is seen as a sexual invitation, so women must keep their eyes downcast. All these behaviours,

100 Political lesbianism and heterosexuality

often seen as natural to the sexes, reflect the power hierarchy of male dominance and serve to maintain it. They are the typical behaviours of the 'genders' of masculine dominance and feminine subordination, and they are the building blocks of the institution of heterosexuality.

Heterosexuality is also supported by social sanctions on women who refuse it. US lesbian feminist Anne Menasche's research shows how various forms of social disapproval function to enforce heterosexuality upon women who have chosen lesbianism. Her fascinating study, through interviews, of why women who had been lesbians returned to heterosexuality, *Leaving the Life* (Menasche, 1999), describes the way in which they were forced to seek heterosexual conversion in order to escape the psychological distress of their outsider status. The women had mostly become lesbians whilst at university in a context in which lesbianism was socially accepted but could not stand the disapproval they were subjected to in the world of work and in their families. She quotes women talking about the importance their mothers attached to their daughters being in a heterosexual relationship and providing grandchildren (ibid.). Lesbianism was all very well as a form of experimentation at university but, in the long run, families wanted to be able to be proud of their offspring and the continuation of their dynasty. Girls and women might not have to face violence from their family or being cut off, though some do, but they are likely to experience considerable emotional pressure and the weight of expectations that cannot be denied. Today the same pressures can lead to a similar outcome for the heterosexual conversion of lesbians, but by a different route: transgenderism, which creates surgically and pharmacologically constructed heterosexuality (Turner, 2017).

Lesbian feminist theorists developed a language to enable them to analyse heterosexuality. Janice Raymond gave us 'hetero-reality', which she defines as 'the worldview that woman exists always in relation to a man' (Raymond, 1986: 3) and which has always 'perceived women together as women alone'. She also offers 'hetero-relations' which she defines as 'the wide range of affective, social, political, and economic relations that are ordained between men and women by men' (Raymond, 1986: 7). The lesbian feminist linguist Julia Penelope has created the word 'heteropatriarchy' to bring into focus the way that the rule of men was instantiated and maintained through the institution of heterosexuality (Penelope, 1986). I used the terms 'heterosexual desire' and 'homosexual desire' in my book *Anticlimax* (2011 [1990]). I argued that sexual responses fashioned around power difference – in sadomasochism and role-playing, for instance, and whether experienced in same- or opposite-sex relations – should be called 'heterosexual', because the term 'hetero' means 'other' or 'different'. Thus, heterosexual desire eroticises difference of power. Similarly, 'homo' means 'same', and can usefully be used to signify sexual responses fashioned around sameness of power or equality, by persons in same- or opposite-sex relations. I did hope, too, to valorise the greater possibilities of equality in same-sex relations by using this term, and to problematise heterosexual ones.

The many ways in which girls and women are dragooned into heterosexuality would repay further study. There is a need for understanding aspects such as forced propinquity with men in the absence of women- or girl-only spaces and the enforcement of sexual response to males through experience of aggressive male sexual initiation from a young age. After the 1990s, though, when some of the work above was carried out, research into heterosexuality as an institution tailed off in consonance with the decline in lesbian feminism and the WLM more generally.

Challenging heterosexuality in practice

The lesbian feminist challenge was not just theoretical. In the UK lesbian feminists influenced local authorities to include a critique of heterosexuality in their approach to lesbian and gay rights, and introduced this critique into the classroom if they were teachers and into girls' work if they were youth workers. The extent of the challenge can be gleaned from the wording of a document called 'Tackling Heterosexism: A Handbook on Lesbian Rights', which was published by the Women's Committee of the Greater London Council in 1986, just before the GLC was abolished by the Conservative government (Harne, 2016). The document says that 'heterosexuality, like the assumed superiority of men, is not natural but acquired', and the fact that 'a majority of women and men choose it as their preferred form of sexuality' is associated with 'persuasion, coercion and threats of ostracization'. It describes the form that the pressure to be heterosexual takes and says that this is so 'intense' that 'most heterosexuals do not even experience any sense of making a choice and so universal is it that most do not even experience it as a pressure'. In this way, lesbian feminist theory, with direct echoes of Adrienne Rich, entered a local authority handbook. The support of the GLC for this radical critique of heterosexuality was an indication of the degree of success that lesbian feminist activism had achieved at this time.

The activism of lesbian feminists was particularly strong in the area of education and youth work (Hutton, 2016). Val Carpenter makes the same point, forcefully: 'It was lesbians who were at the forefront of change when the Girls' Work Movement came to life in the late seventies and early eighties' (Carpenter, 1988: 171). The groups for young women and for young lesbians were radical in ways that would likely seem quite extraordinary now. They did not just ask for tolerance of lesbians, but promoted 'challenging heterosexism' – i.e. the idea that heterosexuality was socially constructed and that young women could choose to be lesbians. Today, specific Lesbian Youth groups are unlikely to exist. Any groups that do function within schools are likely to be quite general and 'queer' in orientation, eschewing the very word 'lesbian' and promoting the idea that girls can be 'gender-binary' or 'gender-fluid', or that young lesbians should be transgender (boys) instead. In place of criticism of heterosexuality, the promotion in schools of transgenderism, which heterosexualises gender nonconforming and potentially lesbian girls, is now officially sanctioned in the UK education system (Transgender Trend, 2016).

Political lesbianism: 'Any woman can be a lesbian' (Dobkin, 1973)

The most controversial aspect of the theorising of heterosexuality was the idea that women could choose to vacate the institution and the practice to become political lesbians. This idea was disturbing to some heterosexual feminists, as we shall see, because, if their orientation was not natural and could be changed, then they might need to defend their political choices. The theorising of heterosexuality was not as prolific in the UK as that which took place in the US, but it was represented by one important paper, 'Political Lesbianism: The Case against Heterosexuality', which was very widely circulated within the WLM and much discussed (see Onlywomen Press, 1981). The paper was created for a conference in 1979, published in the news-letter *WIRES* and then in a pamphlet by Onlywomen Press. It is one of the few lesbian publications to get special mention in histories of the WLM in the UK, on the grounds of its notoriety. The paper was written by the Leeds Revolutionary Feminist Group and was one amongst a number of other radical papers that the group wrote on theorising male violence and male sexuality, and on tactical separatism, for a conference in Leeds in 1979. Unlike feminist conferences today, WLM conferences did not generally feature speakers. Participants wrote short conference papers, typically two sides of A4, individually or in groups, and ran them off on Gestetner machines. They took piles of them to place on tables in the entrance to the venue so that women could choose to attend the workshops set up to discuss the papers that interested them. There was an impressive construction and development of theory by women who were not academics but wrote most prolifically for newsletters and conferences.

The paper was seen as so significant that it warranted reprinting in the national WLM newsletter, *WIRES*. In response to its appearance in *WIRES*, many women, both lesbians and heterosexuals and from different political persuasions (socialist feminist, radical feminist, revolutionary feminist), wrote responses, which were published in subsequent editions of the newsletter. In 1981 the lesbian feminist publisher Onlywomen Press published a pamphlet which contained the original paper together with a selection of the responses – the responses of members of the Onlywomen Press collective and a response from the group of revolutionary feminists who had written the paper – to the controversy that it caused, under the title *Love Your Enemy?* (Onlywomen Press, 1981).

The term 'political lesbianism' was not new. It was used by women in the WLM to refer to those who had abandoned heterosexuality as a matter of political choice and become lesbian feminists. The practice of women choosing to be lesbians was common in the WLM. Radical and revolutionary feminists did not generally believe that sexual orientation was innate and their own experience of becoming lesbians confirmed that it was not. I became a lesbian, for example, because I was persuaded by the reasonable arguments of my feminist sisters that putting men first emotionally and in terms of energy was not consistent with feminist politics. I explain in the interview that I gave for Jeska Rees that 'there's not much point putting your very best energies, emotional energies, into someone who was part of the problem, not part of the solution. It just didn't make any sense, in any way whatsoever' (Rees, 2010: 121). One of my interviewees, who doesn't use the term 'political lesbian' about herself, nonetheless expresses her lesbianism as very clearly a political choice: 'I did understand myself to be making a political choice... [C]learly, I'd been married for 20 years myself, and I didn't find the biology of it offensive... I've made the political choice not to support the patriarchal regime as we have it, in that particular way' ('Kate', interview 2013).

Some women who identified with the term 'political lesbian' were already lesbians before they discovered feminism, but reinterpreted their sexual practice as they placed it within a wider politics. Femi Otitoju explains:

> Becoming a feminist enabled me to see my lesbianism as something that would influence my lifestyle, my life choices as opposed to my sexual – just my sexual practice. I think, prior to that, you know, I'd been sort of led by my loins, I think, but feminism gave me – yeah – a mental, an ethical, perspective, and that allowed me to engage with it in an intellectual way.
>
> *(Femi Otitoju, interview 2013)*

The fact that they were so aware of having made choices made many lesbian feminists less than sympathetic to women who, unlike themselves, were unwilling to leave men but offered no explanation, apart from the fact that it was hard to do so.

The authors of the paper explain that they wrote it because they were fed up with having to lie when asked whether they thought all feminists should be lesbians. To reply in the affirmative might cause offence, and so they were forced to dissimulate: 'Often when we talk about our politics and what it means to say men are the enemy, with other women, we are asked whether we are saying that all feminists should be lesbians' (Onlywomen Press, 1981: 5). They realised the 'topic is explosive' because they knew they were not supposed to say the things they were saying in the paper outside small and trusted groups, 'lest our heterosexual sisters accuse us of woman-hating' (ibid.). The paper states clearly, 'We do think that all feminists can and should be political lesbians', and the definition of a political lesbian is 'a woman-identified woman who does not fuck men. It does not mean compulsory sexual activity with women' (ibid.).

My interviewee Al Garthwaite, who was one of the authors of the 'Political Lesbianism' paper, explains how it came about. By the time the paper was written, she says,

> some of us, we lived, breathed, ate, walked, talked feminism. That was what we did... [W]e were very, very involved in a number of different campaigns, a lot of them around violence against women, and it did seem to us that [political lesbianism] was the way forward for the feminist movement and for women in general to stop being oppressed by men.
>
> *(Al Garthwaite, interview 2013)*

104 Political lesbianism and heterosexuality

She describes the hostile reaction to the paper as 'a huge astonishment'. It was just a paper for a conference, where it aroused some interest, but then it was published in *WIRES* and 'the shit really hit the fan'.

The paper gives an analysis of sexuality formed from discussions and many other conference papers and newsletter entries over the previous couple of years from radical and revolutionary feminists. It takes the position, in common with many radical feminist writings from the UK and US in the 1970s, that heterosexuality and lesbianism are not just sexual preferences and that heterosexuality constitutes an institution through which male domination is organised. It argues that women are dragooned into heterosexuality in order for men to exercise their authority and extract women's unpaid labour in the form of housework, emotional labour and sexual labour (Myron and Bunch, 1975; Brunet and Turcotte, 1988 [1982]). The paper criticises the dominant sexual practice within that institution, penis-in-vagina sex, as not necessarily connected with pleasure for women but playing an important part in maintaining male dominance. It argues that this practice cannot be cleansed of its symbolic meaning under a political system of male dominance and women's subordination because '[o]nly in the system of oppression that is male supremacy does the oppressor actually invade and colonise the interior of the body of the oppressed', and says: 'Attached to all forms of sexual behaviour are meanings of dominance and submission, power and powerlessness, conquest and humiliation.' Its importance is described thus: 'It is specifically through sexuality that the fundamental oppression, that of men over women, is maintained' (Onlywomen Press, 1981: 5).

The paper asks heterosexual feminists to withdraw from sexual relationships with men because those relationships form the infrastructure of the oppressive political system of male dominance: 'Any woman who takes part in a heterosexual couple helps to shore up male supremacy by making its foundations stronger' (ibid.: 6). The heterosexual couple, it argues, is the basic 'political structure of male supremacy', in which 'each individual woman comes under the control of an individual man. It is more efficient by far than keeping women in ghettoes, camps or even in sheds at the bottom of the garden' (ibid.). The paper states, further, that acts of penis-in-vagina sex strengthen male dominance and undermine women's chance of equality because '[e]very man knows that a fucked woman is a woman under the control of men, whose body is open to men, a woman who is tamed and broken' (ibid.). It says that women should give up engaging in penis-in-vagina sex because 'giving up fucking for a feminist is about taking your politics seriously' (ibid.: 8).

Criticism of the paper

Responses to the paper in *WIRES* were mixed, but many expressed considerable anger. These critics said that the paper offended them and that it denied women's experience. Socialist feminist Frankie Rickford says that the paper 'offended and angered me' (ibid.: 11). It was the 'first time' she had seen 'feminists directly deny the principle that every woman's experience is real, and valid' (ibid.). The accusation that the paper denied women's experience is one that was levelled at many aspects of radical/revolutionary feminist theory – the critique of beauty practices, for instance (Jeffreys, 2014 [2005]). It is an argument that means areas of personal life should be off limits to feminist analysis, and fits with socialist and liberal feminist approaches that exempt the personal from scrutiny. Rickford says the paper stymies the attempts of feminist women to analyse their sexual practice: 'The tragedy is that women's tentative attempts to explore and reveal and challenge standard sexual practice have been killed stone dead by the two commandments that if you do it with women you're OK and if you do it with men, you're not' (Onlywomen Press, 1981: 11). Such an assertion shows little acknowledgement of the profound critical analysis of the politics of sexuality that radical and revolutionary feminists were developing at the time, but it does provide an excuse for the determined absence of such scrutiny by heterosexual women.

Another critic of the paper, Sophie Laws, thought that criticism of heterosexual practice was in contradiction to the 'pro-woman line' that she saw as intrinsic to radical feminist politics. She says that the authors had behaved like shock troops of the revolution in their attempts to enforce belief: 'One would think they were trying to be "cadres" in the vanguard Marxist tradition; shining eyes fixed on the glorious future after the revolution, jumpers covered with badges and hearts beating to the rhythm of the right-on line' (ibid.: 12). The paper implies, she says, that 'heterosexual women are either stupid or masochistic'. Ann Pettit is particularly acerbic in her criticism, and says that the paper 'clearly and directly contravenes the demand for the right to a self-defined sexuality. It is also the most patronising, arrogant piece of rubbish I have ever read, including orthodox psychology etc. about women' (ibid.: 14). Another heterosexual woman who was outraged by the paper, Penny Cloutte, accuses the paper's authors of being 'like many sexist men', and is cross that the paper appears to 'tell another how she should live, who she should relate to. There seems to be an attitude about that the WLM is some sort of established church, something external with rules and standards which have to be lived up to' (ibid.). Other women, such as Dianne Grimsditch, say they felt excluded from feminism by the paper, and Debbie Gregory has an even grimmer analysis: 'The political effects of this paper are potentially disastrous. It has made many feminists feel their own struggles are hopeless. It has made many feminists feel the WLM is hopeless. It has made many women feel ripped apart' (ibid.: 43).

The critiques of the paper at the time, such as Rickford's, attribute a great deal of power to one single conference paper written by a small group of women. It is hard to see how the expression of any particular view would function as an authoritarian diktat and prevent others from thinking and developing alternative approaches. Since the paper and its authors had no authority and represented only their own views, the implication that it did may relate to the impact it had on its readers. Readers may have considered the arguments true and found them hard to refute, or they may have been aware that the paper was saying only what a large number of other feminists thought but were not prepared to make public. Sheila Rowbotham, in her brief reflection on the paper 18 years after it was written, argues that the

106 Political lesbianism and heterosexuality

paper expressed a 'perspective that had wider support', and this is why it was not 'effectively challenged' (Rowbotham, 1997: 143).

The heterosexual women who were disturbed by the paper, Al Garthwaite considers, 'were very threatened, I think, because it threatened their own marriages, their own sexual behaviour' (Al Garthwaite, interview 2013). The lesbians who argued against it, she says, were those who had a traditional, and sexological, understanding of lesbianism as biological and innate: 'There's a strong feeling then, and there is now, that lesbians have your sexuality – you're born, it's not made… You've got the gay gene, there's nothing that can be done, and so that's how it is.' Another reason for misgivings was that, although some lesbians were in agreement with the paper's sentiments, they thought it too dangerous to write them down, or they might have been 'just a step too far for them'. They may have felt

> threatened by how they would be seen and whether it would increase preju-
> dice against them, whereas they were being accepted and tolerated at work,
> at home, whatever, in their niche, an oppressed minority, which was fine. But
> an oppressed minority who were actually getting rowdy and saying 'Come
> on' was a different matter.
>
> *(ibid.)*

They may have feared a backlash if lesbians went beyond demanding an end to discrimination and criticised other women's sexual choices.

Beatrix Campbell was inspired by the 'Political Lesbianism' paper to write an angry screed in the socialist feminist journal *Feminist Review* in 1980, excoriating radical feminism, to which she attributed the paper, for making heterosexual women feel uncomfortable. She says that as early as 1973 'the confrontation between socialist feminists and radical feminists had become chronic, and resulted in the hegemony of radical-feminist rhetoric'. This rhetoric consisted of heterosexual women being 'castigated as "sleeping with the enemy"… Heterosexuality as a political problematic was dismissed by radical feminism's dismissal of men. Problem solved' (Campbell, 1980: 3). The effect, she says, was that '[h]eterosexuality was banished to the swamp. Those women unfortunate enough to remain unreconstructed, languishing in the heterosexual jungle were, in effect, accused of…failing politically to prioritise women' (ibid.: 14). In the early1980s socialist feminist critics of the analysis of sexuality and heterosexuality that radical/revolutionary feminists were engaged in tended to attack the ideas as hateful and anti-woman, perhaps with the hope that they could be shut down.

Criticism of the paper by other lesbian feminists

Amongst the myriad complaints against the paper, there were pieces by lesbian feminists which agreed with it strongly. Some of them extended the analysis, such as Justine Jones, who talks about the construction of women's sexuality and why women have masochistic fantasies (Onlywomen Press, 1981: 19). Others point out that, although heterosexual feminists might loudly declaim against the paper, they never addressed its main arguments or explained how their heterosexuality fitted with their feminism, or why it was wrong to see heterosexuality as an institution that supported male dominance. Paula Jennings, for instance, states, 'So far I've come across no analysis of heterosexuality by a heterosexual feminist' (ibid.: 48).

But not all the responses from lesbian feminists were positive. One criticism made of the paper by lesbians who were in other respects supportive was that it unreasonably expanded the category 'lesbian' to include other women who were not involved in sexual relationships with women. Pat, who liked the paper, voices this criticism, saying that the paper's definition of a 'political lesbian' as a 'woman-identified woman who does not fuck men' undervalued the significance of sexuality in lesbian relationships. She says there was 'a danger in the revolutionary feminist position on political lesbianism…that it ignores the importance of women's sexual relations with other women… [A] woman-identified woman who does not fuck men is not a lesbian' (ibid.: 35). A similar criticism of such efforts to expand the category was made of Adrienne Rich's paper 'Compulsory Heterosexual and Lesbian Existence', which posits that women who loved women were on a 'lesbian continuum' whether they related sexually to other women or not (Rich, 1984 [1980]). Janice Raymond responded that Rich's paper was 'morally shortchanging to women who are lesbians and patronising to women who are not lesbians' (Raymond, 1986: 16).

Other lesbian feminist critics disagreed with the paper because they did not think that women could simply become lesbians by making political choices. My interviewees suggested that this response stemmed from a belief in some kind of essential lesbianism. Lynne Harne explains that these lesbians 'saw themselves as what we would call "essential lesbians". They saw themselves as being born lesbians' (Lynne Harne, interview 2013). This idea enabled the creation of a hierarchy in the lesbian feminist community between those lesbians who chose and the 'real' ones, who did not – 'a hierarchy in terms of cultural separatism, where born lesbians were at the top from everybody else' (ibid.). Femi Otitoju explains in her interview that some of the critical reaction did stem from a rejection of the idea that sexuality can be chosen, even by some lesbian feminists themselves: 'Well, because a lot of people…like to believe that one's sexuality is not chosen and…that it's fixed… [T]hey like to romanticise sex, I believe… I think some people see it as not real lesbian…political lesbianism is not real lesbianism' (Femi Otitoju, interview 2013). Femi was a lesbian before she became a feminist but does not believe in essentialism and does think that lesbianism can be chosen: 'I don't feel particularly precious about my kind of gut-level lesbianism.'

Anti-lesbianism in the WLM

Some of the lesbian feminists who supported the 'Political Lesbianism' paper at the time argued that the intensely negative reaction to it betokened a developing mood of anti-lesbianism in the WLM. This, they said, resulted from lesbians going so far as

108 Political lesbianism and heterosexuality

to state a political philosophy that challenged heterosexuality and creating a strong and specifically lesbian feminist culture and politics instead of just asking for toleration. Marlene Packwood, for instance, comments that there was '[c]urrently a time of crisis…arising for lesbians in the Women's Liberation Movement. It seems there is a move on to silence us' (Onlywomen Press, 1981: 26). The lesbians I interviewed, both in the interviews and in print at other times, argued that the reaction to the paper represented a significant shift in the attitude to lesbians in the WLM and revealed in some feminists a latent anti-lesbianism. They considered that, previously, lesbians had been somewhat tolerated because they were seen to represent a persecuted minority who deserved rights and inclusion, but once these lesbians started to articulate a political philosophy that was critical of the institution of heterosexuality, however, and even went so far as to criticise heterosexual women's sexual choices, that tolerance came to an end.

One reaction that was identified at the time by lesbian feminists as representative in its sentiments of the emerging anti-lesbianism was a piece written by Ann Pettit for the WLM magazine *Spare Rib*, which caused such a schism in the collective that it was never published (1979: Lesbian Archive collection, 1/7). It was called '"We Want the Best for You" – For Her Own Good'. The *Spare Rib* collective held the piece back for two years whilst a discussion was conducted about what to do with it. Pettit complained that a separatist feminism dominated the WLM and made 'most women…feel that the movement is of little relevance to them'. She said that it was 'hard to define just <u>how</u> it dominates', but this mainly consisted of what could not be 'said or talked about', such as 'living with men' (ibid., emphasis in original). She opined, 'Personally, I don't see that lesbianism has anything more to do with feminism, <u>necessarily</u>, than has Mrs Thatcher' (ibid., emphasis in original). Pettit was unable to pin down what exactly was oppressive about the behaviour of lesbian feminists but described is as a sort of miasma:

> A 'line' which expresses itself as an atmosphere, a set of attitudes, a whole style of speech, manner and dress, is by its very nebulous nature much harder to challenge than a clearly defined analysis coming from an identifiable group… This in fact is the way that the separatists have come to pervade the movement and dominate its ideas.
>
> *(ibid.)*

Describing herself as a 'friend and lover of men and mother of sons', she said lesbian separatists – a phrase she used in place of 'lesbian feminists' – would have to change: '[S]ome lesbian separatists are going to have to do some thinking about their proselytising, aggressive attitudes to other women' (ibid.).

Pettit's strong negative reaction might signify her recognition that what one of my interviewees, Lynn Alderson, saw as a shift of power had taken place in the WLM, in which lesbians had become much more assertive. Lesbianism had become 'something that was the groovy thing to be as well… [I]t wasn't just right, it was the thing you wanted, and aspired to be, and it became a challenge to every heterosexual' (Lynn Alderson, interview 2013). This shift of power represented the fact that lesbian feminists had created a culture and politics that enabled a new way of being a lesbian and made it possible for women to confidently choose women partners. This new political culture enabled lesbians to throw down a challenge to heterosexual women in relation to their own sexual choices:

> But you know it was the first time that the...balance of power shifted...I think, and it was partly a growing confidence on our part. You know we had spent these years in a way making a lesbian life possible... Nobody had been a lesbian like we were lesbians. Nobody. So, it was a new form of lesbianism that came about as a result of the women's movement.
>
> *(ibid.)*

Many heterosexual women reacted to the challenge by becoming lesbians, she says, but those who did not 'might have thought "Oh well, we could give lesbians their rights, you know", whatever, but they'd never looked at themselves and said: "These women are saying to me that I'm living a contradiction..." Lots of them became lesbians after that debate' (ibid.). Heterosexual women were angry with the paper, she opines, because it 'put them on the spot' about why they continued to be heterosexual.

In the aftermath of the controversy a number of lesbian feminists identified what they considered to be an upsurge of anti-lesbian sentiment in the WLM. Linda Bellos, who was one of my interviewees, stated in 1983 that the attacks on the 'Political Lesbianism' paper were themselves an indication of anti-lesbianism; they were 'actually about having a go at lesbians for being out and shouting about it' (Bellos, *LWLN* 361, 1983, 17 April). She says that lesbians were acceptable if they were 'victims' – i.e. arguing for sympathy because they were excluded or discriminated against – but, 'when we start raising questions about compulsory heterosexuality, tons of shit from heterosexual women pour out'. Julie Bindel, in her interview, agrees with Bellos's 1983 analysis. Her opinion is that the 'Political Lesbianism' paper was seen as threatening because '[i]t was criticising women's choices' (Julie Bindel, interview 2013). Lesbians, Julie argues, had to 'tread carefully', and, when they pointed out the 'contradiction' inherent in being heterosexual as a feminist, they thought 'that what that paper was saying...was you're not proper feminists' (ibid.).

In response to the Anne Pettit piece, three lesbians from the *Spare Rib* collective called a workshop at the National Lesbian Conference in 1981 to discuss the issue. Discussion at the workshop was politically split, and there was a decision to call more workshops of women from all political tendencies, socialist/radical/revolutionary feminists, and those who did not wish to label themselves. The first meeting was entitled 'Anti-Lesbianism in the Women's Liberation Movement' and took place at the women's centre, A Woman's Place, in London. This was attended by a large group (58 are listed as attendees) of lesbians from across the feminist political spectrum, from socialist feminists to revolutionary feminists. The group

110 Political lesbianism and heterosexuality

was named the London Lesbian Offensive Group, or LLOG, with the double 'LL' pronounced in the Welsh way. At the meeting it was suggested that the group be a lesbian 'defence' group, but this was responded to with the argument that it would be better if lesbians were on the offensive. In the minutes of the discussions, participants acknowledge that it was the 'Political Lesbianism' paper that caused a particular outpouring of negativity towards lesbians.

Minutes from the first meeting, taken by Susan Hemmings, say that the need for the group became apparent when Pettit's article was sent to *Spare Rib* two years beforehand (LLOG, 'Minutes of First Meeting', 1981, 5 July, author's collection). It created a crisis for the *Spare Rib* collective, which eventually made a majority decision to publish but to include replies from some members of the collective alongside. Three lesbian members remained opposed to this. The paper was published in *WIRES*, however. The minutes record that there were a series of articles simultaneously in other magazines, including *Company*, *Harpers* and *Cosmopolitan*, which all had a 'feminist veneer' but were 'blatantly anti-lesbian'.

Women's reactions to the 'Political Lesbianism' paper were discussed at the second meeting of LLOG, whose ostensible theme was 'our experiences of anti-lesbianism'. The minutes state that the 'Political Lesbianism' paper kick-started a more intense discussion in the WLM on the politics of heterosexuality and on women's sexual choices, with the paper as a 'focal point':

> One of the writers of the paper was there and expressed surprise that so many of us were using the concept of heterosexuality as an institution and the idea of political lesbianism. Another woman was surprised at <u>her</u> surprise: she felt that new ideas were always filtering through the WLM and we did grow and change. We've had two more years of talking about heterosexuality since the PL paper was first published.
>
> *(LLOG, 'Minutes of Second Meeting', n.d. [1981],*
> *authors' collection, emphasis in original)*

At the next meeting there was a discussion of whether the paper was the 'trigger' for all the anti-lesbianism that the lesbians in attendance considered was going on. The minutes report the feeling of the meeting as being that the paper was not the trigger but was just one example of the 'increased demands' that lesbians were making on women, to which anti-lesbianism was one response (LLOG, 'Minutes', 1981, 20 September, author's collection). They also say that some heterosexual women were defending their sexual practice as being the 'coalface' of political struggle, whereas choosing to become a lesbian was a cop-out: 'Some sisters spoke of the emergence of heterosexuality as a "new radicalism" i.e. heterosexuality as where the struggle is really at' (ibid.).

An article signed by LLOG but with no names attached on 'Anti-Lesbianism in the Women's Liberation Movement' was printed in the *Revolutionary/Radical Feminist Newsletter*, a publication created by the Leeds Revolutionary Feminist Group, in 1982. It gives a clear picture of what the group considered the anti-lesbian sentiment of their heterosexual sisters to consist of (*RRFN* 10, 1982, September). The LLOG article argues that heterosexual feminists claimed they were 'OPPRESSED' by lesbians when they really meant they were 'outnumbered and/or threatened and/ or challenged or criticised' (ibid.: 22, emphasis in original). Heterosexual feminists, LLOG claims, were in the habit of telling lesbians that 'lesbian relationships are a soft option because we as lesbians do not have to struggle in our relationships... because women are equal'. Anti-lesbianism in the WLM took several forms, such as being 'marginalised in the movement as the loony fringe', being accused of 'dominating' just by 'being present, vocal or hardworking' and of 'having more *time* for feminism and political activity because we are not having sexual relationships with men' (ibid.; emphasis in original). Anti-lesbianism also took the form of 'our commitment to women' being 'dismissed as sexually motivated' or 'motivated by more "need" of the movement than het [sic] women'. The article goes so far as to challenge heterosexual feminists to question the 'reasons behind their own inability to love women sexually' and to accept that, since 'caring for and loving women' was an integral part of feminism, their inability to do this was a problem (ibid.: 25).

The demise of radical theorising of sexuality

The radical feminist critique of penis-in-vagina sexual practice evident in the 'Political Lesbianism' paper was further developed in Andrea Dworkin's book *Intercourse* (1987), which proved to be very controversial in its turn. The signal absence of any apparent need on the part of heterosexual feminists to defend or theorise their practice was the subject, more than a decade later than the 'Political Lesbianism' paper, in *Heterosexuality: A Feminism and Psychology Reader*, in which two lesbian feminist academics asked heterosexual women to explain their choices and situations, precisely because heterosexuality had never been subjected to analysis by heterosexual feminists themselves (Wilkinson and Kitzinger, 1993). That volume was followed by *Theorising Heterosexuality*, in 1996, in which both heterosexual and lesbian feminists looked at the way that a critique of heterosexuality could be incorporated into social and political theory (Richardson, 1996). The volume marked the last attempt at making an issue of heterosexuality within the WLM. After that time the radical/revolutionary feminist critique faded away, and is now little known.

Many of us, including me, had thought that the analysis of heterosexuality and how it is constructed would continue apace and become an important element of feminist theory and understanding. Sue Wilkinson and Celia Kitzinger expected this too, as they explain: '[W]e are acutely aware of the need for the continued development of more rigorous and sophisticated analysis of heterosexuality. Arguments first introduced in the early 1970s and 80s...require continually to be updated and their applicability to new social contexts and political situations re-examined' (Wilkinson and Kitzinger, 1993: 25). One new social context is the situation in which a form of heterosexuality is being constructed now by the transgendering of lesbians so that they can appear to be in heterosexual relationships (Jeffreys, 2014). The creation of

112 Political lesbianism and heterosexuality

heterosexuality through drugs and surgery is an application of force that we were unable to imagine at the time of the WLM, but it is reasonably common today. There is vanishingly little feminist political analysis of this situation in the present, however. Wilkinson and Kitzinger call for '[s]ustained analysis…in order to arrive at new insights and develop and extend feminist and psychological theory on heterosexuality' (Wilkinson and Kitzinger, 1993: 25). Rather than that taking place, a psychology industry today, often composed of lesbian practitioners, is fully engaged in heterosexualising lesbians, and there is little or no critical response.

The critique of sexuality and heterosexuality was not continued. By the late 1980s searching analysis of sexuality was scarcely taking place. Julie Bindel bewails this in an article in the radical feminist magazine *Trouble and Strife* in 1988 (Bindel, 1988). The historical moment in which it could take place was short and ended with the so-called feminist 'sex wars' in the 1980s, when socialist feminists and libertarian feminists argued that the correct object of feminist enquiry should be the acquisition of sexual pleasure by any means and that critiques of sadomasochism and pornography were anti-sex (see Jeffreys, 2011 [1990]). No critique of sexuality exists in the present which is as far-reaching as that developed by radical and revolutionary feminists in the US and UK in the 1970s and early 1980s. The 'Political Lesbianism' paper was radical in its statement that heterosexuality was not just a sexual preference but a political institution that provided the foundation for male dominance, and in asking heterosexual women to abandon their relationships with men. Not surprisingly, some heterosexual women determinedly defended their practice by accusing lesbians in the WLM of being oppressive and insulting and insufficiently woman-loving.

The rather extraordinary brouhaha that resulted was attributed by lesbian feminists at the time, both those involved in writing the paper and many others, to an underlying anti-lesbianism that took many forms in the WLM but was ignited to particular fury when lesbians overstepped the mark, and, instead of asking for toleration, threw out a challenge to the heterosexual majority. In a time when radical analysis of sexuality and heterosexuality is absent, and queer theory has eliminated the radical feminist challenge, it may be hard for a new wave of feminists to appreciate the significance of the moment in feminist history that the controversy around the 'Political Lesbianism' paper represents. In the 1980s a backlash took place against the lesbian feminist analysis of sexuality presented here and in the preceding chapter (Jeffreys, 2011 [1990]). The analysis of sexuality was so central to the lesbian feminist revolution that its defeat was a crucial component in the demise of lesbian feminism, which the rest of this book seeks to explain and record.

Bibliography

Bindel, Julie (1988). The State of the Movement: Reflections by Julie Bindel. *Trouble and Strife*, 13: 50–52.

Brown, Rita Mae (1972). Roxanne Dunbar: How a Female Heterosexual Serves the Interests of Male Supremacy. *The Furies*, 1 (1): 5–6. https://library.duke.edu/digitalcollections/wlmpc_wlmms01033.

Brunet, Ariane, and Turcotte, Louise (1988 [1982]). Separatism and Radicalism: An Analysis of the Differences and Similarities. In Hoagland, Sarah Lucia, and Penelope, Julia (eds.), *For Lesbians Only: A Lesbian Separatist Anthology*. London: Onlywomen Press, 448–457.

Bunch, Charlotte (1972). Lesbians in Revolt: Male Supremacy Quakes and Quivers. *The Furies*, 1 (1): 8–10. http://cdm15957.contentdm.oclc.org/cdm/ref/collection/p15957 coll6/id/279.

Campbell, Beatrix (1980). A Feminist Sexual Politics: Now You See It, Now You Don't. *Feminist Review*, 5: 1–18.

Carpenter, Val (1988). Amnesia and Antagonism in the Youth Service. In Cant, Bob, and Hemmings, Susan (eds.), *Radical Records: Thirty Years of Lesbian and Gay History*. London: Routledge, 169–180.

Clarke, Cheryl (1981). Lesbianism: An Act of Resistance. In Moraga, Cherríe, and Anzaldúa, Gloria (eds.), *This Bridge Called My Back: Writings by Political Women of Color*. New York: Kitchen Table Press, 128–137.

Daphne Project (2000). Violence against Lesbians: Education, Research, Public Campaigns. European Commission. https://ec.europa.eu/justice/grants/results/daphne-toolkit/en/ content/violence-against-lesbians-education-research-public-campaigns.

Delphy, Christine, and Leonard, Diana (1992). *Familiar Exploitation: A New Analysis of Marriage in Contemporary Western Societies*. Cambridge: Polity Press.

Dobkin, Alix (1973). View from Gay Head. In *Lavender Jane Loves Women* [album]. New York: Women's Wax Works.

Dworkin, Andrea (1987). *Intercourse*. London: Martin Secker & Warburg.

Giddens, Anthony (2009 [1986]). *Sociology*. Cambridge: Polity Press.

Gottschalk, Lorene (2003). From Gender Inversion to Choice and Back: Changing Perceptions of the Aetiology of Lesbianism over Three Historical Periods. *Women's Studies International Forum*, 26 (3): 221–233.

Graham, Dee L. R. (1994). *Loving to Survive: Sexual Terror, Men's Violence and Women's Lives*. New York: New York University Press.

Harne, Lynne (2016). How to Become a Lesbian in 30 Minutes, Part 1. Lesbian History Group. https://lesbianhistorygroup.wordpress.com/tag/great-london-council.

Hutton, Elaine (2016). How to Become a Lesbian in 30 Minutes, Part 2. Lesbian History Group. https://lesbianhistorygroup.wordpress.com/2016/02.

Henley, Nancy (1977). *Body Politics: Power, Sex, and Non-Verbal Communication*. Englewood Cliffs, NJ: Prentice-Hall.

Jeffreys, Sheila (2011 [1990]). *Anticlimax: A Feminist Perspective on the Sexual Revolution*. Melbourne: Spinifex Press.

Jeffreys, Sheila (2014 [2005]). *Beauty and Misogyny: Harmful Cultural Practices in the West*. Abingdon, UK: Routledge.

Jeffreys, Sheila (2014). *Gender Hurts: A Feminist Analysis of the Politics of Transgenderism*. Abingdon, UK: Routledge.

Menasche, Ann E. (1999). *Leaving the Life: Lesbians, Ex-Lesbians and the Heterosexual Imperative*. London: Onlywomen Press.

Myron, Nancy, and Bunch, Charlotte (eds.) (1975). *Lesbianism and the Women's Movement*. Baltimore: Diana Press.

Okin, Susan Moller (1989). *Justice, Gender and the Family*. New York: Basic Books.

Onlywomen Press (1981). *Love Your Enemy? The Debate between Heterosexual Feminism and Political Lesbianism*. London: Onlywomen Press.

Penelope, Julia (1986). Language and the Transformation of Consciousness. *Law and Inequality: A Journal of Theory and Practice*, 4 (2): 379–391. http://scholarship.law.umn.edu/ cgi/viewcontent.cgi?article=1331&context=lawineq.

Raymond, Janice G. (1986). *A Passion for Friends: Toward a Philosophy of Female Affection.* London: Women's Press.

Rees, Jeska (2010). A Look Back at Anger: The Women's Liberation Movement in 1978. *Women's History Review*, 19 (3): 337–356.

Rich, Adrienne (1984 [1980]). Compulsory Heterosexuality and Lesbian Existence. In Snitow, Ann Barr, Stansell, Christine, and Thompson, Sharon (eds.), *Desire: The Politics of Sexuality.* London: Virago, 212–241.

Richardson, Diane (ed.) (1996). *Theorising Heterosexuality.* Buckingham, UK: Open University Press.

Rowbotham, Sheila (1997). *A Century of Women: The History of Women in Britain and the US.* London: Viking.

Transgender Trend (2016, 18 December). Teaching Transgender Doctrine in Schools. www.transgendertrend.com/teaching-transgender-doctrine-in-schools-a-bizarre-educational-experiment.

Turner, Janice (2017, 12 November). Why Do So Many Teenage Girls Want to Be Like Alex Bertie? *The Times Magazine.* www.thetimes.co.uk/article/meet-alex-bertie-the-transgender-poster-boy-z88hgh8b8.

Wilkinson, Sue, and Kitzinger, Celia (eds.) (1993). *Heterosexuality: A Feminism and Psychology Reader.* London: Sage.

6

SADOMASOCHISM

The challenge to the politics of sexual equality

In this and subsequent chapters I will examine the forces that stopped lesbian feminism in its tracks and began the unwinding of the lesbian revolution. The first to be considered is the considerable backlash that developed in the 1980s to the profound challenge to sexual violence and the construction of sexuality that lesbian feminists had been so influential in creating. The development of a lesbian sadomasochist (S/M) movement in the 1980s stopped the lesbian feminist challenge to dominant male sexuality from making any progress. Lesbian feminists sought to align their relationships and sexual lives with the creation of a feminist revolution by pursuing a politics of equality in love and in sex. They argued that the sexuality of male domination consisted of the eroticising of women's subordination, and this, together with the institution of heterosexuality, formed the lynchpin of women's oppression. Lesbian feminists rejected the ways in which inequality could be eroticised by lesbians, as in butch and femme role-playing and sadomasochism (now more usually called BDSM, or bondage, discipline and sadomasochism).

This critique of sexuality was profoundly challenging. A backlash to these politics developed in the 1980s from within some parts of the feminist and lesbian communities, taking the form of a movement of lesbians who were in favour of sadomasochism and role-playing. They promoted a sexuality of dominance and submission as both natural and progressive. The sadomasochist movement combined with a campaign by libertarian feminists to defend pornography from a feminist challenge, creating the so-called 'sex wars' of the 1980s, in which the newly emerged feminist critique of sexuality was trounced by the powerful forces of male dominance. The critics of the lesbian feminist challenge to the sexual politics of male domination named themselves the 'pro-sex' tendency, and were largely successful in defeating the lesbian feminist attempt to transform the construction of sexuality.

116 Sadomasochism

The sex wars

The lesbian feminist understanding of sexuality that was honed from a movement of liberation was challenged in what were called the 'sex wars' of the 1980s (described in Jeffreys, 2011 [1990]). In the early 1980s the sexual landscape of feminism changed. This was a time in which the global sex industry made a great leap forward, particularly through the relaxation of controls on pornography (Jeffreys, 2011 [1990]; 2009). The growth of the sex industry was supported by the resistance to the feminist challenge to pornography that was mounted by women who described themselves as 'pro-sex'. In the US, women such as those writing in the anthologies *Pleasure and Danger* (Vance, 1984) and *Powers of Desire* (Snitow and Stansell, 1983) made feminists who wanted to eroticise equality out to be anti-sex and prudish. They either defended pornography, on the grounds of free speech, or argued that pornography was empowering to women. The 'pro-sex' camp was introduced to a British audience by the socialist feminist journal *Feminist Review*, in its 'Sexuality' issue in 1982. Some of the US exponents were included, as well as the British writer Rosalind Coward, who opines in a piece that defended pornography that an 'anti-pornography stance' was 'not very useful' (Coward, 1982: 21). One part of the burgeoning sex industry was the creation by some lesbians of their own pornography, such as the US magazine *On Our Backs* (a deliberate riposte to the feminist magazine *Off Our Backs*). New lesbian sex industry magazines promoted an emerging lesbian sadomasochist movement. The 'sex wars' within feminism were against feminists and lesbian feminists who sought to transform sex in order to overturn male domination.

The new lesbian pornography contained precisely similar themes to the material about lesbians which had traditionally been created by male pornographers. Previously lesbians had appeared in pornography only as figments of men's imaginations, in the form of prostituted women simulating sexual activity for male consumers. The new lesbian porn, such as *On Our Backs*, did not deviate from the script. Although it was created by lesbians, the values were similar. I called this development the 'lesbian sexual revolution' and saw it as replicating the problematic values of sexualised misogyny which characterised the supposed sexual revolution created by and for heterosexual men in the 1960s (Jeffreys, 1993). The 'new' lesbian pornography was created from and helped to promote the newly fashionable lesbian sadomasochism. Its violent themes of black leather, whipping and beating came out of the pages of the magazines and into the lesbian community to create new lesbian fashion imperatives. By 1990 London lesbian fashionistas were extolling the virtues and excitements of S/M as the 'in' thing in fashion for the 1990s (Blackman and Perry, 1990, writing in a special issue of *Feminist Review* entitled 'Perverse Politics: Lesbian Issues'). These developments were a very considerable shock to feminists and lesbian feminists, who had expected that their work on creating a sexuality which was based on equality would go from strength to strength and create a feminist sexual revolution. We had to face the fact that we were being strongly opposed from amongst our own ranks, from lesbians who claimed to be feminists yet promoted the eroticising of dominance and submission, humiliation and pain.

The two sides in the 'sex wars' were not equal. The side that described itself as 'pro-sex' – i.e. in favour of pornography and sadomasochism – was aligned with and founded upon centuries of the culture of male sexual violence against women, and upon the industries of pornography and prostitution that were formed to subordinate women in the service of men's pleasures. For this reason, the 'pro-sexers' were hugely well supported and welcomed with open arms by the powers of male domination: by pornographers, the so-called progressive media and the male Left. The feminists who dared to challenge the way in which men's sexuality was constructed and acted out in sexual violence against women, on the other hand, were entirely unfunded, without the support of any masculine institutions and had to invent their script as they went along. They were doing something unprecedented and challenging the foundations of male dominance. They were also developing their ideas mainly in newsletters and at conferences that were women-only and in ways that were shut off from the malestream world. This was good inasmuch as it allowed a freedom of imagination and the ability to theorise beyond the pale of men's authority, but it did mean that the 'pro-sexers', who went straight into the malestream and Left papers and journals with pornographic photos of lesbians in black leather and chains, were unopposed and very influential.

The 'pro-sexers', who supported the male status quo and were much celebrated for doing so in male media, were much more powerful in the malestream world. There was no equality in the marketplace of ideas taking place here. Left and supposedly progressive publications in the 1980s were able to justify their enthusiasm for publishing photos of semi-naked women in black leather and with whips by claiming they were just covering a new and authentic lesbian movement. Lesbian feminists in dungarees and no make-up, who were producing ideas critical of the way male sexuality is constructed and threatening male privileges to use women in prostitution and pornography, were not exciting in the same way. They were, as the US radical feminist theorist Catharine Mackinnon aptly put its when describing the feminist critique of sexuality, 'detumescent' (Mackinnon, 1989a: 130).

Lesbian sadomasochism was a replication of the sexual practice of gay men, which was generally performed in sex clubs and in public. The precursor to gay S/M was a rather small underground fetish scene of heterosexual sadomasochists. I have offered in my book *Unpacking Queer Politics* explanations for the emergence of sadomasochism as the quintessential practice of gay men in the 1970s (Jeffreys, 2003). Not surprisingly, S/M was central to the sexuality of gay men, as they perceived their masculine status as damaged by their homosexuality and eroticised their own powerlessness in response. They were attracted to powerful, aggressive masculinity in the way that women were trained to be. Like women, gay men were overwhelmingly masochists, eroticising the oppression they experienced as gay within a hostile heteropatriarchy. Tops were hard to find, whereas bottoms were extremely plentiful. Though not without its critics, S/M became the mainstream and accepted expression of gay male sexuality and gay male porn (Young, 1995; Levine, 1998).

118 Sadomasochism

The gay male version of sadomasochism was supported by an ideological defence from its practitioners (Young et al.,; Preston, 1993; Dominguez, 1994). The main justification put forward was that S/M was a valuable form of practice because it created a particularly powerful and pleasurable sexual response. It was also promoted as revolutionary and progressive, as the practice of anarchists and others who wanted to abolish sexual repression (Young et al., 1978). Gay sex that did not focus on S/M was called at the time, disparagingly, 'vanilla' sex – i.e. colourless – or 'bambi', and seen as namby-pamby or niminy-piminy (Weeks, 1982; quoted in Jeffreys, 2011 [1990]: 211). S/M sex was called by gay men 'heavy-duty' – i.e. the real thing. But gay male sadomasochists did not bother themselves with detailed justifications, as the lesbians who became involved tended to do, perhaps because the lesbians needed to assuage the contradictions between their practice and their feminism, which were obvious and acute.

The original proponents of lesbian S/M were women in San Francisco who became involved in mixed sadomasochist clubs such as Janus, which was, according to the doyenne of lesbian sadomasochism, Pat (later Patrick) Califia, dominated by gay men (Califia, 1982). The sexual interests of these women transmogrified into a political movement which was directly opposed to lesbian feminist sexual politics. They formed a lesbian S/M group, Samois, and began to organise and publish, starting in 1979 with a publication called *What Color Is Your Handkerchief* (Samois, 1979). This codified the symbols of public gay sadomasochist ritual, in which players wore handkerchiefs of particular colours to indicate their sexual predilection, for a lesbian audience, adding such details as whether the wearer was menstruating as well as whether she was a top or a bottom. Two years later they published a lesbian S/M collection of theory and erotic fiction, *Coming to Power* (Samois, 1982). The leading lights, Gayle Rubin and Pat Califia, organised S/M practitioners from the beginning as a political movement which was based upon feminist forms. Samois members defined themselves as 'feminist lesbians' and constituting 'a lesbian/feminist S/M organisation', set up support and consciousness-raising groups and prioritised 'coming out' based upon the gay liberation movement. Samois defined S/M in such a way as to imply that it was egalitarian: 'A form of eroticism based on a consensual exchange of power' (title page of Samois, 1982). The S/M activists saw themselves as victims of oppression, that oppression coming from lesbian feminists who were critical of a sexuality based on dominance and submission.

The activists defended their position in slightly different ways from gay male practitioners. Samois created an ideology to support the practice which was designed to press feminist buttons, as to S/M being about the empowerment of women, for instance. The activists also defined themselves as having essentialist identities which were similar to those involved in race and class:

> We must have precisely the same dialogues about the texture of our sexuality as we have been having about classism, racism, cultural identity, physical

Sadomasochism **119**

appearance and ability. How do all these differences converge, to make us who we are? We must all ask and answer these questions.

(Davis, 1982: 9)

They saw S/M as an unchangeable personal characteristic. Katherine Davis writes that S/M will make women more and more powerful, saying that 'S/M is a pathway to a more and more powerful self' (ibid.), whilst Juicy Lucy argues that those who are critical of it are 'afraid of sex and afraid of power' (Juicy Lucy, 1982: 38).

From the beginning, S/M dyke ideology denied that lesbian sadomasochism bore any relationship to the real violence from men that women commonly experienced, but pieces within *Coming to Power* clearly gave the lie to this. One piece in the anthology made it quite clear that S/M could be integrated seamlessly into an abusive relationship whilst being justified as just a consensual sexual practice. Susan Farr explains that, in the abuse she dishes out to her girlfriend, 'a cuff says I love you' (Farr, 1982: 184). Farr says she and her girlfriend use violence to punish each other for infidelity. The one suffering from the infidelity can 'escape her feelings' by 'giving the other a beating'. Farr uses this logic to feel justified in giving 'Rae a whipping after she had sex with someone else', which 'expresses directly how angry and jealous I feel' (ibid.: 186). Nonetheless, Pat Califia deplored what she calls the 'confusion between S/M and violence' (Califia, 1982: 259).

Another clear connection with men's violence against women is the fact that proponents were happy to explain that their interest in S/M came from having experienced male violence. They said that S/M provided a way of healing from that abuse. One contributor to *Coming to Power*, Juicy Lucy, for instance, said that she had experienced very many 'beatings' and much 'violence' as a 'straight woman' (Juicy Lucy, 1982). I can remember speaking against S/M at conferences in the 1980s – at the Montreal International Feminist Bookfair in 1988, for instance – where young women would jump up from the audience and say that S/M had healed them from the post-traumatic stress disorder they suffered as a result of men's sexual violence. They said that it enabled them to 'feel' and broke down the defensive wall they had built up to guard against sexual feeling lest it trigger the trauma of the abuse.

Many feminists weighed in with critiques at the time, and the book *Against Sadomasochism* (Linden et al., 1982) contains powerful arguments from very well-known, and mostly lesbian, feminists, including Kathleen Barry, Diana Russell, Audre Lorde and Alice Walker. Sally Roesch Wagner, for instance, asks the important question as to where S/M comes from, and how to account for the development of a 'lesbian-feminist sadomasochistic "liberation" movement' (Wagner, 1982). Like other feminist theorists, she understood sexuality to be socially constructed, and saw sadomasochism as the product of a sadomasochist culture, or what Mary Daly calls the 'sadosociety' (Daly, 1979 [1978]). Feminist critics saw pornography as the major force in constructing S/M, but the depiction of men's violence against women in media and advertising were important too. S/M was a more overt expression of normative sexuality under male dominance. It reproduced the forms of violence

120 Sadomasochism

that terrorised women outside S/M: threat, aggression, rape and torture. But it also showed the basic bone structure of the way sexual response was created.

I argued in several pieces of writing at the time that sexuality under male dominance was constructed to be the eroticising of women's subordination (Jeffreys, 1997 [1985]; 2011 [1990]), for both women and men. The eroticising of power difference was the ordinary basis of heterosexuality, but common amongst gay men and lesbians too. Women had little chance to develop a sexuality of equality because they were born and raised and had their emotional and sexual experiences from a subordinate social status. They did not have power or equality to eroticise, only low status and often actual sexual use and abuse as children and young women. According to this feminist logic, sadomasochists could be seen to be acting out the normative values of heterosexuality rather than being the radical transgressors that they saw themselves to be. This understanding rather undermines the ideology promoted by S/M dykes about how superior and more evolved they were in their sexual practice, as expressed by a Samois member:

> [M]asochism is a highly developed and sophisticated form of sexual expression (it is the only 'deviation' that animals never practice)… It represents a sort of transcendence over the human dilemma… Surprising at it may seem, the highly intellectual character of many masochists is only to be expected when you consider how intellectual the s/m mystique really is.
>
> *(Kolb, 1979: 20–21)*

Ipso facto, lesbian feminist critics were just intellectually limited, or a bit boring.

One justification given for their practice by S/M dykes was that it was OK for lesbians to do it because no men were involved and women were each other's equals. This meant that they could truly consent to the practice and no in-built power imbalances existed. Feminist theorists have shown that there are many problems with the notion that 'consent' in relation to prostitution, pornography, S/M changes the abusive nature of these practices (Pateman, 1989; MacKinnon, 1989b; Jeffreys, 1993). They have pointed out that consent cannot make a practice equal. Indeed, consent is necessary only when a powerful person is about to do something to a less powerful person which is dangerous, as in consent to surgical procedures. It has no place in a sexuality of equality in which the danger of harm is not the foundation of the practice.

One problem with the idea that S/M could be about equality was the way that the practice eroticised many relations of power that needed to be challenged rather than celebrated, not just sex, age and class but also race. Alice Walker, the Black feminist novelist, contributed a powerful chapter to *Against Sadomasochism* in which she argues that S/M was racist because it eroticised and recycled the abuses of slavery. She explains that S/M dykes played out scenarios of master and slave, in which white mistresses paraded Black slaves who were in dog collars and on their knees. This she saw as counter-revolutionary, sexist and racist in the extreme. The Nazi themes of S/M came to the UK through the gay male community, and in the early 1980s in London there was much use of Nazi imagery by S/M gays and S/M lesbians. The swastika was an important S/M symbol and both gay men and lesbians involved in S/M wore it. It was in response to this that I wrote 'Sadomasochism: The Erotic Cult of Fascism', which was published in the US journal *Lesbian Ethics* in 1984 (Jeffreys, 1993 [1984]). I argued that, at a time when white skinhead youths were beating up Black gay men, and particularly disabled gay men, in the toilets at gay clubs in London, it was entirely inappropriate to be promoting the eroticising of fascism. For the majority of the lesbians involved in S/M, these issues were not of great moment. They were having fun trying to be outrageous, and sex was not related to any real-world oppressions in their minds. They were not worried about how to change the way sexuality was constructed in order to end violence against women, or how to challenge racism and fascism. Getting sexually excited and trying to shock lesbian feminists were much more interesting pursuits.

The impact of sadomasochism

S/M became fashionable, and its symbols and appurtenances were ubiquitous in the lesbian community in the 1980s. It morphed into a cultural industry with the creation of lesbian pornography magazines such as *On Our Backs* in the US and the opening of specialist sex clubs and bars. Within a few years lesbian feminists in the UK were trying to hold back a tide of S/M behaviour and display at discos, on marches and parades and at lesbian centres. Newspapers, magazines, entertainment guides, gay and left-wing publications all promoted lesbian S/M as progressive and exciting. They accompanied their coverage with visuals of the sort of imaginary lesbians that had long populated men's pornography. S/M proponents claimed to be the only ones who were open about sex, and the S/M that was so determinedly promoted began to be the only form of 'sex' around. Lesbian sadomasochism occupied the space in which sex could then be spoken about within the WLM. It sucked the air out of the discussion.

One response from lesbian feminists in the UK was to seek to create a conversation about sexuality that would enable S/M to be challenged through the promotion of alternative ideas. Thus, the Lesbian Sex and Sexual Practice Conference was organised for April 1983, with workshops on

> celibacy, feminist erotica, is sex a necessary part of lesbianism, class, friendships, masturbation, philosophy of one night stands, sexual attraction and fantasy, what lesbians do in bed, lesbian culture and image, clothing, role playing, sexual abuse of girls (by men)…Sm, couples, monogamy, lesbian mothers, lesbians and porn, racism, Irish lesbians, lesbian lit and poetry…lesbians and therapy, lesbians and alcohol, lesbian relationships with straight and bisexual women, how responsible are heterosexual feminists for their anti-lesbianism, violence, art.
>
> *(Lesbian Sex and Sexual Practice Conference, publicity leaflet, author's collection)*

122 Sadomasochism

The topics discussed at the conference show the profundity of the conversation about sexuality that was taking place amongst lesbian feminists who rejected S/M at the time. They show that there was plenty to say and do in the area of sexuality without any acceptance that S/M was quintessential lesbian sex.

One of the tasks that lesbian feminists took up was the analysis of where sexual feelings and fantasies came from, with the object of changing them. American lesbian feminist theorist Robin Morgan wrote about being the victim of S/M fantasies, where they came from and how to go about eliminating them in 1977, before any women were claiming that S/M was an empowering sexuality for feminists (Morgan, 1977). I wrote a paper for the 1983 conference entitled 'Sexual Fantasies' (author's collection). Revolutionary feminists such as me considered that the main reason that S/M had such attraction for some lesbians was the ubiquity of masochistic fantasies. I argued that, although S/M activists did not accept social construction and saw fantasies as an indication of an innate sexuality that should not be questioned, in fact masochistic fantasies were very common in women, not anything special that made us particular kinds of people. As I expressed it in my paper, 'We were expected to believe that somewhere inside our heads there existed an innocent romping ground of delight which had got there by magic, or because we were individually so wonderfully creative, or perhaps they were innate.' I said that we needed to ask what experiences had formed them and explained that girls and women learn to turn their subordination into a source of 'emotional and later recognisably sexual satisfaction' which locks them 'tightly into the mesh of our own oppression'.

I explained that this process started so young that 'it can seem to come from within us rather than from outside' and stated that women should not feel guilty that their fantasies are so formed but furious that male dominance has done so much damage. I argued that fantasy life could be changed, and consciousness-raising and laughter were good first places to start: 'Laughter can have a very dampening effect, and so can getting angry.' At this time some of us adopted the practice of creating conference workshops in which we asked women to share the sort of fantasies they had and then sought to show how funny they actually were. We considered that laughter was the best response and would take the power out of the fantasies, which would not be capable of creating such a sexual frisson after a roomful of women had rolled about laughing at them.

In 1984 we set up the group Lesbians Against SadoMasochism (LASM) in London in response to the decision by the new GLC-funded Lesbian and Gay Centre to allow practising and costumed sadomasochists to meet there. LASM argued, for instance, that lesbian mothers should be able to take their children in to use the lesbian floor without having to encounter persons in black leather, studs, swastikas and handcuffs. Many of those of us who were in LASM had already been involved in a lesbian group, Lesbians Against Pornography (LAP), which was formed to oppose pornography, including 'lesbian' pornography produced by lesbians and that created by men.

London lesbian S/M activists in the early 1980s were not interested in just the private practice of their predilection. They created a movement to transform sexuality, promote their practice and silence criticism. The activists invaded meetings in full costume and squared up against lesbian feminists at any events that we organised in response. They carried the attack into lesbian feminist spaces and used their black leather biker costumes and muir caps (associated with the Gestapo) to intimidate. The *London Women's Liberation Newsletter* in 1983 and 1984 contains information about how the S/M movement was affecting feminist events and experience. Women in S/M costume were causing considerable distress to other women in what had been the safe spaces of women's discos and social events. An opinion piece from September 1983 by a Black woman describes what happened when she went to Blisters women's disco at The Fridge. She said a white woman arrived in 'stereo-typed Gestapo gear – the sort you see in movies – unmistakable. Apart from that she had several handcuffs hanging from a leather studded belt round her waist' (LWLN 330, 1983, 23 August). The writer says that she often did not feel comfortable as a Black woman in women's discos because they were mostly white, but this scenario made her particularly 'tense and intimidated'. Some disco organisers at this time instituted 'dress codes' to try to keep the most racist and disturbing displays out of their venues, and this created dissension. Public display was a large part of the appeal for practitioners, but their behaviour forced other lesbians who had no desire to see pornographic/fascist imagery to be unwilling observers. The 'sex wars' around S/M were not simply about what women did in their bedrooms but about the display and promotion of eroticised violence, including the violence of fascism.

S/M lesbians recruited. They were proselytisers for their sexual interest and wanted more women to join the S/M movement, because this gave their ideological onslaught more power and provided more participants in the practice. To recruit they needed to advertise and hold public meetings, and this was unacceptable to feminists running women's newsletters and women's venues. In February 1984 an opinion piece in the *London Women's Liberation Newsletter* criticised the refusal of the collective to print the advertisement for an S/M support group or to give the reasons for this refusal. The writer says that opposition to S/M was 'based on a misunderstanding of the function for us of fantasy and play. I think it's like dreaming…a way of ordering and in some sense controlling frightening and contradictory elements in our lives.' In addition, it showed a failure to 'realise that the reason why women engage in S/M is that it sharply increases sexual pleasure, and for women to pursue their own sexual pleasure is…progressive' (LWLN, 351, 1984, 7 February). In March another lesbian wrote that 'we' should not let 'a few vociferous women police the WLM and stifle honest debate' (LWLN, 355, 1984, 6 March). She supported the advertising of S/M meetings in the newsletter, saying: 'I'd rather S/M lesbians were part of the WLM and engaged in discussion and debate than that they were frozen out.'

The workers at A Woman's Place, the central London women's centre, printed a statement about why they opposed the idea of a 'so called open discussion on sado-masochism' taking place there. They explain that two women whom they thought were from Wages for Housework (a Left-orientated women's group that set up myriad groups to cover women's issues and subvert feminist perspectives) had

124 Sadomasochism

come in to the centre after booking such a meeting and 'intimidated' four workers with 'verbal abuse', and 'at one point one of the Black workers was called a racist for opposing sadomasochism' (LWLN 374, 1984, 17 July). From these descriptions and statements, it is possible to glean the atmosphere of threat and fear that was being created. Something more than simply the right of women to engage in a sexual practice was at stake here. A movement whose members wore fascist regalia was involved in threatening behaviour towards lesbians who were at the very centre of WLM activity in London. Ironically, they operated under the guise of requiring 'support' groups, as if they were themselves an oppressed category of women who needed to draw strength from each other to confront their abusers, whom they identified as feminist anti-violence campaigners.

The next arena on which the S/M lesbians sought to set out their stall was the annual Lesbian Strength march in 1984. An opinion piece in the London news-letter reported that an 'S/M Dykes' banner was carried on the march. The march organising committee was, apparently, unable to ban it because it received no advance notice. The result was that about 20 women stayed away because the banner was included. The writer says she felt 'uneasy, unhappy, uncomfortable being part of a march with that banner. As far as I'm concerned sadomasochism is violence against women' (LWLM 371, 1984, 26 June). Some women who chose to be anonymous had an opinion piece in the same issue, on the other hand, congratulating the Lesbian Strength Committee for not turning away the banner and thereby 'subjug-ating themselves to the demands of a small group of anti-SM propagandists' (ibid.).

Two weeks later the London newsletter carried two opinion pieces about what transpired at a meeting at A Woman's Place which was organised to discuss what happened at the march and work out how best to challenge S/M. Elizabeth Carola described the scene, saying that women from the group Wages for Housework, on this occasion calling themselves S/M Dykes, and other supporters of S/M chose to attend 'all in protofascist gear' and 'criticising feminism, romanticising pornography and prostitution (and in this case sadomasochism and pedophilia) and in general, dominating the meeting' (LWLN, 374, 1984, 17 July). This was accompanied by another opinion piece by me and several others saying that 'lesbians who tried to argue from feminist principles' were 'derided' and called 'scab, Fascist, tool of the State!!!'. Critical feminists, such as me, were accused of being like the National Front (a contemporary UK neo-fascist party) for organising the meeting, which is ironic considering that the S/M dykes were the ones dressed like the Gestapo and the rest of us were in T-shirts and jeans. I well remember the tone of the meeting and the sense of threat that I and my friends felt when faced by a contingent of women in black leather, who entered the small room aggressively and stated that 'SM dykes would be at every meeting, conference etc. to prevent any such discus-sion in the future' (ibid.).

The next arena in which S/M politics was to cause chaos was the London Lesbian and Gay Centre (LLGC). The centre was an important development, in which a large building was renovated in 1984 for the exclusive use of lesbians and gay men, with money from the GLC. A decision was taken before the centre opened that S/M dykes should be allowed to meet there on the floor set aside specifically for lesbian use. In response, Lesbians Against SadoMasochism was set up to organise against this. There was a temporary prohibition on S/M groups meeting at the centre in order that discussion could take place, and in February 1985 there was an open meeting for lesbians at the LLGC to discuss how the new and very important lesbian space should be used (LWLN, 409, 1985, 19 March). A report of the meeting explains: 'A few lesbian-feminists that had managed to find out about the meeting went along to demand that neither S/M groups/individuals nor dykes in fascist/racist/antisemitic clothes and symbols would be allowed to use the women's space, and that the women on the management committee should oppose S/M and offensive clothes for the <u>whole</u> of the Centre' (ibid., emphasis in original). The report of the meeting states that three of the centre management committee members wanted to ban 'offensive clothing' and opposed sadomasochists using the centre as groups, but not as individuals. These three had been subjected to physical threats by sadomasochists, particularly sadomasochist men. Another three women at the meeting were apparently wearing 'offensive regalia', however, including 'long spiked belts and straps, dog collars'. These women said that the regalia could be reclaimed as 'female symbols'. A Jewish daughter of a concentration camp survivor at the meeting 'tried to explain why these things were offensive by describing the sadism in the camps and was told she was disgusting' (ibid.).

A LASM flyer included in the newsletter details the rationale for lesbian feminist opposition to S/M at the centre. It states, 'Sado-masochistic sex is the eroticisation of power, pain and humiliation in a relationship based on domination and subordination. It glorifies the very oppressions many people are trying to struggle against. S/M can involve dangerous, violent activities. S/Ms often wear clothes expressing real power, pain and humiliation, e.g. Nazi-style caps, dog collars, chains. This is racist, anti-semitic, and offensive to all oppressed peoples' (LWLN, 412, 1985, 16 April). LASM asked lesbian feminists to join the LLGC so that they could attend an extraordinary general meeting at the centre a week later, which was to vote on whether S/M groups could meet there and wear their regalia. A report on this meeting stated that a leaflet in the lobby of the centre described the 'feminist community' as 'prescriptive, fascist, moralistic, bland, disgusting' (LWLN, 413, 1985, 23 April). The vote was delayed to a further meeting because, the report states, the gay men present, who mostly favoured the S/M cause, were concerned that they did not have the numbers to win. They organised themselves so that by the next meeting, when the vote was taken, gay men were in the ascendance, and the numbers went 165 to 108 to allow S/M groups to meet. Of the 165, 131 were men, and, of the 108, 82 were women (LWLN, 420, 1985, 12 June).

At that point the centre was largely abandoned by lesbian feminists despite having had a whole floor set aside for women. There was what we called at the time a 'girlcott'. The episode illustrates the problems created when organisations such as the GLC, which was, from noble motives, trying to operate an equal-opportunities agenda, fail to understand that women and gay men have quite different interests and are not just persons of similar bent (see Tobin, 1990). This subsuming of lesbians

126 Sadomasochism

into an overarching category of 'gay' was one of the reasons the LLGC closed within six years of opening. The development of this battle cannot be followed after 1985 through the *London Women's Liberation Newsletter*, however, because the newsletter was destroyed by infighting over identity politics in that year, as we shall see in a later chapter.

The struggle by lesbian feminists to promote a sexuality of equality against the S/M backlash continued, and the 'summer of '88' has been seen by some commentators as a crucial moment in the 'sex wars'. Susan Ardill and Sue O'Sullivan, looking back on that summer from a libertarian perspective in 1989 comment, 'After a couple of years of quietude, events took place in London during the summer of '88 which indicate new shifts in struggles around lesbian sexuality' (Ardill and O'Sullivan, 1989: 126, writing in a special issue of *Feminist Review* entitled 'The Past before Us: Twenty Years of Feminism'). Several events took place in that period in which there was a sharp confrontation between the politics of lesbian feminism and the self-styled 'pro-sex' tendency. One was the summer school which was run as a benefit for the London Lesbian Archive. Another was the visit to London of Joan Nestle, founder of the New York Lesbian Archive, and a proponent of the 'pro-sex' line, particularly around lesbian role-playing. There was also a forum on sadomasochism that was held at Wesley House, the women's centre run by Camden Council in Holborn.

In July 1988 a group of lesbians including the workers from the London Lesbian Archive was preparing to run a Lesbian summer school as a benefit for the archive. Unfortunately, the summer school provided a stage on which opponents of the lesbian feminist analysis of sexuality could protest against lesbian feminists such as me and Janice Raymond. I taught a course on sexuality and Janice gave a talk entitled 'Putting the Politics Back into Lesbianism' (Raymond, 1989), which was apt considering the problems that developed at the event. Two lesbians, Cherry Smyth and Inge Blackman, taught a film course and showed extracts of the movie *She Must be Seeing Things*, which was considered by many participants in the summer school to be pornographic because of its S/M themes, in a plenary session.

An intimation of the assault that was under way against a revolutionary or radical feminist analysis of sexuality was present in the student evaluations of the subject I taught. The evaluations showed that the students in my course were as completely opposed to each other as the two sides of the so-called 'sex wars' were by this stage of the debate on sexuality in the WLM. Whilst some loved the subject, others hated it, and me. The main theme of the negative responses was that I must be suffering from some form of mental illness or propensity for violence against women in order to hold such ideas. In the general comments one respondent said, 'Finally, DON'T invite Sheila Jeffreys again – she has upset so many lesbians with her poignant [sic] narrow-mindedness' (Lesbian Archive summer school evaluations, 1988, author's collection; emphasis in original). Another opined that women like 'Sheila' 'are dangerous'. Others asked, 'Can someone suggest a good therapist for Sheila?', or commented: 'I think Sheila Jeffreys is going to do some injury to herself if she continues to teach in the way she does. She could also do injury to other women, and I'm sure she has done already.' Another said, 'I and a number of other women felt very marginalized, intimidated and abused by Sheila Jeffreys in particular – this woman is clearly unbalanced.' Opposition to a sexuality of eroticised power difference was seen by some at this time as a symptom of mental ill health.

The students who were hostile in the classes were mostly very young, including a group of undergraduates from an East Anglian university. They were a new generation with no knowledge of or interest in the sexual politics of women's liberation. They had a quite different agenda, which included the promotion of butch and femme role-playing. I remember that an older lesbian in my class, which was on the history of lesbian sexuality, was so upset by the behaviour of the youngsters that she stood up in tears to speak of how she had known the role-playing lesbian world of the 1950s and was distressed at the idea that any of it might come back. She was shouted down, probably by those who wrote the sort of evaluation comments above. As Ardill and O'Sullivan note, 'The lesbians who flocked to the summer school, to Joan Nestle's talks, to the panel, the SM debate, and to see *She Must Be Seeing Things* were overwhelmingly white and relatively young.' They sum up the events of the summer with some glee as constituting the routing of the radical feminist commitment to creating a sexuality of equality: 'The rarified purists were experiencing a backlash. To us it seemed as if they were stuck somewhere back in the 1970s, oblivious to new realities' (Ardill and O'Sullivan, 1989: 129).

It was common for the detractors of radical and revolutionary feminism to use the slur that we were racist, rather than engage in the more difficult task of dealing with the ideas that they disagreed with. Ardill and O'Sullivan use this tactic in their discussion of the events of '88. They accuse revolutionary feminists in particular of a 'continual refusal to take real account of race and class' and give as an example the supposedly difficult time that one Black lesbian was given: 'one of the *Seeing Things* organizers was a strong Black lesbian who stood her ground as a Black feminist in the face of all the sound and fury' (ibid.: 128). This was Inge Blackman, who experienced some opposition because she came from a completely different camp on sexual politics, evidence of which is the fact that she later came out as a 'stud' lesbian and adopted a new and more satisfyingly masculine name, Campbell X (Martinez, 2012). The differences were ideological rather than being about race, but accusations of racism were a useful distraction from any consideration of the ideas being put forward.

Another event of that time that escalated the controversy around S/M was a vaunted 'discussion' on sadomasochism organised by practitioners at Wesley House, the women's centre, which also housed the Lesbian Archive. The forum was to be filmed by a lesbian video company, Face to Face productions, which aimed to show the filmed debate at women's centres around the country. I discussed this with Linda Bellos in her interview, and she recalls that both she and I were supposed to be speaking, as we had been invited to provide the opposing view. Most of those speaking were in favour of S/M, however. I intended to speak, nonetheless, until I arrived at Wesley House to see many women arriving on motorbikes and in black leather. The atmosphere looked threatening, and I went up to the Lesbian Archive

128 Sadomasochism

instead with about 30 other lesbians to have our own discussion about how to deal with the problem of S/M. Linda decided to remain on the panel.

The event was reported at length in the entertainment magazine *Time Out* (Baxter, 1988). The air of threat is well attested to in the report: 'At the back of the hall was a large contingent of SM dykes, many looking like extras from '*Madchen in Uniform*' with close-cropped peroxide hair, black leathers, chains and studs.' Near the front were 'what some SMers dismissively refer to as "vanilla dykes" – women who refuse to accept that whips and chains can be part of a loving lesbian relationship'. My departure from the event is described thus: 'One speaker was conspicuously absent – radical feminist Sheila Jeffreys, who took one look at the assembled leather and vanished to form her own anti-SM workshops upstairs.' Linda is quoted as having stated: 'SM is about deriving pleasure from domination and submission. There's something wrong with the glorification of oppression when the world is full of it.' She explains, 'The chains you're wearing around your waists were put around the necks of real Black people.' Apparently, a Jewish woman at the event who was dressed in leathers and studs, and who came from a family of Holocaust survivors, replied to Linda like this: 'I have the right to play with a swastika, and, by playing with it, take the power away from it.' Linda recalls remonstrating, as a Jewish woman herself, with this lesbian (Linda Bellos, interview 2013).

As a result of the promotion and publicity around lesbian S/M, a new image of the lesbian was created. This seems to have been deliberate, and it delighted the practitioners. The report mentions one lesbian claiming that S/M dykes represent lesbians in public and were 'out' in a way that 'vanilla dykes' were not: 'When we get on a tube…the whole world knows we're lesbians. We're out of the closet. Fifty of you could get on a bus in your pastel colours and no one would know you were dykes' (Baxter, 1988). The lesbian feminists of the time were usually quite recognizable, as they did not conform with heterosexual femininity, wearing short hair, no make-up, body hair, jeans, T-shirts and no effeminate clothing. But this, apparently, was not good enough for the S/M lesbians, who wanted the stereotype of the lesbian to be either the dominatrix or the porn victim.

The events of the summer of '88, as Ardill and O'Sullivan point out, represented a moment in which the egalitarian sexual politics of lesbian feminism were publicly trashed and the photogenic qualities of S/M triumphed in public events and the media. In 1990 some of our opponents, including Inge Blackman, who was one of the editors, used an edition of the socialist feminist journal *Feminist Review* to proclaim triumphantly that our politics were dead, and to issue plentiful insults about how puritan, anti-sex, racist and classist we were. One of the articles accused me in particular, and revolutionary feminists in general, of having tried to desex feminism: it was titled 'The De-Eroticization of Women's Liberation: Social Purity Movements and the Revolutionary Feminism of Sheila Jeffreys' (Hunt, 1990). In it Margaret Hunt makes the usual accusation that revolutionary feminists were racist and classist, with, as usual, no examples or evidence. We were, she says, seeking to 'dictate what other women's preferences should be' and needed to listen to people, men and women, with different opinions. Then we would get a better understanding of what 'constitutes oppression'. This would teach us to 'take seriously' forms of 'victimization based on race, class, nationality and immigrant status' and abandon 'the unbelievably reductionist character of the stress on sexuality alone' (ibid.: 43). We might then, Hunt suggests, abandon our inconvenient centring of women and feminism altogether and 'even have to spend some time fighting forms of oppression which affect both men and women'. We might have to 'abandon the idea that there is a universal women's experience', an indication of a line of attack on radical and revolutionary feminism that became extremely common in the 1990s and 2000s, in which our opponents concentrated on the 'politics of difference'. The problem, it seemed, was that our feminism concentrated on women.

Reasons for the success of lesbian sadomasochism

There are a variety of ways to account for the success of sadomasochism in the lesbian version of the 'sex wars'. One was the historical moment: WLM politics were already being challenged by a new generation of women created by the individualist politics of the age of neoliberalism. They were interested in sexual excitement and intensity and in feminism not at all. Another was the vulnerability of lesbians to the promotion of masochism as a revolutionary practice because of the way in which women, under male dominance, imbibed the eroticising of women's subordination. Women grow up under male authority and under the male sexual gaze, and, in many cases, suffering actual sexual violence from men (see Jeffreys, 2011 [1990]). Lesbian S/M offered a way in which women could shed guilt about their capacity to respond sexually to the degradation and abuse. It provided a framework and discipline in which women who had put up barriers to feeling, as a result of men abusing them in childhood, could dare to respond sexually.

Lesbian sadomasochists themselves argued that an important reason for engaging in S/M was child sexual abuse. Some practitioners were open about the way in which their abuse had made them vulnerable and asserted that the rules and discipline involved in S/M made them feel safer when being sexual. An interview conducted by the UK lesbian Sue O'Sullivan with the American safe sex educator Cindy Patton in 1990 suggests that S/M lesbians in the US were much more likely to proclaim publicly that their experience of child sexual abuse and the practice of sadomasochism were connected than those in the UK, because they were less reticent to speak about sex. Patton observes that 'very quickly a fairly large number of male and female SM practitioners emerged in the mid-eighties who talked about having been sexually abused as children' (O'Sullivan, 1990: 125). My interviewee Sandra McNeill describes the way that S/M appealed to lesbian self-mutilators, whom she calls 'quite damaged young women' (Sandra McNeill, interview 2013). She recalls that she and I 'went to a meeting in London where we were trying to understand some of those young women who had got into sadomasochism, and most of them identified as masochists, and this young woman was saying to us 'Well, you know that feeling you get when you can't feel your hands and your feet?', and we said "No"'. The young masochist was describing a phenomenon

130 Sadomasochism

called 'depersonalisation', which is the common experience of women who have been sexually abused and learnt to separate their minds from their bodies in order to survive the experience. Sandra continues,

> I mean, this woman talked about how causing herself pain by self-harming, actually by cutting, made her feel whole again, and so she could feel her hands and her feet. And it was much better if someone else did it to you, it really made you feel whole and it was a sexual turn-on and so it was like making – instead of fighting your oppression it was like making a positive out of it and embracing it.
>
> *(ibid.)*

This, Sandra, suggests, was 'one of the reasons women got into it'.

S/M lesbians themselves assert that they were trained in the practice in gay men's clubs. There was a considerable enthusiasm amongst 'pro-sex' lesbians at the time for imitating gay men, both in adopting their portrayal of masculinity in butch and drag king performances and for their apparently superior sexual practice, particularly the enthusiasm for public sex. Cindy Patton, at the end of her interview, encourages the modelling of lesbian sexuality on that of gay men: 'I think it's possible at this point politically and culturally for lesbians to start looking at gay male porn' (O'Sullivan, 1990: 132). My interviewees also stressed the influence of gay male culture. Julie Bindel considers that it

> seeped into lesbian feminist culture from gay men…that lesbians had run around supporting gay men…and that the merging of the two communities had meant that lots of lesbians who were, quite frankly, bored with the fact that…the height of our movement was no more, were getting involved in some new and exciting experimentation.
>
> *(Julie Bindel, interview 2013)*

She considers that it was a 'Fuck you' gesture to proper feminists, who were saying this is actually 'a long, hard slog', by those who wanted swift rewards from the WLM.

The biggest factor in its success, however, was the fact that S/M fitted completely into the politics of male domination, whereas lesbian feminism was entirely indigestible. It was greatly supported by the strength of gay male politics, which promoted and justified S/M as a specifically gay sexuality and created a powerful and remunerative culture around it. In the 1980s many lesbians forged closer links with gay men in reaction to the AIDS crisis (Phelan, 1994; Bindel, 2014). They felt the need to support their brothers against the ravages of the disease and the popular prejudice against them that resulted, and this greater closeness left lesbians vulnerable to the influence of gay male priorities. The forces of the porn industry and the gay, Left and liberal press all embraced lesbian S/M with great enthusiasm. S/M lesbians were the type they could do business with, the type that populated their fantasies and proved that women's desires were entirely obedient to the dictates of male power, a swooning surrender to violence and abuse. The power of the popular media was a force against which deeply unphotogenic lesbian feminism was powerless.

One S/M proponent who was popular with the media was Della Grace, later Del LaGrace Volcano. She was one of the group of lesbians running the London lesbian S/M club Chain Reaction (Volcano and Halberstam, 1999), and a photographer specialising in lesbian sadomasochism and pornographic images. The *Guardian Weekend* magazine in 1995 carried a lengthy profile of Della by Deborah Orr, which provided an opportunity to run her photos of naked women in black leather scolds' bridles and straps around their breasts, women in black leather corsets and Nazi caps, a woman being held down by the hair whilst another woman is apparently fist-fucking her, and so on (Orr, 1995). Grace's photography and S/M profile were media-friendly in a way that lesbian feminism was not.

The impact of sadomasochism on lesbian feminism

The effect of the S/M movement on lesbian feminism was devastating. Femi Otitoju says that it led to the end of the Lesbian Strength marches, for instance (Femi Otitoju, interview 2013). Lesbian feminists who had taken for granted that their movement was about equality, and considered themselves to be creating a sexual future based upon that principle, experienced grief. Sybil Grundberg says that she 'grieved that it had come up' (Sybil Grundberg, interview 2013). She says that when women took sides for or against S/M it destroyed friendships and networks and damaged the movement profoundly: 'It kind of ripped people up, and ripped up the movement a bit. Women that I wasn't expecting were sort of embracing some of these ideas, so it was a disaster.' Sandra McNeill describes the shock and horror that lesbian feminists such as us experienced when the ideas of Samois started to circulate in the UK: 'It made me feel quite sick, and I instantly thought: this is the death of lesbian feminism. We were arguing for feminists to become lesbians…and I felt that lesbianism was a really positive view of sexuality unlike heterosexuality, between equals' (Sandra McNeill, interview 2013). S/M, she says, 'completely undermined all the work that we, lesbian feminists, were doing around violence against women by men'.

There were some within the WLM who considered that fighting S/M was an unnecessary distraction. They saw it as rather an unimportant side alley for feminists. The radical feminist journal *Trouble and Strife*, for instance, put the shoutline 'Not the Sadomasochism Debate' on the cover of its first issue in 1983, in order to show its disdain. But S/M proved not to be a minor issue at all. The justifications put forward by many gay male and some lesbian practitioners made S/M chic, such that it became the trendy and progressive way to do sex. The huge expansion of the porn industry mainstreamed S/M. It is clear that S/M is very big now in malestream heterosexuality, as indicated by the success of the book and movie *Fifty Shades of Grey* (Dines, 2013; Green, 2015). But, more importantly, the promotion of S/M has been so influential that what were once seen as S/M practices are now routine,

132 Sadomasochism

such as the coercion of girls by male partners into what is called 'rough sex' and anal sex (Marston and Lewis, 2014). The defeat of the lesbian feminist challenge to the eroticising of women's subordination was a serious blow against the possibility of women's equality. One aspect of the S/M backlash that provided another way to attack and overturn lesbian feminist analysis was the promotion of a new form of lesbian butch/femme role-playing which consisted specifically of eroticising power difference. This will be considered in the next chapter.

Bibliography

Ardill, Susan, and O'Sullivan, Sue (1989). Sex in the Summer of '88. *Feminist Review*, 31: 126–134.

Baxter, Sarah (1988). Chain Reaction. *Time Out*, 942: 9.

Bindel, Julie (2014). *Straight Expectations: What Does It Mean to Be Gay Today?* London: Guardian Books.

Blackman, Inge, and Perry, Kathryn (1990). Skirting the Issue: Lesbian Fashion for the 1990s. *Feminist Review*, 34: 67–78.

Califia, Pat (1982). A Personal View of the History of the Lesbian S/M Community and Movement in San Francisco. In Samois (ed.), *Coming to Power: Writings and Graphics on Lesbian S/M*. Boston: Alyson Publications, 243–281.

Coward, Rosalind (1982). Sexual Violence and Sexuality. *Feminist Review*, 13: 9–22.

Daly, Mary (1979 [1978]). *Gyn/Ecology: The Metaethics of Radical Feminism*. London: Women's Press.

Davis, Katherine (1982). What We Fear We Try to Keep Contained. In Samois (ed.), *Coming to Power: Writings and Graphics on Lesbian S/M*. Boston: Alyson Publications, 7–13.

Dines, Gail (2013, 25 October). Don't Be Fooled by *Fifty Shades of Grey*: Christian Grey Is No Heartthrob. *The Guardian*. www.theguardian.com/commentisfree/2013/oct/25/fifty-shades-of-grey-christian-jamie-dornan-fall.

Dominguez, Ivo (1994). *Beneath the Skins: The New Spirit and Politics of the Kink Community*. Los Angeles: Daedalus.

Farr, Susan (1982). The Art of Discipline: Creating Erotic Dramas of Play and Power. In Samois (ed.), *Coming to Power: Writings and Graphics on Lesbian S/M*. Boston: Alyson Publications, 181–189.

Green, Emma (2015, 10 February). Consent Isn't Enough: The Troubling Sex of *Fifty Shades*. *The Atlantic*. www.theatlantic.com/entertainment/archive/2015/02/consent-isnt-enough-in-fifty-shades-of-grey/385267.

Hunt, Margaret (1990). The De-Eroticization of Women's Liberation: Social Purity Movements and the Revolutionary Feminism of Sheila Jeffreys. *Feminist Review*, 34: 23–46.

Jeffreys, Sheila (1993 [1984]). Sadomasochism: The Erotic Cult of Fascism. In Jeffreys, Sheila, *The Lesbian Heresy: A Feminist Perspective on the Lesbian Sexual Revolution*. London: Women's Press.

Jeffreys, Sheila (1993). Consent and the Politics of Sexuality. *Current Issues in Criminal Justice*, 5 (2): 173–183.

Jeffreys, Sheila (1997 [1985]). *The Spinster and Her Enemies: Feminism and Sexuality 1880–1930*. Melbourne: Spinifex Press.

Jeffreys, Sheila (2003). *Unpacking Queer Politics*. Cambridge: Polity Press.

Jeffreys, Sheila (2009). *The Industrial Vagina: The Political Economy of the Global Sex Trade*. Abingdon, UK: Routledge.

Jeffreys, Sheila (2011 [1990]). *Anticlimax: A Feminist Perspective on the Sexual Revolution*. Melbourne: Spinifex Press.

Juicy Lucy (1982). If I Ask You to Tie Me Up, Will You Still Want to Love Me? In Samois (ed.), *Coming to Power: Writings and Graphics on Lesbian S/M*. Boston: Alyson Publications, 29–40.

Kolb, Terry (1979). Masochist's Lib. In Samois (ed.), *What Color Is Your Handkerchief: A Lesbian S/M Sexuality Reader*. Berkeley, CA: Samois, 19–22.

Levine, Martin (1998). *Gay Macho: The Life and Death of the Homosexual Clone*. New York: New York University Press.

Linden, Robin Ruth, Pagano, Darlene R., Russell, Diana E. H., and Star, Susan Leigh (eds.) (1982). *Against Sadomasochism: A Radical Feminist Analysis*. Palo Alto, CA: Frog in the Well Press.

MacKinnon, Catharine A. (1989a). *Toward a Feminist Theory of the State*. Cambridge, MA: Harvard University Press.

MacKinnon, Catharine A. (1989b). Rape: On Coercion and Consent. In MacKinnon, Catharine A., *Toward a Feminist Theory of the State*. Cambridge, MA: Harvard University Press, 171–183.

Marston, Cicely Alice, and Lewis, Ruth (2014). Anal Heterosex among Young People and Implications for Health Promotion: A Qualitative Study in the UK. *British Medical Journal*, 4 (8), DOI: 10.1136/bmjopen2014-004996.

Martinez, Vanessa (2012, 16 July). Exclusive: British Filmmaker Campbell X Talks 'Stud Life'. Indiewire. www.indiewire.com/2012/07/exclusive-british-filmmaker-campbell-x-talks-stud-life-making-of-feature-debut-more-143942.

Morgan, Robin (1977). The Politics of Sado-Masochistic Fantasies. In Robin Morgan, *Going Too Far: The Personal Chronicle of a Feminist*. New York: Random House, 227–240.

Orr, Deborah (1995, 2 July). The Bearded Lady. *The Guardian Weekend*.

O'Sullivan, Sue (1990). Mapping: Lesbianism, AIDS and Sexuality: An Interview with Cindy Patton by Sue O'Sullivan. *Feminist Review*, 34: 120–133.

Pateman, Carole (1989). Women and Consent. In Pateman, Carole, *The Disorder of Women*. Cambridge: Polity Press, 71–89.

Phelan, Shane (1994). *Getting Specific: Postmodern Lesbian Politics*. Minneapolis: University of Minneapolis Press.

Preston, John (1993). *My Life as a Pornographer and Other Indecent Acts*. New York: Masquerade Books.

Raymond, Janice G. (1989). Putting the Politics Back into Lesbianism. *Women's Studies International Forum*, 12 (2): 149–156.

Samois (ed.) (1979). *What Color Is Your Handkerchief: A Lesbian S/M Sexuality Reader*. Berkeley, CA: Samois.

Samois (ed.) (1982). *Coming to Power: Writings and Graphics on Lesbian S/M*. Boston: Alyson Publications.

Snitow, Ann Barr, and Stansell, Christine (eds.) (1983). *Powers of Desire: The Politics of Sexuality*. New York: Monthly Review Press.

Tobin, Ann (1990). Lesbianism and the Labour Party: The GLC Experience. *Feminist Review*, 34: 56–66.

Vance, Carole S. (ed.) (1984). *Pleasure and Danger: Exploring Female Sexuality*. London: Routledge & Kegan Paul.

Volcano, Del LaGrace, and Halberstam, Judith (1999). *The Drag King Book*. London: Serpent's Tail.

Wagner, Sally Roesch (1982). Pornography and the Sexual Revolution: The Backlash of Sadomasochism. In Linden, Robin Ruth, Pagano, Darlene R., Russell, Diana E. H., and

134 Sadomasochism

Star, Susan Leigh (eds.), *Against Sadomasochism: A Radical Feminist Analysis*. Palo Alto, CA: Frog in the Well Press, 23–44.

Young, Ian (1995). *The Stonewall Experiment: A Gay Psychohistory*. London: Cassell.

Young, Ian, Stoltenberg, John, Rosen, Lyn, and Jordan, Rose (1978). Forum on Sadomasochism. In Jay, Karla, and Young, Allen (eds.), *Lavender Culture*. New York: Jove Publications, 85–117.

Zaretsky, Eli (1976). *Capitalism, the Family and Personal Life*. New York: Harper & Row.

7

THE GENDER BACKLASH

Butch/femme role-playing

What is now called 'gender' was referred to as 'sex roles' in the 1970s WLM and feminists saw their task as being to abolish it. Sex roles were seen to constitute the different roles and appearance norms assigned to persons according to the shape of their genitals, and to form the justification and foundation for male domination. The rejection of sex roles was ubiquitous across radical political movements in the 1960s and 1970s. Role-playing was rejected by lesbians and gay men involved in gay liberation, a movement which was influenced by feminist politics. Lesbian feminists argued that role-playing was based upon the stereotyped roles of female-subordinate and male-dominant heterosexuality (Jeffreys, 1993). On this understanding, lesbian feminists eschewed both the outward appearance of 'gender' and the role-defined behaviour that went with it. By the 1980s, however, role-playing was back. The return to lesbian role-playing was a significant aspect of the rejection of lesbian feminism in the 1980s. It offered a form of 'sadomasochism light', with no obvious violence but very obvious eroticising of power difference. In this chapter I will examine the gay and lesbian rejection of roles, and the defeat of the lesbian feminist critique through the rehabilitation of lesbian role-playing and adoption of masculinity in the 1980s.

Lesbian feminist rejection of role-playing

When the Women's Liberation Movement began in around 1970 in the UK, role-playing was still fairly common in some parts of the lesbian community. Lesbian role-playing had been undermined by the rise of unisex and hippiness in the 1960s, and, as the idea of women's equality became a contagion, this form of behaviour suffered further diminution. Lesbians came to lesbian feminism from two directions: gay liberation and the WLM (see Jeffreys, 2003). Both women and men in Gay Liberation Front in the early 1970s were solidly opposed to role-playing in

136 The gender backlash

relationships. They wrote copiously about this and argued that roles imitated the worst aspects of heterosexuality, an institution that they saw as a mainstay of capitalism and the oppression of women (Jeffreys, 2003; Walter, 1980; Jay and Young, 1992). As one male gay liberationist in the UK put it, 'We have been forced into playing roles based upon straight society, butch and femme, nuclear "marriages" which continue within the relationships the same oppression that outside society forces onto its women' (Walter, 1980: 59). Thus, the lesbians who came to lesbian feminism from the GLF were already inoculated by the profound and well-articulated politics of gay liberation against the practice. Lesbians who came to lesbian feminism from the WLM were even more fully inoculated against role-playing by the criticism of sex roles in heterosexual relationships that was so foundational to the feminist politics of the time (Millett, 1970).

Lesbian feminists such as me often socialised in what we called 'straight' bars in the 1970s – i.e. lesbian bars and clubs that served a pre-feminist community of lesbians – and we did sometimes encounter in them expressions of role-playing behaviour. We were puzzled and intrigued, but we felt no need to learn the arcane rules of role-playing in order to fit into this 'gay' culture, because we had a new feminist and lesbian culture in which to thrive. Lesbians who were not yet influenced by feminism, on the other hand, were under pressure to identify themselves as either butch or femme, or could be regarded with suspicion through identifying as 'kiki' – i.e. prepared to consider both butches and femmes as possible partners (Mushroom, 1983). Butch/femme role-playing trumped love and sexual interest. It created an affinity system which required out-marrying (see Bailey and Peoples, 2013: 164). No matter how much a 'butch' wanted to be with a butch or a 'femme' with a femme, they could not.

The rejection of sex roles was an integral part of feminism at the time of the WLM. Indeed, such a rejection was, according to American feminist Anne Koedt, the very definition of radical feminism: 'To me it means the advocacy of the total elimination of sex roles. A radical feminist, then, is one who believes in this and works politically toward that end' (Koedt, 1971). Roles, she said, were 'male political constructs that serve to ensure power and superior status for men'. This understanding was carried seamlessly over into the ideas and practice of lesbian feminism. Both lesbian feminists and gay liberationists rejected butch/femme role-playing because their activism came from the context of a strong women's liberation movement which was founded on a rejection of women's oppression in marriage and in heterosexual relationships. Feminists in the WLM, as well as both women and men in gay liberation, believed that the personal is political, and that the way we interact with others should be based on the kind of world we want to create (Jay and Young, 1992: xxxvii). Creating a future of women's equality was not consistent with the role-playing of inequality. Koedt extended her understanding of the toxicity of role-playing to her analysis of lesbianism, saying: 'A lesbian acting like a man or a gay man acting like a woman is not necessarily sicker than heterosexuals acting out the same roles; but it is not healthy. All role playing is sick, be it "simulated" or "authentic" – according to society's terms' (Koedt, 1971).

The gender backlash **137**

Many other lesbian feminists at the time voiced the same understanding. Del Martin and Phyllis Lyon, the founders of Daughters of Bilitis (DOB), the first political lesbian organisation in the US, were forthright in their rejection of role-playing in their book *Lesbian/Woman* (Martin and Lyon, 1972). They founded DOB in 1955 and had lived through great changes in the way that lesbians related to each other. They explain that the demise of role-playing had been a long time coming: 'We have watched the decline of the butch–femme concept of relationship for sixteen years. It has been a gradual decline... [T]he stereotype has not yet vanished' (ibid.: 81). They attribute the demise to the change that 'has taken place in the way all women (straight or gay) in this country think about sex roles and personal relationships', as a result of the questioning of religion, research on human sexuality and 'liberation movements' (ibid.: 83). The decline in role-playing amongst lesbians reflected the progress that had been made towards equality in heterosexual relationships.

Another foundational text about lesbians was published in the same year: *Sappho was a Right-On Woman*, by Sydney Abbott and Barbara Love (Abbott and Love, 1972). This book, which also rejected roles and marriage outright, was more radical in its feminism. The authors were not extremists, or outliers to lesbian feminism, but absolutely central to it. Both were long-time lesbians who had taken part in both the original WLM organisation, the National Organisation of Women, and in influential lesbian and gay movement political organisations such as the Daughters of Bilitis. They provide a useful explanation of why so many lesbians before the advent of the WLM had used terms such as 'husband' and 'wife' and 'butch' and 'femme' and engaged in role-playing. They say that these lesbians knew no alternative vocabulary to describe their affectional relationships apart from that relating to heterosexuality and they had no other model for how to love one another. Of the terms 'husband' and 'wife', for instance, they say, 'These are the only words in our culture that convey love, trust, permanence, and responsibility in a relationship. The vocabulary of homosexual relationships comes from heterosexuals and is seldom appropriate to homosexual love' (ibid.: 92). Lesbians roleplayed, they say, because, 'Lesbians are raised in a role-playing society' (ibid.).

Interestingly, at the time that Abbott and Love were writing, the desire for marriage and the practice of marriage customs amongst lesbians was seen as something only old lesbians did, and it was assumed this would die out as younger lesbians who were feminists rejected such behaviour. Nowadays, of course, when the campaign for the legalisation of gay marriage has achieved considerable success and is still seen as a fundamental lesbian and gay rights issue, it tends to be younger lesbians who are in favour of such traditional, conservative and heterosexual forms, whilst older lesbian feminists, who experienced the radicalism of the WLM, criticise them.

Abbott and Love argue that one reason some lesbians favoured role-playing was that it relieved their guilt at loving the same sex: 'There is a strong possibility that heavy butch and femme role-playing serves the function of burying guilt. If only men can love women, then a woman who lives existentially as a man will not consciously feel guilty for loving another woman' (ibid.: 96). Many lesbian

138 The gender backlash

commentators have explained that role-playing before the WLM was adopted as a safety measure. If one member of a lesbian couple in public space was indistinguishable from a man, then they were less likely to be harassed as women and as lesbians. As Merrill Mushroom describes, in 1950s America pretending to be heterosexual couples provided protection: 'It was safer to go out on a date with a femme to a straight place if we could pass... Men sometimes beat up lesbians on the street' (Mushroom, 1983: 41). At the time of the WLM, lesbians were not becoming 'transgender', as that was unknown, but the explanations for butch role-playing proposed by Abbott and Love may be useful in understanding the outbreak of transgendering that afflicts lesbian communities today (Jeffreys, 2014).

The power relationship in role-playing

The proponents of revamped butch/femme role-playing in the 1980s argued that it is something specifically and essentially lesbian which does not relate to what takes place between men and women. They not only rejected the argument that role-playing originates in malestream heterosexuality but saw it as insulting (Nestle, 1992b; Munt, 1998b). There is no independent template on which this practice is built, however; rather, it follows the stipulations of heterosexual malestream culture to a large degree, with the butches imitating the behaviour of the powerful class of men and the femmes demonstrating the traditional behaviour of women's subordination. There is plenty of evidence that the role of the femme has historically been one of inferiority, directly reproducing the patterns of women's subordination. Descriptions of straight gay bars in pre-feminist times show that butches were the ones who went to the bar to buy drinks while femmes were expected to sit at the tables gossiping with other femmes. Butches would ask permission of other butches before they asked the femmes who were perceived to belong to them to dance. Rebecca Jennings, a historian of lesbianism in the UK, explains that the impact of feminism made adoption of 'the extremes of masculine and feminine which were central to butch/femme clothing' unnecessary, because lesbians could 'wear trousers and...follow their personal preferences in dress', without question. In addition, feminism caused many to feel 'uncomfortable with the notion of asking a butch's permission to dance with a femme and refused to comply with accepted conventions' (Jennings, 2007: 223). Lesbians who embraced feminism abandoned role-playing and were able to engage enthusiastically in sexual relationships without any resort to the trappings of gendered power difference.

The inequality of power between butches and femmes is illustrated in Ethel Sawyer's work on 'studs' and 'fish' in an African American lesbian community in St. Louis, Missouri, in the 1950s (Sawyer, 1965). The very language used to denote butches or femmes is gendered, of course, but some terms that were in common use make the subordinate and degraded status of the 'femme' particularly clear. In St. Louis the terms in use were 'stud' for butch and 'fish' for femme. These terms are not neutral. 'Studs' represent the highest possible status in hetero masculinity, whereas 'fish' is the term used in gay male culture to refer to women, supposedly based upon the unpleasant smell of women's genitals. Sawyer found plenty of studs to interview but the studs were astonished that she wanted to interview the fish. She explains: 'This status discrepancy between studs and fish…is sufficiently strong that if I felt there might be some difficulty in interviewing a fish, I was able to work it through her stud' (ibid.: 13). Only studs were seen as real lesbians, and they saw no point in anyone talking to their girlfriends. As Abbott and Love point out, 'Oddly enough, the butch may consider herself the Lesbian and her femme a "real woman"' (Abbott and Love, 1972: 97). Lesbians who identified with categories of masculinity such as 'stud' or 'butch' occupied a clearly superior status to those who were identified with femininity, and one aspect of this was that they were seen as the authentic lesbians whilst femmes were a pale imitation.

The reclamation of role-playing in the 1980s

In the 1980s role-playing was re-embraced by some lesbians, and there was a quite extraordinary onslaught by self-proclaimed butches and femmes on the lesbian feminist ideas of equality in relationships. These were more conservative times, when the feminist and gay liberation assaults on marriage, traditional heterosexuality and the way these institutions oppressed women were no longer imaginable. By the 1990s, after all, this conservatism had led to lesbians and gays campaigning to imitate heterosexuals in gay 'marriage'. In the late 1980s and 1990s, as part of the onslaught, a slew of books promoting lesbian role-playing were published. The proponents of role-playing and lesbian historians assert that the book by the American femme Joan Nestle, *A Restricted Country* (1987), was an important influence on the rebirth of role-playing (see the 'Acknowledgments' page of Munt, 1998a).

The first tranche of these books consisted of personal accounts, such as *A Restricted Country* and *Stone Butch Blues* by Lesley Feinberg (Feinberg, 1993). These were followed by edited collections that included personal accounts, poetry, theory and academic articles, such as Joan Nestle's *A Persistent Desire* (Nestle, 1992a), and a British anthology, Sally Munt's *Femme/Butch*, which was published in 1998, by which time role-playing had become fashionable in the UK as well (Munt, 1998a). There were also American collections devoted to either femmeness, or butchness, such as *The Femme Mystique* (Newman, 1995) and *Dagger* (Burana, Roxxie and Due, 1994). Self-appointed lesbian sex therapists played an important role by promoting role-playing as the quintessential way to do lesbian sex. Pat (now Patrick) Califia wrote *Sapphistry*, a lesbian sex guide, before she began to identify as a man (Califia, 1988). Joanne Loulan wrote two volumes of lesbian sex therapy, which have been very influential and are still very much referenced – *Lesbian Sex* (1985) and *Lesbian Passion* (1987) – before writing her paean to role-playing, *Lesbian Erotic Dance: Butch, Femme, Androgyny, and Other Rhythms* (1990). Loulan later returned to heterosexuality.

The anthologies contained pieces by poets, movement activists and a fair representation of heavyweight academics. The academics, many of whom went on to illustrious careers, were not from the social sciences, such as history, sociology,

140 The gender backlash

political science or anthropology. Thus, they had no need to do serious research, provide evidence for their opinions or relate their work to what was going on in the real world. Their interest in role-playing was esoteric; indeed, several contributors lamented that most lesbians were not seriously interested in role-playing or rejected it decisively. This did not deter them. Their usual area of expertise was cultural studies or literature, fields in which the standards of academic rigour are sometimes more relaxed. Judith Halberstam, for instance, became a professor of literature, Sue-Ellen Case specialised in critical studies in theatre, Esther Newton was a professor of American culture, Sally Munt became a professor of cultural studies and Judith Butler became a professor of philosophy and literature. The anthologies contained both pornographic outpourings from the non-academics as well as the romanticisation of role-playing in postmodern language by the academics. What they did share, however, was a cause.

The academic proponents of role-playing used postmodern theory, and the queer theory that was inspired by it, as the foundation of their justification of role-playing (see Jeffreys, 2003). Judith Butler's work was of particular importance (Butler, 1990). Butler says she 'situated herself in relation to butchness' in her early twenties (More, 1999: 286). In her work, as in academic queer theory in general, 'gender' slips free from a feminist understanding that gender forms the foundation of male domination, a material system of oppression, and becomes a free-floating form of appearance norms and behavioural patterns that can be taken up by anyone. This radical uncertainty and looseness of gender is promoted in her work as revolutionary. When men and women take on the 'gender' more usually assigned to the opposite sex, they are portrayed by Butler as creating massive disruption to the social system. She rejects what she calls a 'homophobic radical feminism' which 'can only understand gender trespass and gender transitivity as appropriation, as if something's been stolen from them. Gender is itself a transferable property, it doesn't belong to anyone, and the idea of figuring it as non-transferable property is just a massive mistake' (ibid.: 294). These ideas led to an enthusiastic adoption of drag, role-playing and transgenderism by gay men and lesbians, fuelled by the excitement of believing that these pursuits were radically destabilising to the heteropatriarchy. The revolution that was supposed to be unleashed by these activities failed to materialise. Rather, gender, or the sex roles of masculinity and femininity, were more firmly embedded in not just the lesbian community but in the heterosexual world as well. Not surprisingly, the aping of the gender rules of the heteropatriachy did nothing to overturn male power.

Although a very great deal of publishing effort took place on behalf of role-playing, there was vanishingly little written by those lesbian feminists who were critical, despite the argument by the roleplayers that the feminist critique of roles was all-powerful and dominant and that they were the radicals acting up to power. The only lesbian feminist critique that they cite when sounding off against what they saw as the dreadful anti-sex, conservative, essentialist boring detractors is one article that I wrote in 1987 (Jeffreys, 1987; see Loulan, 1990: chap. 6). Thus, it is my name and my supposedly outrageous opinions which are referred to time and

The gender backlash **141**

again. The overreaction and compendious nature of their outpourings suggest that overturning feminist approaches to sexuality was very important to them; their orgasms were at stake. They were also very successful. The feminist critique was effectively wiped from public memory, and role-playing has rolled on with little naysaying to the present day.

The butch/femme collections promoted the erotic possibilities of role-playing using language more common to that employed in the newly fashionable lesbian sadomasochism. They show clearly that the sex of role-playing provided the excitements of this less extreme form of S/M, through mostly psychological means rather than cutting, beating, blood and gore. The authors argued that role-playing was 'authentic' lesbianism – i.e. how lesbianism had always been until inauthentic lesbian feminism rained on the party. All the writers argued that, however much the role-playing practice seemed clearly to imitate heterosexual forms, it was in fact distinctively lesbian. Elizabeth Lapovsky Kennedy and Madeline Davis in their book on role-playing culture in Buffalo, New York state, in the 1950s, *Boots of Leather, Slippers of Gold*, describe role-playing as 'authentic' lesbianism (Kennedy and Davis, 1993). Butch lesbians did not behave like men, they say; rather, butch lesbians were concerned that their femme partners received sexual pleasure, which real men would never do. They were often very chivalrous, opening doors and lighting cigarettes, and tender towards their girlfriends in a way, they imply, that men would never be. Chivalry was never a sign of women's power, however, but an acknowledgement of women's inferior status. Madeline Davis, a self-defined femme, wrote very masochistic contributions to Joan Nestle's collection, *A Persistent Desire* (1992b), so her self-interest in trying to prove that role-playing was authentic lesbianism is clear.

There is a good deal wrong with the historical picture that the revivalists of role-playing presented. To begin with, the critique of butch and femme and the abandonment of the practice were not, as they claimed, the result of lesbian feminism. The critique was going on in the 1960s as a result of social change towards a greater egalitarianism and fashionable hippiness, before lesbian feminism was born (Abbott and Love, 1972). In addition, the new role-playing was different in several ways. As a result of the changed circumstances, and the general relaxation of roles in malestream society, the necessity for two women to impersonate a heterosexual couple for their safety was no longer such a motivating factor. A new language had been created through lesbian feminism, so that lesbians no longer had to fit themselves and their feelings and practice into a heterosexual straightjacket. The readoption of roles was about something else. It was, as its proponents made very clear, about sadomasochistic sex.

To create the impression that role-playing is something essential and timeless, specifically lesbian and with no relation to male dominance, its proponents tended to adopt a passionate romanticisation, perhaps with the intention of rendering political discussion of the practice impossible. Joan Nestle writes, 'Butch-femme relationships, as I experienced them, were complex erotic and social statements, not phony heterosexual replicas. They were filled with a deeply lesbian language of stance, dress, gesture, love, courage, and autonomy. In the 1950s particularly,

142 The gender backlash

butch-femme couples were the front-line warriors against sexual bigotry' (Nestle, 1992b: 138). Sally Munt, an English academic, was good at this, too. She says that role-playing

> is visual, tactile, and oral, it is a scent, maybe even a taste, and it is about being open to listen, to recognize and receive. Butch/femme is lesbian gender experienced from the inside, it is a mode of articulation *and* a living movement, it is the way our bodies speak our desire. In short butch/femme is a way we can inhabit lesbian desire, a *habitus*.
>
> *(Munt, 1998b: 2)*

These are all rather grand ways of saying that the authors are sexually aroused by power imbalance.

The promotion of role-playing constituted a forceful attack on feminism and lesbian feminism by challenging the profound analysis of the sexuality of male dominance that radical and revolutionary feminists had developed. The feminist critique was very annoying to women who wanted to protect their pleasures and practices from criticism. Feminist theorists such as me (Jeffreys, 2011 [1990]) and Catharine Mackinnon (1989a) argued that the construction of sexuality around the eroticising of women's subordination for men's delight was a fundamental component of male dominance. The roleplayers needed to construct a bulwark, an approach to sexuality which rendered the feminist critique irrelevant, protected the status quo and yet at the same time made their practice seem somehow progressive. Their solution was to promote an alternative politics based on the ideas of the theorist of lesbian sadomasochism Gayle Rubin, and her article 'Thinking Sex' (1984).

This piece was adopted as a foundation stone for lesbian and gay and later queer studies, because it insulated gay male practice and sadomasochism from feminist criticism. It is the very first chapter of the groundbreaking 1993 anthology *The Lesbian and Gay Studies Reader*, and appears in many anthologies of feminist and queer thought thereafter (Abelove, Barale and Halperin, 1993). To defend her sexual preference from feminist criticism, Rubin argues that feminists should not be looking at sex at all. Sex, she says, constituted a totally separate system of oppression which was beyond the remit of feminist thought. In this system it was non-mainstream sexual practices that were oppressed, such as paedophilia and sadomasochism. Feminists, she says, should get back in their box, and stop analysing such matters as gay male sexual practice, which was no concern of theirs. Cherry Smyth from the UK took this approach in the *Butch/Femme* anthology in 1998: 'While feminism located gender oppression as the primary category for understanding power relations, queer defined sexual oppression as its primary site' (Smyth, 1998: 82).

Another way to discredit lesbian feminist analyses was to accuse us of being racist and classist. This was seen as a convenient way to invalidate opponents instead of having to refute their ideas. Amber Hollibaugh and Cherrie Moraga, for instance, ask: 'Why is it that it is largely white middle-class women who form the visible

The gender backlash **143**

leadership in the antiporn movement?' and suggest that these feminists could use their energies better on activism around sex-related issues such as abortion (Hollibaugh and Moraga, 1992 [1983]: 253). Moreover, an accompaniment to the accusation that lesbian feminists who were critical of the eroticizing of power difference were middle class was the justification of role-playing through the assertion that it was authentic working-class lesbian practice (Faderman, 1991; Kennedy and Davis, 1993). This assertion was undermined by the fact that many middle-class lesbians also did roles; Radclyffe Hall is but one example. Equally, many working-class lesbians did not, as Julia Penelope attests (Penelope, 1984). Role-playing was the rule in certain corners of urban lesbian communities and the social spaces they frequented, but it suited the political agenda of roleplayers to assert its ubiquity. At a time when identity politics was in the ascendant, that which purported to be working class was seen as legitimate and positive, and that which was associated with the middle class was seen as the reverse.

The American lesbian historian Lillian Faderman accused lesbian feminist critics of role-playing of being both middle-class and conservative. She was the author of the iconic book of lesbian history, *Surpassing the Love of Men* (Faderman, 1984), which included women who were passionate friends and for whom there could be no proof of a physically sexual relationship in the history of lesbianism. Her book seemed to downplay the importance of physical sexual relations in the definition of lesbianism. But by the 1990s she was attacking what she called 'cultural feminism', a term which she employed for radical or revolutionary feminism, and agreed with the roleplayers and sadomasochists that feminism was not sexy enough. The normalisation of role-playing and S/M were positive developments, she argues: 'The publicity of the debate around s/m served to liberate sexuality somewhat for lesbians who were not tied to the dogmas of cultural feminism; it made them want to experiment with their sexual repertoire' (Faderman, 1991: 263). The 'many young women' who 'claimed butch or femme identities in the 1980s', she says, 'had been fed up with the "proprieties" of lesbian-feminists, cultural feminism, and conservative middle-class lesbians' (ibid.: 264).

Other proponents of role-playing agreed that lesbian feminism was just not sexy. The femme and lesbian psychotherapist Arlene Ishtar states: 'We have limited our options by desexualizing our community' (Ishtar, 1992: 382). The US femme Amber Hollibaugh accuses feminists of having 'neutered' sexuality through criticism of 'roles, S/M fantasy, or any other sexual differences' (Hollibaugh and Moraga, 1992 [1983]: 245). She says lesbian feminists challenged roles because they were 'profoundly afraid of questions of power in bed' (ibid.: 246). She, like other roleplayers, thought feminism was boring because 'it became this really repressive movement, where you didn't talk dirty and you didn't want dirty. It really became a bore' (ibid.: 250).

This is a rather odd attack on a political movement. It is hard to imagine trade unionists or anti-racist activists being criticised for not 'talking dirty' in the same way. But feminism, these lesbians argue, should include pornographic exchanges about getting 'wet' in the course of meetings, speeches and arguments. Feminism

144 The gender backlash

was irredeemably boring because it did not provide the required sexual stimulation to the femmes. The femme therapist Arlene Ishtar opines that, when she slept with lots of 'dykes' in the WLM, 'it was warm and soft and home, but, well, it wasn't hot' (Ishtar, 1992: 380). Madeline Davis says she could not 'understand not being role identified'. She says she believed lesbians who said they were not, but 'all seems so "the same" to me and sort of boring. They're too busy holding hands and swaying and singing about "filling up and spilling over"' (Davis, 1992: 270). The sex therapist JoAnn Loulan explains the feminist rejection of role-playing as being the result of 'homophobia, misogyny, and self-hatred', an approach which leaves no room for political analysis (Loulan, 1990: 24).

These detractors of feminism were not just critical, as political opponents might be, but furious. Hollibaugh is beside herself: 'Sometimes, I don't know how to handle how angry I feel about feminism… I have a personal fury' (Hollibaugh and Moraga, 1992 [1983]: 252). Davis says that lesbian feminism 'really makes me angry' (Davis, 1992: 270). The opposition of roleplayers to criticism could be quite pointed and spiteful towards individuals. Nestle gave a talk in London in the late 1980s about the New York Lesbian Archive, of which she was a founder. My partner and I were in the back row. She said she had read my article 'Butch and Femme: Now and Then' (Jeffreys, 1987), in which I was critical of her views on role-playing, on the plane on the way over, and it had made her cry. She stared at my partner and me and said, very pointedly, that she could not understand the 'eroticism of sameness'. She implied that, because we were not doing role-playing, and both looked like perfectly ordinary lesbian feminists, there could be no passion between us. Her statement could be paraphrased as 'I don't know what they see in each other!'.

The way in which the roleplayers wrote about their practice was pornographic; they just loved 'talking dirty', as they called it. The lesbian feminist critique of roles, on the other hand, was political and employed the political language that feminists had developed: masculinity and femininity, objectification, and so on. The roleplayers replied by talking the language of sadomasochistic sex: about the way their bodies longed and needed very specific humiliating or dominating sexual practices and sensations. The femmes talked about wanting to be 'fucked senseless' and about being 'wet' whilst sitting on bar stools or in other social situations, in a way that was quite incontinent. Joan Nestle speaks of having, as a femme, 'poured out more love and wetness on our bar stools and in our homes than women were supposed to have' (Nestle, 1992b: 138). Madeline Davis writes about her masochistic sexual excitements as a femme: '[T]hat hunger, that desperate need, that desire to be "fucked senseless" and to know that we have, do and would put up with some incredible shit to get it' (Davis, 1992: 268). Mary Frances Platt writes that she was a 'lesbian femme with disabilities' who was 'wise, wild, wet, and wanting' (Platt, 1992: 389). There was a lot of wetness about in these writings. JoAnn Loulan writes in *Lesbian Erotic Dance* about what constituted the dance: 'It's that you are wet and longing for her' (Loulan, 1990: 7). Loulan's book includes many, many pages that could have been entered for the Literary Review's Bad Sex in Fiction Award (except that this was set up two years after her endeavours), including:'You feel your under-pants sticking wetly to your pounding clitoris' (ibid.: 9). Jan Brown writes that 'we all wanted to be fucked senseless' (Brown 1992: 413). Being 'senseless', of course, is not a good condition for a political activist.

Despite the fact that the new prophets of role-playing determinedly denied that butch and femme had any relation to heterosexuality and argued that the practice had no progenitors in the way men and women relate, they nonetheless spoke rather assertively about wanting to be roughly penetrated by cocks, for which they substituted dildos. Brown says, '[S]ome of us wanted to be entered and used by a cock and what that represented' (ibid.). Sally Munt says that what the femme really wants is the '(lesbian) cock' (Munt 1998b: 5). But the sex of role-playing was not just messing around with imitation penises; it was specifically, and in some cases brutally, sadomasochistic. The masochism of the femme is well characterised by Madeline Davis's description of what sex with a butch woman was like:'There is a real interesting dynamic to set up – a master–slave dynamic. When she makes love to you, she is fucking you senseless and being masterful over you, and when you make love to her, you are servicing her… You almost treat the clitoris like the end of a penis' (Madeline Davis, in Davis, Hollibaugh and Nestle, 1992: 262). Joan Nestle gives another example of femme masochism, explaining that she did not just fantasise about scenarios in which she could lux-uriate in humiliation; she found ways to make them real: 'When I was having trouble coming, I fantasized servicing a roomful of butches on my knees. I then found an opportunity to live this desire out and it was wonderful' (ibid.: 266). The problem with lesbian feminists was that they did not appreciate this enthusiastic acting out of the sex of prostitution. They just did not know the rules, which, as Liz O'Lexa explains in the *Femme Mystique* anthology, means believing in 'one who says no and one who says yes' (O'Lexa, 1995: 213). The lesbian feminists, in other words, refused the sexual hierarchies of the heteropatriarchy and thought lesbians could and should behave differently.

Jan Brown wrote that the roleplayers lied to their feminist critics, who she names as Andrea Dworkin and me, by saying, for instance, that role-playing was just about fantasy. In fact, she says, there was no difference between fantasy and reality. The power in their sexual practice was

> in the lust we have to see how close we can get to the edge. It is in the lust to be overpowered, forced, hurt, used, objectified. We jerk off to the rapist, to the Hell's Angel, to daddy, to the Nazi, to the cop, and to all the other images that have nothing to do with the kind of lesbian sex that entails murmurs of endearment, stroking of breasts, and long slow tongue work… We wear the uniform and the gun; we haul our cocks out of our pants to drive into a struggling body…. Sometimes, we need to have a dick as hard as truth between our legs, to have the freedom to ignore 'no' or to have our own 'no' ignored.
>
> *(Brown, 1992: 412)*

146 The gender backlash

Golly; tough talk indeed! It is not surprising that lesbians who were so committed to the values of sexual violence against women were determined to eliminate the uncomfortable analysis of feminists who sought to sexualise equality instead.

Role-playing sex could reasonably be seen as a form of sexual dysfunction, as a recourse of those lesbians who are unable to imagine or practise sex without obvious power differences, often as a result of having been raped in childhood. Roleplayers do, like some sadomasochists, attribute their attachment to the practice to their experience of physical or sexual violence from men, either in childhood or in prostitution. Jan Brown explains that she needs a 'sex where cruelty has value, where mercy does not', because, '[m]any of us graduated from the university of self-destruct. Some of us are street survivors, incest survivors. We lived with abusive boyfriends or drifted through years of substance use' (ibid.: 411). It is possible, though, to learn a different kind of sexual response. The butchest butches of all in pre-feminist times were the 'stone' butches, meaning lesbians who would not allow their femmes to take any sexual initiative or to touch their bodies.

Julia Penelope, a US academic in linguistics and a remarkable lesbian feminist theorist, writes that, in the 1960s, before she discovered lesbian feminism, she acted the role of stone butch (1984). She explains that this was the result of the damage to her sexuality caused by sexual violence in childhood. She was able to come to terms with 'the way in which my incest experiences distorted and atrophied my sexual and emotional responses' in a feminist incest survivors' group. She found feminism an immense liberation. She developed the ability to make love with women outside role-playing, and found 'my intense feelings when I make love, that combination of heat, strength, elation and euphoria that wells up from my gut and fills my body is JOY. What I am experiencing is joy, not 'power'' (ibid.: 33, emphasis in original). This does not sound boring, but to roleplayers and sadomasochists perhaps it is.

The masochism of femmes was not necessarily limited to sexual response, but could extend into the way in which entire relationships were conducted. In *The Femme Mystique* (Newman, 1995), femmes talk about how marvellous femmeness is, and it is clear that they mean subordination – precisely the kind that heterosexual feminists rejected at the time of the WLM. There is a 'back to the '50s' feel about these writings. In the anthology butches take the garbage out and do 'bug duty', but femmes 'pay particular attention to colour schemes'. One femme contributor, Kelly Conway, explains, "Jill has garbage and bug duty… I have made our relationship the number-one priority in my life. I love to cook for her, nurture her, and make our home comfortable. The look on her face when she comes home and the house smells like home cooking and I'm dressed like dessert makes it all worthwhile' (Conway, 1995: 302). She says, 'I am in constant awe of my butch: her strength and intelligence, and the power in her ability to be so gentle…allow [me] to be vulnerable and nurturing' (ibid.). It is hard to imagine such swooning masochism in heterosexual women's publications at that time, but role-playing proponents in the 1990s saw this reinvention of the most oppressive rules of heteroreality as progressive.

Drag king shows

The 1980s role-playing renaissance crucially made butches into heroes. They were seen as the authentic lesbians who defied convention and kept lesbianism going against the odds, as those who were prepared to stand up and stand out and be seen as lesbians. Along with worshipping butches, the femmes wrote about how difficult it was that, because they looked indistinguishable from feminine heterosexual women, their lesbianism was not visible and could be seen as less authentic. The butches characterised lesbianism and, despite the protestations of femmes, they did not. The romanticising of butchness was promoted particularly in one aspect of the reembracing of role-playing in the 1990s: drag king shows. In the 1990s drag kinging began as a form of entertainment in lesbian communities in the US and the UK. The photographer Del LaGrace Volcano, an American in the UK, and the queer theorist Judith "Jack" Halberstam, an Englishwoman in the US, author of the 1998 book *Female Masculinity* (Halberstam, 1998), published a book of photos accompanied by a short text about the drag king phenomenon (Volcano and Halberstam, 1999). Inspired by the fact that gay men had a whole history and culture around drag queens, who performed in clothing associated with women, some lesbians set up drag king shows and competitions in which women, not always lesbians, dressed up as men.

They favoured masculine-looking men and often imitated working-class male stereotypes, because working-class men were seen as more authentically masculine. Drag kinging formed a halfway house between the return of role-playing with the adoption of masculinity by 'butch' identifying lesbians, in the 1980s, and the development of the transgendering of lesbians, which took off in the 1990s. Masculinity is the behaviour of the powerful sex class, so it was exciting to some lesbians to adopt it, though there could be some variety in the way that they did this. Halberstam explains in the preface to *The Drag King Book* that 'Del identifies variously as hermaphrodyke, transman, and other complicated self-constructed identities. I identify as a trans-butch or a drag butch, in other words, a butch who is at the transitive edge of female masculinity' (ibid.: 1).

In the 1990s the performance of masculinity became fashionable and feted in the media, which enjoyed seeing lesbians living up to the stereotype that they really wanted to be men. Halberstam notes this popularity: 'Drag Kings have been featured everywhere recently – *Marie Claire*, *New York Post*, *London Times*, *Penthouse Magazine*, *The Face*' (Halberstam, 1999: 7). Drag kinging was a godsend to a media that still delighted in seeing lesbians as wannabe men. In the foreword to the book Volcano acknowledges that drag kinging had never been a part of lesbian culture in the way that drag queens had been important in gay male culture; it was a new invention. Women dressing up in men's clothing to entertain the public was common historically, as in the career of the music hall artist Vesta Tilley, but women doing this to entertain other women, specifically, was not, and it had no part in lesbian life (Gardner, 2010).

148 The gender backlash

Volcano and Halberstam comment that the lesbians who took part in drag king competitions emulated what they saw as the most gross and ultra-masculine behavior, often involving farting, and they 'showed their arses, made coarse noises, belched, spat and slouched off the stage' (Volcano and Halberstam, 1999: 71). They engaged, they say, in what were often 'heavily working-class renditions of dominant masculinity'. Although many of the women who took part in drag king workshops were heterosexual women who wanted to experience the luxuries of shedding effeminate clothing in a sympathetic environment, those who took part in the competitions, especially in London, Volcano and Halberstam say, were all butch lesbians and/or in the process of transition to hormonally and surgically constructed manliness. Some, she says, traced their decision to transgender 'back to their involvement in Drag King cultures, but others suggest that Drag King experimentation just confirmed desires they already had' (ibid.: 127).

The attainment of masculinity meant that they needed to adopt masculine behaviours even when they were inconvenient, such as not allowing themselves to enjoy dancing because, apparently, men did not do that. Volcano quotes one drag king as saying, in apparent seriousness, 'For example, butches don't often let themselves dance. There's something very stiff about being butch, and when I dance I do it in a mock femme way, or I do a kind of fag dance because to dance as a butch is very difficult' (ibid.: 131). When asked why the drag kings limited themselves to the imitation of working-class masculinity, one drag king replied: 'Well, men in suits are just too boring to imitate with their suits and parted hair, there's no theatre there' (ibid.: 137). Vesta Tilley, on the other hand, dressed up as a very wide variety of male types, including dapper men in suits. In drag king performances it was traditional, patriarchal stereotypes of masculinity that appealed, not any kind of empathetic new incarnation that might be less of a problem for women.

The promotion of role-playing was very concerted and comprised a determined and pointed attempt by some lesbians to overturn any advances lesbian feminists had made to create a new model for how relationships could be conducted – i.e. without ritualised inequality and heteropatriarchal roles. They succeeded to a large extent. Histories of lesbianism, such as that by Lillian Faderman, regularly subject lesbian feminists to quite savage criticism for their attempts to support egalitarian lesbian relationships (Faderman, 1991). This influential version of the history now portrays lesbian feminists as bullies who were hostile to other lesbians. Prominent American lesbians, such as the therapist Arlene Lev, talk of how lesbian feminists oppressed the roleplayers, saying that 'lesbian feminist politics' drove 'butch-femme' identities 'underground' in the 1970s (Lev, 2008).

Today the feminist critique has been overwhelmed, and the term 'butch' is in quite general use in online lesbian and feminist media as a term for strong and proud lesbians. The efforts of the roleplayers supported an extremely harmful development for lesbians. The promotion of traditional masculinity has led, via drag kinging and other routes, to a situation in which many young and some older lesbians are seeking lifelong chemical use and life-changing and risky surgeries so that they may 'transgender' and become simulacra of men (Jeffreys, 2014). This practice takes these lesbians back to the period before the WLM, when the scientists of sex promoted the idea that lesbians really wanted to be men or possessed the brains of men within the bodies of women. Gender has won. The overwhelming determination by feminists to abolish 'gender' or 'sex roles' in the 1970s has been defeated, only to be replaced by a public embrace – in the form of policies and legislation and an industry of profitable medical support – of lesbians becoming 'men' (ibid.). The 'sex wars' over pornography and sadomasochism were not the only source of internecine warfare within lesbian feminism in the 1980s. The next chapter will look at another of these forces of destruction: the wielding of 'identity politics'.

Bibliography

Abbott, Sidney, and Love, Barbara (1972). *Sappho Was a Right-On Woman: A Liberated View of Lesbianism*. New York: Stein & Day.

Abelove, Henry, Barale, Michèle Aina, and Halperin, David (eds.) (1993). *The Lesbian and Gay Studies Reader*. New York: Routledge.

Bailey, Garrick, and Peoples, James (2013). *Essentials of Cultural Anthropology*. Florence, KY: Wadsworth, Cengage Learning.

Brown, Jan (1992). Sex, Lies and Penetration: A Butch Finally 'Fesses Up. In Nestle, Joan (ed.), *The Persistent Desire: A Femme-Butch Reader*. Boston: Alyson Publications, 410–415.

Burana, Lily, Roxxie and Due, Linnea (eds.) (1994). *Dagger: On Butch Women*. Pittsburgh: Cleis Press.

Butler, Judith (1990). *Gender Trouble: Feminism and the Subversion of Identity*. New York: Routledge.

Califia, Pat (1988). *Sapphistry: The Book of Lesbian Sexuality*. Tallahassee, FL: Naiad Press.

Case, Sue-Ellen (1998). Making Butch: An Historical Memoir of the 1970s. In Munt, Sally (ed.), *Butch/Femme: Inside Lesbian Gender*. London: Cassell, 37–45.

Conway, Kelly (1995). Stop Me before I Bake Again. In Newman, Leslea (ed.), *The Femme Mystique*. Boston: Alyson Publications, 300–302.

Davis, Madeline (1992). Epilogue, Nine Years Later. In Nestle, Joan (ed.), *The Persistent Desire: A Femme-Butch Reader*. Boston: Alyson Publications, 270–271.

Davis, Madeline, Hollibaugh, Amber, and Nestle, Joan (1992). The Femme Tapes. In Nestle, Joan (ed.), *The Persistent Desire: A Femme-Butch Reader*. Boston: Alyson Publications, 254–267.

Faderman, Lillian (1981). *Surpassing the Love of Men: Romantic Friendship and Love between Women from the Renaissance to the Present*. New York: William Morrow.

Faderman, Lillian (1991). *Odd Girls and Twilight Lovers: A History of Lesbian Life in Twentieth-Century America*. New York: Columbia University Press.

Feinberg, Leslie (1993). *Stone Butch Blues: A Novel*. Ithaca, NY: Firebrand Books.

Gardner, Lynn (2010, 13 May). Ladies as Gentlemen: The Crossdressing Women of Edwardian Musical Theatre. *The Guardian*. www.theguardian.com/music/2010/may/13/cross-dressing-women-musical-theatre.

Halberstam, Judith (1998). *Female Masculinity*. Durham, NC: Duke University Press.

Halberstam, Judith (1999). Preface. In Volcano, Del LaGrace, and Halberstam, Judith, *The Drag King Book*. London: Serpent's Tail, 1–8.

Halberstam, Judith, and Hale, C. Jacob (1998). Butch/FTM Border Wars. *GLQ: A Journal of Lesbian and Gay Studies*, 4 (2): 283–286.

150 The gender backlash

Hollibaugh, Amber, and Moraga, Cherríe (1992 [1983]). What We're Rollin' around in Bed with: Sexual Silences in Feminism. In Nestle, Joan (ed.), *The Persistent Desire: A Femme-Butch Reader*. Boston: Alyson Publications, 243–253.

Ishtar, Arlene (1992). Femme-Dyke. In Nestle, Joan (ed.), *The Persistent Desire: A Femme-Butch Reader*. Boston: Alyson Publications, 378–383.

Jay, Karla, and Young, Allan (1992). Introduction to the Second Edition. In Jay, Karla, and Young, Allan (eds.), *Out of the Closets: Voices of Gay Liberation*. London: Gay Men's Press, vii–lix.

Jeffreys, Sheila (1987). Butch and Femme: Now and Then. *Gossip*, 5: 65–95 [reprinted in Lesbian History Group (ed.) (1989), *Not a Passing Phase: Reclaiming Lesbians in History 1840–1985*. London: Women's Press, 158–187].

Jeffreys, Sheila (1993). *The Lesbian Heresy: A Feminist Perspective on the Lesbian Sexual Revolution*. London: Women's Press.

Jeffreys, Sheila (2003). *Unpacking Queer Politics*. Cambridge: Polity Press.

Jeffreys, Sheila (2011 [1990]). *Anticlimax: A Feminist Perspective on the Sexual Revolution*. Melbourne: Spinifex Press.

Jeffreys, Sheila (2014). *Gender Hurts: A Feminist Analysis of the Politics of Transgenderism*. Abingdon, UK: Routledge.

Jennings, Rebecca (2007). *Tomboys and Bachelor Girls: Narrating the Lesbian in Post-War Britain 1945–71*. Manchester: Manchester University Press.

Kennedy, Elizabeth Lapovsky, and Davis, Madeline (1993). *Boots of Leather, Slippers of Gold: The History of a Lesbian Community*. New York: Routledge.

Koedt, Anne (1971). Lesbianism and Feminism. Chicago: CWLU. Available at CWLU Herstory Project, www.cwluherstory.org/classic-feminist-writings-articles/lesbianism-and-feminism.html (accessed 5 September 2016).

Lev, Arlene (2008). More than Surface Tension: Femmes in Families. *Journal of Lesbian Studies*, 12 (2/3): 127–144.

Loulan, JoAnn (1985). *Lesbian Sex*. San Francisco: Spinsters Ink Books.

Loulan, JoAnn (1987). *Lesbian Passion: Loving Ourselves and Each Other*. San Francisco: Spinsters Ink Books.

Loulan, JoAnn (1990). *Lesbian Erotic Dance: Butch, Femme, Androgyny, and Other Rhythms*. San Francisco: Spinsters Ink Books.

MacKinnon, Catharine A. (1989). *Toward a Feminist Theory of the State*. Cambridge, MA: Harvard University Press.

Martin, Del, and Lyon, Phyllis (1972). *Lesbian/Woman*. New York: Bantam Books.

Millett, Kate (1972 [1970]). *Sexual Politics*. London: Abacus.

More, Kate (1999). Never Mind the Bollocks: 2. Judith Butler on Transsexuality. In More, Kate, and Whittle, Stephen (eds.), *Reclaiming Genders: Transsexual Grammars at the Fin de Siècle*. London: Cassell, 285–302.

Munt, Sally (ed.) (1998a). *Butch/Femme: Inside Lesbian Gender*. London: Cassell.

Munt, Sally (1998b). Introduction. In Munt, Sally (ed.), *Butch/Femme: Inside Lesbian Gender*. London: Cassell, 1–11.

Mushroom, Merrill (1983). Confessions of a Butch Dyke. *Common Lives, Lesbian Lives*, 9: 39–42.

Nestle, Joan (1987). *A Restricted Country*. Ann Arbor, MI: Firebrand Books.

Nestle, Joan (ed.) (1992a). *The Persistent Desire: A Femme-Butch Reader*. Boston: Alyson Publications.

Nestle, Joan (1992b). The Femme Question. In Nestle, Joan (ed.), *The Persistent Desire: A Femme-Butch Reader*. Boston: Alyson Publications, 138–146.

Newman, Leslea (ed.) (1995). *The Femme Mystique*. Boston: Alyson Publications.

O'Lexa, Liz (1995). Let Me Be the Femme. In Newman, Leslea (ed.), *The Femme Mystique*. Boston: Alyson Publications, 213–215.

Penelope, Julia (1984). Whose Past Are We Reclaiming? *Common Lives, Lesbian Lives*, 13: 16–36.

Platt, Mary Frances (1992). Reclaiming Femme…Again. In Nestle, Joan (ed.), *The Persistent Desire: A Femme-Butch Reader*. Boston: Alyson Publications, 388–389.

Roof, Judith (1998). Lesbian Feminism Meets 1990s Butch-Femme. In Munt, Sally (ed.), *Butch/Femme: Inside Lesbian Gender*. London: Cassell, 27–36.

Roz, Paula, Rachel, Della, Edith, Susan, Perry, Patty and Christine (1980). Don't Call Me Mister, You Fucking Beast! In Walter, Aubrey (ed.), *Come Together: The Years of Gay Liberation 1970–73*. London: Gay Men's Press, 164.

Rubin, Gayle (1984). Thinking Sex: Notes for a Radical Theory of the Politics of Sexuality. In Vance, Carole S. (ed.), *Pleasure and Danger: Exploring Female Sexuality*. London: Routledge & Kegan Paul, 267–319.

Sawyer, Ethel (1965). A Study of a Public Lesbian Community, Washington University, Department of Sociology–Anthropology. Available at http://elisechenier.com/wp-content/uploads/2016/02/Ethel-Sawyer-A-Study-of-a-Public-Lesbian-Community-1965.pdf.

Smyth, Cherry (1998). How Do We Look? Imaging Butch/Femme. In Munt, Sally (ed.), *Butch/Femme: Inside Lesbian Gender*. London: Cassell, 82–89.

Victoria and Albert Museum (n.d.). Vesta Tilley. www.vam.ac.uk/content/articles/v/vesta-tilley (accessed 9 November 2016).

Volcano, Del LaGrace, and Halberstam, Judith (1999). *The Drag King Book*. London: Serpent's Tail.

Walter, Aubrey (ed.) (1980). *Come Together: The Years of Gay Liberation 1970–73*. London: Gay Men's Press.

8

IDENTITY POLITICS AND THE DESTRUCTION OF LESBIAN FEMINISM

'The CIA couldn't have done it better' (Rahila of Southall Black Sisters, 1986)

This chapter examines another force that contributed to the demise of lesbian feminism. This is the way in which identity politics was used by some women to cause chaos in the women's and lesbian community and in groups that ran crucial feminist and lesbian resources. In the late 1970s and 1980s issues of 'identity politics', based on class, race, disability, fat oppression and other categories, came to occupy feminist and lesbian feminist concerns in such a way that some commentators, and many of my interviewees, were prepared to see them as playing a central part in the demise of lesbian feminism and the WLM. Indeed, 'Rahila', from the Black feminist group Southall Black Sisters, wrote in the feminist newspaper *Outwrite* in 1986 about the ways in which identity politics, particularly around race, were destroying the WLM. She says, 'The CIA couldn't have done it better' (Rahila, Southall Black Sisters, *Outwrite*, 47, May 1986). 'Identity politics' as it played out in the WLM did not mean the serious consideration of the oppressions of race and class. These were of great concern for feminists at the time. Many of those who joined the WLM came from the male Left and were cognizant of these issues, and they were, like the women of Southall Black Sisters, likely to have structuralist understandings of all forms of oppression rather than seeing them as emanating from particular individuals or groups of women. Identity politics, on the other hand, saw class and race as individual identities, made other women into the enemy and contributed to the disintegration of lesbian and feminist institutions and practices.

In the 1980s there was serious consideration of the ways in which class and race affected women and lesbians and efforts to address them, which was quite different from that which took place around identity politics. In the 1970s and 1980s racism and the fight against it came to prominence in British politics. The organisations Rock Against Racism and the Anti-Nazi League fought resurgent far Right organisations, such as the National Front. As a result of these developments left-wing activists sought to take the anti-racist struggle into local government, and a 'sea change' in attitudes and practices relating to race and sex discrimination took place, which James Heartfield calls the 'equal opportunities revolution' (Heartfield, 2017). Very important changes took place in local government, with the adoption of equal opportunities policies designed to advance Black and white women, and Black men in the workplace. The developments of that time have become de rigueur, with equal opportunities politics in some form a standard feature of modern management. These changes were the result of the strength and successes of the feminist and Black movements from the 1960s onwards. Feminists took up and campaigned for the new class and race politics through local government, and this move was called by feminist political scientists 'municipal feminism' (Ross, 2018). Although their successes were considerable in relation to local government, when the equal opportunities policies that they introduced were extended to WLM and lesbian organisations that were funded by local councils, some difficulties were created. The priorities of local governments were sometimes in conflict with those of the organisations they funded.

The term 'identity politics' was not used in the WLM in the UK until sometime after its creation in the US by the socialist feminist Black lesbian group the Combahee River Collective in 1978, and, when it was used, it was not with a positive connotation (Combahee River Collective, 1983 [1978]). Radical feminist commentators in the 1980s and later used this term mainly as a pejorative to describe the way in which varieties of these politics were being deployed with destructive effects (McNeil, 1996). The main problem created by a focus on identity politics in the form in which it developed within the WLM was that it entailed a transfer of attention from seeing men as the enemy to the identification of some groups of women as the enemies of women. Women began to 'identify' themselves in meetings and in print in terms of class, race, disability, motherhood status, etc., so that they might have more authority. 'Woman' and 'lesbian' did not feature in these lists and were not considered important 'identities'.

In 1989 Harriet Wistrich and Julie Bindel described the effect of identity politics on the WLM like this: 'The politics of women's liberation has been disappearing under a cloud of "isms"; challenging male supremacy now comes a very poor second to the accumulation of oppression points within the feminist community' (Wistrich and Bindel, 1989: 3). Although myriad forms of destruction were wrought by these politics, the most momentous was the destruction of the *London Women's Liberation Newsletter* and the Lesbian Archive. The newsletter was the foundation of feminist organising and community creation in London, and it ended in 1985. For lesbians, the destruction of the London Lesbian Archive, which imploded at the end of 1988, was a devastating blow. The demise of both these institutions will be considered here

Origin of 'identity politics'

The well-known Black American lesbian Barbara Smith, who is a socialist feminist, says that the first usage of the term 'identity politics', appeared in the significant

154 Identity politics

paper 'The Combahee River Collective Statement' of 1978, which she wrote along with her twin sister Beverley Smith and other women (Combahee River Collective, 1983 [1978]). It was created to enable the group to describe the way in which their identities as Black lesbians were inextricably intertwined with their identities as women, and could not be separated (see Jones and Eubanks, 2014: 53). Barbara Smith, interviewed by a number of other feminists, explains what she means by 'identity politics'. She says, '[B]efore we began to assert identity politics and the importance of a Black feminist stance, we were, by and large, invisible' (ibid.: 54). She explains: 'Identity politics is, then, the political analysis and practice that arises out of careful attention to the lived realities of experiencing interlocking oppressions' (ibid.: 42).

The perspective on which Smith's politics are based is not that of lesbian feminism, and she makes some disparaging remarks about lesbian separatist politics. As a socialist feminist, Smith considers that feminists should both work in coalition with other oppressed groups of people to achieve their aims and make any sacrifices of their most cherished political principles and practices that may be necessary to do so. She is opposed to separatism because this is not the coalitionism which she favours, and is particularly opposed to lesbian separatism because this puts women and particularly lesbians first. She describes lesbian separatism as a variety of 'identity politics' and criticises it for not placing enough emphasis on all other oppressed people, such as particular groups of men, who are not 'white' lesbians:

> Lesbian separatism was a kind of identity politics that frequently did not take into account that there were many, many people in this country and around the globe who were terribly and horribly oppressed and didn't happen to be white lesbians. They weren't really interested in that, because they saw one major contradiction, which was patriarchy… [C]oalition politics are really, really vital.
>
> *(Smith in ibid.: 55)*

There were, of course, Black lesbians involved in lesbian separatism who completely disagreed with Smith that separatism is unsuited to Black women (Lee, 1988 [1981]). Her views represent but one political tendency within feminism at that time, but it was an influential one because it was supported by all the considerable contempt for autonomous, women-only, feminist and lesbian organising that exists in masculine culture and politics, and this gave it clout.

Within political science and academia, the term has come to be used to denote a great variety of politics and bears little resemblance to the way in which the Combahee River Collective originally intended it. The term lends itself to infinite expansion around forms of personal identification. Within feminist theory it has been overtaken in popularity by the term 'intersectionality' (Crenshaw, 1991), which has a similar meaning and tends to be expanded well beyond its usefulness in the same way. It is used, for instance, by male-bodied transgender activists in the present to guilt-trip women and feminists and intrude their variety of identity politics into feminist concerns (Cox, 2014). These men say that they must be respected as 'women' by feminists who are intersectional, because they are one of the sections.

The adoption of identities

In the 1980s there was some pressure upon feminists and lesbian feminists to adopt identities, primarily of race or class. There was a good deal that white feminists needed to learn about racism and about working with Black feminists in this period. Linda Bellos, for instance, explains in her interview that white feminists did need to understand that their assumptions and behaviour related to a particular culture and could be exclusionary: 'Lots of white middle-class women brought their culture into the room, and the culture was of white supremacy. And I don't mean consciously; not consciously "I am better" but that…they had patronising views about Black women' (Linda Bellos, interview 2013). Alongside the challenge that was taking place to assert the importance of Black women's experience and priorities, though, some women wielded identity politics in destructive ways. Linda, who took a job at the feminist magazine *Spare Rib* in 1981, has written about what she considered 'the limitations of identity politics' (Bellos, n.d., accessed 2017). She says she 'had no problem with the idea of identity politics' itself, but with the way it was understood as part of a hierarchy of oppression. She says, 'I recall being described as "doubly" or "triply oppressed", as were many other women of colour. The more boxes of oppression a person ticked the more visible they became but this didn't necessarily mean they were heard or listened to.' She thought the situation became quite dire: 'I still think identity politics has grown into a form of competitive victimhood which to my mind is neither healthy nor even feminist.' One form of the competition was about which was a 'worse' form of oppression, race or class, and this could be extended to whether being an incest survivor was a more victimised category than either.

Harriet Wistrich and Julie Bindel explain that, by 1989, identity politics had had a damaging effect on the WLM. They comment that recognition that power imbalances exist between women is positive: 'It is certainly a progression that power imbalances between women are more often considered and on the agenda of feminism these days' (Wistrich and Bindel, 1989: 3). They go on to say, however, that 'there is a crucial difference between recognising power imbalances between women and respecting <u>all</u> differences of experience, circumstance and perspective between women', which leads to the disappearance of 'the politics of women's liberation' as women seek to establish authority in meetings and writings by listing the forms of oppression they suffer. The effect, they say, was that '[a] feminism for political change has been transformed into an antagonistic set of communities submerged in fixed identities' (ibid., emphasis in original).

The rise of identity politics took place in stages as new 'isms' were articulated and recognised. Class politics came first, and considerable divisions around class were identified and created in the late 1970s. This was followed by race, which was swiftly followed in its turn by disability. Fat politics and other more rarefied varieties

156 Identity politics

could then be attached to the model. Not all 'isms' were equal, however. In the early 1980s some Jewish feminists, and some gentile supporters, sought to raise the profile of anti-Semitism as a form of oppression, but this was not seen as legitimate and was contested vigorously in a way that other 'isms' were not (Attar, 1983).

Class was adopted as an identity by some lesbian feminists from the late 1970s. The way in which this took place provides a template for understanding the adoption of other identities. In the early 1970s WLM, class oppression was still mostly understood by feminists as a structural problem related to economics and to capitalism. As identity politics became more influential, discussion around class changed, and women started to 'identify' as working class and set up working-class women's groups and newsletters, and, by the early 1980s, working-class lesbians were organising in similar ways. The grounds on which women self-identified were slippery. Some women identified according to the status of their fathers, though they had themselves changed status through going to grammar schools and having university educations. There were many discussions on such questions.

Some women sought to wield a working-class identity to get their voices heard and taken seriously. They would identify themselves as working class before they spoke at a meeting, for instance, so that their views carried more weight. Lynn Alderson expressed her disquiet at the way that this worked in 1977 in the *London Women's Liberation Newsletter*:

> To accuse a woman of being either middle or working class and to ask her to reveal her class origins instead of answering the point she is making (or explaining the connection) seems to me to frustrate what could be an important discussion in the movement and to be personally intimidating and guilt-tripping rather than opening up the very real issues involved.
>
> *(Alderson, LWLN 31, 1977, 28 September)*

The hurling of accusations about classist behaviour could become quite vituperative and harmful to the survival of women's conferences and organisations, but some who had adopted class identity sought to justify it by saying that middle-class women had caused the outburst, by showing their privilege, for instance.

Marlene Packwood, who identified as a working-class woman, sought to explain the degree of aggressive and disruptive behaviour that class identity politics could lead to, in the radical feminist journal *Trouble and Strife* (Packwood, 1983). She says that some women who identified as working class engaged in problematic behaviour towards other women, which could include swearing and bullying, and that they argued that this was natural behaviour for working-class women who were driven to distraction by the behaviour of middle-class women. She had, mistakenly, she reports, at times been 'angry with the coarse rebellion of working class women which occurred from time to time in the WLM', in which, 'working class anger sometimes comes out sharply and with jagged edges. It presents itself in the form of hurled insults, accusations of snooty middle-class values, drunken working-class women calling middle-class women snobby, arrogant, dismissive bitches at conferences and workshops.' But her lack of sympathy, she says, was caused by the fact that she went to a grammar school, where she got infected with middle-class values.

Packwood saw middle-class women as subordinating their working-class sisters, and her point of view does represent much of the argumentation going on at the time: 'One thing is utterly clear – one class is subordinate to the other' (ibid., 8). In her analysis, 'middle-class' women in the WLM are portrayed as a powerful clique. She makes a number of demands of these women, which include 'redistribution of wealth' amongst feminists and that they should help working-class women up onto the battlements of culture, which they were successfully assailing. They should 'open up to other women areas of the spheres and institutions they are now beginning to have access to: education and the law, the medical profession and the press, television, publishing' (ibid.: 11). In fact, at that time very few women had influential access to these masculine fortresses.

Those who took a more structural rather than individualist approach to class developed more practical ways of dealing with it. They addressed inequality rather than focusing on individual identity. Jan McLeod describes in her interview the ways in which economic class was dealt with in the collective which set up Rape Crisis in Glasgow (Jan McLeod, interview 2013). She explains that Rape Crisis in Glasgow was formed by women who identified as socialist feminists, which is different from what happened in England, where work against violence against women was led by radical feminists. As socialist feminists, she says, 'class was like a very strong thing in our discussion at the RCC [rape crisis centre], and we used to have all sorts of very political principles about what we would or wouldn't do'. This led to procedures to ensure women could afford travel expenses to access services and childcare. Unlike the situation in London and some other parts of England, class did not create big divisions, which she attributes to a strong socialist orientation on the part of those who joined the collective: 'I think it's because of the socialist feminist and the trade union links; there were quite a lot of women there that came from a working-class background...' Class was also addressed, she says, in the recognition that 'if you're poorer it is harder to escape it, or that if you're really poor there is a high chance that your family and friends are poor'. Although collective members discussed class and race and disability, and the discussions could be painful, they did not create the atmosphere of blame and anger that was seen in other places. In relation to race as well, the sort of internal strife that affected London feminists was not seen in Glasgow. When Jan McLeod went to meetings about violence against women in England, she says that 'the English women would scream and cry, and very often it was about racism', to the extent that '[t]o be quite honest, we used to come back and go 'Bloody Hell'... We weren't familiar with the struggles that Black women were having. [...] [T]o us it was a bit like – oh, gosh – quite dramatic or whatever' (ibid.).

The use of identity politics as a form of one-upwomanship caused harm to groups and friendship circles, but there were ways in which it was wielded that created much greater damage. The interpersonal hostility could lead to harassment and even violence to property, as we shall see. When this politics was formalised in

158 Identity politics

WLM or lesbian organisations, it could lead to their fragmentation and destruction. It would be good, particularly for those of us who lived through this maelstrom and were damaged by it, to be able to explain why it took place, but that is not easy to do. I shall suggest some forms of explanation here that feminist theorists and my interviewees have put forward and give examples of events that took place that could fit these frameworks.

Why did identity politics take hold?

Horizontal hostility

The main explanation created by feminists for the development of aggression between women is the idea of horizontal hostility. This term was first used by the Black US feminist Florynce Kennedy in 1970: 'Horizontal hostility may be expressed in sibling rivalry or in competitive dueling... [It is] misdirected anger that rightly should be focused on the external causes of oppression' (Kennedy, 1970: 495). Kennedy's explanation for the behaviour is that oppressed people were unable to adjust to the circumstances of freedom and knew only how to be oppressed or to oppress: 'Oppressed people are frequently very oppressive when first liberated. And why wouldn't they be? They know best two positions. Somebody's foot on their neck or their foot on somebody's neck' (ibid.). The term has since been taken up to explain Black-on-Black violence by male youth in the US, and to explain many other instances in which members of oppressed groups are aggressive towards their peers, because it is much safer than risking penalties, such as physical violence or the punishment of powerful institutions, by attacking the oppressors.

American lesbian separatist philosopher Julia Penelope wrote about the way in which horizontal hostility was creating destruction amongst lesbians in 1990. She defines the term as 'the anger, frustration, and mistrust directed by members of an oppressed group, often inappropriately, toward other members of the same group' (Penelope, 1992: 60). She argues that this hostility is directed towards those who are 'more visible and vocal' (ibid.), and the labels most used in the name-calling are '*Nazi, racist, ageist* and *classist*' (ibid.: 66, emphasis in original). The name-calling of a lesbian can leave her isolated, she says, and often other lesbians who may have been her friends will join in the criticism to deflect the hostility from themselves and appear virtuous. She explains that another arena of name-calling is the so-called 'sex wars', in which sadomasochists direct multiple accusations at those who want to call the construction of sexuality in to question: '*Nazis, fascists, sex police...anti-sex, puritans...moralists*' (ibid.: 68, emphasis in original). She argues that name-calling is a '*power* play', aimed at controlling the 'behaviors, thoughts and actions' of those who are targeted, and a form of '*verbal abuse*' (ibid., emphasis in original). She asks that lesbians take responsibility for the way that they feel in relation to another lesbian, and, instead of saying that the other woman 'intimidates' them, for example, they should examine their own feelings and past experience to find out why they feel that way rather than blaming and abusing the other woman. One of the reasons that such name-calling was a problem, she says, is that it 'trivializes the real physical and social dangers posed by white supremacist groups like the Ku Klux Klan, the skinheads, and the neo-Nazis' (ibid.: 69).

My interviewees offer a range of explanations for the horizontal hostility that took place amongst British lesbian feminists. Al Garthwaite explains that women and lesbians were under intense pressure in the streets, where they lived with groups of men 'throwing stones at you and…shouting nasty things at you when you come home…harassing you on the street'. Under such pressure these lesbians turned on their own, as they had no power to deal with the men who were the cause of the stress: 'It's sort of like a civil war situation, and in civil wars families turn in on each other and it takes generations to get that sorted out, and I think the same thing was happening' (Al Garthwaite, interview 2013). This sort of behaviour did not happen in male-dominated political movements such as the trade union movement, she suggests, because male trade unionists were probably not under the same sort of intense pressure as the lesbians were.

Some lesbians, even some who identified as working class themselves, saw the attacks on other feminists using 'isms' as being a way to discredit politics with which they disagreed but with which they were unable to argue in other ways. Carol Jones, for instance, replied to a piece about class by one of its proponents in the London newsletter, saying that the politics under attack 'thick and fast' in magazines such as *City Limits* and *Time Out*, and in the newsletter, was that which named 'men as the enemy and male sexuality as the problem'. She says,

> These attacks are coming in the form of lies: calling revolutionary feminists 'right wing' and 'white and middle class'… So, the term 'right wing, white, middle class' has become a term of abuse to throw at any woman who attacks pornography and other forms of male violence, and whose politics are threatening to the left. As a working class revolutionary feminist I am sick of being called 'right wing' because I name men as the enemy.
>
> *(LWLN 359, 1984, 3 April)*

Julie Bindel also argues that accusations of classism were used to attack revolutionary feminism: '[U]nfortunately, it was the first identity, I think, that was ever used as a stick to beat proper, hard-core revolutionary feminism' (Julie Bindel, interview 2013).

Julie says that such accusations originate in the male Left, which always accused feminists in general of being middle class, even when they were extremely posh themselves. Women of the Left tended to use this tactic to attack feminism as a bourgeois issue: '[W]e were seen as the bourgeois who were messing around with bigger issues that would just divide the Left, and that we should wait until after the revolution' (ibid.). Al Garthwaite suggests that individual feminists began to use identity labels in order to 'cause trouble', or for what they could 'gain from it': 'Every conversation it seemed was prefaced by "Speaking as a lesbian mother", "Speaking

160 Identity politics

as a working-class woman", "Speaking as a Black woman" – you know: "Speaking as a…lesbian mother, I can't stand white bread"' (Al Garthwaite, interview 2013).

The horizontal hostility approach helps to explain why this identity politics did not have such a devastating effect on male-dominated political groups and organisations such as the trade union movement and the Black movement. Men were not as powerless or as without recourse as women, who had been largely excluded from the political process, were. When I asked why race identity politics did not get taken to the same extreme in male-dominated movements such as the trade union movement and the Black movement, Linda said she thought this was because it was feminists who had 'started with a critique that the personal is political', which was, she opines, 'taken too far… [P]eople took it to a point which was, frankly, self-indulgent' (Linda Bellos, interview 2013). Femi Otitoju explains that the issue of race was dealt with in the WLM in a way that was not replicated within masculinist Black politics at the time. She says that at a non-feminist meeting, when she apologised for being late because she was at a women's centre meeting, a man told her she 'needed to decide whether I was Black or whether I was a woman and what my priorities were. Very, very clear…very simple.' In the WLM this approach would be unacceptable, Femi says, because women 'cared more', so that 'I couldn't look at a woman and say: "Well, you need to decide whether you're Black or whether you're a woman or whether you're disabled". Black people have no problem; Black men have no problem saying that to me' (Femi Otitoju, interview 2013).

Within the lesbian community there was sometimes horizontal hostility between lesbians in the name of class which went beyond verbal bullying to include more seriously criminal behaviour. One example is the use of guilt-tripping to get feminists seen as middle class to hand over their chequebooks and credit cards so that fraud could take place. Al Garthwaite describes this happening in London and Leeds: 'They were relying on middle-class guilt on behalf of other women to provide them with credit cards or chequebooks or stealing them from them. And then using them in shops or to get money… To get them the life of Riley' (Al Garthwaite, interview 2013). Apart from petty crime, acts of violence took place, such as throwing bricks through the windows of women perceived to be 'middle class'. Al describes this as happening in Leeds on more than one occasion. All of it was damaging to the culture and community that lesbian feminists were intent upon creating and caused mistrust and disillusionment.

Tyranny of structurelessness

One reason why it was possible for acrimonious identity politics to wreak havoc on WLM groups and resources was that feminists rejected hierarchical organisation and sought to operate on the basis of consensus. US feminist Jo Freeman calls the problems this principle caused the 'tyranny of structurelessness' (Freeman, 1972 [1970]). Women's groups eschewed the structures practised by the male Left, with officeholders and lines of authority, because they were influenced by anarchist principles and committed to equality. This left groups such as the London Lesbian

Archive and the Women's Liberation Newsletter Collective vulnerable to coups, as Freeman explains: 'The more un-structured a group it is, the more lacking it is in informal structures; the more it adheres to an ideology of "structurelessness", the more vulnerable it is to being taken over by a group of political comrades' (ibid.: 24). Linda Bellos explains how this worked in relation to the newsletter. She says that identity politics became a kind of 'competition', and this was partly the result of the fact that 'we didn't have leadership, we didn't have an editorial board... We worked collectively... [T]here was a lot of guilt' (Bellos, n.d.). She says, 'We got so into shouting about being excluded, and women were excluded, there was no doubt about it in my mind, women were, but that became the agenda rather than what we could do collectively and how we might do things collectively in ways that were inclusive.'

The events that took place around the *London Women's Liberation Newsletter* provide a good example of the way the tyranny of structurelessness works to forestall solutions to interpersonal dispute, particularly when exacerbated by the guilt-tripping of identity politics. The newsletter relied for 12 years on an open and constantly changing collective of volunteers, who decided upon content, enforced policies such as the principle that there should be no personal attacks, typed and duplicated contributions and did the mail-out. In all this time there was no sense that involvement was more than a form of quite hard work which was enlivened by companionship and a sense of taking part in vital WLM activity. It did not matter, therefore, if there was no formal structure and no one was in charge. But this very informality left it extremely susceptible to any women or group of women who wanted to exert their authority, or take it over for their own advantage. This lack of structure was crucial to the way in which the newsletter ended in 1985. The identity politics that devastated the newsletter were those of disability and race.

In the early 1980s an identity politics based upon disability began to have a considerable impact on the *London Women's Liberation Newsletter*. Feminist disability activists in the group Sisters Against Disablement (SAD) were far ahead of political and popular culture at the time in demanding access for women with disabilities to public spaces. It took a long time for local government politics to catch up, and disability access to public services is still frequently to be found wanting. SAD's demands were ahead of their time, and they were simply not possible for the volunteers producing the newsletter, or individual women wanting to organise meetings, to fulfil, and the effects were destructive. They demanded that all feminist meetings, conferences and events be held in places where there was good disability access, and that any woman or group advertising a meeting in the London newsletter should publish details of the venue in answer to a lengthy 'access code', which SAD provided, covering any issues that could be of importance to women with a range of disabilities. Since public venues did not provide this information, feminists organising meetings had to scope out venues ahead of time with tape measures, and note down not just measurements but the types of floor coverings and taps and a host of other factors. The detailed access code responses for each meeting took up many pages of the newsletter, whereas a meeting announcement would previously

162 Identity politics

have occupied, at most, a short couple of sentences. The newsletter volunteers had to type up entries and print them manually using Gestetner machines, which took a great deal of time even without tens of extra pages of access code responses.

Whereas, in the beginning, compliance with filling in the access code was voluntary, by August 1983 it had become compulsory (LWLN 330, 1983, 28 August). At this time the code consisted of one page of A4 with points 'A' to 'T'. It started with questions about parking, including ramps, many details about doors, including widths, and whether they were heavy or light, revolving and opened inwards or outwards. It included floor surfaces, three questions about lighting, seven about seating and questions about participation, including eight about note takers and signers. The code included whether a crèche was provided and asked eight questions about that.

Fulfilling these demands could be quite time-consuming for organisers, who had to cross London (which could take more than an hour), arrange to get into a building to do the measuring and fact-finding, get home and type up the information for the newsletter. In addition, many meetings took place in women's homes at that time, and women would either have to provide such information about their taps and carpets or give up home meetings out of discouragement. When asked about how the politics of disability affected lesbian feminism, Julie Bindel opines: 'It was hideous.' She says that SAD activists 'should never in a million years have been able to represent in any way the proper radical disability rights movement', because they were putting blame on 'women who were not identifying as disabled. They were bullying, they were unreasonable' (Julie Bindel, interview 2013).

In principle, all the SAD access code questions are valid, and if they were asked by women with disabilities of public venues it would be reasonable for a local government officer to do a survey and provide an answer. For individual feminists organising meetings, however, it was an impossible task. For the voluntary group getting out the newsletter every fortnight, it was likely to be very hard to find the volunteer labour to record the newsletter and send out cassettes for women with hearing difficulties, for instance. But the demands could not be said to be too onerous or unreasonable. Such was the susceptibility of movement activists by this time to guilt-tripping around identity politics that the demands were seen as inescapable. The result was that women no longer sought or were unable to advertise WLM meetings and events, and these activities ground to a halt.

The ongoing problem around disability was accompanied by the wielding of race identity politics in a competition for power around the newsletter, and this was an even more destructive issue than disability identity politics for this hugely important resource. Race politics was employed to effect a coup: the policy decision by the collective in January 1985 that 'only women who are Black/Irish/Jewish/of Colour can work on the production of the newsletter' (LWLN 423, 1985, 3 July). Up till that time the collective had always been open. The introduction of this policy was a coup which put control in the hands of a particular group of women who self-identified as members of these categories. Elizabeth Carola explains in the newsletter what happened (LWLN 422, 1985, 26 June). She says that there had been a constant decline in subscriptions to a point lower than any in its 12-year history, and the problem was that the collective was 'being arrogant and destructive'. Its attitude was thus: 'We Are Right, and if you don't agree, You Are Ablist, Racist and/or…Wrong.' This attitude led women to 'stop reading the newsletter'. She says the collective's attitude of 'confrontation and attack' as the only way it knew to deal with racism and ableism in the WLM was 'pure male left', and showed 'the same antagonistic attitude towards non-ethnic minority women in the newsletter that many of us have towards men'.

In response to the fact that the newsletter was in terminal decline, an 'open' meeting of the newsletter collective was held in June 1985 at which the now closed group was asked to resign in order that the newsletter could be saved. The group defended its policy, saying it had had to introduce it because of the racist behaviour of other women. The collective members proceeded to hurl abuse at the women who were criticising them, and the accusations demonstrate precisely the bullying tone that their detractors were complaining about: 'By objecting to the N/L policies on able-bodied chauvinism and racism you are refusing to give up your power to oppress women with disabilities who are Black/Irish/Jewish/of Colour' (LWLN 422, 1985, 26 June). The next edition of the newsletter, labelled 'Crisis Edition', contained the minutes of the open meeting, which stated that the collective had resigned but had ruled that none of the other women present who wanted to form a new collective and save the newsletter could do so because the 'next collective (had) to be exclusively women who are Black/of Colour, Irish and Jewish' (LWLN 423, 1985, 3 July). An emergency collective brought out a few more issues, until in September it reported that there was not much content coming in and that it was broke. The last issue had six pages of content and 14 pages of access codes.

Readers may wonder why we lesbians, me included, were unable to assert ourselves sufficiently to counter this bullying and save such an important resource. The problem was that there was no mechanism to do so. The survival of the newsletter relied on a voluntary collective, and there were no rules as to how it should be run. When the group that described itself as 'Black/Irish/Jewish/of Colour' conducted its coup, using bullying and guilt-tripping to effect it, there was no way in which other women could act to counter it. The newsletter was the main medium of communication. It carried discussions and advertised political meetings and social activities for the women's and lesbian community in London, and its demise was a body blow to the WLM and to lesbian feminism.

External pressures

The deployment of identity politics within the lesbian feminist community was attributed by some of my interviewees to the pressures from outside that were having an impact on the WLM in the 1980s. One of these, Al Garthwaite explains, was the increasingly hostile political climate of Thatcherism, which caused women to turn on each other as they faced pressure to survive. Being a lesbian feminist was not a good 'career move' (Al Garthwaite, interview 2013). Moreover, she says,

164 Identity politics

some women were just 'complete bullies'. Julie Bindel blames the sort of politics then being practised by mainly left-wing local authorities, which funded women's organisations and then inflicted upon them their own priorities:

> Many women's organisations operated through a kind of femo-cratic regime, and of course, within local government, there's a tick box: you've got to employ people who are Black, and in wheelchairs, and who are single parents, and – you know – who live somewhere where 20 per cent of the population are below the poverty line.

> *(Julie Bindel, interview 2013)*

The crisis at the Lesbian Archive illustrates Julie's point well, because the internal strife developed around class, race and sadomasochism. The archive was set up in 1984 by volunteers. The decision was made to seek funding from the Greater London Council, and later by the London Boroughs Grants Scheme, and these funders imposed their own priorities, such as the requirement that the workers and management committees it supported should have a representation of Black women, with no regard to political nuance. This created the stage for serious conflict. The task of the Lesbian Archive was never seen as being just about the collection of material. It was set up by lesbian feminist separatists, and the politics was very important from the outset. There was an explicit commitment to anti-pornography and anti-sadomasochism politics, for instance. The policy was that, although it might have materials from the other side of the 'sex wars', such as those related to lesbian pornography and lesbian sadomasochism, in the collection, because this aspect of lesbian history needed to be included for the purposes of authenticity, these would not be promoted or displayed. The intention was that the archive should be women-only and open to all women who wanted to consult the materials. So long as the archive remained in the hands of a radical feminist lesbian collective of volunteers it was united. The project was seen as so important that collective members talked of being prepared to put all the materials under their beds if they were under threat rather than lose them. When the decision was made to apply for funding, however, the archive became subject to pressures beyond the control of its lesbian feminist progenitors, and serious divisions arose.

In mid-1988 a grave dispute arose between the two paid workers and the majority of the 'collective', which was by then calling itself a management committee and seeking to turn itself into a responsible employer to meet the demands of the funders. The dispute escalated to such a pitch that the workers removed all the financial documents, froze the bank account and left the archive. The result was that they were eventually sacked with two months' wages in lieu for gross misconduct. Lines of authority were badly confused, and feminist principles of collectivism and equality caused considerable problems in this situation. The dispute began over class and continued to encompass race politics and sadomasochism. The management committee saw the politics of prospective workers as the first priority – i.e. they needed to be lesbian feminists. The paid workers had different priorities which are likely to have been influenced or imposed by the funders. They were put in a position where they were serving two entities: a lesbian feminist management committee and an unnuanced equal opportunities policy from the funders. They designed a new application form for use in filling a new position, the wording of which the majority of those in the committee objected to. It required applicants to identify themselves according to their identities: class, race and physical abilities.

The Lesbian Archive worker who was responsible for putting the identity categories into the form gave her reasons for doing so. One was that this was a regular practice on such forms, a claim with which others vigorously disagreed. For including disability, she proffered the reason that 'if there are two Black women and one of them is disabled, it could be important to know this, the same with class – it's good to have a profile of the person we are choosing in relation to what we need' (minutes of Lesbian Archive meeting, 1988, 25 August, author's collection). She said that the 'background' of a person was important because it would suggest 'what sort of attitudes they have', or 'kinds of skills or knowledge', and that class identification would mean they would have 'a knowledge of that culture', whatever that may be.

Critical committee members pointed out that there was no recognised definition of working-classness, and that would make it very difficult for women who were supposed to 'define themselves' to know how to identify. One committee member explained that some women who grew up working class would no longer see themselves as such. Some, she said, saw themselves as classless and some came from countries that did not have the same sort of class system as the UK. Another said that she would identify as working class 'if pushed' but felt uncomfortable because she had 'the advantages of education'. The admission of such complexities made the idea of class identification look less obviously progressive. The worker expressed outrage at the criticisms that were being raised by the majority of those present to the questions about identity. She said, 'I'm just shocked really by the attitude of this collective. Every other feminist and lesbian group in this city recognises class and race as political issues. It's appalling that we are not allowed to recognise it' (minutes of Lesbian Archive meeting, 1988, 25 August, author's collection). Another lesbian, in support of the worker, said that critics of such identity politics wanted to 'wipe out other people's experience', and it was 'bloody disgusting'. The majority of the management group, however, remained convinced that all archive workers must have lesbian and feminist politics, whatever their other qualifications for the position.

Race identity politics became important because of the concern felt by some within the collective that it was all-white and that it needed to be more inclusive of Black women. The collective had contained one Black woman in the beginning, Linda Bellos, but a couple of years later she was no longer active in the group. The archive had two workers who were white, and when the decision was reached that another worker should be appointed there was a discussion about how to put into the advertisement that applications from Black lesbians would be welcome. The same issues arose as with the inclusion of class identity. The majority of those in the management committee felt it was important that all applicants should represent

166 Identity politics

the radical feminist politics of the archive and that questions should be asked in interviews to elicit this information. Some, however, felt that a Black lesbian worker should be appointed whether she had radical feminist politics or not, since it was so important to have Black representation and there might not be any Black applicants with the right politics. This issue became extremely polarised, with accusations of racism being directed towards those who considered that the politics of a prospective worker were of prime importance.

The dispute was exacerbated by a conflict over sadomasochism, discussed in a previous chapter. This conflict, which was around the showing of the movie *She Must Be Seeing Things* at the Lesbian Archive summer school in the summer of 1988, brought things to a head. The significance of the political difference between the workers, who endorsed the showing of the movie, and the management committee, which knew nothing about its content, was hidden beneath accusations of racism. In October 1988 the archive was in crisis about the attitude of the workers towards the management committee. At a collective meeting, at which the harm caused by the movie to the reputation of the archive and to that of the summer school attendees who were disturbed by it was discussed, the majority of the management committee asked the workers to agree not to take decisions that affected the archive, such as showing such a movie, without the knowledge and express approval of the committee. The workers refused to agree to this and walked out of the collective meeting (minutes of special meeting of the Lesbian Archive Collective, 1988, 1 September, author's collection). By this point there was a situation of non-cooperation between the workers and the employing body/management committee, which led to their dismissal. The management committee issued a statement in December 1988 to explain its actions, stating that the response of the workers to their dismissal was to 'distract attention from the issue of sexual violence onto that of the supposed racism of the management committee' ('Statement from Our Side: The Dispute at the Lesbian Archive', 1988, December: Marion, Carol, Margaret, Elaine and Sheila, author's collection).

The upshot of the dispute was that the management committee retained the company, Orinda, that had been set up to run the archive and other projects, whilst the workers and their supporters kept the archive and appointed a Black lesbian worker, Linda King, who worked for just four weeks and saw her job as being to mitigate the 'racism' of the Lesbian Archive. She produced a report entitled *We Have Always Been Here*, which was introduced by the 'LAIC's Interim Support Group and Co-worker' (King, Linda, n.d., Lesbian Archive and Information Centre, author's collection). Her 'co-worker', one of the original two white workers, says in an introduction that the dispute in 1988 'focussed on the issue of changing the racist nature of the Lesbian Archive', which had a 'history of racism' (ibid.: 3). King reports on what she considers to be the failings of 'white lesbians', who think they are 'superior' to Black women: 'White reasoning precludes an examination of their own cultural racism and assumptions about how and when change should occur' (ibid.: 9). She gives ten recommendations to support 'the transition of the LAIC from a racist resource to a representative service'. She explains that she found working in this racist resource to be difficult, because there were times 'when the pressure of unspoken racism expressed through the body language and silence chilled my blood' (ibid.: 11). The archive carried on for two years until it lost funding, at which point the materials were moved to the Glasgow Women's Library, where they are mostly still not available to view after 25 years. There is currently no lesbian archive in the UK.

The decision by the London Lesbian Archive to seek local government funding could, in retrospect, be seen to be a mistake, and this is not the only way to run an archive. Indeed, the New York Lesbian Archive had a policy from the beginning of never seeking public funding and surviving on donations from other lesbians and volunteer labour. For 15 years it was situated in the apartment of one of the founders, Joan Nestle, until a building was purchased for it from donations (Lesbian Herstory Archives, n.d.). Thus the New York archive was not trammelled with the demands and regulations of external funders, and it survives whereas the London archive did not.

Identity politics, then, was not necessarily about taking class, race and disability seriously. It was used for some very destructive purposes. Some feminists and lesbian feminists used 'isms' to boost their authority in meetings and groups, and, in some cases, they used 'isms' to justify abusive behaviour. They used them to attack those with whom they had political differences, because accusations of racism, for instance, could be more effective that open disagreement on pornography. In some cases, the deployment of identity politics was imposed on feminist and lesbian feminist organisations by outside forces – i.e. local government funders who were not sympathetic to the idea that politics should be more important than equality categories. By the mid- to late 1980s identity politics was contributing to bitter infighting and the implosion of very important feminist and lesbian feminist resources, such as the London newsletter and the Lesbian Archive.

In 1986 the Black feminist group Southall Black Sisters (SBS) stated vehemently that identity politics was damaging to the WLM. The group wrote a centre-page spread in *Outwrite* newspaper that year lamenting the dire state of the movement entitled 'Masses of Women but Where's the Movement?'. SBS said that the Black feminist movement in the UK had grown considerably but was being harmed by some who engaged in hostility towards other feminists over identity politics and personalised race and class as identities rather than opposing them as structures of oppression. The group said there was 'a vociferous (small but loud) part of this new radical movement which, instead of organising against Thatcher, turned against the women's movement and forced it to fragment away into an infinity of internal fights. Real political conflicts such as racism, classism, able bodiedism etc., were articulated' in a 'bourgeois way (i.e. personal experience)' and this had 'paralysed the movement'. SBS commented that 'the CIA couldn't have done better' (Rahila, *Outwrite*, 47, 1986, May).

Inge Blackman, the Black lesbian who used accusations of racism against those, such as me, who she disagreed with over the Lesbian Archive summer school, pronounced triumphantly in 1990 that identity politics had defeated the lesbian

168 Identity politics

feminist critique of sexuality: 'Now that political lesbianism no longer calls the shots within feminism and the concept of a unified sisterhood has all but disappeared, it is conceivable that feminism is fading and that a "post-feminist" state is evolving' (Blackman and Perry, 1990: 77). It was specifically identity politics, she considers, that had effected this rout of the 'revolutionary feminists'. It happened because 'identity politics has left these groups fragmented… All this has forced feminism to question its assumption of gender's universality' (ibid.).

In subsequent decades the WLM has been portrayed as a white, middle-class, racist movement which deservedly failed because of the determination not to recognise 'identity politics' or intersectionality. These detractors are likely to be those who do not share the politics of radical and revolutionary feminists and are happy to use such accusations to discredit them. Considering the extraordinary lengths to which the discussion and attempts to accommodate these identity politics went at the time, it might more reasonably be argued that many women in the WLM cared very much indeed about race, class and disability but not in ways which were productive. Rather, many were guilt-stricken that they were unable to protect themselves, or the resources that were so important to them, from attacks on these grounds. The internecine hostilities within the WLM and lesbian feminism were responses to outside forces such as the battles against racism that were being conducted in progressive politics at that time and the exigencies of the new political climate of Thatcherism. In the next and final chapter, the focus moves onto these external forces, which made it extremely difficult for a lesbian feminist movement formed in a very different political context to survive.

Bibliography

Attar, Dena (1983). An Open Letter on Anti-Semitism and Racism. *Trouble and Strife*, 1: 13–16.

Bellos, Linda (n.d.). The Limitations of Identity Politics. British Library, 'Spare Rib'. www.bl.uk/spare-rib/articles/the-limitations-of-identity-politics#sthash.wDiJGsZr.dpuf (accessed 21 October 2017).

Blackman, Inge, and Perry, Kathryn (1990). Skirting the Issue: Lesbian Fashion for the 1990s. *Feminist Review*, 34: 67–78.

Combahee River Collective (1983 [1978]). The Combahee River Collective Statement. In Smith, Barbara (ed.), *Home Girls: A Black Feminist Anthology*. New York: Kitchen Table Press, 272–282.

Cox, Laverne (2014, 11 March). Laverne Cox Talks about Intersectionality at Harvard. YouTube. www.youtube.com/watch?v=jY3F1pIxHMA11.

Crenshaw, Kimberlé (1991). Mapping the Margins, Identity Politics, and Violence against Women of Color. *Stanford Law Review*, 43 (6): 1241–1299.

Freeman, Jo (1972 [1970]). The Tyranny of Structurelessness. *Second Wave*, 2 (1): 20–25.

Heartfield, James (2017). *The Equal Opportunities Revolution*. London: Repeater Books.

Jones, Alethia, and Eubanks, Virginia (eds.) (2014). *Ain't Gonna Let Nobody Turn Me Around: Forty Years of Movement Building with Barbara Smith*. Albany, NY: State University of New York Press.

Kennedy, Florynce (1970). Institutionalized Oppression vs. the Female. In Morgan, Robin (ed.), *Sisterhood Is Powerful: An Anthology of Writings from the Women's Liberation Movement*. New York: Vintage Books, 492–500.

Lee, Anna (1988 [1981]). A Black Separatist. In Hoagland, Sarah Lucia, and Penelope, Julia (eds.), *For Lesbians Only: A Separatist Anthology*. London: Onlywomen Press, 83–91.

Lesbian Herstory Archives (n.d.). A Brief History. www.lesbianherstoryarchives.org/history.html (accessed 5 April 2017).

McNeil, Sandra (1996). Identity Politics. In Harne, Lynne, and Miller, Elaine (eds.), *All the Rage: Reasserting Radical Lesbian Feminism*. London: Women's Press, 52–58.

Packwood, Marlene (1983). The Colonel's Lady and Judy O'Grady: Sisters under the Skin? *Trouble and Strife*, 1: 7–12.

Penelope, Julia (1992). Do We Mean What We Say? Horizontal Hostility and the World We Would Create. In Penelope, Julia (ed.), *Call Me Lesbian: Lesbian Lives, Lesbian Theory*. Freedom, CA: Crossing Press, 60–77.

Ross, Freya Johnson (2018). From Municipal Feminism to the Equality Act: Legislation and Gender Equality Work in UK Local Government 1980–2010. *Women's Studies International Forum*, 66: 1–8.

Wistrich, Harriet, and Bindel, Julie (1989). An Ism of One's Own. *Revolutionary/Radical Feminist Newsletter*, 19, Autumn.

9

GRIEF

The demise of lesbian feminism

The loss of the WLM, women's culture and lesbian feminism was experienced as a major disaster by many lesbians who lived through that time. The emotional toll has been particularly well described by lesbian feminists from the US, writing in the journal *Trivia* in two issues dedicated to the question 'are lesbians going extinct?'. The editor, Lise Weil, describes the enormity of what was lost when that which she calls a 'movement of lovers' went into decline:

> What's easy to forget [is] how BIG it was, the change we (Lesbians) stood for – and in many cases brought about – back when we were busy reinventing the world. As big and as powerful as the energy produced by two women's bodies in love, which to me at the time was clearly the most creative force in the universe.
>
> *(Weil, 2010, emphasis in original)*

So important was lesbian feminism to Weil that, she says, 'when I look down on the life I'm living now it pales in the light of then'. She quotes US lesbian Maureen Brady, expressing the significance of the loss poignantly: 'It has often seemed that life nearly stopped after the movement stopped being a central force.' The dominant theme of the *Trivia* issues was the grief of the veterans of lesbian feminism at its demise. This final chapter looks at the way in which the changed political context contributed to this devastating loss.

Lesbian feminism declined in the US and in other countries, not just in the UK, so a UK-based explanation will not suffice to explain this. Lesbian feminism declined in concert with the Women's Liberation Movement, and both, as is the case with other social movements, declined in response to forces from outside, as well as internal divisions (Davenport, 2014). This book has looked at the internal divisions in some detail, but the outside forces have not been given so much attention. I will remedy that here, examining the development of individualistic, anti-egalitarian neoliberal politics in the US and in the UK, which had a devastating effect on left-wing and progressive politics in general, including the WLM and lesbian feminism. In the UK, the conservative turn included the passage in 1988 of legislation to prevent what the then government called 'the promotion of homosexuality', which had a chilling effect on lesbian and gay politics. The intellectual response to neoliberal politics was the development of a libertarian ideology, post-structuralism and its derivative in terms of lesbian and gay politics, namely queer theory. The intellectual climate changed dramatically, from one in which revolution was seen as desirable and possible to one in which those who still believed in such things were dismissed and pooh-poohed as simplistic fools and hopeless romantics. For feminists and lesbians, the new turn of mind was particularly catastrophic. Women who adopted postmodernism cast scorn on the idea that the word 'woman' could have any meaning, saying that it was 'essentialist' (Brodribb, 1992). The advance of women's studies and feminism into the academy was fatally undermined by these developments.

The internal divisions were largely a response to these outside forces. The internal divisions, as we have seen, include the development of pro-sex industry politics, to the detriment of the anti-violence and anti-pornography aspects of lesbian feminism. This was exemplified in what have been called the 'sex wars' between feminists in the 1980s, which were examined in previous chapters. But the 'sex wars' were the result of the growth of the sex industry in the malestream world. The versions that affected lesbian feminism, such as 'lesbian' pornography, reflected what was happening outside, where neoliberal policies led to the removal of any constraints on the burgeoning of a global sex industry, which carried major harms to women from Thailand to Toronto (Jeffreys, 2009). The forces that destroyed the WLM and lesbian feminism did not originate from within those movements but were embraced by some feminists and lesbians, with devastating results.

When did lesbian feminism die?

The scope of the WLM and women's/lesbian culture was so considerable, and reached into so many corners of the public and private lives of lesbians, that it is not possible to identify a specific date for the demise. When my interviewees were asked about this, they suggested various dates from the mid-1980s through to the late 1990s. These dates depended on when they realised that it was over, or when significant institutions crumbled or disappeared. The date at which the women's or lesbian culture faded away is different from the date at which the politics developed by lesbian feminists – theory and practice about male sexuality and sexual violence, heterosexuality and political lesbianism – became extinct. The political ideas were under attack from the early to mid-1980s, at a time when feminist bookstores, bands and theatre were still thriving. For instance, when I moved from London to Melbourne in 1991, I was delighted to be able to live on a street where there was evidence of the continued existence of a women's and lesbian culture. There was

172 The demise of lesbian feminism

a women's art gallery opening, there was a café on the street run by out lesbians, and a feminist bookstore and a feminist gift shop were around the corner. Within a few years they were all gone. Some feminist and lesbian resources have lingered on, amidst harsh opposition from men's rights activists, until much more recently. The remnants that survived included, until 2015, when it was finally harried into abeyance, the Michigan Women's Music Festival in the US.

Femi Otitoju puts the demise as early as 1984 (Femi Otitoju, interview 2013). She chose that date, she says, because it was around that time that the Greater London Council, which was funding many women's and lesbian groups and services, began to enforce an equal opportunities policy, which consisted of requiring funded organisations to have a representation of women from equality categories amongst their workers. The acceptance of funding by the GLC, she said, meant that feminists lost their ability to 'organise autonomously' in favour of 'the dependency on the money and the paid workers'. This could lead to the problem of organisations having to appoint workers to conform to an equality policy rather than for their politics. The effect could be that 'you fill these institutions or, worse still, just have a few of these women who have no feminist politics' (ibid.).

Lynne Harne argues that lesbian feminism 'dispersed' in the 1980s. She prefers the word 'dispersal' to 'demise' because it better conveys the gradual process by which this took place, and dates the dispersal to the early to mid-1980s. She explains that she left London in 1981, and by the time she returned, in 1984/5, there was no longer a movement, meaning that there wasn't 'a self-conscious body that organised meetings [that] called itself that. There was plenty of activism… But the movement, that wonderful, joyous explosion, had gone.' Although there were 'some things…still going on in the early 1990s', they 'began to…die' (Lynne Harne, interview 2013). Al Garthwaite explains that, although identity politics had caused great damage to lesbian feminism by the mid-1980s, there was a revival of sorts in the late 1980s as lesbians were jolted into action by the need to oppose legislation introduced by Margaret Thatcher's Conservative government to outlaw 'the promotion of homosexuality', under section 28 of the Local Government Act (1988). She considers that the real decline happened in the 1990s, but, she points out, lesbian feminists continued to be active in the areas of women's services, in local government and in universities, even though there was no longer a movement: 'Certain things had become much more mainstream, so there were lesbian feminists working in refuges… [T]here were women's committees, there were women's officers in universities, and they kept the flame going, so to speak. The women's officers kept the new Reclaim the Night marches going through the '90s' (Al Garthwaite, interview 2013).

There seems to be general agreement, though, that by the late 1980s the marvel that had been lesbian feminism was in serious decline, and by the 1990s lesbian feminist theorists were seeking to explain this (Jeffreys, 1993; Kitzinger and Perkins, 1993; Harne and Hutton, 1996). I wrote my 1993 book *The Lesbian Heresy: A Feminist Perspective on the Lesbian Sexual Revolution* from the slow-burning grief that many lesbian feminist activists had been feeling since the 'sex wars' in the mid- to late 1980s. What I call the 'lesbian sexual revolution' entailed the promotion of lesbian sadomasochism and a newly constructed industry of pornography created by lesbians, many of whom had been exploited in the malestream sex industry, for other lesbians. Similar concerns caused my interviewees Lynne Harne and Elaine Hutton to produce the edited collection *All The Rage: Reasserting Radical Lesbian Feminism* in 1996. In this book, writers seek to explain the decline. Elaine Hutton, for instance, writes about what she considered one factor, which is the disappearance of feminist and lesbian publications and the creation of feminism-free lesbian publications from gay male publishers such as *Diva*, which incorporated masculine and malestream views of what lesbians should be. We wrote from our feelings of despair and to understand what had happened to our lesbian feminist world.

The emotional effect of the demise

Like the US lesbian feminists quoted at the opening of this chapter, their counterparts in the UK were desolated by the demise of lesbian feminism. Julie Bindel remembers

> getting very, very despondent and bitter and angry at around the time – it was about '87 and '88... And Lynn Alderson had come around for dinner, ...and she said: 'There's no longer a women's movement; we've got to wait for the next movement.' And I remember like it was yesterday, and I went berserk.
>
> *(Julie Bindel, interview 2013)*

Al Garthwaite speaks of being extremely depressed at the demise of lesbian feminism. She says she became 'really, really depressed... I became very depressed, and remained depressed for some years.' The aspect that was most depressing was the development of sadomasochism, 'because lesbian feminists' had been 'offering something that was positive and different from role-playing' and 'heterosexual norms', whereas the sadomasochists were 'just...whipping each other, and that was greatly depressing' (Al Garthwaite, interview 2013).

The effect could be not just emotional but a threat to economic survival. Lynne Harne explains that, when the Greater London Council was abolished by the Conservative government in 1986, 'I lost my job...and...all the groups I was politically active in were beginning to die away gradually' (Lynne Harne, interview 2013). She reports being devastated by the advent of queer politics: 'I think we felt...really defeated by the lesbians who had embraced queer politics and pornography.' The adoption of sex industry practices and products was particularly depressing. She remembers

> in the early '90s going to a festival with a friend in Clissold Park, and there was this lesbian stall with all these dildos on it – just penises, basically. I was thinking this is the absolute end. If this...is what lesbianism is, this is the absolute end of – and how dare they? [...]I mean, it was awful.
>
> *(ibid.)*

174 The demise of lesbian feminism

'Kate' talks of the devastating impact of the changed political climate in the late 1980s on many aspects of her life, such as what she was able to achieve in her work as an academic and in the bringing up of her children: 'It wasn't just lesbian feminism drying up; it was everything that I minded about, that I was trying to achieve politically, through my job. And through the way that I brought up the kids' ('Kate', interview 2013). 'Life became,' she says, 'much more brutal, and much more frightening, because there were all kinds of things that you had to be extremely careful, or not to say quite as overtly as one once would.' The changed political climate was responsible for more than just the loss of lesbian feminism, 'Lesbian feminism copped it, but so did a whole range of other things', which included there being 'much more challenge', so that, 'if kids in lectures said things that were unacceptable, other students would pick it up. So, there was a lot that went with that. That made life much more frightening, drafty, chilly' (ibid.). This chilly climate was the effect of the conservative turn in politics.

The conservative turn in politics

A conservative turn in politics created a political backlash in direct opposition to the developing lesbian and gay politics of the 1980s. In 1979 the Conservative government headed by Margaret Thatcher was elected, and over the next decade a savage assault was unleashed against the progress that feminists, lesbians and gay men had made in the policy and practice of local government, and the provision of services. The Conservatives then remained in power until 1997. By the mid-1980s the new government had gained the confidence to enact an agenda of 'conservatising' not just state institutions such as the railways, through privatisation, but the whole way in which citizens related to each other, and the tone of the society. The post-war social compact, of state responsibility for its citizens and the welfare state, was overthrown in favour of a harsher atmosphere of individual responsibility and competition. The backlash was spearheaded by the right-wing press and carried out by the Tory government. These right-wing forces used the issue of lesbian and gay rights to encourage the spleen of Conservative voters and to attack the Labour Party and what was called by the media the 'loony Left' (Jones and Mahony, 1989). It was hard for Labour politicians to support the social liberalism that undergirded local authority provision for lesbians and gays while anti-gay hatred was being stirred up amongst their potential voters in white working-class constituencies.

The first salvo in the pillorying of lesbian and gay activism took place in 1983, in response to the publication by Gay Men's Press of a book for children by a Danish heterosexual woman author, Susanne Bösche, called *Jenny Lives with Eric and Martin*. Bösche wrote the book to encourage discussion between children and adults about the issue of children living with gay parents (Bösche, 2000). It was a black and white picture book which showed a girl child engaging in everyday pursuits with the two gay men she lived with. Its publication caused an outcry from the right-wing press and Tory politicians, as Colin Clews describes: '*The Sun*, as part of its ongoing campaign against 'Loony Left' Labour authorities ran the frontpage headline, *"Vile Book*

In School: Pupils See Pictures Of Gay Lovers", claiming that the book was available in school libraries.' He explains that the report about school libraries containing the book was a lie, 'because the book, wasn't – nor ever had been – but then *The Sun* has never let the facts get in the way of a good story' (Clews, 2012).

The right-wing campaign against the book fuelled the conservative backlash, which was in response to the success of tireless lesbian and gay activists in the early 1980s in trade unions, in local authorities and the Labour Party to change attitudes and get a recognition of lesbian and gay rights. 1985 was a significant year for the success of this struggle. It saw the publication of a charter on lesbian and gay rights by the GLC, called 'Changing the World', and the opening of the first Lesbian and Gay Centre in London, funded by the GLC. In that year both the Trades Union Congress and the Labour Party conference passed resolutions on lesbian and gay rights. All of this was achieved against a continuous backdrop of considerable opposition in the right-wing press, which was emboldened by increased hostility to gay men in reaction to the AIDS epidemic. Davina Cooper describes the government backlash in relation to the policy and practice of the London borough of Haringey, where she was a councillor (Cooper, 1989). She was also a member of groups that were formed to support the 'positive images' policy adopted by the council in 1986, after the setting up of the council's first lesbian and gay unit. The idea behind positive images was that they would counteract the discrimination suffered by lesbians and gay men.

The response to Haringey's plan for lesbians and gays was a debate in the House of Lords on 28 July, in which the education secretary set up an inquiry. In the middle of a considerable backlash in the conservative press, an election took place in 1987. A nominally independent group called the Committee for a Free Britain launched a series of adverts which give a taste of the extreme hostility being whipped up against lesbians and gay men. One of the adverts contained a photo of a woman with the words 'My name is Betty Sheridan. I'm married with two children. *And I'm scared.* If you vote Labour they'll go on teaching my kids about GAYS AND LESBIANS instead of giving them proper lessons' (quoted in Cooper, 1989: 52; emphasis in original). Meanwhile, a press statement from the Conservative Party in Tottenham, which is part of the borough of Haringey, described the borough's lesbian and gay unit as 'a greater threat to family life than Adolf Hitler' (quoted in ibid.: 57). Newspapers such as the *Daily Mail* and *The Sun* were heavily involved, in the early 1980s, in ridiculing any advances by lesbians and gays, and seeking to stimulate outrage amongst the straight populace. The press campaign culminated in a piece of legislation which was designed to prevent further progress, section 28 of the Local Government Act in 1988, which prohibited 'the promotion of homosexuality'. The precise wording of the legislation was as follows:

Local authorities shall not:

(a) promote homosexuality or publish material for the promotion of homosexuality;
(b) promote the teaching in any maintained school of the acceptability of homosexuality as a pretended family relationship.

176 The demise of lesbian feminism

Section 28 did not result in legal cases, and no one was prosecuted in the period before its repeal in 2003 (Gillan, 2003). But its effect was to chill the political climate and cast a shadow on all the politics that gay activists were involved in around local government and the areas controlled by it, such as education.

It was lesbian feminist activism, however, that posed the greatest degree of challenge to conservative prejudices. Many lesbians became involved, alongside gay men, in the opposition to section 28. Indeed, the most memorable protest against the legislation was conducted by three lesbians who abseiled from the public gallery onto the floor of the House of Lords in outrage at its passing (Brown, 2017). The politics of the lesbian campaigners was very different from that of the gay men, however. The male gay activists had regularly worked against lesbian feminist ideas and practice in local authority activism. In relation to the new legislation, they chose to defend themselves by making claims that the lesbian feminists totally disagreed with, such as that homosexuality was innate and biological and thus could not be, successfully, 'promoted'. They retreated to a politics of biological determinism, which they honed in response to the wave of gay-hating unleashed as the AIDS epidemic hit. This politics asserts that homosexuals are just 'born that way' and therefore deserve respect like any other of god's creatures. This was the politics that the local authorities usually took up when they wanted to be 'progressive', as Cooper explains: 'Haringey Council treated sexual orientation as another aspect of the borough's cultural diversity: a fixed immutable characteristic. Steve King, council leader, stated, "Nobody can be taught to be lesbian or gay"' (Cooper, 1989: 67). This was entirely different from the politics of lesbian feminists, who challenged the institution of heterosexuality, asserting that any woman can, and perhaps should, be a lesbian and that there was no point just seeking toleration when a revolution was called for.

Lesbian feminist commentators consider that section 28 was the response to the much more challenging work of lesbians, rather than just the assimilationist approach of gay men. The mid-1980s was the moment when the campaigning activities of lesbian feminists were just beginning to gain traction. Margaret Jackson asserts that the government move to legislate against the promotion of homosexuality was in response to the way lesbian feminists were developing theory and action against the institutionalisation of heterosexuality: 'The Conservative government's recent and unprecedented attempt to intervene in sex education in schools can be seen as a response to the challenge to the institution of heterosexuality which has been developing within the current phase of feminism' (Jackson, 1989: 18). Sue Sanders and Gill Spraggs, too, attribute the right-wing backlash to the successes of lesbian feminists in getting Labour-controlled councils to put in place feminist and pro-lesbian policies: 'The policies of the so-called 'loony Left'…began to develop following many years' hard work and agitation by lesbian activists' (Sanders and Spraggs, 1989: 83).

After the legislation had been adopted, the climate of lesbian feminist activism was chilled. Although there was general agreement that the way the legislation was framed could not easily be used to circumscribe the pro-lesbian and pro-gay

The demise of lesbian feminism **177**

policies and practices of local authorities, there was much fear and tension and the social climate was changed. The chilling effect of the changing political climate is well described by Lynne Harne: 'Do you remember the *Daily Mail* and the *Daily Express* were saying the GLC is…funding all these black lesbian disabled feminists and is not concerned about ordinary women' (Lynne Harne, interview 2013). Lynne explains the importance of the feminist activism that had taken place through the GLC by pointing out that it did, after feminist campaigning, 'get sexist advertising banned on the Tube'. This, she thinks was 'one of the best things that the GLC ever did'.

My interviewee 'Kate' explains that the closing down by Margaret Thatcher's government of institutions and services that had provided shelter to lesbian and feminist politics made women feel threatened and exposed, and changed what they were able to say. The Inner London Education Authority (ILEA) was abolished in 1990. It had promoted a great deal of equality work through schools and teacher education in universities. Thereafter, 'Kate' says, teachers and lecturers had to be 'very careful', lest they appear in the *Daily Mail* being quoted as 'loony Lefties' ('Kate', interview 2013). The effect of this backlash was that 'life got extremely difficult for people in the public services – or women in the public services particularly, who were trying to change practices in institutions outside their own particular fold'. The conservative backlash undermined lesbian feminism in other ways, too. As well as leading to the abolition of the GLC and the ILEA, which had supported and funded lesbian projects, it also led to a tightening up of the rules as to who could claim benefits, so that economic survival for many lesbian feminist activists who had worked full-time for the movement without pay became much more difficult.

The changing political climate of the late 1980s put other feminist institutions and resources in jeopardy too, such as feminist bookstores, which were important community hubs, and the practice of squatting. Chris Wall identifies the end of the lesbian squatting community as arriving in 1977, when the Conservatives gained control of the Greater London Council and embarked on a policy of transferring GLC-owned properties to the inner London boroughs and ending the practice of giving out licenses to squat (Wall, 2017). Squatters were given the opportunity to get rehoused in council flats or to set up housing co-ops to keen control of their houses. Despite these changes, lesbian squatting continued in some areas to the end of the 1990s.

The Conservative government took against state funding for alternative bookshops. There were parliamentary questions about such funding, and, as Lucy Delap explains, Thatcher 'declared herself utterly revolted' by the materials on sale in 1988 in a Haringey radical bookshop which received grants from Haringey Council (Delap, 2016: 189). The passing of section 28 chilled the climate for feminist and lesbian bookselling, as schools and libraries ceased to buy books from them. Other factors in the demise included the fact that, as feminist publishing became more established, malestream bookstores began to stock the titles, and this took patronage away from the feminist stores. A factor quite specific to the demise of feminist and alternative bookstores in general was the Net Book Agreement,

178 The demise of lesbian feminism

introduced in 1991, which set a minimum price for selling British books and led to the discounting of books by supermarkets and chain bookstores, with the result that smaller players could not compete. Lucy Delap points out that Thatcher-era austerity and central attacks on local government in the mid- to late 1980s caused 'significant damage to bookselling' across the board (Delap, 2016: 192).

Queering lesbian feminism

The verb 'to queer', before it was taken up by gay male theorists, meant 'to harm or cause damage', and the advent of queer politics and queer theory certainly damaged lesbian feminism. Queer theory took up the ideas created in the 1980s by the theorists of postmodernism. The change in the intellectual climate in the academy that these bodies of masculine thought represented made it hard even to articulate feminism and lesbian feminism. This change came in two tranches: postmodernism in the early 1980s and queer theory in the early 1990s. Theorists who adopted postmodernism, most usually called post-structuralism when applied to theory, promoted the ideas of a band of French male intellectuals such as Jacques Derrida, Jacques Lacan and Michel Foucault (Brodribb, 1992). The ideas were expressed in a manner that was hard to understand, but the import was to dismiss movements for social transformation such as socialism and feminism as unsophisticated relics of an old-fashioned way of thinking – i.e. that social change could be achieved by movements of the oppressed. The idea that there could be a better future, which could be worked towards, was called 'teleological' and much derided. The very idea that you could speak about 'women' was questioned. The concept of 'women' was seen as 'essentialist' – i.e. believing in fixed categories – because, for postmodernists, everything was entirely flexible and in a state of flux.

Postmodern ideas particularly infected the way in which sexuality was thought about, because the favourite theorist was Michel Foucault, who was gay and wrote *The History of Sexuality* in three volumes (Foucault, 1978). Not only were the main postmodern theorists men, but they had no consciousness that women existed or needed to be thought about. Their ideas were adopted by some feminists, and this made them more respectable within the academy. They entered the sneering game of superiority that postmodern theorists played with poor, benighted politicos such as socialists, radical feminists and lesbian feminists. For the radical feminists who had entered or sought to enter academia in the 1980s through the adoption of women's studies as an academic discipline or through feminist scholarship in other areas, postmodernism was a serious blow. The take-up of the ideas of postmodern feminists, such as the queer theorist Judith Butler, in the academy made life for radical feminists very difficult. They became the darlings of the male establishment, because they paid homage to these men and effectively raised the drawbridge against radical feminists through editorship of scholarly journals, through hiring practices, through teaching and through writing against us (Bell and Klein, 1996: sect. 3). Although some radical feminist academics did go on to forge successful careers in this increasingly hostile climate, many more found the odds stacked against them.

The demise of lesbian feminism **179**

My interviewee 'Kate' is incisive in her description of the effect of postmodernism on the situation of feminists in the universities. She calls it 'all this post-modern up your jumper', and connects its arrival with the neoliberal takeover of political space at the time:

> It was connected… The rise of individualism, through the neoliberal take-over – it wasn't just social justice that went, it was all the sociologies, if you like, that went with them. You couldn't talk about social divisions and power because it was all more nuanced than that. You couldn't say anything about anything. Except the text. I can remember saying that at a conference, and a guy talked about rape as a text, and I went ballistic.
>
> *(Kate, interview 2013)*

The US social movements historian Barbara Epstein argues that the adoption of 'high theory', which, from the 1980s onwards, meant postmodernism or queer theory, combined with the enforcement of neoliberal policies in universities, was very damaging to feminism and helped to bring the 'women's movement' to an end. She wrote in 2001: 'In the arena of high theory, the most prestigious sector of academic feminism, competition and the pursuit of status are all too often uppermost' (Epstein, 2001). She says: 'The pursuit of status, prestige, and stardom has turned feminist and progressive values on their head. Instead of the 1960s' radical feminist critique of hierarchy, we have a kind of revelling in hierarchy and in the benefits that come with rising to the top of it.'

Radical feminists rejected postmodern theory (Brodribb, 1992; Bell and Klein, 1996). We were protected from falling under its thrall by a profound scepticism about what male-dominated universities and male intellectuals considered proper theory – i.e. the wisdom of male dominance. The intellectual fathers produced ideas from their own heads and with no reference to women or the suffering we experienced at the hands of men. The creation of radical feminist theory was stimulated by the criticism and rejection of these male theorists, such as Marx and Freud, and later Derrida, Lacan and Foucault. Radical feminist theorists did not use men's theory as a reference point and did not cite men in their writings, unless a particular man who had learnt from feminist thought made a really interesting contribution, and that was very rare. Radical feminists said that theory for feminism needed to come from the consideration of women's experience, and that men in ivory towers who created ideas from their own experience as members of the dominant class in relation to women were worth examining in order to take their ideas apart, but not to provide a foundation for our thinking.

The second onslaught on feminist politics, this time specifically lesbian feminist politics, was the advent of queer theory. By the time this took place, in the early 1990s, lesbian feminism was well past its peak, because of many of the forces described in this book and in this chapter. Its impact was to entirely remasculinise lesbian and gay theory, so that lesbian feminist insights were wiped out and the word 'lesbian' stowed in a side cupboard (see Walters, 1996). Male gay activists constructed queer

180 The demise of lesbian feminism

politics in the early 1990s as an in-your-face riposte to the exacerbated hatred of gay men that arose in response to the AIDS epidemic, and lesbians did not figure in it. From a lesbian perspective, this male-designed politics was deeply problematic. Lesbian feminists used the term 'lesbian' to make lesbians visible, so that by the early 1980s it was usual for mixed gay politics to not only include the word but to put it first, as in 'lesbian and gay', in the names of conferences, journals, etc. Queer politics submerged the separate existence and personhood of lesbians within that of men, by using a new generic term: 'queer'. 'Queers' were male, and if women wanted to get in on the act they had to adopt a descriptor; they were 'queer women', as the term 'queer men' was not used because it was not necessary. Queer theory was an application of postmodern theory to queer politics.

The term 'lesbian', which had always been so important to the visibility of lesbians and our very different experience and politics, gradually fell out of use, so that, at the time of writing, many lesbians internationally are lamenting the 'disappearing' L-word (Morris, 2016). Queer politics and theory were entirely gay-male-orientated. As I explain in my book *Unpacking Queer Politics* (2003), the agenda was about the promotion and protection of a male sexuality focussed upon objectification and exploitation and centred on themes of public sex and pornography. When women who identified as feminists took up these ideas, they undermined feminist scholarship. The most well-known female figure of queer theory, Judith Butler, argues that performing as some 'gender' other than the one you had enforced upon you – i.e. men cross-dressing and lesbians acting butch – was transgressive and transformative (Butler, 1990). Instead, it empowered the ideology of male cross-dressers who started the transgender activist movement, which does, in the present, equate the socially constructed sex roles that gender represents with biological sex. This deliberate obfuscation has enabled them to get legislation changed to recognise them as 'women' and create havoc by destroying the protections and affirmative-action policies that feminists had struggled for decades to achieve (Jeffreys, 2014).

Alix Dobkin, the renowned lesbian feminist songwriter and singer from the US, commented in 2016 on the impact of queer and gender studies (Dobkin and Tatnall, 2016). She says that men felt left out of women's studies, so demanded its substitution by gender studies, with the result that

> [t]he final nail in the coffin of women being distinct was hammered in. Now students were concerning themselves with the variety of sexes available to them... Who were women? Who were men? Sex designation became a choice. Somehow the connection to patriarchy...got lost... 'Gender' replaced women in the academy and 'queer' disappeared Lesbians in the community.
>
> *(ibid.: 226)*

The effect of these changes on the intellectual zeitgeist was to create a very hostile climate for lesbian feminist academics and students. This changed climate was consolidated by the management revolution that hit universities in the 2000s, through the practice of corporatisation.

The demise of lesbian feminism **181**

Professionalisation of women's studies

In response to these forces, the field of women's studies was professionalised and lost its name and focus. In the late 1970s and 1980s many lesbian feminists, including me, were involved in teaching women's and lesbian studies outside universities. We taught evening classes under the umbrella of the Workers' Educational Association, or extramural classes attached to universities but at one remove. In the 1990s many of these same lesbians, me included, were able to move into tenured positions in universities as women's studies courses were set up in these institutions, and feminist and lesbian approaches to geography, politics, law and sociology were incorporated into traditional subjects. In the halcyon days of women's studies, young women and older women coming back into education could experience exciting and radical feminist education at BA and MA level, which could make them into feminists or strengthen their feminist politics. This all changed in the 1990s, because the academy was a strongly masculine sphere that was not welcoming to feminist education for long.

Rosemary Auchmuty and I used to teach women's history evening classes together in the early 1980s. Rosemary explains the excitement of moving into the academy in the early 1990s:

> And what was interesting about the jobs that we went into [was that] we'd been critiquing, we'd been writing and all those things, and now we were actually inside the academy… We were doing women's studies, we were doing lesbian studies, we were doing lesbian feminist approaches, and so on.
>
> *(Rosemary Auchmuty, interview 2013)*

This process, she says, was linked to the demise of lesbian feminism because, once lesbians were in the academy, they had to make compromises: 'Well, the connection is that you can't be "pure"… Well, up to a point what you produce has got to be in the service of the academy.' Lesbian feminists such as Rosemary and I went into the academy from activism, with very different ideas on pedagogy from the malestream world, but being inside the academy did affect us. The 'latitude' that Rosemary says that she had in the university came to an end, she considers, at the end of the 1990s. At that time women's studies and lesbian studies were being shut down: 'They didn't last that long…and then it was gone, I mean – that was it.' Rosemary points out that, even before that time, the student body had changed, from feminists and lesbians who were keenly interested and involved in lesbian feminist politics to a new cohort who rejected those same politics; 'In the early days I used to get people who would read – because I used to set them – the political lesbian paper, and they would read it and they'd become lesbians. I mean, you know, we used to have these debates… [T]hat certainly wasn't going to happen after that' (ibid.). Where women's studies courses were not shut down they were forced, or chose so that they might survive, to change their name to 'gender studies'. This removed the focus from women and fitted with the postmodern and queer emphasis on 'gender' rather than women's oppression as the focus of their rather esoteric endeavours.

182 The demise of lesbian feminism

These processes were exacerbated by the corporatisation of the universities. In the late 1990s and 2000s the higher education sector in the UK came under increasing pressure from neoliberal ideologues and government funding cuts to corporatise. Corporatisation made universities into semi-private businesses. They were expected to make a profit, instead of existing according to liberal principles as to the social benefit of education for its own sake. Courses were cut that did not fit the new model, particularly those relating to women's studies or anything overtly political and critical of dominant culture and politics. Management structures became more muscular and bullying, creating masculine work cultures that were in contradiction to women's interests. To get or maintain academic jobs, aspirants were required to pursue and acquire outside funding, becoming cash cows for their institutions. Grant-awarding bodies that distributed this funding acted as gatekeepers, able to determine what research was done, and it was not going to be radical or lesbian feminist. As the Australian law professor Margaret Thornton explains, these processes have effected a remasculinisation of the academy, such that the ideal academic has now become 'a "technopreneur" - a scientific researcher with business acumen who produces academic capitalism' (Thornton, 2013: 127). All of this was problematic for the pursuit of any critical research and teaching in universities (Nair, 2017). Even where feminist teachers managed to survive, they were likely to have to move into more malestream areas and drop or marginalise their feminist interests. A climate which was already hostile to radical feminist ideas became positively toxic. Little remained of the climate of the 1980s, when women's studies courses and feminist research and teaching were incorporated into universities.

The professionalisation of women's services

Many lesbians founded or chose to work in services against male violence, such as women's refuges and rape crisis centres. Jan McLeod, from Glasgow, where she was a stalwart of the Glasgow Rape Crisis Centre for decades, suggests that one reason for the demise of lesbian feminism might be the professionalisation of these women's services (Jan McLeod, interview 2013). She says that lesbians were in the majority in the women's organisations founded in the 1970s and 1980s and 'heavily influenced' their practices and ideologies. These lesbians 'had a rather unique [sic] experience and huge skills and abilities for things like campaigning and organising and all sorts of stuff'. But when the organisations changed they

> became professionalised and they got funding, and there is just a huge difference between being a voluntary group and – you know – working on that collective and on a consciousness-raising level and being a funded group. [...] [B]ut when you get considerable amounts of money you have to provide a professionalised service, and there is no time, or very little time, for the things that applied to collective working and feminism.

> *(ibid.)*

The lesbians who set up and maintained women's services found they had little time for feminist activism.

My interviewees discussed the way in which the achievement of local government funding for women's services could contribute to the demise of lesbian feminist activism. Two institutions in London were abolished by the Conservative government in the 1980s, because they were perceived to be too left-wing: the Greater London Council, in 1986, and the Inner London Education Authority, in 1990. Both had funded and promoted women's equality and women's services. I discussed in the last chapter whether the London Lesbian Archive was negatively affected by getting funding, with the effect that it collapsed in acrimony, whereas the New York Lesbian Archive, which never sought external funding, survives. Jan McLeod considers that some of the demands entailed by getting funding for women's services could undermine activism, and Femi Otitoju (Femi Otitoju, interview 2013) speaks of the effect of the funders' priorities having a potentially negative effect. Some of my interviewees were much more positive, however. Lynn Alderson considers that local government funding was crucial in enabling women's services to survive during the backlash. She says, 'I actually think that local government…became a stronghold because, once we got Thatcher in, life was impossible. She went for us deliberately. She went specifically for us' (Lynn Alderson, interview 2013). Lesbians in local government and women's services were supported by their employers and funders, so that, Lynn says, 'we hung on in there and the council hung on in there with us, and by and large didn't just sack us to save the money'. Lynn, like many other lesbians, was working in local government equal opportunity units, and though, as she says, 'I wouldn't call it radical politics', she does think

> that the kind of equal opportunity politics had its uses in terms of looking at services, changing the ethos of a community, that kind of thing, and it was a genuine attempt to bring in race, class, women, disability – a whole range of those areas where people were disadvantaged, and to do something about that.
>
> *(ibid.)*

For decades women's anti-violence services served as reservoirs of lesbian feminism, where the ideas and practices could be to some extent preserved. Most recently, these reservoirs have come under threat (Laville, 2014). Because of the neoliberal priorities of the UK government, austerity and small statism, local authorities have been forced to tender out their refuges for women escaping men's violence to the lowest bidder. The successful bidders are likely to be charities that have no feminist understanding. They can put in cheap bids because they rely on volunteers or have charitable status to avoid taxes, so that feminist organisations are unable to compete. The new managers may be successful because they tender for services that do not even include refuges but other less effective methods of helping women. At the same time, many refuges have been closed because of funding cuts.

There were many forces involved in the demise of lesbian feminism. In previous chapters I looked at forces that harmed lesbian feminism from the inside, the politics of sadomasochism and the politics of identity. In this chapter I have examined the forces from outside, such as major changes in the political turn of mind, austerity, anti-egalitarian conservatism and changes in the theoretical zeitgeist, such as post-modernism and queer theory, which marginalised feminism in general. Although there is much hesitation amongst my interviewees and other commentators to put a date to the moment when the demise of lesbian feminism took place, it is quite evident today that this has happened. In the following postscript I give a picture of the extremely hostile climate that now exists for lesbians and lesbian feminism and argue that there is a great need to recreate this movement.

Bibliography

Bell, Diane, and Klein, Renate (eds.) (1996). *Radically Speaking: Feminism Reclaimed.* Melbourne: Spinifex Press.

Bösche, Susanne (2000, 31 January). Jenny, Eric, Martin and Me. *The Guardian.* www.theguardian.com/books/2000/jan/31/booksforchildrenandteenagers.features11 (accessed 3 January 2018).

Brodribb, Somer (1992). *Nothing Mat(t)ers: A Feminist Critique of Postmodernism.* Melbourne: Spinifex Press.

Brown, Jessica (2017). Here's Why the 'Sexual Avengers' Stuck a Sign to the House of Lords. *The Independent.* https://indy100.com/article/sexual-avengers-plaque-house-of-lords-lesbian-protest-section-28-7595256.

Butler, Judith (1990). *Gender Trouble: Feminism and the Subversion of Identity.* New York: Routledge.

Carpenter, Val (1988). Amnesia and Antagonism in the Youth Service. In Cant, Bob, and Hemmings, Susan (eds.), *Radical Records: Thirty Years of Lesbian and Gay History.* London: Routledge, 169–180.

Chesler, Phyllis (1972). *Women and Madness.* New York: Avon.

Clews, Colin (2012, 28 June). 1983. Book: Jenny Lives with Eric and Martin. Gay In the 80s. www.gayinthe80s.com/2012/06/1983-book-jenny-lives-with-eric-and-martin.

Cooper, Davina (1989). Positive Images in Haringey: A Struggle for Identity. In Jones, Carol, and Mahony, Pat (eds.), *Learning Our Lines: Sexuality and Social Control in Education.* London: Women's Press, 46–78.

Davenport, Christian (2014). *How Social Movements Die: Repression and Demobilization of the Republic of New Africa.* Cambridge: Cambridge University Press.

Delap, Lucy (2016). Feminist Bookshops, Reading Cultures and the Women's Liberation Movement in Great Britain, c. 1974–2000. *History Workshop Journal,* 81: 171–196.

Dixon, Jane, Salvat, Gilly, and Skeates, Jane (1989). North London Young Lesbian Group: Specialist Work within the Youth Service. In Jones, Carol, and Mahony, Pat (eds.), *Learning Our Lines: Sexuality and Social Control in Education.* London: Women's Press, 232–248.

Dobkin, Alix, and Tatnall, Sally (2016). The Erasure of Lesbians. In Barrett, Ruth (ed.), *Female Erasure: What You Need to Know about Gender Politics' War on Women, the Female Sex and Human Rights.* Pacific Palisades, CA: Tidal Time Publishing, 225–228.

Epstein, Barbara (2001). What Happened to the Women's Movement? *Monthly Review,* 53 (1): 1–13.

Foucault, Michel (1978). *The History of Sexuality,* vol. I. London: Allen Lane.

Gillan, Audrey (2003, 17 November). Section 28 … Gone but Not Forgotten. *The Guardian.* www.theguardian.com/politics/2003/nov/17/uk.gayrights.

Harne, Lynne (2016). How to Become a Lesbian in 30 Minutes, Part 1. Lesbian History Group. https://lesbianhistorygroup.wordpress.com/tag/great-london-council.

Harne, Lynne, and Hutton, Elaine (1996). *All the Rage: Reasserting Radical Lesbian Feminism.* London: Women's Press.

Hutton, Elaine (2016). How to Become a Lesbian in 30 Minutes. Part 2. Lesbian History Group. https://lesbianhistorygroup.wordpress.com/2016/02.

Jackson, Margaret (1989). Sexuality and Struggle: Feminism, Sexology and the Social Construction of Sexuality. In Jones, Carol, and Mahony, Pat (eds.), *Learning Our Lines: Sexuality and Social Control in Education.* London: Women's Press, 1–22.

Jeffreys, Sheila (1993). *The Lesbian Heresy: A Feminist Perspective on the Lesbian Sexual Revolution.* London: Women's Press.

Jeffreys, Sheila (2003). *Unpacking Queer Politics.* Cambridge: Polity Press.

Jeffreys, Sheila (2009). *The Industrial Vagina: The Political Economy of the Global Sex Trade.* Abingdon, UK: Routledge.

Jeffreys, Sheila (2014). *Gender Hurts: A Feminist Analysis of the Politics of Transgenderism.* Abingdon, UK: Routledge.

Jones, Carol, and Mahony, Pat (eds.) (1989). *Learning Our Lines: Sexuality and Social Control in Education.* London: Women's Press.

Kitzinger, Celia, and Perkins, Rachel (1993). *Changing Our Minds: Lesbian Feminism and Psychology.* New York: New York University Press.

Laville, Sandra (2014, 3 August). Domestic Violence Refuge Provision at Crisis Point, Warn Charities. *The Guardian.* www.theguardian.com/society/2014/aug/03/domestic-violence-refuge-crisis-women-closure-safe-houses.

Morris, Bonnie (2016). *The Disappearing L: Erasure of Lesbian Spaces and Culture.* Albany, NY: State University of New York Press.

Nair, Yasmin (2017, 7 June). The Dangerous Academic Is an Extinct Species. Current Affairs. www.currentaffairs.org/2017/04/the-dangerous-academic-is-an-extinct-species.

Raymond, Janice G. (1986). *A Passion for Friends: Towards a Philosophy of Female Affection.* London: Women's Press.

Sanders, Sue, and Spraggs, Gill (1989). Section 28 and Education. In Jones, Carol, and Mahony, Pat (eds.), *Learning Our Lines: Sexuality and Social Control in Education.* London: Women's Press, 79–128.

Thornton, Margaret (2013). The Mirage of Merit: Reconstitution the 'Ideal Academic'. *Australian Feminist Studies,* 28 (76): 127–143.

Wall, Chris (2017, 18 May). Sisterhood, Sawdust and Squatting: Radical Lesbian Lives in 1970s Hackney. Lesbian History Group. https://lesbianhistorygroup.wordpress.com/2017/05/18/sisterhood-sawdust-and-squatting-radical-lesbian-lives-in-1970s-hackney-christine-wall.

Walters, Suzanna Danuta (1996). From Here to Queer: Radical Feminism, Postmodernism, and the Lesbian Menace (or, Why Can't a Woman Be More Like a Fag?). *Signs,* 21 (4): 830–869.

Weil, Lise (2010). Are Lesbians Going Extinct? (Editorial). *Trivia: Voices of Feminism,* 10. www.triviavoices.com/issue-10-are-lesbians-going-extinct-1.html.

POSTSCRIPT

The erasure of lesbians

At the time of writing this book it is very hard for lesbians in the UK or the US to find any women's or lesbian spaces. Almost all the resources I talk about in previous chapters have been lost: feminist bookstores, women's centres, clubs and discos, archives, poetry and writing groups, presses, festivals and conferences. The word 'lesbian' is barely used in public, and many euphemisms are used by lesbians to conceal their lesbianism, such as 'queer' and 'non-binary'. This situation is being called by concerned lesbian feminists 'the erasure of lesbians' (Dobkin and Tatnall, 2016). There is no space here to present a detailed history of what happened to lesbian politics in the period between the decline of lesbian feminism in the 1990s and the spatial and conceptual desert that exists today. I shall, instead, describe some of the challenges faced by lesbian feminists now who are beginning the task of recreating a lesbian feminist movement.

The loss of lesbian spaces

In the last decade the issue of the loss of lesbian spaces, and therefore lesbian community and culture, became an issue in feminism and in lesbian and gay and fashionable online magazines. This problem was flagged in two issues of the American feminist journal *Trivia*, in 2010, titled 'Are Lesbians Going Extinct?' (Weil, 2010). In these issues, lesbian feminists mourn how much they had once had. The disappearance of all the places in which lesbians could meet, socialise, hold discussions, perform, listen to music, dance, buy books, exhibit artworks had, as the last of these resources closed down, finally become a matter of more general concern. The disappearance of lesbian language, spaces, community and culture was named 'lesbian erasure', and, as a writer at the feminist online magazine *A Room of Our Own* put it in 2015, 'This is about the erasure of lesbians, which is pandemic. Lesbian erasure is global: lesbians are being erased from every aspect of society, in both state-sponsored male violence and individuated violence' (Brownworth, 2015). Bonnie Morris's book *The Disappearing L: Erasure of Lesbian Spaces and Culture* (2016) details the extent of the backlash against lesbian feminism in the US, culminating in the loss of the Michigan Music Festival in 2015.

Lesbian meeting places had to change to 'gender-neutral' venues under pressure from queer and trans-identified people, mainly men, who complained about them being transphobic and exclusionary (Cox, 2016). Susan Cox gives a breakdown of the losses in the feminist online magazine *Feminist Current*, explaining: 'San Francisco, known as one of the most prominent LGBT communities in the world, doesn't have *a single lesbian bar*, and New York City's lesbian spaces have dwindled severely. There are no explicitly lesbian bars in Vancouver (Lick – once the city's only lesbian bar – closed in 2011)' (ibid., emphasis in original). She points out that gay men are not experiencing this problem, and their resources are intact. Lesbian magazines and online resources have closed down too (Binstock, 2016). Social media, which had been touted as such an advantage for feminist organising, compared with the Xeroxing and telephone trees of the WLM, turned out to be problematic for lesbian feminism in many ways (Megarry, 2014). The administrators of Facebook, mostly male, regularly ban references to lesbians and other expressions of feminist politics that irritate them (Evernote, 2017; Morgan, 2017). Telephone trees offered the advantage of not being surveilled by angry men. Currently, lesbian meetings and social events cannot easily be advertised openly for fear that men, and particularly men who cross-dress and transgender, will seek to intrude or disrupt. The London Lesbian History Group, which started to meet regularly again in 2015 after a hiatus of 20 years, cannot be open about its venue. This is in stark contrast to the situation in the late 1970s, when I published my name, address and phone number in the London newsletter to advertise a meeting in my flat. Such openness now is not possible because of the threat of men's violence.

The disappearing L-word

The disappearance of the word 'lesbian' and the reluctance of new and younger lesbians to use it prevent lesbians organising and make it very hard to create lesbian culture. Words are important, and the very basis of the ability to theorise or act politically. That for which there is no word cannot be articulated. The word 'lesbian' places a flag on political territory and states that it is possible for a woman to commit herself emotionally and sexually to another woman. It is hard to think of another word, apart perhaps for the word 'dyke', that will allow this concept to exist in the imagination. It establishes that women who love women are not gay men, not part of the category 'queer', but possessed of a quite separate way of being in the world that is based on the fact that they are women – biologically female – and raised as members of the female sex, which is subject to male domination.

Use of the word 'lesbian' was undermined by the development of queer politics in the 1990s, as explained in the last chapter (Jeffreys, 1994). Since the early 1990s many lesbians have eschewed the word 'lesbian' in favour of describing themselves

188 Postscript

as 'queer', which is a vague term that may seem safer because it is not sex-specific. In 2010, on the liberal feminist website Feministing, a lesbian called Miriam explained why she, and the website, found 'queer' a better word than 'lesbian':

> Queer is not as specific as words like lesbian or gay, and it does not explain exactly either your gender or the gender of your partner. Lesbian implies pretty clearly that you are a woman who partners with other women. You might identify as genderqueer, trans or gender non-conforming, so that kind of specificity might not fit well. Or you might partner with people across the gender spectrum...
>
> *(Miriam, 2010)*

The word 'lesbian' is rejected here because it identifies a woman's sex and the sex of her partner. It is insufficiently vague and does not include sex with men.

This proliferation of euphemisms enables new lesbians to avoid a term that has become, since the eclipse of lesbian feminism, unpopular because it is seen as 'exclusive'. Christina Cautericci of Slate explained in 2016 that the term 'lesbian' is seen as 'inaccurate and gauche' amongst young women because it implies that a woman might not want sexual relations with men. She suggests how its use can be avoided: 'The word *lesbian*, insofar as it means a woman who is primarily attracted to women, does not correctly describe our reality. My personal queer community comprises cisgender and transgender women; transgender men and transmasculine people; and people who identify as non-binary or genderqueer' (Cautericci, 2016). There are many lists of 'non-binary', genderfluid or genderqueer celebrities online, mostly in the entertainment industry. One such is the lesbian film director Jill Soloway, who chooses not to use the L-word and identifies as a 'gender non-conforming queer person, who prefers to be referenced with gender-neutral pronouns (they/them/their)' (Freeman, 2017: 6). The scarcity of new lesbian role models in popular culture as a result of this kind of obfuscation creates difficulties for those young and older women who might like to choose womanloving now.

Not any woman can be a lesbian

'Any woman can be a lesbian' is the refrain from the classic Alix Dobkin song 'View from Gay Head', recorded in 1973 (Dobkin, 1973). The song is an anthem to that extraordinary and joyful journey which Alix and so many thousands of other women, including me, took into the world of lesbians and lesbianism at the time of the WLM. Today that journey would be very difficult, because not only is there barely a lesbian world to move into but there is much opposition in the online lesbian community to the idea that a woman who has been heterosexual can or should become a lesbian at all. There is a resurgence of the nineteenth-century sexological idea that lesbianism is an innate condition. The understanding that sexuality is not fixed enabled thousands of women to leave heterosexuality at the time of the WLM and become lesbians. As feminist social constructionist influence waned, the biological determinism that was always more favoured by gay men came to prominence again. Lorene Gottschalk conducted research into the way that lesbians understood how they came to be lesbians over three decades, the 1970s, the 1980s and the 1990s (Gottschalk, 2003). She discovered that belief in the ability to choose was dominant in the early period, only to be overtaken by a pessimistic essentialism as the hope of revolution died in succeeding decades. How women understand their lesbianism depends upon philosophical context. The contemporary essentialism tends to be intertwined with a belief in essential gender, in which the most lesbianly lesbians, the true or 'gold star' lesbians, see themselves as 'butch'. Those who identify as 'butch' tend to be the most hostile to the idea of political lesbianism, and to say that those who make political choices to be lesbians are just not real ones.

The butch lesbian blogger Dirt, who is no feminist, goes further, saying that women who have ever related sexually to men can never become lesbians. She has written a series of articles on her blog calling significant lesbian feminist theorists and activists who had heterosexual experience before they chose for women 'straightbians'. She includes me, Adrienne Rich, Julie Bindel, Rita May Brown and many others. She says that I am not and have never been a lesbian because I was once heterosexual; rather, I am a 'straightbian' (Dirt, 2017). Although not all 'real' butch lesbians are as hostile as Dirt, the idea that lesbianism consists of innate butchness and that any lesbians who do not see themselves as butch are inauthentic is quite commonly employed in the online lesbian world. The feminist blogger Purple Sage, for instance, considers that butchness is an innate characteristic: 'Being butch is a lifelong personality trait. A butch begins life as a tomboy and is immediately obvious as being different... It's because she has an unmistakable personality, that comes with ways of thinking and relating and certain mannerisms that are automatic to her that she cannot turn off' (Purple Sage, 2016). This sort of jockeying for position and for authenticity, for the status of 'real ones', creates bitter divisions between lesbians. It also creates a barrier to heterosexual women choosing to become lesbians. The promotion of essentialism and butchness makes swathes of lesbians disappear who are not seen to have the appropriate biography and characteristics. It is harmful to the possibility of creating lesbian feminist community and politics, which cannot develop when the idea of essential lesbianism is wielded to prevent women imagining that they could choose to love women.

Lesbians are really men

One significant trend that has contributed greatly to the disappearance of lesbians, the word 'lesbian' and lesbian spaces is the transgender rights movement, which I analysed extensively in my last book, *Gender Hurts: A Feminist Analysis of the Politics of Transgenderism* (2014). The movement was created in the 1990s by heterosexual male cross-dressers, largely as a result of the Internet, which enabled men with this fetish to network around their interests, build an industry of pornography,

190 Postscript

specialised clothing, equipment and services and promote the fantasy that a person might 'really' be a member of the opposite sex. It encouraged unhappy lesbians to believe that they could become chemically and surgically constructed heterosexual men. American sociology professor Arlene Stein acknowledged in 2010 that the determination of many lesbians to transgender was transforming the lesbian community (Stein, 2010). She is sanguine about this, saying that these lesbians will probably stay attached to the lesbian community, and that that community will just become more diverse, though her article is titled 'The Incredible Shrinking Lesbian World', which does not sound positive. Stein is referring to adult lesbians transgendering to become straight. A more worrying trend is the transgendering of girls who are attracted to other girls in their teens, before they are able to understand that they can be lesbians.

There has been a great increase in the number of children, those under 18 years old, being referred to gender identity clinics in the UK, from 314 in 2011 to 2,016 in 2016 (Turner, 2017). Children referred to gender identity clinics with what is called gender dysphoria in the UK are now 70 per cent female, and, amongst their number, the majority are 'same-sex attracted' teenagers (Gender Identity Referral Service, 2017). This is in stark contrast with the situation in past decades, when boys far outnumbered girls. The girls and young women are being subjected to drugs and surgery before they are of the age at which they would usually recognise that they are lesbians. Clinical research shows that the girls are being referred at later ages than the boys, from 12 to 18, rather than as children, at a time when they are likely to have experienced sexual attraction, but they identify attraction to the same sex as meaning that they are boys, and all those featuring in recent research said they were 'heterosexual' (Steensma et al., 2010; Steensma et al., 2013). The majority of the girls, 95 to 100 per cent, who are 'persisters' – i.e. continue to identify as the opposite sex after puberty – are those who are, as the studies say, 'same-sex attracted'. It would be hard to find a greater distinction between what is happening to young girls who are attracted to other girls today and what was happening in London in the 1980s. Whereas there were once lesbian youth groups and the teaching of heterosexuality as socially constructed, there is now state-sponsored medical violence against young lesbians through treatment by the public health service that is in direct opposition to their rights as girls and as lesbians.

The harm to these young potential lesbians is severe. The drug Lupron that children are given to delay puberty is risky and causes considerable harm (Jewett, 2017; Hruz, Myer and McHugh, 2017). One of the harms of delaying puberty is that it sterilises the girls who are treated in this way, as ova do not develop. Other harms are caused by the necessary lifelong use of cross-sex hormones from age 16 onwards, and by the numerous surgeries such young women may suffer, from breast amputation to hysterectomy, and even in some cases the construction of non-functioning imitation penises from other parts of their bodies (Jeffreys, 2014). I have called this treatment of children who do not conform to gender stereotypes/sex roles 'gender eugenics'. It may also reasonably be called 'conversion therapy', a term which is usually used to refer to attempts to prevent homosexuality in persons who have not 'transgendered', since harmful and lifelong drug and surgical treatments are aimed at converting young lesbians into heterosexual males. It is a profound human rights catastrophe, and something that could not have been imagined at the time of the lesbian feminist movement.

One of the most urgent tasks of a revived lesbian feminist movement must be to oppose this violence against lesbians, and this is beginning to happen. Some of those who have transgendered through drugs and/or surgery are 'detransitioning', or going back to understanding that they are women and lesbians as they realise the harm they have done to their bodies. They are reasserting their lesbian pride, and may be an advance guard of the new generation of lesbian feminists (Autonomous Womyn's Press, 2015).

Lesbians are a male fantasy

The harm inflicted upon lesbians by the transgender rights movement goes beyond the transgendering of girl children for the crime of loving girls to the harassment and bullying of lesbians by the heterosexual male cross-dressers who are the main proponents of transgenderism (Jeffreys, 2014). The cross-dressers fantasise that they are women for sexual excitement. The support of their claim to womanhood by legislatures and the medical profession has led to a dangerous overturning of women's rights to women-only spaces such as toilets and changing rooms in schools and public places, as well as many harms to women's status (Jeffreys, 2016). At the start of 2018 there were media reports of male cross-dressers' success in removing the single-sex status of an iconic women's space that had for decades been a place for lesbians to socialise and exercise, the historic Hampstead Ladies' Pond in London (Petter, 2018). The City of London Corporation announced it would allow male cross-dressers to use the area, though it was arguably superfluous to their needs as there were two other ponds – one for men and one that was mixed – available for their use.

Apart from the removal of women's spaces, the most immediate harm to lesbians from these men is sexual coercion. The idea of being able to sexually use lesbians is an important part of their sexual fantasies; there is, after all, a popular genre of pornography in which women are portrayed as 'lesbians' for men's delight. Cross-dressers go further than just consuming 'lesbianism' in porn and seek excitement by pretending that they are actually 'lesbians', a delusion supported by the fact that they remain heterosexual and sexually attracted to women. The cross-dressers pressurise and threaten lesbians into admitting them not just into lesbian spaces but into their bodies. Male transgender activists use the term 'the cotton ceiling' to refer to the underwear of lesbians who do not want to be penetrated by their penises, in reference to the 'glass ceiling' – i.e. the barrier to women's advancement in their careers. In a blog post on Transgender Forum, entitled 'The Cotton Ceiling', one

192 Postscript

of these men bewails the reluctance of lesbians to have sex with him despite all his approaches and entreaties:

> I will press on, however. I am no quitter. I am a rebel. I don't accept things just because that's 'the way they are.' I will continue the quest for my fair maiden. The Cotton Ceiling must be broken. We are not perverted men seeking to rape lesbians and turn them into slaves to the patriarchy. We – ARE women. We ARE females. We ARE people. We have feelings.
>
> *(Steele, 2015; emphasis in original)*

The great majority of men who transgender retain their genitals and demand, because they have adopted the identity 'lesbian', traditional penis-focused sexual intercourse with lesbians, women who specifically reject the idea of sex with male partners (Jeffreys, 2014).

The forms of vilification that men's rights activists use, many if not most of whom seem from their obsessions to be male heterosexual cross-dressers, are extreme, and many are too disturbing to be quoted here. A website created to track these men's abuse called Terf Is a Slur lists innumerable examples from their Twitter accounts, however (Terf Is a Slur, n.d.). Angry male transgender activists have developed an insulting language for women, for feminists and for lesbians who oppose the notion that they can really be women. They call women 'cis women', in comparison with their own cross-dressing selves, whom they call 'transwomen'. The word 'terf' (transexclusionary radical feminist) is used by these men to vilify women, principally lesbian feminists, who refuse their demands and maintain that men cannot become women by an act of will. Most of the tweets invoke or threaten violence, such as slapping, shooting or punching these uppity women, or causing them to 'die in fire', cave their heads in with rocks or slit their throats. There is much reference to wanting 'terfs' to 'choke' on the men's penises, or what they call their 'girl dicks'. The threats of hundreds of men are recorded here, and there is a special large section showcasing their anger about the recalcitrance of lesbians in the form of the 'cotton ceiling'.

The men's rage has led to them holding or threatening to hold protests outside any venues at which those they see as 'terfs' seek to speak or hold events, and, on one occasion at Hyde Park Corner in 2017, a male trans activist attacked a woman he suspected of being critical of transgenderism and knocked her to the ground (Turner, 2017). This degree of rage creates a very different atmosphere and degree of difficulty for lesbian feminists today. To organise, write, socialise, in online or in geographical spaces, they must deal with a degree of threats and abuse which simply did not exist in previous decades.

A new lesbian feminism

At this low moment in lesbian feminist politics there is evidence of a new beginning in the UK. In 2017 many media outlets that were previously determined to keep any feminist criticism out of their pages began to publish pieces critical of the anti-woman social changes that the male cross-dressers are demanding, such as having gender-neutral passports, rendering sex identification in the census optional and, in effect, eliminating the material reality of womanhood. Surprisingly, this change in what could be spoken about was led by *The Times* newspaper (Turner, 2017). A new upsurge of feminism is happening, in part at least in outraged reaction to the extent of the demands the male cross-dressers are making, and the extent of their influence. As part of this new wave of feminism, women are coming out about their lesbianism or coming out as lesbians. At the time in which I did the interviews for this book this was not so clear, and there is no doubt that some of my interviewees would speak differently today about the opportunities for a new wave of lesbian feminism. The times are different now in many ways, however, and there could be no precise replication of that which we created in the 1970s. I hope that this book, rather than causing despair in a new generation of lesbians at what has been lost, will offer some inspiration in the new stage of the lesbian revolution that is already under way.

Bibliography

Autotomous Womyn's Press (2015). *Blood and Visions: Womyn Reconciling with Being Female*. San Diego: Autotomous Womyn's Press.

Binstock, Rae (2016, 20 December). Why Lesbian Spaces Will Always Be in Danger of Closing, and Why Some Will Always Survive. Slate. www.slate.com/blogs/outward/2016/12/20/why_do_lesbian_spaces_have_such_a_hard_time_staying_in_business.html.

Brownworth, Victoria A. (2015, 5 March). Erasure the New Normal for Lesbians. A Room of Our Own. www.aroomofourown.org/erasure-the-new-normal-for-lesbians-by-vabvoc.

Cautericci, Christina (2016, 20 December). For Many Young Queer Women, Lesbian Offers a Fraught Inheritance. Slate. www.slate.com/blogs/outward/2016/12/20/young_queer_women_don_t_like_lesbian_as_a_name_here_s_why.html.

Cox, Susan (2016, 26 December). Lesbian Spaces Are Still Needed, No Matter What the Queer Movement Says. Feminist Current. www.feministcurrent.com/2016/12/26/lesbian-spaces-still-needed-no-matter-what-queer-movement-says.

Dirt (2016). Sheila Jeffreys: Where Straightbian and Butch/Femme Collide. http://dirtywhiteboi67.blogspot.co.uk/2016/06/sheila-jeffreys-where-straightbian-and.html?m=1.

Dobkin, Alix (1973). View from Gay Head. In *Lavender Jane Loves Women* [album]. New York: Women's Wax Works.

Dobkin, Alix, and Tatnall, Sally (2016). The Erasure of Lesbians. In Barrett, Ruth (ed.), Female Erasure: *What You Need to Know about Gender Politics' War on Women, the Female Sex and Human Rights*. Pacific Palisades, CA: Tidal Time Publishing, 225–228.

Evernote (2017, 2 July). Mass Silencing. www.evernote.com/shard/s717/sh/711e2438-de46-48ff-81fe-a02b714296d0/fa0c991f172b2ea4.

Freeman, Hadley (2017, 21 May). Transparent's Jill Soloway: 'The Words Male and Female Describe Who We Used to Be'. *The Guardian*. www.theguardian.com/tv-and-radio/2017/may/21/transparents-jill-soloway-the-words-male-and-female-describe-who-we-used-to-be.

Gender Identity Referral Service (2017). Referral Figures for 2016–17. National Health Service. http://gids.nhs.uk/number-referrals.

194 Postscript

Gottschalk, Lorene (2003). From Gender Inversion to Choice and Back: Changing Perceptions of the Aetiology of Lesbianism over Three Historical Periods. *Women's Studies International* Forum, 26 (3): 221–233.

Hruz, Paul W., Mayer, Lawrence S., and McHugh, Paul R. (2017). Growing Pains: Problems with Puberty Suppression in Treating Gender Dysphoria. *The New Atlantis*, 52: 3–36. www.thenewatlantis.com/publications/growing-pains.

Jeffreys, Sheila (1994). The Queer Disappearance of Lesbians. *Women's Studies International Forum*, 17 (5): 459–472.

Jeffreys, Sheila (2014). *Gender Hurts: A Feminist Analysis of the Politics of Transgenderism*. Abingdon, UK: Routledge.

Jeffreys, Sheila (2016). Transgender Equality versus Women's Equality: A Clash of Rights. Written Evidence Submitted to the UK Transgender Equality Inquiry, October 14, 2015. In Barrett, Ruth (ed.), *Female Erasure: What You Need to Know about Gender Politics' War on Women, the Female Sex and Human Rights*. Pacific Palisades, CA: Tidal Time Publishing, 56–63.

Jewett, Christina (2017, 2 February). Drug Used to Halt Puberty in Children May Cause Lasting Health Problems. STAT. www.statnews.com/2017/02/02/lupron-puberty-children-health-problems.

Megarry, Jessica (2014). Online Incivility or Sexual Harassment? Conceptualising Women's Experiences in the Digital Age. *Women's Studies International Forum*, 47: 46–55.

Miriam (2010, 16 June). What's the Difference between Lesbian and Queer? Feministing. http://feministing.com/2010/06/16/whats-the-difference-between-lesbian-and-queer.

Morgan, Joe (2017, 1 July). Why Is Facebook Banning Lesbians for Using the Word 'Dy★e'? Gay Star News. www.gaystarnews.com/article/facebook-banning-lesbians-using-word-dye/#gs.yBzMsXc.

Morris, Bonnie (2016). *The Disappearing L: Erasure of Lesbian Spaces and Culture*. Albany, NY: State University of New York Press.

Petter, Olivia (2018, 1 January). Transgender Women Face Angry Reaction for Using Hampstead Ladies' Pond. *The Independent*. www.independent.co.uk/life-style/trans-gender-women-hampstead-heath-ladies-pond-kenwood-kate-moss-a8136581.html.

Purple Sage (2016, 4 December). Butch as a Personality Type. https://purplesagefem. wordpress.com/2016/12/04/butch-as-a-personality-type.

Steele, Amanda F. (2015, 20 April). The Cotton Ceiling. Transgender Forum. www.tgforum. com/wordpress/index.php/the-cotton-ceiling.

Steensma, Thomas D., Biemond, Roeline, de Boer, Fijgje, and Cohen-Kettenis, Peggy T. (2010). Desisting and Persisting Gender Dysphoria after Childhood: A Qualitative Follow-up Study. *Clinical Child Psychiatry*, 16 (4): 499–516.

Steensma, Thomas D., McGurie, Jenifer K., Kreukels, Baudwijntje, Beekman, Anneke, and Cohen-Kettenis, Peggy T. (2013). Factors Associated with Desistence and Persistence of Childhood Gender Dysphoria: A Quantitative Follow-up Study. *Journal of the American Academy of Child and Adolescent Psychiatry*, 52 (6): 582–590.

Stein, Arlene (2010). The Incredible Shrinking Lesbian World and Other Queer Conundra. *Sexualities*, 13 (1): 21–32.

Terf Is a Slur (n.d.). Documenting the Abuse, Harassment and Misogyny of Transgender Identity Politics. https://terfisaslur.com (accessed 26 September 2017).

Turner, Janice (2017, 12 November). Why Do So Many Teenage Girls Want to Be Like Alex Bertie? *The Times Magazine*. www.thetimes.co.uk/article/meet-alex-bertie-the-transgender-poster-boy-z88hgh8b8.

Weil, Lise (2010). Are Lesbians Going Extinct? (Editorial). *Trivia: Voices of Feminism*, 10. www .triviavoices.com/issue-10-are-lesbians-going-extinct-1.html.

BIBLIOGRAPHY

Unpublished primary sources

Newsletters

Revolutionary/Radical Feminist Newsletter (*RRFN*).

Women's Information and Referral Enquiry Service (*WIRES*): the national women's liberation movement newsletter.

London Women's Liberation Newsletter (*LWLN*): this newsletter went by slightly different names and the numbering sequence changed at irregular intervals. For the sake of simplicity, I have called all the incarnations of the London newsletter that came out of the London Women's Liberation Workshop, and later A Woman's Place, *LWLN*.

These newsletters were consulted in the Women's Library, now at the London School of Economics and Political Science, at Feminist Archive North at the Brotherton Library, University of Leeds, and at Glasgow Women's Library.

Published primary sources

Feminist and lesbian magazines and journals

Arena Three
Feminist Review
Gossip
Trouble and Strife
Lesbian Ethics (US)

Non-feminist media sources

City Limits
Spare Rib
The Guardian
Time Out

Special and Private Collections

Lesbian Archive collection, Glasgow Women's Library.
Author's collection, containing press cuttings, meetings minutes, conference papers and flyers.
Lynne Keys' collection, containing meeting minutes.

Secondary sources

Abelove, Henry, Barale, Michèle Aina, and Halperin, David (eds.) (1993). *The Lesbian and Gay Studies Reader*. New York: Routledge.

Abbott, Sidney, and Love, Barbara (1972). *Sappho Was a Right-On Woman: A Liberated View of Lesbianism*. New York: Stein & Day.

AFP (2017, 3 July). Sweden's Bråvalla Music Festival Cancelled Next Year after Sex Attacks. *The Guardian*. www.theguardian.com/world/2017/jul/03/swedens-bravalla-music-festival-cancelled-next-year-after-sex-attacks.

Alderson, Lynn (2016, 8 December). Sisterwrite Bookshop. Lesbian History Group. https://lesbianhistorygroup.wordpress.com/2016/12/08/sisterwrite-bookshop-lynn-alderson.

Allen, Jeffner (ed.) (1990). *Lesbian Philosophies and Cultures*. Albany, NY: State University of New York Press.

Allen, Paula (1970). *Free Space: A Perspective on the Small Group in Women's Liberation*. New York: Times Change Press.

Ardill, Susan, and O'Sullivan, Sue (1989). Sex in the Summer of '88. *Feminist Review*, 31: 126–134.

Attar, Dena (1983). An Open Letter on Anti-Semitism and Racism. *Trouble and Strife*, 1: 13–16.

Autotomous Womyn's Press (2015). *Blood and Visions: Womyn Reconciling with Being Female*. San Diego: Autotomous Women's Press.

Bailey, Garrick, and Peoples, James (2013). *Essentials of Cultural Anthropology*. Florence, KY: Wadsworth, Cengage Learning.

Bailey, J. Michael, and Triea, Kura (2007). What Many Transgender Activists Don't Want You to Know. *Perspectives in Biology and Medicine*, 50 (4): 521–534.

Barrett, Michèle (1980). *Women's Oppression Today: Problems in Marxist Feminist Analysis*. London: Verso Books.

Barry, Kathleen (1979). *Female Sexual Slavery*. New York: New York University Press.

Bart, Pauline, and Moran, Eileen Geil (eds.) (1993). *Violence against Women: The Bloody Footprints*. Newbury Park, UK: Sage.

Baxter, Sarah (1988). Chain Reaction. *Time Out*, 942: 9.

Bell, Diane, and Klein, Renate (eds.) (1996). *Radically Speaking: Feminism Reclaimed*. Melbourne: Spinifex Press.

Bellos, Linda (n.d.). The Limitations of Identity Politics. British Library, 'Spare Rib'. www.bl.uk/spare-rib/articles/the-limitations-of-identity-politics#sthash.wDiJGsZr.dpuf (accessed, 21 October 2017).

Bindel, Julie (1988). The State of the Movement: Reflections by Julie Bindel. *Trouble and Strife*, 13: 50–52.

Bindel, Julie (2014). *Straight Expectations: What Does It Mean to Be Gay Today?* London: Guardian Books.

Binstock, Rae (2016, 20 December). Why Lesbian Spaces Will Always Be in Danger of Closing, and Why Some Will Always Survive. Slate. www.slate.com/blogs/outward/2016/12/20/why_do_lesbian_spaces_have_such_a_hard_time_staying_in_business.html.

Bishop, Helen (1992). Writing Our Own History: Dial-A-Dyke. *Trouble and Strife,* 25: 45–52.

Blackman, Inge, and Perry, Kathryn (1990). Skirting the Issue: Lesbian Fashion for the 1990s. *Feminist Review,* 34: 67–78.

Bloodroot Collective (1988). Bloodroot: Brewing Visions. *Lesbian Ethics,* 3 (1): 3–22.

Bösche, Susanne (2000, 31 January). Jenny, Eric, Martin and Me. *The Guardian.* www.theguardian.com/books/2000/jan/31/booksforchildrenandteenagers.features11 (accessed 3 January 2018).

British Library (n.d.). Sisterhood and After. British Library. www.bl.uk/sisterhood# (accessed 30 January, 2018).

Brodribb, Somer (1992). *Nothing Mat(t)ers: A Feminist Critique of Postmodernism.* Melbourne: Spinifex Press.

Brown, Jan (1992). Sex, Lies and Penetration: A Butch Finally 'Fesses Up. In Nestle, Joan (ed.), *The Persistent Desire: A Femme-Butch Reader.* Boston: Alyson Publications, 410–415.

Brown, Jessica (2017). Here's Why the 'Sexual Avengers' Stuck a Sign to the House of Lords. *The Independent.* https://indy100.com/article/sexual-avengers-plaque-house-of-lords-lesbian-protest-section-28-7595256.

Brown, Rita Mae (1972). Roxanne Dunbar: How a Female Heterosexual Serves the Interests of Male Supremacy. *The Furies,* 1 (1): 5–6. https://library.duke.edu/digitalcollections/wlmpc_wlmms01033.

Browne, Sarah (2012). 'A Veritable Hotbed of Feminism': Women's Liberation in St Andrews, Scotland, *c.*1968–*c.*1979. *Twentieth Century British History,* 23 (1): 100–123.

Browne, Sarah (2014). *The Women's Liberation Movement in Scotland.* Manchester: Manchester University Press.

Brownian, Carrie-Ann (2016, 13 October). Transing the Dead: The Erasure of Gender-Defiant Role Models from History. 4th Wave Now. https://4thwavenow.com/tag/radclyffe-hall.

Brownmiller, Susan (2000). *In Our Time: Memoir of a Revolution.* New York: Dial Press.

Brownworth, Victoria A. (2015, 5 March). Erasure the New Normal for Lesbians. A Room of Our Own. www.aroomofourown.org/erasure-the-new-normal-for-lesbians-by-vabvoc.

Bruley, Sue (2013). Consciousness-Raising in Clapham: Women's Liberation as 'Lived Experience' in South London in the 1970s. *Women's History Review,* 22 (5): 717–738.

Brunet, Arianne, and Turcotte, Louise (1988 [1982]). Separatism and Radicalism: An Analysis of the Differences and Similarities. In Hoagland, Sarah Lucia, and Penelope, Julia (eds.), *For Lesbians Only: A Lesbian Separatist Anthology.* London: Onlywomen Press, 448–457.

Bunch, Charlotte (1972). Lesbians in Revolt: Male Supremacy Quakes and Quivers. *The Furies,* 1 (1): 8–10. http://cdm15957.contentdm.oclc.org/cdm/ref/collection/p15957coll6/id/279.

Burana, Lily, Roxxie and Due, Linnea (eds.) (1994). *Dagger: On Butch Women.* Pittsburgh: Cleis Press.

Burford, Barbara (1986). *The Threshing Floor.* London: Sheba Feminist Publishers.

Burford, Barbara, Pearse, Gabriela, Nichols, Grace, and Kay, Jackie (1985). *A Dangerous Knowing: Four Black Women Poets.* London: Sheba Feminist Publishers.

Butler, Judith (1990). *Gender Trouble: Feminism and the Subversion of Identity.* New York: Routledge.

Califia, Pat (1982). A Personal View of the History of the Lesbian S/M Community and Movement in San Francisco. In Samois (ed.), *Coming to Power: Writings and Graphics on Lesbian S/M.* Boston: Alyson Publications, 243–281.

Califia, Pat (1988). *Sapphistry: The Book of Lesbian Sexuality.* Tallahassee, FL: Naiad Press.

Campbell, Beatrix (1980). A Feminist Sexual Politics: Now You See It, Now You Don't. *Feminist Review,* 5: 1–18.

198 Bibliography

Caprio, Frank (1954). *Female Homosexuality*. London: Peter Owen.

Card, Claudia (1995). *Lesbian Choices*. New York: Columbia University Press.

Carmen, Gail, Shaila and Pratibha (1984). Becoming Visible: Black Lesbian Discussions. *Feminist Review*, 17: 53–72.

Carmen, Gail, Neena and Tamara (1987). Becoming Visible: Black Lesbian Discussions. In Feminist Review (ed.), *Sexuality. A Reader*. London: Virago, 216–244.

Carpenter, Val (1988). Amnesia and Antagonism in the Youth Service. In Cant, Bob, and Hemmings, Susan (eds.), *Radical Records: Thirty Years of Lesbian and Gay History*. London: Routledge, 169–180.

Case, Sue-Ellen (1998). Making Butch: An Historical Memoir of the 1970s. In Munt, Sally (ed.), *Butch/Femme: Inside Lesbian Gender*. London: Cassell, 37–45.

Cautericci, Christina (2016, 20 December). For Many Young Queer Women, Lesbian Offers a Fraught Inheritance. Slate. www.slate.com/blogs/outward/2016/12/20/young_queer_women_don_t_like_lesbian_as_a_name_here_s_why.html.

Chesler, Phyllis (1972). *Women and Madness*. New York: Avon.

Cholmeley, Jane (n.d.). Oral Histories/Jane Cholmeley. London Metropolitan Archives. www.speakoutlondon.org.uk/oral-histories/jane-cholmeley (accessed 5 January 2018).

Claire (2017, 22 February). Lezbehonest about Queer Politics Erasing Lesbian Women. Sister Outrider. https://sisteroutrider.wordpress.com/2017/02/22/lezbehonest-about-queer-politics-erasing-lesbian-women.

Clarke, Cheryl (1981). Lesbianism: An Act of Resistance. In Moraga, Cherríe, and Anzaldúa, Gloria (eds.), *This Bridge Called My Back: Writings by Political Women of Color*. New York: Kitchen Table Press, 128–137.

Clarke, Cheryl (1983). The Failure to Transform: Homophobia in the Black Community. In Smith, Barbara (ed.), *Home Girls: A Black Feminist Anthology*. New York: Kitchen Table Press, 190–201.

Clews, Colin (2012, 28 June). 1983. Book: Jenny Lives with Eric and Martin. Gay In the 80s. www.gayinthe80s.com/2012/06/1983-book-jenny-lives-with-eric-and-martin.

Clews, Colin (2017). *Gay in the 80s: From Fighting for Our Rights to Fighting for Our Lives*. Leicester: Troubador Press.

Combahee River Collective (1983 [1978]). The Combahee River Collective Statement. In Smith, Barbara (ed.), *Home Girls: A Black Feminist Anthology*. New York: Kitchen Table Press, 272–282.

Commons Select Committee (2016, 13 September). 'Widespread' Sexual Harassment and Violence in Schools Must Be Tackled. Parliament UK. www.parliament.uk/business/committees/committees-a-z/commons-select/women-and-equalities-committee/news-parliament-2015/sexual.

Conway, Kelly (1995). Stop Me Before I Bake Again. In Newman, Leslea (ed.), *The Femme Mystique*. Boston: Alyson Publications, 300–302.

Cooper, Davina (1989). Positive Images in Haringey: A Struggle for Identity. In Jones, Carol, and Mahony, Pat (eds.), *Learning Our Lines: Sexuality and Social Control in Education*. London: Women's Press, 46–78.

Coote, Anna, and Campbell, Beatrix (1982). *Sweet Freedom: The Struggle for Women's Liberation*. Oxford: Basil Blackwell.

Coughlan, Sean (2010, 31 March). Majority of Young Women in University. BBC News. http://news.bbc.co.uk/1/hi/education/8596504.stm.

Coughlan, Sean (2010, 10 April). University Applications up 16.5 Percent. BBC News. http://news.bbc.co.uk/1/hi/education/8619922.stm.

Coveney, Lal, Jackson, Margaret, Jeffreys, Sheila, Kay, Lesley, and Mahony, Pat (eds.) (1984). *The Sexuality Papers: Male Sexuality and the Social Control of Women*. London: Hutchinson.

Coward, Rosalind (1978). Re-Reading Freud: The Making of the Feminine. *Spare Rib*, May: 43–46.

Coward, Rosalind (1982). Sexual Violence and Sexuality. *Feminist Review*, 13: 9–22.

Cox, Laverne (2014, 11 March). Laverne Cox Talks about Intersectionality at Harvard. YouTube. www.youtube.com/watch?v=jY3F1pIxHMA11.

Cox, Susan (2016, 26 December). Lesbian Spaces Are Still Needed, No Matter What the Queer Movement Says. Feminist Current. www.feministcurrent.com/2016/12/26/lesbian-spaces-still-needed-no-matter-what-queer-movement-says.

Crenshaw, Kimberlé (1991). Mapping the Margins, Identity Politics, and Violence against Women of Color. *Stanford Law Review*, 43 (6): 1241–1299.

Daly, Mary (1979 [1978]). *Gyn/Ecology: The Metaethics of Radical Feminism*. London: Women's Press.

Daly, Mary (1984). *Pure Lust: Elemental Feminist Philosophy*. London: Women's Press.

Daly, Mary (1985 [1968]). *The Church and the Second Sex*. Boston: Beacon Press.

Daly, Mary (1985 [1973]). *Beyond God the Father: Toward a Philosophy of Women's Liberation*. Boston: Beacon Press.

Davis, Katherine (1982). What We Fear We Try to Keep Contained. In Samois (ed.), *Coming to Power: Writings and Graphics on Lesbian S/M*. Boston: Alyson Publications, 7–13.

Daphne Project (2000). Violence against Lesbians: Education, Research, Public Campaigns. European Commission. https://ec.europa.eu/justice/grants/results/daphne-toolkit/en/content/violence-against-lesbians-education-research-public-campaigns.

Davenport, Christian (2014). *How Social Movements Die: Repression and Demobilization of the New Republic of Africa*. Cambridge: Cambridge University Press.

Davis, Madeline (1992). Epilogue, Nine Years Later. In Nestle, Joan (ed.), *The Persistent Desire: A Femme-Butch Reader*. Boston: Alyson Publications, 270–271.

Davis, Madeline, Hollibaugh, Amber, and Nestle, Joan (1992). The Femme Tapes. In Nestle, Joan (ed.), *The Persistent Desire: A Femme-Butch Reader*. Boston: Alyson Publications, 254–267.

De Beauvoir, Simone (1972 [1949]). *The Second Sex*. London: Penguin Books.

Delap, Lucy (2016). Feminist Bookshops, Reading Cultures and the Women's Liberation Movement in Great Britain, c. 1974–2000. *History Workshop Journal*, 81: 171–196.

Delphy, Christine, and Leonard, Diana (1992). *Familiar Exploitation: A New Analysis of Marriage in Contemporary Western Societies*. Cambridge: Polity Press.

Dines, Gale (2010). *Pornland: How Porn Has Hijacked Our Sexuality*. Melbourne: Spinifex Press.

Dines, Gail (2013, 25 October). Don't Be Fooled by *Fifty Shades of Grey*: Christian Grey Is No Heartthrob. *The Guardian*. www.theguardian.com/commentisfree/2013/oct/25/fifty-shades-of-grey-christian-jamie-dornan-fall.

Dirt (2016). Sheila Jeffreys: Where Straightbian and Butch/Femme Collide. http://dirtywhiteboi67.blogspot.co.uk/2016/06/sheila-jeffreys-where-straightbian-and.html?m=1.

Dirt (2017). Unstraightening Lesbian: Removing the Heterosexual Lens Next Series. https://dirtywhiteboi67.blogspot.co.uk/2017/12/unstraightening-lesbian-removing.html.

Dixon, Jane, Salvat, Gilly, and Skeates, Jane (1989). North London Young Lesbian Group: Specialist Work within the Youth Service. In Jones, Carol, and Mahony, Pat (eds.), *Learning Our Lines: Sexuality and Social Control in Education*. London: Women's Press, 232–248.

Dixon, Janet (1988). Separatism: A Look Back at Anger. In Cant, Bob, and Hemmings, Susan (eds.), *Radical Records: Thirty Years of Lesbian and Gay History*. London: Routledge, 69–84.

Doan, Laura (2001). *Fashioning Sapphism: The Origins of a Modern English Lesbian Culture*. New York: Columbia University Press.

200 Bibliography

Dobkin, Alix (1973). View from Gay Head. In *Lavender Jane Loves Women* [album]. New York: Women's Wax Works.

Dobkin, Alix and Tatnall, Sally (2016). The Erasure of Lesbians. In Barrett, Ruth (ed.), *Female Erasure: What You Need to Know about Gender Politics' War on Women, the Female Sex and Human Rights*. Pacific Palisades, CA: Tidal Time Publishing, 225–228.

Docuaddict (2012, 31 May). The Road to Greenham 'Changed the Course of My Life'. Disarming Grandmothers. https://disarminggrandmothers.wordpress.com/2012/05/31/the-road-to-greenham-changed-the-course-of-my-life.

Dominguez, Ivo (1994). *Beneath the Skins: The New Spirit and Politics of the Kink Community*. Los Angeles: Daedalus.

Dworkin, Andrea (1981). *Pornography: Men Possessing Women*. London: Women's Press.

Dworkin, Andrea (1987). *Intercourse*. London: Martin Secker & Warburg.

Dworkin, Andrea (1988 [1977]). Biological Superiority: The World's Most Dangerous and Deadly Idea. In Dworkin, Andrea, *Letters from a War Zone: Writings 1976–1987*. London: Secker & Warburg, 110–116.

Echols, Alice (1989). *Daring to Be Bad: Radical Feminism in America 1967–1975*. Minneapolis: University of Minnesota Press.

Ellis, Henry Havelock (1927). *Sexual Inversion*. Philadelphia: F. A. Davis.

Ellis, Henry Havelock (1936). *Studies in the Psychology of Sex*, vol. I. London: William Heinemann Medical.

Enjeti, Anjali (2014, 9 May). The Last 13 Feminist Bookstores in the US and Canada. Paste Magazine. www.pastemagazine.com/blogs/lists/2014/05/the-last-13-feminist-bookstores-in-the-us-and-canada.html.

Epstein, Barbara (2001). What Happened to the Women's Movement? *Monthly Review*, 53 (1): 1–13.

Evernote (2017, 2 July). Mass Silencing. www.evernote.com/shard/s717/sh/711e2438-de46-48ff-81fe-a02b714296d0/fa0c991f172b2ea4.

Faderman, Lillian (1981). *Surpassing the Love of Men: Romantic Friendship and Love between Women from the Renaissance to the Present*. New York: William Morrow.

Faderman, Lillian (1985). *Scotch Verdict*. London: Quartet.

Faderman, Lillian (1991). *Odd Girls and Twilight Lovers: A History of Lesbian Life in Twentieth-Century America*. New York: Columbia University Press.

Farnham, Margot (1990). Tyne and Tide: A Lesbian Life Story. Margot Farnham Interviews Helen Lilly. *Trouble and Strife*, 18: 47–52.

Farr, Susan (1982). The Art of Discipline: Creating Erotic Dramas of Play and Power. In Samois (ed.), *Coming to Power: Writings and Graphics on Lesbian S/M*. Boston: Alyson Publications, 181–189.

Feinberg, Leslie (1993). *Stone Butch Blues: A Novel*. Ithaca, NY: Firebrand Books.

Figes, Eva (1970). *Patriarchal Attitudes: Women in Revolt*. New York: Stein & Day.

Forrest, Katherine V. (1984). *Daughters of a Coral Dawn*. Tallahassee, FL: Naiad Press.

Foucault, Michel (1978). *The History of Sexuality*, vol. I. London: Allen Lane.

Freeman, Hadley (2017, 21 May). Transparent's Jill Soloway: 'The Words Male and Female Describe Who We Used to Be'. *The Guardian*. www.theguardian.com/tv-and-radio/2017/may/21/transparents-jill-soloway-the-words-male-and-female-describe-who-we-used-to-be.

Freeman, Jo (1972 [1970]). The Tyranny of Structurelessness. *Second Wave*, 2 (1): 20–25.

Freire, Paulo (1970). *The Pedagogy of the Oppressed*. New York: Herder and Herder.

Friedan, Betty (1963). *The Feminine Mystique*. New York: W. W. Norton.

Frye, Marilyn (1983 [1977]). Some Reflections on Separatism and Power. In *The Politics of Reality: Essays in Feminist Theory*. Freedom, CA: Crossing Press, 95–109.

Frye, Marilyn (1983). *The Politics of Reality: Essays in Feminist Theory*. New York: Crossing Press.

Frye, Marilyn (1993). Lesbian Sex. In Frye, Marilyn, *Willful Virgin: Essays in Feminism*. New York: Crossing Press, 76–92.

Fryer, Peter (1984). *Staying Power: The History of Black People in Britain*. London: Pluto Press.

Gage, Caroline (2010). The Inconvenient Truth about Teena Brandon. Trivia: Voices of Feminism. www.triviavoices.com/the-inconvenient-truth-about-teena-brandon.html (accessed 28 October 2017).

Gardiner, Jill (2003). *From the Closet to the Screen: Women at the Gateways Club, 1945–1985*. London: Pandora.

Gardner, Lynn (2010, 13 May). Ladies as Gentlemen: The Crossdressing Women of Edwardian Musical Theatre. *The Guardian*. www.theguardian.com/music/2010/may/13/cross-dressing-women-musical-theatre.

Gearhart, Sally (1978). *The Wanderground: Stories of the Hill Women*. Watertown, MA: Persephone Press.

Gender Identity Referral Service (2017). Referral Figures for 2016–17. National Health Service. http://gids.nhs.uk/number-referrals.

Giddens, Anthony (2009). *Sociology*. Cambridge: Polity Press.

Gillan, Audrey (2003, 17 November). Section 28 … Gone but Not Forgotten. *The Guardian*. www.theguardian.com/politics/2003/nov/17/uk.gayrights.

Gottschalk, Lorene (2003). From Gender Inversion to Choice and Back: Changing Perceptions of the Aetiology of Lesbianism over Three Historical Periods. *Women's Studies International Forum*, 26 (3): 221–233.

Graham, Dee L. R. (1994). *Loving to Survive: Sexual Terror, Men's Violence and Women's Lives*. New York: New York University Press.

Grassroots Feminism (2009, 21 December). Sheba Feminist Publishers. www.grassrootsfeminism.net/cms/node/593 (accessed 18 December 2017).

Green, Emma (2015, 10 February). Consent Isn't Enough: The Troubling Sex of *Fifty Shades*. *The Atlantic*. www.theatlantic.com/entertainment/archive/2015/02/consent-isnt-enough-in-fifty-shades-of-grey/385267.

Green, Frankie (2012). Talk given at the 'Music and Liberation' exhibition at Space Station 65 Gallery, London, 1 December. https://womensliberationmusicarchive.co.uk/talks-presentations-interviews.

Green, Frankie (2014). Talk given at the 'Feminist Archives and Activism: Knowing Our Past – Creating Our Future' workshop at the 'Feminism in London' conference, London, 25 October. https://womensliberationmusicarchive.co.uk/talks-presentations-interviews.

Green, Frankie (2015). Talk given at the 'History of Feminist Activism' event, London, 11 March. https://womensliberationmusicarchive.co.uk/talks-presentations-interviews.

Griffin, Susan (1981). *Pornography and Silence*. London: Women's Press.

Halberstam, Judith (1998). *Female Masculinity*. Durham, NC: Duke University Press.

Halberstam, Judith (1999). Preface. In Volcano, Del LaGrace, and Halberstam, Judith, *The Drag King Book*. London: Serpent's Tail, 1–8.

Halberstam, Judith, and Hale, C. Jacob (1998). Butch/FTM Border Wars. *GLQ: A Journal of Lesbian and Gay Studies*, 4 (2): 283–286.

Hall, Radclyffe (1982 [1928]). *The Well of Loneliness*. London: Virago.

Hall Carpenter Archives Lesbian Oral History Group (1989). *Inventing Ourselves: Lesbian Life Stories*. London: Routledge.

Hanmer, Jalna, and Saunders, Sheila (1984). *Well-Founded Fear: A Community Study of Violence to Women*. London: Hutchinson.

Harne, Lynne (2016). How to Become a Lesbian in 30 Minutes, Part 1. Lesbian History Group. https://lesbianhistorygroup.wordpress.com/tag/great-london-council.

202 Bibliography

Harne, Lynne, and Hutton, Elaine (1996). *All the Rage: Reasserting Radical Lesbian Feminism.* London: Women's Press.

Hartman, Heidi (1979). The Unhappy Marriage of Marxism and Feminism: Towards a More Progressive Union. *Capital and Class*, 3 (2): 1–33.

Heartfield, James (2017). *The Equal Opportunities Revolution.* London: Repeater Books.

Henley, Nancy (1977). *Body Politics: Power, Sex, and Non-Verbal Communication.* Englewood Cliffs, NJ: Prentice-Hall.

Hess, Katharine, Langford, Jean, and Ross, Kathy (1988 [1980]). Comparative Separatism. In Hoagland, Sarah Lucia, and Penelope, Julia (eds.), *For Lesbians Only: A Separatist Anthology.* London: Onlywomen Press, 125–131.

Hite, Shere (1977). *The Hite Report: A Nationwide Study of Female Sexuality.* Sydney: Summit Books.

Hoagland, Sarah Lucia, and Penelope, Julia (eds.) (1988). *For Lesbians Only: A Separatist Anthology.* London: Onlywomen Press.

Hoagland, Sarah Lucia (1988a). *Lesbian Ethics: Toward New Value.* Palo Alto, CA: Institute for Lesbian Studies.

Hoagland, Sarah Lucia (1988b). Introduction. In Hoagland, Sarah Lucia, and Penelope, Julia (eds.), *For Lesbians Only: A Separatist Anthology.* London: Onlywomen Press, 1–14.

Hoagland, Sarah Lucia (1992). Introduction. In Penelope, Julia, *Call Me Lesbian: Lesbian Lives, Lesbian Theory.* Freedom, CA: Crossing Press, xi–xvii.

Holland, Janet, Ramazanoglu, Caroline, Sharp, Sue, and Thomson, Rachel (1998). *The Male in the Head: Young People, Heterosexuality and Power.* London: Tufnell Press.

Hollibaugh, Amber, and Moraga, Cherríe (1983). What We're Rollin' around in Bed with: Sexual Silences in Feminism. In Snitow, Ann Barr, and Stansell, Christine (eds.), *Powers of Desire: The Politics of Sexuality.* New York: Monthly Review Press, 394–406.

Home Office (1957). *Report of the Committee on Homosexual Offences and Prostitution* [known as the Wolfenden Report]. London: Her Majesty's Stationery Office.

Hruz, Paul W., Mayer, Lawrence S., and McHugh, Paul R. (2017). Growing Pains: Problems with Puberty Suppression in Treating Gender Dysphoria. *The New Atlantis*, 52: 3–36. www.thenewatlantis.com/publications/growing-pains.

Hunt, Margaret (1990). The De-Eroticization of Women's Liberation: Social Purity Movements and the Revolutionary Feminism of Sheila Jeffreys. *Feminist Review*, 34: 23–46.

Hutton, Elaine (2016). How to Become a Lesbian in 30 Minutes, Part 2. Lesbian History Group. https://lesbianhistorygroup.wordpress.com/2016/02.

Ishtar, Arlene (1992). Femme-Dyke. In Nestle, Joan (ed.), *The Persistent Desire: A Femme-Butch Reader.* Boston: Alyson Publications, 378–383.

Jackson, Margaret (1989). Sexuality and Struggle: Feminism, Sexology and the Social Construction of Sexuality. In Jones, Carol, and Mahony, Pat (eds.), *Learning Our Lines: Sexuality and Social Control in Education.* London: Women's Press, 1–22.

Jackson, Stevi (1983). The Desire for Freud: Psychoanalysis and Feminism. *Trouble and Strife*, 1: 32–41.

Jay, Karla, and Young, Allen (eds.) (1992 [1972]). *Out of the Closets: Voices of Gay Liberation.* New York: New York University Press.

Jay, Karla, and Young, Allan (1992). Introduction to the Second Edition. In Jay, Karla, and Young, Allan (eds.), *Out of the Closets: Voices of Gay Liberation.* London: Gay Men's Press, vii–lix.

Jeffreys, Sheila (1977, 5 April). The Need for Revolutionary Feminism: Against the Liberal Takeover of the Women's Liberation Movement. Paper presented at 9th National

Women's Liberation Conference, London. Available at Feministes Radicales: www.feministes-radicales.org/2012/05/20/the-need-for-revolutionary-feminism (accessed 19 December 2017).

Jeffreys, Sheila (1987). Butch and Femme: Now and Then. *Gossip*, 5: 65–95 [reprinted in Lesbian History Group (ed.) (1989), *Not a Passing Phase: Reclaiming Lesbians in History 1840–1985*. London: Women's Press, 158–187].

Jeffreys, Sheila (1989). Does It Matter If They Did It? In Lesbian History Group (ed.), *Not a Passing Phase: Reclaiming Lesbians in History 1840–1985*. London: Women's Press, 19–28.

Jeffreys, Sheila (1993a). Consent and the Politics of Sexuality. *Current Issues in Criminal Justice*, 5 (2): 173–183.

Jeffreys, Sheila (1993b). *The Lesbian Heresy: A Feminist Perspectives on the Lesbian Sexual Revolution*. London: Women's Press.

Jeffreys, Sheila (1993c [1984]). Sadomasochism: The Erotic Cult of Fascism. In Jeffreys, Sheila, *The Lesbian Heresy: A Feminist Perspective on the Lesbian Sexual Revolution*. London: Women's Press.

Jeffreys, Sheila (1994). The Queer Disappearance of Lesbians. *Women's Studies International Forum*, 17 (5): 459–472.

Jeffreys, Sheila (1997 [1985]). *The Spinster and Her Enemies: Feminism and Sexuality 1880–1930*. Melbourne: Spinifex Press.

Jeffreys, Sheila (2003). *Unpacking Queer Politics*. Cambridge: Polity Press.

Jeffreys, Sheila (2009). *The Industrial Vagina: The Political Economy of the Global Sex Trade*. Abingdon, UK: Routledge.

Jeffreys, Sheila (2011 [1990]). *Anticlimax: A Feminist Perspective on the Sexual Revolution*. Melbourne: Spinifex Press.

Jeffreys, Sheila (2012). *Man's Dominion: the Rise of Religion and the Eclipse of Women's Rights*. Abingdon, UK: Routledge.

Jeffreys, Sheila (2014 [2005]). *Beauty and Misogyny: Harmful Cultural Practices in the West*. Abingdon, UK: Routledge.

Jeffreys, Sheila (2014). *Gender Hurts: A Feminist Analysis of the Politics of Transgenderism*. Abingdon, UK: Routledge.

Jeffreys, Sheila (2016). Transgender Equality versus Women's Equality: A Clash of Rights. Written Evidence Submitted to the UK Transgender Equality Inquiry, October 14, 2015. In Barrett, Ruth (ed.), *Female Erasure: What You Need to Know about Gender Politics' War on Women, the Female Sex and Human Rights*. Pacific Palisades, CA: Tidal Time Publishing, 56–63.

Jennings, Rebecca (2007a). *Tomboys and Bachelor Girls: Narrating the Lesbian in Post-War Britain 1945–71*. Manchester: Manchester University Press.

Jennings, Rebecca (2007b). *A Lesbian History of Britain: Love and Sex between Women since 1500*. Oxford: Greenwood World Publishing.

Jewett, Christina (2017, 2 February). Drug Used to Halt Puberty in Children May Cause Lasting Health Problems. STAT. www.statnews.com/2017/02/02/lupron-puberty-children-health-problems.

Johnson Reagon, Bernice (1983). Coalition Politics: Turning the Century. In Smith, Barbara (ed.), *Home Girls: A Black Feminist Anthology*. New York: Kitchen Table Press, 356–368.

Jones, Alethia, and Eubanks, Virginia (eds.) (2014). *Ain't Gonna Let Nobody Turn Me Around: Forty Years of Movement Building with Barbara Smith*. Albany, NY: State University of New York Press.

Jones, Carol, and Mahony, Pat (eds.) (1989). *Learning Our Lines: Sexuality and Social Control in Education*. London: Women's Press.

204 Bibliography

Juicy Lucy (1982). If I Ask You to Tie Me Up, Will You Still Want to Love Me. In Samois (ed.), *Coming to Power: Writings and Graphics on Lesbian S/M.* Boston: Alyson Publications, 29–40.

Kay, Jackie (ed.) (1984). *A Dangerous Knowing: Four Black Women Poets.* London: Sheba Feminist Publishers.

Keating, Shannon (2017, 12 February). Can Lesbian Identity Survive the Gender Revolution? Buzzfeed. www.buzzfeed.com/shannonkeating/can-lesbian-identity-survive-the-gender-revolution?utm_term=.ljGkWRM0Z#.cmLYQgGpq.

Kelly, Liz (1988). *Surviving Sexual Violence.* Cambridge: Polity Press.

Kennedy, Elizabeth Lapovsky, and Davis, Madeline (1993). *Boots of Leather, Slippers of Gold: The History of a Lesbian Community.* New York: Routledge.

Kennedy, Florynce (1970). Institutionalized Oppression vs. the Female. In Morgan, Robin (ed.), *Sisterhood Is Powerful: An Anthology of Writings from the Women's Liberation Movement.* New York: Vintage Books, 492–500.

Kitzinger, Celia, and Perkins, Rachel (1993). *Changing Our Minds: Lesbian Feminism and Psychology.* London: Onlywomen Press.

Klein, Viola (1946). *The Feminine Character: History of an Ideology.* London: Kegan Paul.

Koedt, Anne (1971). Lesbianism and Feminism. Chicago: CWLU. Available at CWLU Herstory Project, www.cwluherstory.org/classic-feminist-writings-articles/lesbianism-and-feminism.html (accessed 5 September 2016).

Koedt, Anne (1974 [1970]). The Myth of the Vaginal Orgasm. In The Radical Therapist Collective (ed.), *The Radical Therapist.* London: Penguin Books, 133–142.

Kolb, Terry (1979). Masochist's Lib. In Samois (ed.), *What Colour Is Your Handkerchief: A Lesbian S/M Sexuality Reader.* Berkeley, CA: Samois, 19–22.

Laville, Sandra (2014, 3 August). Domestic Violence Refuge Provision at Crisis Point, Warn Charities. *The Guardian.* www.theguardian.com/society/2014/aug/03/domestic-violence-refuge-crisis-women-closure-safe-houses.

Lee, Anna (1988 [1981]). A Black Separatist. In Hoagland, Sarah Lucia, and Penelope, Julia (eds.), *For Lesbians Only: A Separatist Anthology.* London: Onlywomen Press, 83–91.

Lee, Anna (1988 [1983]). The Tired Old Question of Male Children. In Hoagland, Sarah Lucia, and Penelope, Julia (eds.), *For Lesbians Only: A Separatist Anthology.* London: Onlywomen Press, 312–314.

Lesbian Ethics (1985). Non? Monogamy? A Readers' Forum. *Lesbian Ethics,* 1 (2): 79–105.

Lesbian Herstory Archives (n.d.). A Brief History. www.lesbianherstoryarchives.org/history.html .

Lesbian History Group (1989). *Not a Passing Phase: Reclaiming Lesbians in History 1840–1985.* London: Women's Press.

Lev, Arlene (2008). More than Surface Tension: Femmes in Families. *Journal of Lesbian Studies,* 12 (2/3): 127–144.

Levine, Martin (1998). *Gay Macho: The Life and Death of the Homosexual Clone.* New York: New York University Press.

Linden, Robin Ruth, Pagano, Darlene R., Russell, Diana E. H., and Star, Susan Leigh (eds.) (1982). *Against Sadomasochism: A Radical Feminist Analysis.* Palo Alto, CA: Frog in the Well Press.

Livia, Anna (1987). *Bulldozer Rising.* London: Onlywomen Press.

Lockyer, Bridget (2013). An Irregular Period? Participation in the Bradford Women's Liberation Movement. *Women's History Review,* 22 (4): 643–657.

London Revolutionary Feminist Anti-Pornography Group (1985 [1978]). Pornography. In Rhodes, Dusty, and McNeill, Sandra (eds.), *Women against Violence against Women.* London: Onlywomen Press, 13–18.

Long, Julia (2012). *Anti-Porn: The Resurgence of Anti-Pornography Feminism*. London: Zed Books.

Lorde, Audre (1982). *Zami: A New Spelling of My Name*. Freedom, CA: Crossing Press.

Lorde, Audre (1984a). *Sister Outsider: Essays and Speeches by Audre Lorde*. Freedom, CA: Crossing Press.

Lorde, Audre (1984b [1978]). Uses of the Erotic: The Erotic as Power. In Lorde, Audre, *Sister Outsider: Essays and Speeches by Audre Lorde*. Freedom, CA: Crossing Press, 53–59.

Louise, Valentine (1988). Fear. In Hoagland, Sarah Lucia, and Penelope, Julia (eds.), *For Lesbians Only: A Separatist Anthology*. London: Onlywomen Press, 181–186.

Loulan, JoAnn (1985). *Lesbian Sex*. San Francisco: Spinsters Ink Books.

Loulan, JoAnn (1987). *Lesbian Passion: Loving Ourselves and Each Other*. San Francisco, CA: Spinsters Ink Books.

Loulan, JoAnn (1990). *Lesbian Erotic Dance: Butch, Femme, Androgyny, and Other Rhythms*. San Francisco: Spinsters Ink Books.

MacDonald, Jocelyn (2017, 13 January). Today's Shameless Lesbians Won't Be Queered. *Feminist Current*. www.feministcurrent.com/2017/01/13/todays-shameless-lesbians-wont-queered.

Mackay, Finn (2014). Reclaiming Revolutionary Feminism. *Feminist Review*, 106: 95–103.

Mackay, Finn (2015). *Radical Feminism: Feminist Activism in Movement*. Basingstoke, UK: Palgrave Macmillan.

MacKinnon, Catharine A. (1989a). *Toward a Feminist Theory of the State*. Cambridge, MA: Harvard University Press.

MacKinnon, Catharine A. (1989b). Rape: On Coercion and Consent. In MacKinnon, Catharine, *Toward a Feminist Theory of the State*. Cambridge, MA: Harvard University Press, 171–183.

MacKinnon, Catharine A. (2006). *Are Women Human? And Other International Dialogues*. Cambridge, MA: Harvard University Press.

McNeil, Sandra (1996). Identity Politics. In Harne, Lynne, and Miller, Elaine (eds.), *All the Rage: Reasserting Radical Lesbian Feminism*. London: Women's Press, 52–58.

Mama, Amina (1995). *Beyond the Masks: Race, Gender and Subjectivity*. London: Routledge.

Marston, Cicely Alice, and Lewis, Ruth (2014). Anal Heterosex among Young People and Implications for Health Promotion: A Qualitative Study in the UK. *British Medical Journal*, 4 (8), DOI: 10.1136/bmjopen2014-004996.

Martin, Del, and Lyon, Phyllis (1972). *Lesbian/Woman*. New York: Bantam Books.

Martinez, Vanessa (2012, 16 July). Exclusive: British Filmmaker Campbell X Talks 'Stud Life'. *Indiewire*. www.indiewire.com/2012/07/exclusive-british-filmmaker-campbell-x-talks-stud-life-making-of-feature-debut-more-143942.

Megarry, Jessica (2014). Online Incivility or Sexual Harassment? Conceptualising Women's Experiences in the Digital Age. *Women's Studies International Forum*, 47: 46–55.

Menasche, Anne (1999). *Leaving the Life: Lesbians, Ex-Lesbians and the Heterosexual Imperative*. London: Onlywomen Press.

Miller, Elaine (1998). Zero Tolerance in Wonderland: Some Political Uses of Imagination. In Hutton, Elaine (ed.), *Beyond Sex and Romance? The Politics of Contemporary Lesbian Fiction*. London: Women's Press, 152–174.

Miller, Isabel (1971). *Patience and Sarah*. New York: McGraw-Hill.

Millett, Kate (1972 [1970]). *Sexual Politics*. London: Abacus.

Miriam (2010, 16 June). What's the Difference between Lesbian and Queer? *Feministing*. http://feministing.com/2010/06/16/whats-the-difference-between-lesbian-and-queer.

Mitchell, Juliet (1974). *Psychoanalysis and Feminism*. London: Allen Lane.

206 Bibliography

Mohin, Lilian (1979). *One Foot on the Mountain: Anthology of British Feminist Poetry 1969–1979*. London: Onlywomen Press.

Mohin, Lilian (1984). Lesbian Radical Feminism: The Only Radical Feminism? (Letters). *Trouble and Strife*, 3: 6–8.

Mohin, Lilian (1986). *Beautiful Barbarians: Lesbian Feminist Poetry*. London: Onlywomen Press.

Moore, Lisa L. (2013, 23 August). It Is an Apple. An Interview with Judy Grahn. Los Angeles Review of Books. https://lareviewofbooks.org/article/it-is-an-apple-an-interview-with-judy-grahn/#!.

More, Kate (1999). Never Mind the Bollocks: 2. Judith Butler on Transsexuality. In More, Kate, and Whittle, Stephen (eds.), *Reclaiming Genders: Transsexual Grammars at the Fin de Siècle*. London: Cassell, 285–302.

Moraga, Cherríe and Anzaldúa, Gloria (eds.) (1981). *This Bridge Called My Back: Writings by Radical Women of Color*. New York: Kitchen Table Press.

Morgan, Joe (2017, 1 July). Why Is Facebook Banning Lesbians for Using the Word 'Dy★e'? Gay Star News. www.gaystarnews.com/article/facebook-banning-lesbians-using-word-dye/#gs.yBzMsXc.

Morgan, Robin (1977a). *Going Too Far: The Personal Chronicle of a Feminist*. New York: Random House.

Morgan, Robin (1977b). The Politics of Sado-Masochistic Fantasies. In Morgan, Robin, *Going Too Far: The Personal Chronicle of a Feminist*. New York: Random House, 227–240.

Morris, Bonnie (2016). *The Disappearing L: Erasure of Lesbian Spaces and Culture*. Albany, NY: State University of New York Press.

Munt, Sally (1998). Introduction. In Munt, Sally (ed.), *Butch/Femme: Inside Lesbian Gender*. London: Cassell, 1–11.

Mushroom, Merrill (1983). Confessions of a Butch Dyke. *Common Lives, Lesbian Lives*, 9: 39–42.

Myron, Nancy, and Bunch, Charlotte (eds.) (1975). *Lesbianism and the Women's Movement*. Baltimore: Diana Press.

Namjoshi, Suniti (1981). *Feminist Fables: A Retelling of Myths*. London: Sheba Feminist Publishers.

Nair, Yasmin (2017, 7 June). The Dangerous Academic Is an Extinct Species. Current Affairs. www.currentaffairs.org/2017/04/the-dangerous-academic-is-an-extinct-species.

Nestle, Joan (1987). *A Restricted Country*. Ann Arbor, MI: Firebrand Books.

Nestle, Joan (ed.) (1992a). *The Persistent Desire: A Femme-Butch Reader*. Boston: Alyson Publications.

Nestle, Joan (1992b). The Femme Question. In Nestle, Joan (ed.), *The Persistent Desire: A Femme-Butch Reader*. Boston: Alyson Publications, 138–146.

Newman, Leslea (ed.) (1995). *The Femme Mystique*. Boston: Alyson Publications.

Nick (1980 [1972]). The Myth of Sexual Attraction. In Walter, Aubrey (ed.), *Come Together: The Years of Gay Liberation 1970–73*. London: Gay Men's Press, 176–177.

Okin, Susan Moller (1989). *Justice, Gender and the Family*. New York: Basic Books.

O'Lexa, Liz (1995). Let Me Be the Femme. In Newman, Leslea (ed.), *The Femme Mystique*. Boston: Alyson Publications, 213–215.

Onlywomen Press (1981). *Love Your Enemy? The Debate between Heterosexual Feminism and Political Lesbianism*. London: Onlywomen Press.

Oram, Alison (2007). *Her Husband Was a Woman: Women's Gender-Crossing in Modern British Popular Culture*. Abingdon, UK: Routledge.

Orr, Deborah (1995, 2 July). The Bearded Lady. *The Guardian Weekend*.

O'Sullivan, Sue (1990). Mapping: Lesbianism, AIDS and Sexuality: An Interview with Cindy Patton by Sue O'Sullivan. *Feminist Review*, 34: 120–133.

Packwood, Marlene (1983). The Colonel's Lady and Judy O'Grady: Sisters under the Skin? *Trouble and Strife*, 1: 7–12.

Pateman, Carole (1989). Women and Consent. In Pateman, Carole, *The Disorder of Women*. Cambridge: Polity Press, 71–89.

Peachey, Paul (2015, 22 August). Women in Manual Trades: Pioneering Tradeswoman's Charity Faces Closure despite Shortage of Skilled Construction Workers. *The Independent*. www.independent.co.uk/news/uk/home-news/women-in-manual-trades-pioneering-tradeswomans-charity-faces-closure-despite-shortage-of-skilled-10467368.html.

Penelope, Julia (1984). Whose Past Are We Reclaiming? *Common Lives, Lesbian Lives*, 13: 16–36.

Penelope, Julia (1986). Language and the Transformation of Consciousness. *Law and Inequality: A Journal of Theory and Practice*, 4 (2): 379–391. http://scholarship.law.umn.edu/cgi/viewcontent.cgi?article=1331&context=lawineq.

Penelope, Julia (1988). The Mystery of Lesbians. In Hoagland, Sarah Lucia, and Penelope, Julia (eds.), *For Lesbians Only: A Separatist Anthology*. London: Onlywomen Press, 506–546.

Penelope, Julia (1990). *Speaking Freely: Unlearning the Lies of the Fathers' Tongues*. New York: Pergamon Press.

Penelope, Julia (1992a). The Lesbian Perspective. In Penelope, Julia (ed.), *Call Me Lesbian: Lesbian Lives, Lesbian Theory*. Freedom, CA: Crossing Press, 39–51.

Penelope, Julia (1992b). Do We Mean What We Say? Horizontal Hostility and the World We Would Create. In Penelope, Julia (ed.), *Call Me Lesbian: Lesbian Lives, Lesbian Theory*. Freedom, CA: Crossing Press, 60–77.

Petter, Olivia (2018, 1 January). Transgender Women Face Angry Reaction for Using Hampstead Ladies' Pond. *The Independent*. www.independent.co.uk/life-style/transgender-women-hampstead-heath-ladies-pond-kenwood-kate-moss-a8136581.html.

Phelan, Shane (1994). *Getting Specific: Postmodern Lesbian Politics*. Minneapolis: University of Minneapolis Press.

Platt, Mary Frances (1992). Reclaiming Femme…Again. In Nestle, Joan (ed.), *The Persistent Desire: A Femme-Butch Reader*. Boston: Alyson Publications, 388–389.

Poirot, Kristan (2009). Domesticating the Liberated Woman: Containment Rhetorics of Second Wave Radical/Lesbian Feminism. *Women's Studies in Communication*, 32 (3): 263–292.

Potts, Billie (1988 [1982]). Owning Jewish Separatism and Lesbian Separatism. In Hoagland, Sarah Lucia, and Penelope, Julia (eds.), *For Lesbians Only: A Separatist Anthology*. London: Onlywomen Press, 149–158.

Preston, John (1993). *My Life as a Pornographer and Other Indecent Acts*. New York: Masquerade Books.

Purple Sage (2016, 4 December). Butch as a Personality Type. https://purplesagefem.wordpress.com/2016/12/04/butch-as-a-personality-type.

Purvis, June (2004). Inspiring Women: Remembering Mary Stott (1907–2002). *Women's History Review*, 13 (4): 517–520. www.tandfonline.com/doi/pdf/10.1080/09612020400200408.

Radford, Jill (1998). Lindsay Gordon Meets Kate Brannigan – Mainstreaming or Malestreaming: Representations of Women Crime Fighters. In Hutton, Elaine (ed.), *Beyond Sex and Romance? The Politics of Contemporary Lesbian Fiction*. London: Women's Press, 81–105.

208 Bibliography

Radford, Jill, and Russell, Diana (1992). *Femicide: The Politics of Woman Killing*. Farmington Hills, MI: Twayne Publishers.

Radicalesbians (1972 [1970]). The Woman-Identified Woman. In Jay, Karla, and Young, Allen (eds.), *Out of the Closets: Voices of Gay Liberation*. New York: New York University Press, 172–177.

Raymond, Janice G. (1986). *A Passion for Friends: Towards a Philosophy of Female Affection*. London: Women's Press.

Raymond, Janice G. (1994 [1979]). *The Transsexual Empire: The Making of the She-Male*. New York: Teachers' College Press.

Rees, Jeska (2010). A Look Back at Anger: The Women's Liberation Movement in 1978. *Women's History Review*, 19 (3): 337–356.

Rhodes, Dusty, and McNeill, Sandra (eds.) (1985). *Women against Violence against Women*. London: Onlywomen Press.

Rich, Adrienne (1977). *The Meaning of Our Love for Women Is What We Have Constantly to Expand: Speech at New York Lesbian Pride Rally June 26, 1977*. New York: Out & Out Books.

Rich, Adrienne (1979). *Women and Honour: Notes on Lying*. London: Onlywomen Press.

Rich, Adrienne (1984 [1980]). Compulsory Heterosexuality and Lesbian Existence. In Snitow, Ann, Stansell, Christine, and Thompson, Sharon (eds.), *Desire: The Politics of Sexuality*. London: Virago, 212–241.

Richardson, Diane (ed.) (1996). *Theorising Heterosexuality*. Buckingham, UK: Open University Press.

Romito, Patrizia (2008). *A Deafening Silence: Hidden Violence against Women and Children*. Bristol: Policy Press.

Roof, Judith (1998). Lesbian Feminism Meets 1990s Butch-Femme. In Munt, Sally R. (ed.), *Butch/Femme: Inside Lesbian Gender*. London: Cassell, 27–36.

Rosen, Ruth (2000). *The World Split Open: How the Modern Women's Movement Changed America*. New York: Viking.

Rosenberg, Carroll Smith (1975). The Female World of Love and Ritual: Relations between Women in Nineteenth Century America. *Signs*, 1 (1): 1–20.

Ross, Freya Johnson (2018). From Municipal Feminism to the Equality Act: Legislation and Gender Equality Work in UK Local Government 1980–2010. *Women's Studies International Forum*, 66: 1–8.

Rowbotham, Sheila (1972). The Beginning of the Women's Liberation Movement in Britain. In Wandor, Michelene (ed.), *The Body Politic: Women's Liberation in Britain 1969–1972*. London: Stage 1, 91–102.

Rowbotham, Sheila (1997). *A Century of Women: The History of Women in Britain and the US*. London: Viking.

Roz, Paula, Rachel, Della, Edith, Susan, Perry, Patty and Christine (1980). Don't Call Me Mister, You Fucking Beast! In Walter, Aubrey (ed.), *Come Together: The Years of Gay Liberation 1970–73*. London: Gay Men's Press, 164.

Rubin, Gayle (1984). Thinking Sex. Notes for a Radical Theory of the Politics of Sexuality. In Vance, Carole S. (ed.), *Pleasure and Danger: Exploring Female Sexuality*. London: Routledge & Kegan Paul, 267–319.

Russ, Joana (1975). *The Female Man*. New York: Bantam Books.

Russell, Diana (1975). *The Politics of Rape: The Victim's Perspective*. New York: Stein & Day.

Samois (ed.) (1979). *What Color Is Your Handkerchief: A Lesbian SM Sexuality Reader*. Berkeley, CA: Samois.

Samois (ed.) (1982). *Coming to Power: Writings and Graphics on Lesbian S/M*. Boston: Alyson Publications.

Sanders, Sue, and Spraggs, Gill (1989). Section 28 and Education. In Jones, Carol, and Mahony, Pat (eds.), *Learning Our Lines: Sexuality and Social Control in Education*. London: Women's Press, 79–128.

Sarachild, Kathie (1978). Psychological Terrorism. In Redstockings (ed.), *Feminist Revolution*. New York: Random House.

Sawyer, Ethel (1965). A Study of a Public Lesbian Community, Washington University, Department of Sociology–Anthropology. Available at http://elisechenier.com/wp-content/uploads/2016/02/Ethel-Sawyer-A-Study-of-a-Public-Lesbian-Community-1965.pdf.

Schonfeld, Rosemary (1982 [1979]). Self-Defence. In *Out of Bounds* [album]. London: Ova Music.

Schonfeld, Rosemary (2017, 15 September). Ova: The Radical Feminist Band. Lesbian History Group. https://lesbianhistorygroup.wordpress.com/2017/09/15/ova-the-radical-feminist-band-rosemary-schonfeld.

Scott, Sarah, and Payne, Tracey (1984). Underneath We're All Lovable. *Trouble and Strife*, 3: 20–24.

Segal, Lynne (1987). *Is the Future Female? Troubled Thoughts on Contemporary Feminism*. London: Virago.

Setch, Eve (2002). The Face of Metropolitan Feminism: The London Women's Liberation Workshop, 1969–1979. *Twentieth Century British History*, 13 (2): 171–190.

Shulman, Sheila (1983). When Lesbians Came Out in the Movement: Interview by Lynn Alderson. *Trouble and Strife*, 1: 51–56.

Sisterhood and After Research Team (2013). Girls in Formal Education. British Library. www.bl.uk/sisterhood/articles/girls-in-formal-education.

Smyth, Cherry (1998). How Do We Look? Imaging Butch/Femme. In Munt, Sally (ed.), *Butch/Femme: Inside Lesbian Gender*. London: Cassell, 82–89.

Snitow, Ann Barr, and Stansell, Christine (eds.) (1983). *Powers of Desire: The Politics of Sexuality*. New York: Monthly Review Press.

Spinster, Sydney (1988 [1982]). The Liberation of Lesbian Separatist Consciousness. In Hoagland, Sarah Lucia, and Penelope, Julia (eds.), *For Lesbians Only: A Separatist Anthology*. London: Onlywomen Press, 97–121.

Staggenborg, Suzanne, and Taylor, Verta (2005). Whatever Happened to the Women's Movement? *Mobilization*, 10 (1): 37–52.

Stanley, Liz (1982). Male Needs: The Problems and Problems of Working with Gay Men. In Friedman, Scarlet, and Sarah, Elizabeth (eds.), *On the Problem of Men: Two Feminist Conferences*. London: Women's Press, 190–212.

Steele, Amanda F. (2015, 20 April). The Cotton Ceiling. Transgender Forum. www.tgforum.com/wordpress/index.php/the-cotton-ceiling.

Steensma, Thomas D., Biemond, Roeline, de Boer, Fijgje, and Cohen-Kettenis, Peggy T. (2010). Desisting and Persisting Gender Dysphoria after Childhood: A Qualitative Follow-up Study. *Clinical Child Psychiatry*, 16 (4): 499–516.

Steensma, Thomas D., McGurie, Jenifer K., Kreukels, Baudwijntje, Beekman, Anneke, and Cohen-Kettenis, Peggy T. (2013). Factors Associated with Desistence and Persistence of Childhood Gender Dysphoria: A Quantitative Follow-up Study. *Journal of the American Academy of Child and Adolescent Psychiatry*, 52 (6): 582–590.

Stein, Arlene (2010). The Incredible Shrinking Lesbian World and Other Queer Conundra. *Sexualities*, 13 (1): 21–32.

Sutton, Jo, and Hanmer, Jalna (1984). Writing Our Own History: A Conversation about the First Years of Women's Aid between Jo Sutton and Jalna Hanmer. *Trouble and Strife*, 4: 55–60.

210 Bibliography

Tallen, Bette S. (1988 [1983]). Lesbian Separatism: A Historical and Comparative Perspective. In Hoagland, Sarah Lucia, and Penelope, Julia (eds.), *For Lesbians Only: A Separatist Anthology*. London: Onlywomen Press, 132–143.

Taylor, Verta, and Rupp, Leila J. (1993). Women's Culture and Lesbian Feminist Activism: A Reconsideration of Cultural Feminism. *Signs*, 19 (1): 32–63.

Terf Is a Slur (n.d.). Documenting the Abuse, Harassment and Misogyny of Transgender Identity Politics. https://terfisaslur.com (accessed 26 September 2017).

Thornton, Margaret (2013). The Mirage of Merit: Reconstitution the 'Ideal Academic'. *Australian Feminist Studies*, 28 (76): 127–143.

Tobin, Ann (1990). Lesbianism and the Labour Party: The GLC Experience. *Feminist Review*, 34: 56–66.

Transgender Trend (2016, 18 December). Teaching Transgender Doctrine in Schools. www.transgendertrend.com/teaching-transgender-doctrine-in-schools-a-bizarre-educational-experiment.

Turner, Janice (2017, 12 November). Why Do So Many Teenage Girls Want to Be Like Alex Bertie? *The Times Magazine*. www.thetimes.co.uk/article/meet-alex-bertie-the-transgender-poster-boy-z88hgh8b8.

Unfinished Histories (2013a). Beryl and the Perils. www.unfinishedhistories.com/history/companies/beryl-and-the-perils.

Unfinished Histories (2013b). Hormone Imbalance. www.unfinishedhistories.com/history/companies/hormone-imbalance.

Unfinished Histories (2013c). Theatre of Black Women. www.unfinishedhistories.com/history/companies/theatre-of-black-women.

Unfinished Histories (n.d. – a). Kate Crutchley. www.unfinishedhistories.com/interviews/interviewees-a-e/kate-crutchley.

Unfinished Histories (n.d. – b). Siren. www.unfinishedhistories.com/interviews/interviewees-a-e/siren.

Vance, Carole S. (ed.) (1984). *Pleasure and Danger: Exploring Female Sexuality*. London: Routledge & Kegan Paul.

Volcano, Del LaGrace, and Halberstam, Judith (1999). *The Drag King Book*. London: Serpent's Tail.

Wagner, Sally Roesch (1982). Pornography and the Sexual Revolution: The Backlash of Sadomasochism. In Linden, Robin Ruth, Pagano, Darlene R., Russell, Diana E. H., and Star, Susan Leigh (eds.), *Against Sadomasochism: A Radical Feminist Analysis*. Palo Alto, CA: Frog in the Well Press, 23–44.

Walker, Alice (1982). A Letter of These Times, or Should This Sadomasochism Be Saved? In Linden, Robin Ruth, Pagano, Darlene R., Russell, Diana E. H., and Star, Susan Leigh (eds.), *Against Sadomasochism: A Radical Feminist Analysis*. Palo Alto, CA: Frog in the Well Press, 205–208.

Wall, Chris (2017, 18 May). Sisterhood, Sawdust and Squatting: Radical Lesbian Lives in 1970s Hackney. Lesbian History Group. https://lesbianhistorygroup.wordpress.com/2017/05/18/sisterhood-sawdust-and-squatting-radical-lesbian-lives-in-1970s-hackney-christine-wall.

Walter, Aubrey (ed.) (1980). *Come Together: The Years of Gay Liberation 1970–73*. London: Gay Men's Press.

Walters, Suzanna Danuta (1996). From Here to Queer: Radical Feminism, Postmodernism, and the Lesbian Menace (or, Why Can't a Woman Be More Like a Fag?). *Signs*, 21 (4): 830–869.

Weil, Lise (2010). Are Lesbians Going Extinct? (Editorial). *Trivia: Voices of Feminism*, 10. www.triviavoices.com/issue-10-are-lesbians-going-extinct-1.html.

West, Keon (2014, 6 June). Why Do So Many Jamaicans Hate Gay People? *The Guardian.* www.theguardian.com/commentisfree/2014/jun/06/jamaica-music-anti-gay-dancehall-homophobia.

Whitbread, Helena (ed.) (1988). *The Secret Diaries of Miss Anne Lister.* London: Virago.

Wilkinson, Sue, and Kitzinger, Celia (eds.) (1993). *Heterosexuality: A Feminism and Psychology Reader.* London: Sage.

Wistrich, Harriet, and Bindel, Julie (1989). An Ism of One's Own. *Revolutionary/Radical Feminist Newsletter,* 19, Autumn.

Wittig, Monique (1980). The Straight Mind. *Feminist Issues,* 1 (1): 103–111.

Wittig, Monique (1992). *The Straight Mind and Other Essays.* Boston: Beacon Press.

Wittig, Monique, and Zeig, Sandre (1979). *Lesbian Peoples: Material for a Dictionary.* New York: Avon.

Women's Liberation Music Archive (n.d.). Siren. https://womensliberationmusicarchive. co.uk/t (accessed 28 October 2017).

Womensgrid – Women's Groups News (2016, 9 May). Women and Manual Trades Relaunches as Women on the Tools! www.womensgrid.org.uk/groups/?p=4201.

Worrow, Eileen (2010, 26 May). Barbara Burford Obituary. *The Guardian.* www.theguardian. com/society/2010/may/26/barbara-burford-obituary.

Young, Ian (1995). *The Stonewall Experiment: A Gay Psychohistory.* London: Cassell.

Young, Ian, Stoltenberg, John, Rosen, Lynn, and Jordan, Rose (1978). Forum on Sadomasochism. In Jay, Karla, and Young, Allen (eds.), *Lavender Culture.* New York: Jove Publications, 85–117.

Zaretsky, Eli (1976). *Capitalism, the Family and Personal Life.* New York: Harper & Row.

Zehra (1987). Different Roots, Different Routes. *Trouble and Strife,* 10: 11–15.

Zimmerman, Bonnie (1990). *The Safe Sea of Women: Lesbian Fiction 1969–1989.* Boston: Beacon Press.

Zimmerman, Bonnie (2007). A Lesbian-Feminist Journey through Queer Nation. *Journal of Lesbian Studies,* 11 (1/2): 37–52.

INDEX

Abbott, Sydney 137–139
African American lesbian community
   138–139
Against Sadomasochism 119, 120
Alderson, Lynn: boy children issue 70;
   fancying 91; feminist bookstores 39–40;
   monogamy 90; women-only spaces 61;
   women's services 183; working-class
   identity 156
Allen, Jeffner 87
*All The Rage: Reasserting Radical Lesbian
   Feminism* (Harne and Hutton) 173
anal sex 132
Anticlimax (Daly) 88
anti-lesbianism 107–111
archival research 8–9
Ardill, Susan 126, 127
Arena Three (magazine) 16–18
arson threat 41
Arts Council 40
Auchmuty, Rosemary 7, 51, 181
authentic lesbianism 141
A Woman's Place (AWP) 72, 109, 123
AWP *see* A Woman's Place

Barry, Kathleen 85, 119
Bart, Pauline 85
BDSM *see* bondage, discipline and
   sadomasochism
Beautiful Barbarians (Mohin) 38
Beauty and Misogyny (Jeffreys) 83
Bellos, Linda 109, 155, 161, 165
Beryl and the Perils, lesbian theatre
   group 48

Bindel, Julie: demise of lesbian feminism
   173; gay male culture 130; identity
   politics 155, 164; as lesbian feminist 31;
   non-monogamy 90; 'Political Lesbianism'
   paper 109; revolutionary feminism 159;
   as separatist 61, 73; sexuality and 112;
   straightbian 189
biomythology 37
Bishop, Helen 51
Black feminist politics 2
Black lesbian feminism 28–30; conferences
   and groups 29; definition of 29; in
   separatism 65–68
Black Lesbian Group 66–67, 153
Blackman, Inge 126, 127, 167
bondage, discipline and sadomasochism
   (BDSM) 115
bookstores, lesbian feminist 39–41
Boots of Leather (Kennedy and Davis) 141
Bösche, Susanne 174
Boston, Jane 49
boy children, in separatism 69–71
Brady, Maureen 170
Brannigan, Kate 38
Brent Women's Centre Festival 50
British lesbian feminist theory 80
British Library project 6
Brixton Black Women's Group 28
Brossard, Nicole 38
Brown, Jan 145–146
Brown, Rita Mae 97, 189
Browne, Sarah 6
Brownmiller, Susan 18
Bruley, Sue 8

Index **213**

Brunet, Ariane 98
Bulldozer Rising (Livia) 37
Bunch, Charlotte 97
Burford, Barbara 37
butch/femme role-playing *see* role-playing
Butler, Judith 140, 178, 180
Butterworth, Sue 39–40

Califia, Pat (Patrick) 118, 139
Call Me Lesbian (Penelope) 78
Campaign for Homosexual Equality (CHE) 19, 21, 64
Campbell, Beatrix 36, 106
Caprio, Frank 80–81
Card, Claudia 87
Carola, Elizabeth 124, 162
Carpenter, Val 101
Century of Women, A (Rowbotham) 5
Changing Our Minds (Kitzinger and Perkins) 42, 92
Chapman, Diana 17
CHE *see* Campaign for Homosexual Equality
Chiaroscuro (Kay's play) 50
Cholmeley, Jane 39–41
cis women 192
City Limits (magazine) 47, 159
Clarke, Cheryl 67, 81
class politics 155–156
Clews, Colin 174–175
Cloutte, Penny 105
Combahee River Collective 153–154
Come Together (GLF magazine) 90
Coming to Power 118–119
Common Woman, The (Grahn) 39
Company (magazine) 110
'Compulsory Heterosexuality and Lesbian Existence' (Rich) 35, 98, 107
conferences, lesbian culture 50
conscientization 56
conservative politics 174–178
conversion therapy 191
Conway, Kelly 146
Cooper, Davina 175, 176
Coward, Rosalind 116
Cox, Susan 187
cross-dressers 71, 191
Crutchley, Kate 49
cultural feminism 143
cultural institutions 50–52
cultural separatism 62
culture *see* lesbian culture; women's culture

Dagger 139
Daily Express (newspaper) 177

Daily Mail (newspaper) 175, 177
Daly, Mary: erotic love *vs.* friendship 88; *Gyn/Ecology* 76; lesbian feminist theory 2, 77–79; sadosociety 83, 119; separatism and 57; women-only organising 60
Dangerous Knowing: Four Black Women Poets, A (Kay) 38
Daring to be Bad (Echols) 5
Daughters of a Coral Dawn (Forrest) 37
Daughters of Bilitis (DOB) 137
Davis, Katherine 119
Davis, Madeline 141, 144–145
'De-Eroticization of Women's Liberation, The: Social Purity Movements and the Revolutionary Feminism of Sheila Jeffreys' (Hunt) 128
Delap, Lucy 39–40, 177–178
depersonalisation 130
Derrida, Jacques 178–179
Devil's Dykes, lesbian theatre group 48
Disappearing L, The: Erasure of Lesbian Spaces and Culture (Morris) 44, 187
discos, lesbian culture 47–48
Dixon, Janet 60–1, 63
Dobkin, Alix 180, 188
Drag King Book, The (Halberstam) 147
drag king phenomenon 147–149
Dreher, Sarah 37
Drill Hall, theatre venue 49
Dunbar, Roxanne 97
Dworkin, Andrea 59, 76, 85, 145

Earlham Street Workshop 24
Eaves Disco 47
Echols, Alice 5
education: lesbian feminism 27–28; WLM and 27
Education Act 1962 27
Ellis, Edith Lees 15
Ellis, Henry Havelock 15, 79
Endangered Species group 50
Epstein, Barbara 179
Equal Opportunities Act 1975 47, 58
erotic love *vs.* friendship 88
essential self 91
ethics, lesbian perspective 86–87
extremist 7

Face, The 147
Faderman, Lillian 14, 143, 148
Fairbanks, Natasha 49
Farr, Susan 119
Fawcett Society 72
Feinberg, Lesley 139
Female Homosexuality (Caprio) 80

214 Index

female inverts 15
Female Man, The (Russ, Joanna) 37
Female Masculinity (Halberstam) 147
Feminine Mystique, The (Friedan) 4
feminist bookstores 39–41
Feminist Current (magazine) 187
Feminist Fables: A Retelling of Myths (Namjoshi) 37
feminist press 41–42
feminist psychology 92
Feminist Review (journal) 31, 66, 68, 106, 116, 128
feminist separation 64
feminist therapy 92
feminist veneer 110
Femme/Butch (Munt) 139
Femme Mystique, The 139, 146
Fifty Shades of Grey (movie) 131
For Lesbians Only, 42, 59
Forrest, Katherine 37
Foucault, Michel 78, 178–179
Free Space 57
Freeman, Jo 160
Freire, Paulo 56
Freud, Sigmund 78, 91, 179
Freudianism 78
Friedan, Betty 4, 22
friendship: erotic love *vs.* 88; lesbian perspective 82–83
Frye, Marilyn: 'Lesbian Sex' 88; manloving 82; separatism 63–65; as Separatist teachers 57; talk about lesbians and gay men 21; US academic lesbian feminist 87
Furies, The (magazine) 97

Garthwaite, Al 22, 25, 69–70, 103, 106, 159–160, 163, 172–173
Gay Liberation Front (GLF) 1, 19, 22–23, 43
gay male culture 130
gay men: lesbian separation from 19–22; role-playing 19–20; separatism and 64
Gay Men's Press 174
Gay Women's Group 23
Gay Women's Liberation 26
Gearhart, Sally Miller 37
gender: difference 99; eugenics 191; as transferable property 140
gender-binary 101
gender-fluid 101
Gender Hurts: A Feminist Analysis of the Politics of Transgenderism (Jeffreys) 189
genderqueer 188
general hostility 40
GLC *see* Greater London Council

GLF *see* Gay Liberation Front
Going Too Far 60
Gordon, Lindsay 38
Gossip: A Journal of Lesbian Feminist Ethics (journal) 87
Gottschalk, Lorene 189
Graham, Dee 99
Grahn, Judy 38–39
Greater London Council (GLC) 45, 164, 172–173, 175, 177, 183
Green, Frankie 43, 44
Griffin, Susan 76, 85
Grimsditch, Dianne 105
Grundberg, Sibyl: non-monogamy 90; psychiatry *vs.* psychology 51; sadomasochism 131
Guardian Weekend (magazine) 131
gut-level lesbianism 107
gyn/affection 83
Gyn/Ecology (Daly) 76, 79

Halberstam, Judith 140, 147–148
Hall, Radclyffe 8, 15, 35
Hanmer, Jalna 85
Hardy, Sara 49
Haringey Council 176–177
Haringey radical bookshop 177
Harne, Lynne 31, 93, 107, 172–173, 177
Harpers and *Cosmopolitan* (magazine) 110
Hart, Deborah 41
Heartfield, James 153
Hemmings, Susan 110
heteropatriarchy 100
heteroreality 83, 100
hetero-relations 100
heterosexism, challenging 101
heterosexual desire 100
heterosexuality: construction of 98–101; description of 96; as political institution 96–98; in practice 101; theorising of 77
Heterosexuality: A Feminism and Psychology Reader 111
Hill, Tony 38
History of Sexuality, The (Foucault) 178
HLRS *see* Homosexual Law Reform Society
Hoagland, Sarah 57, 78, 87
Hollibaugh, Amber 142–143
homophobic radical feminism 140
homosexual desire 100
Homosexual Law Reform Society (HLRS) 16
homosexual sex 88
homosexuality 15
horizontal hostility 158–160

Hormone Imbalance, lesbian theatre
group 48
Hunt, Margaret 128
Hutton, Elaine 84, 173

identity politics: adoption of 155–158;
external pressures 163–168; horizontal
hostility 158–160; origin of 153–155;
overview of 152–153; race 162, 165;
tyranny of structurelessness 160–163;
see also politics
ILEA *see* Inner London Education
Authority
'Incredible Shrinking Lesbian World, The'
(Stein) 190
Inner London Education Authority (ILEA)
177, 183
intellectual separation 57
interpersonal hostility 157
intersectionality 154
Ishtar, Arlene 143–144

Jackson, Margaret 176
Jackson, Stevi 91
Jeffreys, Sheila 4, 83, 117, 126–128, 180, 189
Jennings, Paula 107
Jennings, Rebecca 15, 138
Jenny Lives with Eric and Martin
(Bösche) 174
Jewish Lesbian Feminist Group 24
Jewish Separatism 69
Jo, Bev 87
John, Helen 70–71
Jones, Allen 50
Jones, Carol 159
Jones, Justine 106

Katyachild, Maria 71
Kay, Jackie 38
Kelly, Liz 85
Kennedy, Elizabeth Lapovsky 141
Kennedy, Florynce 158
King, Linda 166
Kitzinger, Celia 77, 92, 111
Koedt, Anne 136
Ku Klux Klan 159

Lacan, Jacques 78, 178–179
Langley, Esme 16
LAP *see* Lesbians Against Pornography
LASM *see* Lesbians Against SadoMasochism
Latin American Women's Group
meeting 50
Laurieston Hall Women's Arts Festival,
Scotland 50

Laws, Sophie 105
Leaving the Life (Menasche) 100
Lee, Anna 70
Leeds Lesbian Newsletter 31
Leeds Revolutionary Feminists 42, 62, 67,
102, 110
lesbian(s): African American community
138–139; bars and clubs 136; definition
of 80–82; erasure 186–187; existence
35; male fantasy 191–192; as men
189–191; name-calling 158; naming
30–32; political 8, 96; pornography 116;
role-playing *see* role-playing; separation
from gay men 19–22; sexological
version of 15
Lesbian and Gay Studies Reader, The 142
Lesbian Archive collective 1, 8, 9, 32, 51–52,
126, 127, 153, 164–166
Lesbian Choices (Card) 87
lesbian culture: conferences 50; cultural
institutions 50–52; discos 47–48; feminist
bookstores 39–41; feminist press 41–42;
lesbian theatre 48–50; literature 36–38;
music 44–47; poetry 38–39; squatting
42–44; women's culture 34–35; women's
theatre 48–50
*Lesbian Erotic Dance: Butch, Femme,
Androgyny, and Other Rhythms* (Loulan)
139, 144
Lesbian Ethics (Silveira) 87, 92, 121
lesbian feminism: Black lesbian feminism
28–30; class and education 27–28; culture
and community 32; death of 171–173;
development of 22–26; documenting
history of 7–8; emotional effect of
173–174; future of 192–193; historical
context of 26–30; methodology
8–9; political policy of 22; queer theory
178–180; through radical feminism 3–5;
through revolutionary feminism 3–5;
WLM and 18–19; writing history of 5–7
lesbian feminist rejection, role-playing
135–138
lesbian feminist thought 77–80
*Lesbian Heresy, The: A Feminist Perspective on
the Lesbian Sexual Revolution* 172
Lesbian History Group 1, 8, 32, 37, 51–52
Lesbian Line 26, 50–51
Lesbian Line Women's Disco 47
Lesbian Passion (Loulan) 139
Lesbian Peoples: Material for a Dictionary
(Wittig and Zeig) 57
lesbian perspective: definition of lesbian
80–82; ethics 86–87; feminist sex
88–91; friendship 82–83; lesbian

216 Index

feminist thought 77–80; overview of 76–77; rejection of therapy 91–93; sexual violence 83–86
Lesbian Philosophies and Cultures (Allen) 87
lesbian separatism 68–69
lesbian sex: feminist sex and 88–91; in HLRS 16; lookism 89, 90; non-monogamy 89–90
Lesbian Sex (Loulan) 139
lesbian sex therapy 139
lesbian sexual revolution 172–173
Lesbian Teachers' Newsletter 31
Lesbian/Woman (Lyon and Martin) 137
Lesbians Against Pornography (LAP) 1, 122
Lesbians Against SadoMasochism (LASM) 1, 122, 125
lesbianism: authentic 141; change of climate 16–18; before flood 13–16; as lavender herring 22; separatism and 63–65
Lev, Arlene 148
LHG *see* London Lesbian Offensive Group
liberal feminism 3–4
lifestyle separatism 61–62
Lilly, Helen 27
Lister, Ann 14
literature, lesbian culture 36–38
Livia, Anna 37, 87
LLGC *see* London Lesbian and Gay Centre
LLOG *see* London Lesbian Offensive Group
Local Government Act (1988) 172, 175
Lockyer, Bridget 6
London Lesbian and Gay Centre (LLGC) 124
London Lesbian Offensive Group (LLOG) 1, 3, 7, 9, 110–111
London Revolutionary Feminist Anti-Pornography group 86
London Times 147
London Women's Liberation Newsletter (LWLN) 10, 18, 126, 153; disco advertisement 47–48; lesbians writing and organising meetings 22–23; S/M movement 123; in transsexualism 71; tyranny of structurelessness 161
London Women's Liberation Rock Band 44
London Women's Liberation Workshop 6, 18, 22–23
Long, Pauline 71
lookism 89
Lorde, Audre: biomythology and 37; Black feminist politics 2; male domination thinkers 79; as radical feminist theorists 76; sadomasochism 119; understanding of erotic 89

Louise, Valentine 59
Loulan, Joanne 139, 144
Love, Barbara 137–139
Loving to Survive (Graham) 99
Lucy, Juicy 119
Lupin Sisters 45–46
L-word 187–188
Lyon, Phyllis 137

McDermid, Val 37–38
Mackay, Finn 6
MacKinnon, Catharine 4, 117, 142
McLeod, Jan: Rape Crisis 157, 182; sexual violence 84–85
McNeil, Sandra: fancying people 91; lifestyle separatism 61–62; non-monogamy 90; sadomasochism 129–130, 131; transsexuals and WLM 72; women-only groups 85; women-only organising 58; women-only spaces 60
male fantasy 191–192
male sexuality 20–21
malestream squatting 42
Mama, Amina 28
manloving 82
Marie Claire 147
Martin, Del 137
Marx, Karl 78, 179
Marxism 4, 18, 78
Marxist economic theory 4
Marxist feminists 26
masculine separation 64
masculinity 99
masochism 120
Menasche, Anne 100
middle-class women: education 27–28; identity 157; literacy 14; romantic friendships for 14
Miller, Elaine 37
Miller, Isabel 35
Millett, Kate 76
Miner, Valerie 37
Minorities Research Group (MRG) 16–18
misunderstanding of separatism 62–3
Mohin, Lilian: Onlywomen Press and 2, 41; radical feminism 4
Montreal International Feminist Bookfair 119
Moraga, Cherrie 142–143
Morgan, Robin 60, 122
Morris, Bonnie 44, 187
MRG *see* Minorities Research Group
Ms (magazine) 60
municipal feminism 153

Munt, Sally 139, 140, 142, 145
Mushroom, Merrill 138
music, lesbian culture 44–47
'Mystery of Lesbians, The' (Penelope) 87

name-calling lesbians 158
Namjoshi, Suniti 37
National Abortion Campaign day school 50
National Lesbian Conference 1974 31,
    72, 109
National Lesbian Newsletter 31
National Organization of Women
    (NOW) 4, 22
necromancers 79
'Need for Revolutionary Feminism,
    The: Against the Liberal Takeover of
    the Women's Liberation Movement'
    (Jeffreys) 4
Nestle, Joan 139, 141, 144–145, 167
New York Lesbian Archive 126, 144,
    167, 183
New York Post 147
Newton, Esther 140
non-monogamy 89–90
Northern Women's Liberation Rock
    Band 44, 45
*Not a Passing Phase: Reclaiming Lesbians in
    History 1840–1985* 51–52
NOW *see* National Organization
    of Women

objectification 90
Okin, Susan Moller 97
O'Lexa, Liz 145
On Our Backs (magazine) 116
One Foot on the Mountain (Mohin) 38, 41
Onlywomen Press 2, 38, 41–42, 102;
    Changing Our Minds 42; *For Lesbians Only*
    42; *One Foot on the Mountain* 41; *Women
    against Violence against Women* 42; *Women
    and Honour: Notes on Lying* 41
Oram, Alison 15
Organisation of Women of Africa and
    African Descent (OWAAD) 28–29
Orr, Deborah 131
O'Sullivan, Sue 126, 127, 129
Other Women's Disco 47
Otitoju, Femi: Greater London Council
    172; horizontal hostility approach 160;
    Lesbian Strength marches 131; political
    lesbian 103; rejection of sexuality 107;
    separatism 68; sexual relationship 91;
    sexual violence 84; women's services
    funding 183
Outwrite (newspaper) 29, 152, 167

Oval House, theatre venue 49
OWAAD *see* Organisation of Women of
    Africa and African Descent

Packwood, Marlene 108, 156–157
Pandora publisher 41
Pankhurst, Christabel 47
Parker, Pat 38
*Passion for Friends, A: Toward a Philosophy of
    Female Affection* (Raymond) 82–83, 85, 92
Patience and Sarah (Miller) 35
Patriarchy Study Group 84
Patton, Cindy 129–130
Payne, Tracey 91
Penelope, Julia: *Call Me Lesbian* 78;
    heteropatriarchy 100; horizontal hostility
    158; lesbian perspective 77; politics
    87; role-playing 143; separatism 60; as
    Separatist teachers 57; sexuality and
    sexual violence 146
Penthouse Magazine 147
Perkins, Rachel 92
Persistent Desire, A (Nestle) 139
Pettit, Ann 108–109
phallocratic technology 79
Pizzey, Erin 25–26
Place for Us, A (Miller) 35
Platt, Mary Frances 144
Pleasure and Danger 116
poetry, lesbian culture 38–39
Poirot, Kristan 5
'Political Lesbianism' paper 41, 102–104;
    criticism by other lesbian feminists
    106–107; criticism of paper 104–106
political lesbians 8, 96
politics: Black feminist 2; class 155–156;
    conservative 174–178; identity *see*
    identity politics; race identity 162, 165
Pornography: Men Possessing Women
    (Dworkin) 59
postmodern theory 179
Potts, Billie 69
Powers of Desire 116
professionalisation: women's services
    182–184; women's studies 181–182
pro-sex/pro-sexers 115–117
pro-woman line 105
'Psychoanalysis of Edward the Dyke, The'
    (Grahn) 38
Purvis, June 72
pyrotechnics 77

Quaye, Terry 46
queer theory, lesbian feminism 178–180,
    187–188

218 Index

race identity politics 162, 165
Radford, Jill 85
radical feminism 3–5, 23, 136; homophobic 140
Radical Feminism: Feminist Activism in Movement (Mackay) 6
Radicalesbians 81
Rape Crisis 157
Raymond, Janice: Coalition Against Trafficking 85; gender difference 99; hetero-reality 100; as insider outsider 63; lesbian sexuality 18; protest against lesbian feminists 126; as radical feminist theorists 76; therapism 92; *The Transsexual Empire* 72; women's friendship 82–83
Read, Cynthia 16
Reagon, Bernice Johnson 65
reclamation, role-playing 139–146
Red Lesbians 23
Rees, Jeska 6, 102
Restricted Country, A (Nestle) 139
Revolutionary and Radical Feminist Newsletter (RRFN) 31, 80, 110
revolutionary feminism 3–5, 159
Rich, Adrienne 7, 38, 98; erasure 98; heterosexuality 98; lesbian continuum 107; lesbian existence 35; lesbian feminist theory 2; local authority handbook 101; nascent feminist political content 82; as radical feminist theorists 76; straightbians 189; theoretical works 41–42
Rickford, Frankie 104–105
Rock Against Racism 48, 152
Rock Against Sexism event 48
role-playing 19–20; drag king phenomenon 147–149; lesbian feminist rejection of 135–138; power relationship in 138–139; reclamation of 139–146; sex 146
Room of One's Own, A (Woolf) 80
rough sex 132
Rowbotham, Sheila 5, 18–19, 105–106
Rubin, Gayle 118, 142
Runnalls, Jana 45–46
Rupp, Leila 2
Russ, Joanna 37
Russell, Diana 85, 119

Sackville-West, Vita 15, 51
SAD *see* Sisters Against Disablement
sadomasochism: gay male version of 118; general impact of 121–129; impact on lesbian feminism 131–132; reasons for lesbian 129–131; S/M movement 115–121

'Sadomasochism: The Erotic Cult of Fascism' 121
sadomasochism light 135
sadomasochist (S/M) Dykes 120, 124, 125, 128
sadomasochist (S/M) movement 115–132
sado-masochistic sex 125, 144
sadosociety 83
Safe Sea of Women, The (Zimmerman) 36
Sage, Purple 189
saliromania 84
Sanders, Sue 176
Sapphistry (Califia) 139
Sappho Discos 47
Sappho was a Right-On Woman (Abbott and Love) 137
Schonfeld, Rosemary 45–46
Scotch Verdict (Faderman) 14
Scott, Sarah 91
Self-Defence (song by Schonfeld) 46
separatism: boy children and 69–71; description of 55; end of 73; feminist *vs.* masculine separation 64; Going too far? 60–62; intellectual separation 57; lesbian *vs.* other 68–69; lesbianism and 63–65; lifestyle 61–62; as luxury for white women 65–68; misunderstanding of 62–63; overview of 55–56; profound form of 60; tactical *vs.* cultural 62; theory of 56–57; transsexualism and 71–72; women-only organising 57–60; women-only space 57–60
'Separatism and Radicalism' (Brunet and Turcotte) 98
Separatist teachers 57
Setch, Eve 6, 18
sex: anal 132; class 4, 78; homosexual 88; lesbian *see* lesbian sex; lesbian perspective 88–91; role-playing 146; rough 132; sado-masochistic 125, 144
Sex Discrimination Act 1975 40
sex roles 135
sex wars 3, 112, 115–121, 158, 164
'Sexual Fantasies' (Morgan) 122
Sexual Offences Act 1967 16
Sexual Politics (Millett) 76
sexual violence, lesbian perspective 83–86
Sexuality Papers, The 84
She Must be Seeing Things (movie) 126, 166
Shulman, Sheila 20, 24–25, 41, 61
Silveira, Jeanette 87
Silver Moon bookstore 39–40
Siren, theatre group and band 48–49
Sisters Against Disablement (SAD) 161–162

Sisterwrite bookstore 39–40
Slippers of Gold (Kennedy and Davis) 141
Smith, Barbara 153–154
Smith, Beverley 154
Smyth, Cherry 126, 142
socialist feminism 3
Soloway, Jill 188
'Some Reflections on Separatism and Power' (Frye) 63
South London Women's Art Centre 45
Southall Black Sisters (SBS) 152, 167
Spare Rib (magazine) 108, 155
specialised lesbian groups: Brixton Black Women's Group 28; Jewish Lesbian Feminist Group 24; Turkish Lesbian Group 30
Spinster, Sydney 57, 87
Spraggs, Gill 176
squatting, lesbian culture 42–44
Stanley, Liz 21, 64
Stein, Arlene 190
Stoltenberg, John 85
Stone Butch Blues (Feinberg) 139
Stott, Mary 72
straight mind 56, 77
straightbians 189
Sun, The (newspaper) 175
Surpassing the Love of Men (Faderman) 143
Switsur, Julie 16

'Tackling Heterosexism: A Handbook on Lesbian Rights' 101
tactical separatism 62
Tallen, Bette 63, 69
Taylor, Verta 2
technopreneur 182
Teena, Brandon 8
Thatcher, Margaret 22, 174, 177
Thatcherism 163
theatre, lesbian culture 48–50
Theatre of Black Women 49–50
Theorising Heterosexuality 111
theory of separatism 56–57
therapism 92
'Thinking Sex' (Rubin) 142
Thornton, Margaret 182
Threshing Floor, The (Burford) 37
Time Out (magazine) 47, 128, 159
Times, The (newspaper) 193
Tipton, Billy 8
transexclusionary radical feminist 192
transphobia 17
Transsexual Empire, The (Raymond) 72
transsexualism 71–72

transwomen 192
Trebilcot, Joyce 62, 87
Trethewey, Debs 49
Trivia (journal) 3, 170, 186
Trouble and Strife (journal) 30, 91, 112, 131, 156
Turcotte, Louise 98
Turkish Lesbian Group 30

Unpacking Queer Politics (Jeffreys) 117, 180
upper-class women 14

'vanilla' sex 118
Vile Book In School: Pupils See Pictures Of Gay Lovers (Clews) 174–175
Virago press 41–42
Volcano, Del LaGrace 147–148

Wagner, Sally Roesch 119
Walker, Alice 119, 120
Wall, Chris 42–44, 177
Wanderground, The (Gearhart) 37
Well of Loneliness, The (Hall) 15, 35
West, Keon 67
What Color Is Your Handkerchief 118
Wilkinson, Sue 77, 111
Wilson, Barbara 37
Winter, Jude 49
Wistrich, Harriet 153, 155
Wittig, Monique 56, 57, 77, 78
WLM *see* Women's Liberation Movement
Wolfenden report 16
woman-identification 82
woman-identified woman 107
'Woman- Identified Woman, The' 82
Women Against Nukes meeting 50
Women Against Rape meeting 50
Women against Violence against Women 42, 84–85
Women and Caring Jobs meeting 50
Women and Honour: Notes on Lying (Rich) 41
Women and Manual Trades 43
Women and Mental Health group 50
Women in Manual Trades meeting 50
women-loving women 14
women-only gigs 46
women-only organising 57–60
women-only principle 58
women-only space 57–60
Women's Aid 25–26
Women's Arts Alliance collective 50
Women's Committee of the Greater London Council 101

women's culture: importance of, 34–5; patriarchal culture 35

Women's Information and Referral Enquiry Service (WIRES) 10, 42, 102

'Women's Intellectual Terrorist Conspiracy from Hell' (W.I.T.C.H.) 87

Women's Liberation Movement (WLM): anti-lesbianism 107–111; in Bradford, Yorkshire 6; British Library project 6; creating culture and social and political community 1; education and 27; in Scotland 6; in US 2; *see also* lesbian culture; lesbian feminism; lesbian perspective

Women's Liberation Music Archive online 44

Women's Monthly Event 48

Women's Press, The 41, 59

women's romantic friendships 14

women's services, professionalisation 182–184

women's studies, professionalisation 181–182

women's theatre 48–50

Woolf, Virginia 80

Workers' Educational Association 50, 181

working-class identity 156

working-class women 15; describing clubs 16; education 27–28; identity 156; uprising of 18

Zami: A New Spelling of My Name (Lorde) 37

Zeig, Sandre 57

Zimmerman, Bonnie 34, 36, 35